D1591485

DISCARD

BASEBALL RATINGS

ALSO BY CHARLES F. FABER
AND FROM MCFARLAND

Spitballers:
The Last Legal Hurlers of the Wet One (2006)

The American Presidents
Ranked by Performance (2000, paperback 2006)

Baseball Pioneers:
Ratings of Nineteenth Century Players (1997)

BASEBALL RATINGS

The All-Time Best Players at Each Position, 1876 to the Present

THIRD EDITION

Charles F. Faber

McFarland & Company, Inc., Publishers

Jefferson, North Carolina, and London

LIBRARY OF CONGRESS CATALOGUING-IN-PUBLICATION DATA

Faber, Charles F.
Baseball ratings : the all-time best players at each position,
1876 to the present / Charles F. Faber.— 3d ed.
p.   cm.
Includes index.

ISBN: 978-0-7864-3414-5
softcover : 50# alkaline paper ∞

1. Baseball players— United States— Biography.
2. Baseball players— Rating of — United States.   I. Title.
GV865.A1F28 2008   796.357092'2 — dc22   2008001638

British Library cataloguing data are available

©2008 Charles F. Faber. All rights reserved

*No part of this book may be reproduced or transmitted in any form
or by any means, electronic or mechanical, including photocopying
or recording, or by any information storage and retrieval system,
without permission in writing from the publisher.*

Cover photograph ©2008 Shutterstock

Manufactured in the United States of America

*McFarland & Company, Inc., Publishers
Box 611, Jefferson, North Carolina 28640
www.mcfarlandpub.com*

Acknowledgments

It is customary for the author of a book to extend thanks to those persons who have assisted him in his work. I shall do that. First, however, I wish to pay tribute to three men, now deceased, who had nothing directly to do with this book, but who helped start me on a lifetime of research and writing about baseball.

Verlin McAlister was my uncle. In a time when most small towns in Iowa had a semipro or amateur baseball club, Verlin was a pitcher and first baseman for the Blakesburg Boosters, his hometown club. I still have newspaper clippings from games he played in the early 1930s. When I was about 12 years old he gave me a copy of *Spalding's Official Baseball Guide,* 1928 edition. I had never seen a baseball guide before. I was enthralled. What a treasure trove of information! But the book ended with the 1927 season. Immediately I set out to bring it up to date and later to treat the data in new and different ways. I have never stopped.

Tait Cummins was the sports editor of the *Cedar Rapids Gazette.* When I was a teenaged college student, he gave me my first sportswriting job, covering industrial league and high school basketball. More than a boss, Tait was a good friend and a mentor. From him I learned how to write about sports.

Earl Whitehill was a former major league pitcher with over 200 victories to his credit. When I wrote my first pieces about baseball, he invited me into his home, and, over a cup of tea, read my articles and discussed with me not the quality of my writing but some of the technical aspects of the game. The fact that this seasoned veteran found my ideas worth discussing encouraged me to continue writing about the game.

My first book of baseball ratings was published by McFarland in 1985. I appreciate the encouragement of friends at the University of Kentucky who urged me to submit the manuscript for publication. For many years my late wife, Patricia Faber, provided much needed love and support. My gratitude to her is great indeed.

As for the present book, my grandson, Zach Webb, read parts of the manuscript and offered constructive criticism. My daughter, Mindy Faber, assisted with accessing Library of Congress photographs. Zach, Mindy, and my son Danny Faber helped solve computer problems that threatened to delay completion of the manuscript. My granddaughter, Kyffin Webb, provided valuable assistance. Patricia Kelly helped me secure photographs from the National Baseball Hall of Fame and Museum. I have made liberal use of data published in various baseball encyclopedias, ranging from

Hy Turkin and S. C. Thompson's *The Official Encyclopedia of Baseball* (New York: A. S. Barnes and Company, 1951) through the nine editions of the Macmillan publication, and the 2004 volume by the same title, edited by Pete Palmer and Gary Gillette and published by Barnes and Noble. In addition, the information found on-line at *Baseball-Reference.com* has been quite useful.

Contents

Preface

Who was the greatest baseball player of all time? The greatest hitter, the best fielder, the top pitcher? Questions such as these have long been debated by baseball fans, usually with more heat than light. How is it possible to compare a home run slugger with a singles hitter who compiles a higher batting average? How can the exploits of a hitter from the deadball era be rated against the feats of a player who bats a livelier ball? How can the accomplishments of fielders equipped with tiny gloves, or none, be compared with the achievements of present-day players and the webbed, cushioned gloves they employ?

The immodestly named Faber System permits valid comparisons of the performance of ballplayers across the decades. The first book utilizing this system was titled *Baseball Ratings* and was published by McFarland in 1985, the first of many baseball books published by that house. In this initial work only those position players who played most of their careers after 1900 were rated. In 1995 the second edition of *Baseball Ratings* was published. The book was revised and expanded to include pitchers and position players who had become eligible for listing after the publication of the first edition. Neither of these volumes included players who spent the majority of their major league careers before 1901; those ratings were at last presented in *Baseball Pioneers*, published by McFarland in 1997. The present volume combines data from the previous volumes and applies the Faber System to all the major leagues from 1876 through 2006. An addition to the newest work is the inclusion of on-base-percentage as one of the components of the batting ratings. Fielding records for outfielders are adjusted to give extra credit for assists. Certain adjustments have been made to some of the 19th-century ratings to take into account shorter playing seasons and a shorter pitching distance prior to 1893. Detailed explanations of and rationales for adjustments are provided at appropriate places in the book.

In 1869 the Cincinnati Red Stockings became the first team openly to consist entirely of salaried players. In 1871 the first professional league was formed, the National Association of Professional Base Ball Players. Although the circuit had many quality players, it suffered from organizational problems, as well as many other shortcomings, and lasted only five years. During those five seasons, 23 different teams played in the league, but only three lasted the entire time. A major problem was clubs starting the season but dropping out before the end of the year. Not once did every team in the league play a complete schedule. In 1875, for example, the league granted a franchise to a club in Keokuk, Iowa. Located in a rural area far from any center of population, Keokuk counted only 12,776 residents in the 1870 census. Not surprisingly, the club folded after only 13 games. Even so, it outlasted one of the two Baltimore clubs that started the 1873 season. The Marylands lasted for only six games. In 1969 the Special Records Committee determined that the National Association should not be classified as a major league for records purposes. I agree with that decision. The uneven schedules played by teams in that circuit make the data almost useless for rankings.

In 1876, the National Association was replaced by a better organized circuit, the National League of Professional Base Ball Clubs, which survives today as one of our two existing major leagues. For purposes of this book, the National League will be considered the first major league. From 1882 through 1891 the American Association was a worthy rival to the older loop. The Players' League survived only one season (1890), but the majority of its players had proven their abilities in one of the other circuits, so it too is considered a major league. The same is true of the Federal League, which had major league standing in 1914 and 1915. Of course, since 1901 the American League has had equal status with the National.

On the other hand, the Union Association, which challenged the majors in 1884, was unable to attract enough established major leaguers to fill more than 18 percent of its rosters. Therefore, it is not considered a major league in this publication. Although the Special Records Committee accepted major league status for the Union Association, it's hard to agree with that decision. The loop suffered from the same problems as the old National Association. Half of the 12 clubs in the league did not play a full schedule, several playing as few as 25 games. The main reason to discount data from the Union Association, however, is the low caliber of competition. For example, Fred Dunlap led the Association with a .412 batting average and an on-base percentage of .448. He also led the league in slugging average, home runs, runs scored, and runs batted in. A legitimate big league player, Dunlap dominated the Union Association but never led the National League in any of those categories during nearly a decade in the older circuit. Using data from the 1884 season would unfairly skew his ranking.

Ratings are presented for each major league for each year from 1876 through 2006. All infielders and outfielders appearing in at least two-thirds of the scheduled games and all backstops catching in at least half of the schedule are included. For each player with five or more such years, career records are computed. Career rankings are presented for each position in rank order all the way from number one down to the least successful. Rankings are given separately for hitting, for fielding, and for a combination of the two.

In addition, ratings are computed for all pitchers involved in 15 or more decisions in a season. Of central importance to the Faber System is a procedure by which the strength of the pitcher's team is taken into account. Pitchers on last-place teams can thereby be compared with hurlers on championship clubs. Ratings for relief pitchers are also included.

The book is divided into six sections: Hitters, Fielders, Players (Hitting and Fielding), Starting Pitchers, Closers and Middle Relievers. Each section opens with a detailed explanation of methodology, so any reader with access to the raw data can replicate them. A listing of the yearly leaders in each league follows, along with rankings of career leaders.

In most cases players are identified by the name by which they were best known during their playing days. George Ruth is Babe, Harold Reese is Pee Wee, and Urban Faber is Red. Charles Hartnett and Charles Stengel are Gabby and Casey, respectively. Richard Allen started his career as Richie, but preferred to be called Dick, so he is Dick Allen in this book. Stanislaus Kowalewski played ball as Stan Coveleskie and that is how we identify him, despite the practice recent writers have of dropping the final e from his surname.

1

HITTERS

In rating hitters, one must look at the fundamental purpose of hitting — that is, to produce runs for the team. There are two ways to do this. One way is to get on base, advance around the bases, and score the run oneself. The other way is to drive a teammate across the plate. Either method produces one run for the team. A run scored and a run batted in have equal value. Each is worth exactly one point, no more, no less. A leadoff batter who through his hits, walks, and speed scores 120 runs has made a contribution of equal value to a cleanup hitter whose long-ball clouting drives in 120 runs. In neither case are the runs the results of the sole effort of a single man. The leadoff man usually must depend on a teammate to knock him in if he is going to score. The cleanup hitter seldom gets a run batted in unless there is a man on base when he comes to the plate. An exception to this rule is when the batter hits a home run. In this case the run is scored through the efforts of a single batter. Therefore, the Faber System gives extra credit for home runs.

In addition to runs scored or runs batted in and home runs, the system also recognizes batting averages and on-base percentage. Baseball is a game of tradition, and for many years the batting average was considered the most important statistic. Many non-sports publications, such as the *World Almanac*, have for many years provided lists of batting champions; i.e. leaders in batting average. The 1916 battle for the title between Ty Cobb and Nap Lajoie with a Chalmers automobile as the prize sparked one of the greatest controversies of the decade when the St. Louis Browns played deep on the last day of the season, allowing Lajoie to beat out seven bunts in the doubleheader. Charges of chicanery again surfaced in 1976 when George Brett edged out Hal McRae for the batting championship on the last day of the season. On a more positive note, baseball fans remember the exploits of Ted Williams in the season-ending doubleheader of 1941 when he became the last man to hit over .400 in a season. In 2006 many fans followed the successful efforts of Joe Mauer in becoming the first American League catcher to win the circuit's batting crown.

Over the past several decades the home run and the RBI have assumed equal importance to the batting average in the opinion of fans, while the runs scored number has fallen somewhat by the wayside. Thus we have the coveted Triple Crown for the hitter who leads the league in batting average, home runs, and RBIs in the same year. Some recent home run accomplishments have spurred excitement and controversy equal to the batting races mentioned above. Baseball, more than any other sport, has a coterie of fans who take statistics very seriously. A new field of sabermetrics (named for the Society of American Baseball Researchers) has sprung up. Some scholars of the game advocate that on-base percentage (OBP) should replace the batting average (BA) in calculations. They have a point. If getting on base leads to a run it matters not how the runner reached base, whether by hit, walk, hit by pitch, or other means. When leading off an inning this is certainly true. But if there are runners on base, a hit is surely better than a walk for it has at least the potential of advancing the runners closer to home plate. Both the BA and the OBP are incorporated in our system. As the base hit is a component of both the batting average and the on-base percentage, the system justifiably gives more weight to the hit than to the walk.

Thus the rating system involves five components—runs scored, runs batted in, home runs, batting average, and on-base percentage. The exact formula is explained below.

Season Records

For each batter a yearly point total is compiled by adding the number of runs scored or runs batted in (whichever is higher), the number of home runs, and a figure derived from the batting average and on-base percentage. The latter number is constructed by getting rid of the decimal points by multiplying each figure by 1000, adding the results together, and dividing by two to get an average. (Some statisticians object to averaging averages, but it is a common practice in sabermetrics.) For example, in 2006 Albert Pujols scored 119 runs, batted in 137, hit 49 home runs, had a .331 batting average and .431 in-base percentage. To get his total for the year we add 137 plus 49 plus 381 (the average of 331 and 431). His total is 557 points. In most seasons the point totals of all players appearing in two-thirds or more of their team's games in a season are compiled and a league mean is computed for each year. (In seasons of 154 games and 162 games, 100 games is used as the minimum instead of two-thirds of the team's games. Because of the demands of the position, catchers may become eligible by playing in one-half of their team's games.) Use of this method makes it possible to compare the relative strengths of batters from different eras. During the 1907 season, for instance, the National League as a whole had a batting average of .243, an OBP of .308, hit a total of 140 home runs, and scored 4189 runs, an average of fewer than seven runs per game. In contrast, National Leaguers in 1930 hit for an average of .303 with a .360 OBP, hit 892 four-baggers, and scored 7025 runs, well over an average of eleven runs per game. The Faber System shows that the mean total points of eligible players in 1907 was 356, compared to 449 for the average 1930 player, a difference of 93 points. Thus, a 1930 hitter would have to attain an additional 93 points to equal the output of his 1907 counterpart. The 512 points that Honus Wagner achieved in 1907 through his batting average of .350, OBP of .408, 98 runs scored, and 8 home runs is a better performance than Freddie Lindstrom's 1930 total of 551 points, acquired through a .379 batting average, a .425 OBP, 127 runs scored, and 22 home runs. Impressive though the Giant third baseman's numbers are, he exceeded the league mean by "only" 102 points, whereas the Pirate shortstop led the league with 156 points above the mean. This method of rating batters to fair to hitters of all eras.

Career Ratings

In all computations involving more than a single season, a hitter is first given a credit of 50 points for each year counted. Thus, the average hitter has a total of 50 points rather than zero points per year. The rationale for this is that the player who participates in two-thirds or more of his team's games during a season is usually a better hitter than the pitchers and benchwarmers who fill out the roster. A league mean based on regular players is assumed to be about 50 points higher than one based on the average of all players. A player's career rating is determined by adding 50 points per year to the total amount that he is above or below the league mean during each of his ten best seasons. Don Kessinger, a smooth-fielding shortstop, mostly with the Chicago Cubs in the 1960s and 1970s, was a competent big league hitter. He was not quite as productive as the average full-time player, but year after year he attained respectable numbers. The 50 point rule gives him a total of 460 points for his best ten years, a number more reflective of his ability than the −40 he would have received without the rule. Dozens of other examples could be given, but perhaps one will suffice.

Ten seasons are enough to establish the quality of a batter. If he continues to excel after ten years, it can only enhance his stature, not diminish it. For example, in 1983 Pete Rose at the age of 42 had a sub-par season. He hit .245 with an OBP of .316, no homers, and only 52 runs scored and 45 batted in, for a total of 333 points, far below the league mean of 382. This performance does not diminish his standing. It is not included in his career record, for that record is based on his best ten years. Incidentally, those were not his first ten years in the majors. Pete was not a great natural hitter. He achieved his status as one of the premier hitters of the game only after many years of extraordinary effort, through the kind of drive and enthusiasm that earned him the nickname "Charlie Hustle." During his first two seasons with the Reds, Pete's totals were unimpressive. These seasons were included in his career total until he had completed seasons better than them; then they were dropped from his career record. The rule is *the best ten years count*, thus giving a more accurate picture of the player who improves with experience, as well as the one who plays past his prime. By the end of Pete's first ten seasons in the majors, he had compiled 1303 points. Had his career ended then, Rose would be ranked 98th on our list of the all-time greatest hitters. However, Pete continued to improve through the 1981 season, by which time he had attained 1576 points, moving him up to 40th place in our rankings. The 1981 season was Pete's 19th in the majors. Few players last that long, let alone have one of their best years at that point. After that year Pete's performance declined, but his career rating did not change. He had established his stature as a hitter.

Another factor taken into account in computing a hitter's career record is the fact that it is possible to participate in 100 or more games in a season and yet not be a full-time player. For example, players who are used primarily as pinch hitters or inserted in the late innings as defensive replacements do not have as great an opportunity to score runs or bat them in as players who participate in the entire game. To protect such players from an unjustly low rating, any season beyond the minimum of five years is dropped from the player's career record if his times at bat are fewer than four multiplied by the number of games his team played.

With the exception noted above about times at bat, the rules for compiling a career record are:

1. *A minimum of five seasons of sufficient games must be played.*
2. *For players with five through ten years, all seasons must be counted.*
3. *For players with more than ten years, only the best ten years will be included in the career record.*

Extended Careers

Although using a player's best ten years may be the most appropriate way to compute his career record, it is not the only way. The system permits any number of variations to be used. For example, the best eight, or twelve, or fifteen, or whatever seasons could be substituted. Or the entire career could be used. In this publication any time the term "career" is used without a modifier, it refers to a player's best ten years (or all eligible seasons if he had fewer than ten such years.) If a player's entire career is used it will be referred to as an "extended career" or "all eligible seasons."

In 1894 Hugh Duffy hit .440, a mark recognized as the highest batting average in major league history (Library of Congress).

Using all eligible seasons often yields a somewhat different ranking than using the ten best. Going back to our example of Pete Rose, we see that Charlie Hustle had 1576 points in his best ten years, which occurred from 1965 through 1981. If we count all his seasons to that point, he had attained 2389 points. During his remaining four seasons he compiled an additional 163 points, bringing his total to 2552 points, acquired in 23 seasons. Among all major league hitters

Pete's career ranking, based on his best ten years, is 40th place. In the extended career rankings, based on all eligible seasons, his rank is 12th. Even though Pete had several sub-par seasons, his performance was never as much as 50 Faber System points below the league mean, so he gained at least a few points each year he played. Thus, he ranks much higher in extended career ratings than he does in career rankings. On the other hand, players whose productivity deteriorates sharply in their declining years fare less well. Those whose entire career spans only 10 or 12 years also fall behind in extended career rankings.

Points Per Season

Another way of figuring the quality of a batter's performance is to calculate the average number of points attained per season played. Whereas the extended career method usually rewards players for longevity, the points per season method often penalizes longtime players. The player who can hit as well in his twenty-third major league season as he did in his best years is very rare indeed. Pete Rose, for example, averaged 157.6 points per year during his best years, but during his extended career, on which our points per season rankings are based, his average fell to 110.0. He does not come close to making the top 50 in this category.

The average points per season statistic is a way of recognizing great hitters whose careers have been abbreviated due to injury or other misfortune. The star-crossed Turkey Mike Donlin, for example, never makes any lists of all-time best hitters, despite his .334 BA, his .402 OBP, and 95 runs scored and six home runs per year in a dead-ball era. A broken leg, a suspension, a year-long holdout, and other disputes with management limited his career. Only through the points per season statistic (151.4) can he get the recognition he merits. This category also spotlights current players who have not yet played enough years to reach the top of any other charts. Not that he lacks recognition, but the amazing 207.2 points per season racked up by Albert Pujols in his first six years shows that he will be ranked as one of the greatest hitters of all time — if he keeps it up for a few more years. However, points per season is a very volatile statistic for active players. Their numbers can go up or down in a hurry. We like Albert's chances of becoming one of the all-time greats, but only time will tell.

Leading Hitters by Year

National League

In 1876, the first year of the National League, Ross Barnes of the Boston Red Caps established a high standard. He hit .429, had an on-base percentage of .462, scored 56 runs, batted in 59, and hit one home run. His 504 Faber System points exceeded the league mean by 184, a mark that was not matched until King Kelly compiled 218 points in 1886. Kelly's record stood as the circuit's best for over 100 years until Barry Bonds bettered it in 2001 and again in 2002 and 2004. Rogers Hornsby, Hack Wilson, Stan Musial, and Mark McGwire are the only other National league hitters to top the 200 points mark, with the Rajah doing it three times. Hornsby led the league nine times, while Musial and Bonds each were the circuit's hitter of the year eight times.

In 1894 Hugh Duffy established a record .440 batting average, a mark that still stands as the best ever in the majors. However, he was not the league leader in Faber System points, for in that very same year Billy Hamilton had an on-base percentage of .522 and an incredible 198 runs scored.

LEADING NATIONAL LEAGUE HITTERS BY YEAR

Year	Hitter	AB	Runs	Hits	HR	RBI	BA	OBP	Total	Points
1876	Ross Barnes	322	56	138	1	59	.429	.462	504	184
1877	Jim O'Rourke	265	68	96	0	23	.362	.407	453	123
1878	Paul Hines	257	42	92	4	50	.358	.363	415	106
1879	Paul Hines	409	81	146	2	52	.357	.369	446	123
1880	George Gore	322	70	116	2	47	.360	.399	452	147
1881	Cap Anson	343	67	137	1	82	.399	.442	504	176
1882	Cap Anson	348	69	126	1	83	.362	.397	464	132
1883	Dan Brouthers	425	85	159	3	97	.374	.397	480	129
1884	King Kelly	452	120	160	13	95	.354	.414	517	170
1885	Roger Connor	455	102	164	1	65	.371	.435	505	151
1886	King Kelly	451	155	175	4	79	.388	.483	595	218
1887	Sam Thompson	545	118	203	11	166	.372	.416	570	164
1888	Cap Anson	515	101	177	12	84	.344	.406	485	137
1889	Mike Tiernan	499	147	167	10	73	.335	.447	549	142
1890	Billy Hamilton	496	133	161	2	49	.325	.430	513	119
1891	Billy Hamilton	527	141	179	2	60	.340	.453	540	144
1892	Cupid Childs	558	136	177	3	53	.317	.443	519	130
1893	Ed Delahanty	595	145	219	19	146	.368	.423	561	130
1894	Billy Hamilton	558	198	225	2	60	.403	.522	662	190
1895	Billy Hamilton	517	166	201	7	74	.389	.490	613	169
1896	Jesse Burkett	580	160	240	6	72	.410	.461	602	166
1897	Willie Keeler	564	145	239	0	74	.424	.464	589	149
1898	John McGraw	519	143	176	0	53	.342	.475	547	147
1899	John McGraw	399	140	156	1	33	.391	.547	610	190
1900	Elmer Flick	545	106	200	11	110	.367	.441	525	101
1901	Jesse Burkett	597	139	228	10	75	.382	.440	562	170
1902	Ginger Beaumont	541	100	193	0	67	.357	.404	481	115
1903	Ginger Beaumont	613	137	209	7	68	.341	.390	510	118
1904	Honus Wagner	490	97	171	4	75	.349	.423	487	124
1905	Cy Seymour	581	95	219	8	121	.377	.429	532	159
1906	Honus Wagner	516	103	175	2	71	.339	.416	483	124
1907	Honus Wagner	515	98	180	6	82	.350	.408	483	146
1908	Honus Wagner	568	100	201	10	109	.354	.415	504	163
1909	Honus Wagner	495	92	168	5	100	.339	.420	486	130
1910	Sherry Magee	519	110	172	6	123	.331	.445	517	141
1911	Jimmy Sheckard	539	121	149	4	50	.276	.434	480	96
1912	Heinie Zimmerman	557	95	207	14	99	.372	.418	508	108
1913	Gavvy Cravath	525	78	179	19	128	.341	.407	520	128
1914	Gavvy Cravath	499	76	149	19	100	.299	.402	470	92
1915	Gavvy Cravath	522	89	149	24	115	.285	.393	478	121
1916	Hal Chase	542	66	184	4	92	.339	.425	437	84
1917	George Burns	597	103	180	5	45	.302	.380	447	96
1918	Heinie Groh	493	86	158	1	37	.320	.395	445	96
1919	George Burns	534	86	162	2	46	.303	.396	438	76
1920	Rogers Hornsby	589	96	218	9	94	.370	.431	516	127
1921	Rogers Hornsby	592	131	235	21	126	.397	.458	580	174
1922	Rogers Hornsby	623	141	250	42	152	.401	.459	624	200
1923	Rogers Hornsby	424	89	163	17	83	.384	.459	528	104
1924	Rogers Hornsby	536	121	227	25	94	.424	.507	612	207
1925	Rogers Hornsby	504	133	203	39	143	.403	.489	628	205

Year	Hitter	AB	Runs	Hits	HR	RBI	BA	OBP	Total	Points
1926	Hack Wilson	529	97	170	21	109	.321	.406	499	96
1927	Rogers Hornsby	568	133	205	26	125	.361	.448	564	158
1928	Rogers Hornsby	486	99	188	21	94	.387	.498	563	147
1929	Rogers Hornsby	602	156	229	39	149	.380	.459	615	199
1930	Hack Wilson	585	146	208	56	191	.356	.454	652	203
1931	Chuck Klein	594	121	200	31	121	.337	.398	530	117
1932	Chuck Klein	650	153	226	38	137	.348	.404	566	164
1933	Chuck Klein	606	101	223	28	120	.368	.422	543	161
1934	Mel Ott	582	119	190	35	135	.326	.415	541	138
1935	Arky Vaughan	499	108	192	19	99	.385	.491	515	116
1936	Mel Ott	534	120	175	22	135	.328	.448	556	151
1937	Joe Medwick	633	111	237	31	154	.374	.414	579	187
1938	Mel Ott	527	116	164	36	116	.311	.442	529	143
1939	Johnny Mize	564	104	197	28	108	.349	.444	532	133
1940	Johnny Mize	579	111	182	43	137	.314	.404	539	152
1941	Pete Reiser	536	117	184	14	76	.343	.406	506	123
1942	Mel Ott	549	118	162	30	93	.295	.415	503	137
1943	Stan Musial	617	108	220	13	81	.357	.425	512	138
1944	Stan Musial	568	112	197	12	94	.347	.440	518	132
1945	Tommy Holmes	636	125	224	28	117	.352	.420	539	151
1946	Stan Musial	624	124	228	16	103	.365	.434	540	166
1947	Ralph Kiner	565	118	177	51	127	.313	.417	543	133
1948	Stan Musial	611	135	230	39	131	.376	.450	587	200
1949	Stan Musial	612	124	205	36	123	.338	.438	552	154
1950	Stan Musial	555	105	192	28	109	.346	.437	529	111
1951	Stan Musial	578	124	205	32	108	.355	.449	557	151
1952	Stan Musial	578	105	194	21	91	.336	.432	510	124
1953	Duke Snider	590	132	198	42	126	.336	.419	552	147
1954	Ted Kluszewski	573	104	187	49	141	.326	.407	557	146
1955	Duke Snider	538	126	166	42	136	.309	.418	542	138
1956	Duke Snider	542	112	158	43	101	.292	.399	500	117
1957	Hank Aaron	615	118	198	44	132	.322	.378	520	134
1958	Willie Mays	600	121	208	29	96	.397	.419	533	144
1959	Hank Aaron	629	116	223	39	123	.355	.401	540	149
1960	Eddie Mathews	548	108	152	39	124	.277	.397	500	121
1961	Frank Robinson	545	117	176	37	124	.323	.404	525	124
1962	Frank Robinson	609	134	208	39	136	.342	.421	557	163
1963	Hank Aaron	631	121	201	44	130	.319	.391	529	168
1964	Willie Mays	578	121	171	47	111	.296	.383	508	136
1965	Willie Mays	558	118	177	52	112	.317	.398	528	167
1966	Dick Allen	524	112	166	40	110	.317	.396	509	129
1967	Roberto Clemente	585	103	209	23	110	.357	.399	512	145
1968	Willie McCovey	523	81	153	36	105	.293	.378	477	122
1969	Willie McCovey	491	101	157	45	126	.320	.453	558	184
1970	Billy Williams	636	137	205	42	126	.322	.391	537	145
1971	Joe Torre	634	97	230	24	137	.363	.421	554	191
1972	Billy Williams	574	95	191	37	122	.333	.398	526	158
1973	Willie Stargell	522	106	156	44	119	.299	.392	509	127
1974	Joe Morgan	512	107	150	22	67	.293	.427	489	120
1975	Joe Morgan	498	107	163	17	94	.327	.466	521	138
1976	Joe Morgan	472	113	151	27	111	.320	.444	522	151

Year	Hitter	AB	Runs	Hits	HR	RBI	BA	OBP	Total	Points
1977	George Foster	615	124	197	52	149	.320	.382	552	161
1978	Dave Parker	581	102	194	30	117	.334	.394	511	141
1979	Keith Hernandez	610	116	210	11	105	.344	.417	508	123
1980	Mike Schmidt	548	104	157	48	119	.286	.380	502	130
1981	Mike Schmidt	354	78	112	31	91	.316	.435	498	146
1982	Al Oliver	617	90	204	22	109	.321	.392	493	113
1983	Dale Murphy	589	131	178	31	121	.302	.393	515	133
1984	Ryne Sandberg	631	114	200	19	84	.314	.367	474	96
1985	Pedro Guerrero	487	99	156	33	87	.320	.422	503	126
1986	Mike Schmidt	552	97	160	37	119	.290	.390	496	128
1987	Tony Gwynn	589	119	218	7	87	.370	.496	535	142
1988	Will Clark	575	102	162	29	109	.282	.386	472	101
1989	Kevin Mitchell	543	100	158	47	125	.291	.388	512	149
1990	Barry Bonds	519	104	156	33	114	.301	.406	501	119
1991	Barry Bonds	510	95	149	25	116	.292	.410	492	120
1992	Barry Bonds	473	109	147	34	103	.311	.456	527	157
1993	Barry Bonds	539	129	181	46	123	.336	.458	569	175
1994	Jeff Bagwell	400	104	147	39	116	.368	.451	565	191
1995	Dane Bichette	579	102	197	40	128	.340	.364	520	125
1996	Ellis Burks	613	142	211	40	128	.344	.408	558	162
1997	Larry Walker	568	143	208	49	130	.366	.452	601	193
1998	Mark McGwire	509	130	152	70	147	.299	.470	602	203
1999	Larry Walker	438	108	166	37	115	.379	.458	571	160
2000	Todd Helton	580	138	216	42	147	.372	.463	609	198
2001	Barry Bonds	476	129	156	73	137	.328	.515	632	229
2002	Barry Bonds	403	117	149	46	110	.370	.582	639	249
2003	Barry Bonds	390	111	133	45	90	.341	.529	591	197
2004	Barry Bonds	373	129	135	45	101	.362	.609	660	274
2005	Albert Pujols	591	129	195	41	117	.330	.430	550	171
2006	Ryan Howard	581	104	182	58	149	.312	.425	576	174

American Association

Pete Browning of the Louisville Eclipse led the American Association in Faber System hitting points in the league's inaugural year of 1882. He led again in 1885, the only man to lead the circuit more than once. The outstanding batting feat of the association's ten-year existence was accomplished by Tip O'Neill of the St. Louis Browns with 216 points, derived from a batting average of .435, an OBP of .490, and an amazing 167 runs scored, along with 14 home runs and 123 runs batted in. He is one of only a few players ever to lead a

James Edward "Tip" O'Neill was baseball's first triple crown winner. In 1887 the Canadian-born outfielder not only led the American Association in batting average, home runs, and runs batted in, but he also led in runs scored, on-base percentage, slugging average, hits, doubles, triples, and total bases. His .435 batting average is the second highest ever recorded in the major leagues (Library of Congress).

major league in every category used in our rankings. The Canadian-born outfielder also led the circuit in hits, doubles, triples, and slugging average.

Leading American Association Hitter by Year

Year	Hitter	AB	Runs	Hits	HR	RBI	BA	OBP	Total	Points
1882	Pete Browning	288	67	109	5	n.a.	.378	.430	476	159
1883	Ed Swartwood	413	86	147	3	n.a.	.356	.394	464	123
1884	Long John Reilly	448	114	152	11	91	.339	.366	478	138
1885	Pete Browning	481	98	174	9	73	.362	.393	485	134
1886	Henry Larkin	565	133	180	2	74	.319	.390	490	114
1887	Tip O'Neill	517	167	225	14	123	.435	.490	644	216
1888	Hub Collins	527	133	162	2	53	.307	.373	471	108
1889	Harry Stovey	556	152	171	19	119	.308	.393	564	115
1890	Tommy McCarthy	548	137	192	6	69	.350	.430	522	110
1891	Tom Brown	589	177	189	5	71	.321	.397	541	141

Players' League

In its one year of existence the Players' League was led by Roger Connor, a long-time National League star, who now is deservedly in the Hall of Fame.

Leading Players' League Hitter

Year	Hitter	AB	Runs	Hits	HR	RBI	BA	OBP	Total	Points
1890	Roger Connor	484	133	169	14	103	.349	.450	546	127

American League

Nap Lajoie of the Philadelphia Athletics dominated the American League hitters in 1901, the circuit's first year as a major league. He led the league in almost every hitting category except triples and compiled 198 Faber System points, a record that was not broken until 1915 when Ty Cobb accumulated 206 points. The record set by the Georgia Peach was broken by Babe Ruth with 247 points in 1920. The next year the Bambino upped the mark to 254 points, which still stands as an American League record. The 200 point level was reached by the Sultan of Swat in six of his nine league-leading season. Ted Williams reached that number four times; Lou Gehrig and Jimmie Foxx did it twice each; Ty Cobb and Mickey Mantle one time apiece. Cobb and Williams each led the league eight times.

Leading American League Hitters by Year

Year	Hitter	AB	Runs	Hits	HR	RBI	BA	OBP	Total	Points
1901	Nap Lajoie	544	145	232	14	125	.426	.463	602	198
1902	Ed Delahanty	473	103	178	10	93	.376	.453	528	128
1903	Patsy Dougherty	490	107	195	4	59	.331	.372	463	95
1904	Nap Lajoie	554	92	211	5	102	.381	.413	502	157
1905	Topsy Hartsel	533	87	147	0	48	.276	.409	430	83
1906	George Stone	581	91	208	6	71	.358	.417	485	129
1907	Ty Cobb	605	97	212	5	119	.350	.380	489	139
1908	Ty Cobb	581	86	188	4	108	.324	.367	458	117
1909	Ty Cobb	573	116	216	9	107	.377	.431	529	181
1910	Ty Cobb	506	106	194	8	91	.383	.456	535	169

Two of the top hitters of the American League's first two decades were Ty Cobb (*left*) and Shoeless Joe Jackson. Jackson hit .408 in 1911 but lost the batting championship to Cobb, who collected 12 titles from 1907 through 1919 (Library of Congress).

Year	Hitter	AB	Runs	Hits	HR	RBI	BA	OBP	Total	Points
1911	Ty Cobb	591	147	248	8	127	.420	.467	599	190
1912	Tris Speaker	580	136	222	10	90	.383	.464	570	176
1913	Joe Jackson	528	109	197	7	71	.373	.460	533	162
1914	Eddie Collins	526	122	181	2	85	.344	.452	522	159
1915	Ty Cobb	563	144	208	3	99	.369	.486	575	206
1916	Tris Speaker	546	102	211	2	79	.386	.470	532	154
1917	Ty Cobb	588	107	225	7	102	.383	.444	528	172
1918	Ty Cobb	421	83	161	3	64	.382	.440	499	140
1919	Babe Ruth	432	103	139	29	114	.322	.456	532	143
1920	Babe Ruth	540	177	204	59	171	.378	.512	663	247
1921	Babe Ruth	457	158	172	54	137	.376	.533	675	254
1922	George Sisler	586	134	246	8	105	.420	.467	586	163
1923	Babe Ruth	522	152	205	41	131	.393	.545	662	248
1924	Babe Ruth	549	143	200	46	121	.378	.513	635	211
1925	Harry Heilmann	573	97	225	13	134	.393	.457	572	133
1926	Babe Ruth	495	139	184	47	150	.372	.516	644	244
1927	Lou Gehrig	584	149	218	47	175	.373	.474	646	226
1928	Babe Ruth	536	163	173	54	142	.323	.463	610	191
1929	Babe Ruth	499	121	172	46	154	.345	.430	588	162
1930	Lou Gehrig	581	143	220	41	174	.379	.473	642	207
1931	Babe Ruth	534	149	199	46	163	.373	.495	643	221
1932	Jimmie Foxx	585	151	213	58	169	.364	.469	644	223
1933	Jimmie Foxx	573	125	204	48	163	.356	.449	614	191
1934	Lou Gehrig	579	128	210	49	165	.363	.465	628	195
1935	Hank Greenberg	619	121	203	36	170	.328	.411	576	150
1936	Lou Gehrig	579	167	205	49	152	.354	.478	632	174
1937	Hank Greenberg	494	137	200	47	183	.337	.436	610	178
1938	Jimmie Foxx	565	139	197	50	175	.349	.462	631	173
1939	Jimmie Foxx	467	130	168	35	105	.360	.464	577	154
1940	Hank Greenberg	573	129	195	41	150	.340	.433	578	161
1941	Ted Williams	456	135	185	37	120	.406	.553	652	240
1942	Ted Williams	522	141	186	36	137	.356	.499	604	208
1943	Rudy York	571	90	155	34	118	.271	.366	471	96
1944	Bob Johnson	525	106	170	17	106	.324	.431	501	113
1945	Nick Etten	565	77	161	18	111	.285	.387	465	91
1946	Ted Williams	514	142	176	38	123	.342	.497	600	210
1947	Ted Williams	528	125	181	32	114	.343	.499	578	186
1948	Ted Williams	509	124	188	25	127	.369	.497	585	176
1949	Ted Williams	566	150	194	43	159	.343	.490	619	213
1950	Walt Dropo	559	101	150	34	144	.322	.378	528	106
1951	Ted Williams	531	109	169	30	126	.318	.464	547	142
1952	Al Rosen	567	115	171	28	105	.302	.387	478	96
1953	Al Rosen	599	115	201	43	145	.336	.422	567	176
1954	Ted Williams	386	93	133	29	89	.345	.513	551	174
1955	Al Kaline	588	121	200	27	102	.340	.421	529	136
1956	Mickey Mantle	533	132	188	52	130	.353	.464	588	174
1957	Mickey Mantle	474	121	173	34	94	.365	.512	594	210
1958	Mickey Mantle	519	127	158	42	97	.304	.443	543	168
1959	Eddie Yost	521	115	145	21	61	.278	.435	493	113
1960	Mickey Mantle	527	119	145	40	94	.275	.399	527	114
1961	Norm Cash	535	119	193	41	132	.361	.487	591	190

Year	Hitter	AB	Runs	Hits	HR	RBI	BA	OBP	Total	Points
1962	Mickey Mantle	377	96	121	30	89	.321	.486	520	130
1963	Carl Yastrzemski	570	91	183	14	68	.321	.418	475	109
1964	Mickey Mantle	465	92	141	35	111	.303	.423	509	137
1965	Tony Oliva	576	107	185	16	98	.321	.378	473	104
1966	Frank Robinson	576	122	182	49	122	.316	.410	534	179
1967	Carl Yastrzemski	579	112	189	44	121	.326	.418	477	135
1968	Carl Yastrzemski	539	90	162	23	74	.301	.426	541	165
1969	Harmon Killebrew	555	106	153	49	140	.276	.427	531	168
1970	Carl Yastrzemski	566	125	186	40	102	.329	.452	556	179
1971	Bobby Murcer	529	94	175	25	94	.331	.427	498	126
1972	Dick Allen	506	90	156	37	113	.308	.420	514	162
1973	Reggie Jackson	539	99	158	32	117	.293	.383	487	115
1974	Jeff Burroughs	554	84	167	25	118	.301	.397	492	129
1975	John Mayberry	554	95	161	34	106	.291	.416	494	123
1976	Rod Carew	605	97	200	9	90	.331	.396	466	100
1977	Rod Carew	616	128	239	14	100	.388	.449	561	176
1978	Jim Rice	677	121	213	46	139	.315	.370	528	153
1979	Fred Lynn	531	116	177	39	122	.333	.423	539	158
1980	George Brett	449	87	175	24	118	.390	.454	564	187
1981	Rickey Henderson	423	89	135	6	35	.319	.408	460	99
1982	Robin Yount	635	129	210	29	114	.331	.379	513	127
1983	Wade Boggs	582	100	210	5	74	.361	.444	508	126
1984	Eddie Murray	588	97	180	26	110	.306	.410	497	126
1985	Rickey Henderson	547	146	172	24	72	.314	.419	537	144
1986	Don Mattingly	677	117	238	31	113	.352	.394	521	146
1987	Wade Boggs	551	108	200	24	89	.363	.461	544	150
1988	Wade Boggs	584	128	214	5	58	.366	.476	554	178
1989	Wade Boggs	621	113	205	3	54	.330	.430	496	124
1990	Rickey Henderson	489	119	159	28	61	.325	.439	529	158
1991	Frank Thomas	559	104	178	32	109	.318	.453	527	145
1992	Frank Thomas	573	108	185	24	115	.323	.439	520	146
1993	John Olerud	551	109	200	24	107	.363	.473	551	158
1994	Frank Thomas	399	106	141	38	101	.353	.487	564	179
1995	Edgar Martinez	511	121	182	29	113	.356	.479	568	162
1996	Frank Thomas	527	110	184	40	134	.349	.459	578	155
1997	Frank Thomas	530	110	184	35	125	.347	.456	562	147
1998	Albert Belle	609	113	299	49	152	.328	.399	565	162
1999	Manny Ramirez	522	131	174	44	165	.333	.442	597	177
2000	Carlos Delgado	569	115	170	41	137	.344	.470	595	177
2001	Jason Giambi	520	109	178	38	120	.342	.477	568	158
2002	Alex Rodriguez	624	125	187	57	142	.300	.392	545	135
2003	Carlos Delgado	570	117	172	42	145	.302	.426	551	150
2004	Vladimir Guerrero	612	124	206	39	126	.337	.391	529	123
2005	Alex Rodriguez	605	124	194	48	130	.321	.421	549	153
2006	David Ortiz	558	115	160	54	137	.287	.413	541	125

Federal League

In both of its two seasons as a major league the Players' League was led in hitting by Benny Kauff. Known as the "Ty Cobb of the Federal League," the young man was not only an outstanding hitter, but also a speedster, leading the league in stolen bases both years. Although he was never convicted of any crime, he was banned by Commissioner Kenesaw Mountain Landis in 1920 and was out of organized baseball at the age of 30. He is one of those who rank much higher in points per season than in career rankings.

LEADING FEDERAL LEAGUE HITTER BY YEAR

Year	Hitter	AB	Runs	Hits	HR	RBI	BA	OBP	Total	Points
1914	Benny Kauff	571	120	311	8	95	.370	.447	537	155
1915	Benny Kauff	483	92	165	12	83	.342	.446	498	131

Leading Hitters by Career

Of all the thousands of baseball players who have played in the major leagues over the past 130 years only three — Cliff Johnson, Matt Franco and David Ortiz — are eligible under our criteria to be ranked among hitters without playing at least one-half of their team's games at the same position in the field during any of those seasons. While positions are, to be technical about it, fielding positions, hitters are also identified with the field positions they most often play. Therefore, we list Johnson as a catcher and Ortiz as a first baseman. Except for the pinch hitter and the designated hitter, a player must be listed at a field position in order to bat. So we tend to think of hard-hitting first basemen, slugging outfielders, and so on, regardless of the technical accuracy of such terminology. A Silver Slugger Award is even presented to the man voted as the best hitter at each position.

In this section the top hitters at each position are identified, with the ranking derived from the point totals collected during the career of the batter, regardless of how many years he played at the position in question. For example, Ernie Banks is ranked as the fifth best hitting shortstop of all time, even though many of his points may have been collected during years in which he played first base. Each player is ranked according to his primary fielding position. There is also a separate listing for designated hitters.

First Base

On a career basis (best years) Lou Gehrig ranks as the best hitting first baseman of all time. He leads first sackers in runs scored, hits, runs batted in, and batting average. Mark McGwire has the most home runs and Cap Anson compiled the best on-base percentage. Gehrig won the Triple Crown in 1934, led the league in OBP five times, in RBIs five times, and in home runs thrice. He holds the American League record for the most runs batted in during a season with 184 ribbies in 1934. According to our system he was the best hitter in the league four times. The American League gave him the Most Valuable Player Award in 1927, and the baseball writers voted him the award in 1936. Jimmie Foxx ranks second. He won the Triple Crown in 1934 and was our choice as the best hitter in the league four times. He led the American League in batting twice, in OBP three times, in home runs four times, and won the RBI crown three times. He was thrice named the American League's Most Valuable Player. Third and fourth places in the career rankings are occupied by two pioneer batsmen, Dan Brouthers and Cap Anson. Next in line come three modern-day hitters, Frank Thomas, Jeff Bagwell, and Todd Helton. Johnny Mize, Roger Connor, and Harmon Killebrew round out the top ten.

In the extended career rankings, Cap Anson, with his 20 eligible seasons, rises to the top, even though he did not have the best record in any of the hitting categories. Gehrig leads in runs, runs batted in, batting average, and on-base percentage. Eddie Murray leads in hits,

Lou Gehrig is the best hitting first baseman of all time. The Yankees star leads first sackers in batting average, runs batted in, and runs scored (National Baseball Hall of Fame Library, Cooperstown, New York).

while Rafael Palmeiro has the most home runs. Anson was the best hitter in the National League three times, led in batting average twice and in OBP thrice. Although the RBI was not an official statistic in Anson's time, modern researchers have established that he led the league in this category eight times. Cap is followed by Gehrig and Foxx, each of whom had fewer eligible seasons. In fourth place is Murray. Another 20-year man, Palmeiro is fifth, Connor is sixth, and Rod Carew with 17 seasons, many of them at second base, ranks seventh. The remaining spots in the top ten are filled by Thomas, Bagwell, and Killebrew, all of whom also made the top ten in career rankings.

When the players are ranked according to points per season, a newcomer — Albert Pujols — heads the list. Three other presently or recently active players are in the top ten — Helton, Thomas, and Bagwell. Where these players will rank when their careers are complete remains to be seen. Two old reliables, Gehrig and Foxx, are second and fourth, respectively. Brouthers is seventh, McGwire eighth, and Mize ninth. That leaves one place for a player not previously mentioned. Hank Greenberg is fifth. The reason he did not make the other listings is that he lost one season because of a broken wrist and five years due to military service in World War II, leaving him only nine eligible seasons. Gehrig is tops in runs scored, hits, runs batted in, batting average, and on-base percentage. McGwire has more home runs per season than any other first baseman.

In looking at these rankings one is impressed by the record of Lou Gehrig. The Iron Horse ranks first in career hitting, second in extended career, and second in points per season. Jimmie Foxx is only one or two spots behind Gehrig in each of these categories. No one else ranks in the best seven in all the rankings, but Bagwell, Thomas, and Brouthers all make the top ten.

FIRST BASE CAREER (BEST YEARS)

Player	Best years		AB	Runs	Hits	HR	RBI	BA	OBP	Points
1. Lou Gehrig	1927–37	10	5797	1428	2056	392	1560	.355	.462	2247
2. Jimmie Foxx	1929–42	10	5448	1269	1879	418	1388	.345	.450	1942
3. Dan Brouthers	1882–92	10	4651	1078	1622	79	649	.349	.422	1842
4. Cap Anson	1876–90	10	4079	829	1406	61	902	.345	.465	1801
5. Frank Thomas	1991–2003	10	5343	1057	1690	364	1180	.316	.438	1775
6. Jeff Bagwell	1993–2003	10	5537	1148	1690	365	1156	.305	.416	1728
7. Todd Helton	1998–2006	9	5013	1005	1674	281	985	.334	.430	1703
8. Johnny Mize	1936–48	10	5183	959	1680	297	1096	.324	.410	1683
9. Roger Connor	1880–92	10	4540	974	1498	72	704	.330	.400	1578
10. Harmon Killebrew	1959–71	10	5429	917	1441	431	1155	.265	.387	1576

FIRST BASE EXTENDED CAREER (ALL ELIGIBLE SEASONS)

Player	Eligible Seasons		AB	Runs	Hits	HR	RBI	BA	OBP	Points
1. Cap Anson	1876–97	20	8534	1597	2807	92	1746	.329	.398	2729
2. Lou Gehrig	1925–38	14	7935	1878	2700	493	1989	.340	.448	2716
3. Jimmie Foxx	1928–42	15	7719	1688	2527	524	1827	.327	.431	2610
4. Eddie Murray	1977–96	20	11169	1614	3218	501	1899	.288	.363	2257
5. Rafael Palmeiro	1988–2003	18	10178	1622	2941	552	1793	.289	.376	2137
6. Roger Connor	1880–96	17	7714	1607	2448	137	1311	.329	.398	2118
7. Rod Carew	1967–85	17	8795	1355	2890	86	956	.329	.396	2061
8. Frank Thomas	1991–2006	13	6818	1285	2096	446	1463	.307	.431	2028
9. Harmon Killebrew	1959–74	15	7332	1200	1907	543	1478	.260	.382	2019
10. Jeff Bagwell	1991–2004	14	7697	1506	2289	446	1510	.297	.412	1988

FIRST BASE POINTS PER SEASON

Player	Eligible Seasons		AB	Runs	Hits	HR	RBI	BA	OBP	Points
1. Albert Pujols	2001–06	6	582	125	173	42	126	.332	.419	207.2
2. Lou Gehrig	1925–38	14	567	134	193	35	142	.340	.448	192.9
3. Todd Helton	1998–2006	9	557	112	186	31	109	.334	.434	189.2
4. Jimmie Foxx	1928–42	15	512	113	168	35	124	.327	.431	174.0

Player	Eligible Seasons		AB	Runs	Hits	HR	RBI	BA	OBP	Points
5. Hank Greenberg	1933–47	9	534	109	157	35	130	.314	.412	156.7
6. Frank Thomas	1991–2006	13	524	99	161	34	113	.307	.431	156.0
7. Dan Brouthers	1881–94	13	476	111	164	8	94	.345	.427	148.2
8. Mark McGwire	1987–99	11	489	92	130	46	111	.261	.394	144.1
9. Johnny Mize	1936–51	12	492	88	156	27	101	.316	.405	143.8
10. Jeff Bagwell	1991–2004	14	550	108	164	32	108	.297	.412	142.0

Second Base

By whatever measure one chooses to use, Rogers Hornsby is the greatest hitting second baseman of all time. In his best ten years he had more hits, more runs batted in, a higher batting average and a higher on-base percentage than any other achieved in a comparable period. Charlie Gehringer leads in runs scored, and Jeff Kent has the most home runs. Hornsby's .424 batting average in 1924 is the highest recorded in the major leagues since 1901, and his lifetime average of .358 in the highest in the National League. He won the Triple Crown in 1922 and again in 1925. He led the league in on-base percentage and in slugging nine times; in batting average seven times; in runs scored five times; four times each in hits, doubles, and runs batted in; three times in bases on balls; and twice in triples and home runs. Although the Most Valuable Player award was given only occasionally during Hornsby's career, he won the honor twice. In career standings he easily leads all second basemen, followed by Hall of Famers Eddie Collins, Nap Lajoie, and Joe Morgan. Craig Biggio ranks fifth, followed by Gehringer, Roberto Alomar, Kent, Ryne Sandberg, and Jackie Robinson.

For an extended career of 15 eligible seasons Hornsby again leads all second basemen, although Eddie Collins with 19 seasons is a close second. Rajah leads in runs batted in, batting average, and on-base percentage. Gehringer is tops in runs scored, with one run more than Biggio. Collins leads in hits and Kent in homers. With but one exception the top ten extended career hitters are the same as those who had the best ten years. The one exception is the addition of Lou Whitaker to the elite group. Because Jackie Robinson was 28 years old before he broke the color barrier, he spent fewer years in the major leagues than other top players and did not make the top ten in extended career listings with a total of only ten seasons in the majors.

By a wide margin Hornsby tops the rankings of second basement in hitting points per season. Collins is second. Robinson moves all the way up to third, and old timer Hardy Richardson enters the rankings in fourth place. Familiar names fill spots five through ten — Biggio, Morgan, Lajoie, Gehringer, Alomar, and Kent. Hornsby leads in runs batted in, batting average, and on-base percentage. Gehringer scored the most runs per season, Collins had the most hits, and Kent the most home runs.

SECOND BASE CAREER (BEST YEARS)

Player	Best years		AB	Runs	Hits	HR	RBI	BA	OBP	Points
1. Rogers Hornsby	1917–29	10	5445	1185	2089	248	1126	.384	.459	1959
2. Eddie Collins	1909–24	10	5435	1093	1893	32	738	.348	.439	1624
3. Nap Lajoie	1897–1912	10	4957	872	1775	47	985	.358	.400	1567
4. Joe Morgan	1965–32	10	5272	1006	1524	177	704	.289	.408	1428
5. Charlie Gehringer	1926–40	10	5974	1260	1999	136	1018	.335	.404	1322
6. Craig Biggio	1992–2004	10	5972	1124	1772	172	686	.297	.388	1308
7. Roberto Alomar	1989–2001	10	5561	1020	1755	148	795	.316	.392	1270
8. Jeff Kent	1994–2005	10	5447	896	1608	267	1062	.295	.362	1185
9. Ryne Sandberg	1982–92	10	6066	980	1743	223	788	.287	.352	1177
10. Jackie Robinson	1947–56	10	4877	947	1518	137	734	.311	.409	1165

SECOND BASE EXTENDED CAREER (ALL ELIGIBLE SEASONS)

Player	Eligible Seasons		AB	Runs	Hits	HR	RBI	BA	OBP	Points
1. Rogers Hornsby	1916–31	15	7752	1527	2809	294	1434	.362	.449	2503
2. Eddie Collins	1908–26	19	9849	1730	3217	46	1275	.327	.423	2453
3. Joe Morgan	1965–84	19	9195	1635	2499	268	1170	.272	.391	1986
4. Craig Biggio	1989–2006	17	10236	1762	2904	278	1120	.284	.367	1773
5. Nap Lajoie	1897–1916	16	8186	1288	2902	60	1321	.355	.398	1662
6. Charlie Gehringer	1926–41	16	8784	1763	2818	183	1419	.321	.404	1659
7. Roberto Alomar	1988–2003	16	8902	1490	2679	206	1110	.301	.372	1603
8. Lou Whitaker	1978–94	17	8289	1345	2288	230	1038	.276	.360	1403
9. Jeff Kent	1992–2006	15	7564	1200	2189	345	1380	.289	.356	1395
10. Ryne Sandberg	1982–97	14	8614	1262	2269	270	997	.285	.344	1354

SECOND BASE POINTS PER SEASON

Player	Eligible Years		AB	Runs	Hits	HR	RBI	BA	OBP	Points
1. Rogers Hornsby	1916–31	15	517	102	187	20	96	.362	.449	166.9
2. Eddie Collins	1908–26	19	518	91	169	2	67	.327	.423	129.1
3. Jackie Robinson	1947–56	10	488	95	152	14	73	.311	.409	116.5
4. Hardy Richardson	1879–90	11	438	100	135	5	64	.308	.347	110.4
5. Joe Morgan	1965–84	19	484	86	132	14	62	.272	.391	104.5
6. Craig Biggio	1989–2006	17	602	104	171	16	66	.284	.367	104.3
7. Nap Lajoie	1897–1916	16	512	81	156	4	83	.355	.398	103.9
8. Charlie Gehringer	1926–41	16	549	110	176	11	89	.321	.404	103.7
9. Roberto Alomar	1988–2003	16	556	93	167	13	69	.301	.372	100.2
10. Jeff Kent	1992–2006	15	504	80	146	23	92	.289	.356	93.0

Shortstop

Among major league shortstops Honus Wagner has the best career record, topping all shortstops in batting average and on-base percentage. According to Faber System ratings he was the best hitter in the National League six times, including four consecutive seasons from 1906 through 1909. He led the National League in batting average eight times, in two-base hits seven times, in slugging six times, in runs batted in five times, in on-base percentage four times, in triples three times, and in runs and hits twice each. Two currently active players—Alex Rodriguez and Derek Jeter—rank second and third, respectively. A-Rod has the most runs scored, home runs, and runs batted in, while Jeter leads in hits. Hall of Famers Arky Vaughan, Ernie Banks, Robin Yount, and Cal Ripken occupy places fourth through seventh. In eighth spot is Julio Franco, who has not played shortstop for several years, but still has more years at that position than at any other. The last two places in the top ten go to Barry Larkin and Alan Trammell.

For an extended career Wagner again leads all shortstops, ranking first in runs scored, hits, runs batted in, and batting average. Rodriguez leads in home runs, and Arky Vaughan has the best on-base percentage. Cal Ripken moves up to second place in the rankings, followed by Rodriguez, Yount, Banks, Vaughan, and Franco. Oldtimer George Davis accumulated enough points in his 18 years to move into eighth position. Jeter is ninth and Old Aches and Pains—Luke Appling—holds down the final position in the top ten.

Despite playing the last few seasons at third base, Alex Rodriguez is ranked as the best hitting shortstop in points per season. He has the most runs scored, home runs, and runs batted in. A-Rod has won the Silver Slugger Award at shortstop seven times and at third base once. Twice he has been named the American League's Most Valuable Player. Honus Wagner holds the runnerup spot in points per year and leads in batting average. In third place is another active player who has vacated the shortstop position for another location on the field — Nomar Garciaparra. Vaughan, Ripken, and Jeter (who has the most hits per season) are fourth through sixth. Oldtimer Hughie Jennings leads in on-base percentages and ranks seventh in points. Despite 18 years as a major league player, Jennings had only seven eligible seasons. Four times he appeared in only one game during the season, and two other times he was in fewer than ten games. During 11 of his 18 seasons he played in fewer than 100 games, but when he did play a full season he put up some good numbers. Johnny Pesky, Ernie Banks, and Vern Stephens are the remaining members of the top ten hitting shortstops on a points per season basis.

SHORTSTOP CAREER (BEST YEARS)

Player	Best years		AB	Runs	Hits	HR	RBI	BA	OBP	Points
1. Honus Wagner	1900–09	10	5263	1019	1844	45	956	.350	.416	1730
2. Alex Rodriguez	1997–2006	10	5984	1239	1847	436	1242	.309	.381	1608
3. Derek Jeter	1997–2006	10	6160	1089	1954	173	775	.317	.390	1314
4. Arky Vaughan	1933–43	10	5381	977	1737	85	769	.323	.402	1306
5. Ernie Banks	1955–69	10	5891	897	1666	359	1104	.283	.341	1277
6. Robin Yount	1978–89	10	5719	947	1749	168	824	.306	.361	1249
7. Cal Ripken	1982–94	10	6086	945	1740	245	919	.286	.353	1144
8. Julio Franco	1985–86	10	5461	864	1687	121	967	.309	.365	1123
9. Barry Larkin	1988–2004	10	5156	991	1553	148	665	.304	.380	1099
10. Alan Trammell	1979–83	10	5069	827	1542	135	679	.304	.368	1086

SHORTSTOP EXTENDED CAREER (ALL ELIGIBLE SEASONS)

Player	Eligible Years		AB	Runs	Hits	HR	RBI	BA	OBP	Points
1. Honus Wagner	1898–1916	19	9967	1686	3288	97	1670	.330	.393	2549
2. Cal Ripken	1982–2001	18	10871	1552	2987	398	1582	.275	.344	2118
3. Alex Rodriguez	1996–2006	11	6571	1339	2023	459	1326	.308	.388	1692
4. Robin Yount	1974–93	20	11008	1632	3142	251	1406	.285	.342	1665
5. Ernie Banks	1954–69	16	9081	1273	2498	495	1580	.275	.334	1632
6. Arky Vaughan	1932–43	12	6373	1217	2532	91	879	.319	.402	1450
7. Julio Franco	1983–2005	17	8195	1228	2461	62	1130	.300	.360	1443
8. George Davis	1890–1908	18	8962	1538	2652	73	1437	.296	.363	1378
9. Derek Jeter	1996–2006	11	6742	1272	2138	183	853	.317	.388	1319
10. Luke Appling	1932–49	15	8054	1217	2652	73	1437	.296	.363	1378

SHORTSTOP POINTS PER SEASON

Player	Eligible Years		AB	Runs	Hits	HR	RBI	BA	OBP	Points
1. Alex Rodriguez	1996–2006	11	597	122	184	42	121	.308	.388	153.8
2. Honus Wagner	1898–1916	19	525	89	173	5	88	.330	.393	134.2
3. Nomar Garciaparra	1997–2006	7	587	106	190	26	105	.324	.376	130.4
4. Arky Vaughan	1932–43	12	531	94	169	8	73	.319	.402	121.3
5. Cal Ripken	1982–2001	18	604	86	166	22	88	.275	.344	117.7
6. Derek Jeter	1996–2006	11	613	116	194	17	78	.317	.388	119.9
7. Hughie Jennings	1892–1900	7	508	116	166	2	93	.327	.412	114.0
8. Johnny Pesky	1942–53	8	541	101	170	2	48	.312	.377	107.6
9. Ernie Banks	1954–69	16	568	80	156	31	99	.275	.334	102.0
10. Vern Stephens	1942–54	11	531	84	154	21	99	.289	.356	98.1

Wade Boggs leads all third basemen in career hitting. He has the highest batting average, the most hits, and the highest on-base percentage among third sackers with ten or more eligible seasons at the hot corner (National Baseball Hall of Fame Library, Cooperstown, New York).

Third Base

Wade Boggs leads all third basemen in career hitting. He has the most hits, and the best batting average and the highest on-base percentage of players with ten eligible seasons. He won five batting championships and led the American League in on-base percentage six times. Mike Schmidt ranks second. The Phillies thirdsacker led the National League in home runs seven times, in slugging five times, in runs batted in four times, and in on-base percentage three times. He tops Eddie Mathews by one as the career leader in home runs. Third ranking Edgar Martinez is better known as a designated hitter but he played more years at the hot corner than at any other position. Fourth and fifth and sixth spots are occupied by George Brett and Chipper Jones. Sixth place goes to Paul Molitor, who leads our list in runs scored. Eddie Mathews ranks seventh and Ron Santo is eighth. In ninth place is Stan Hack, the only third baseman in the top ten to start his major league career before World War II. Rounding out the top ten is Ken Boyer.

When all eligible seasons are taken into account George Brett moves to the head of the class. He won three batting titles, led in on-base percentage once, and led in hits and slugging three times each. His .390 batting average in 1980 is the highest in the major leagues since Ted Williams hit .406 in 1941. He leads third basemen in extended career hits, home runs, and runs batted in Boggs is third in these rankings and leads in batting average and OBP. Fourth-ranking Molitor leads in runs scored. He is followed by Mathews, Martinez, Jones, and Santo. Ninth place in the extended career rankings goes to a player who did not make the previous list — Darrell Evans. Stan Hack is tenth in the rankings.

When third basemen are ranked by hitting points per season, a different player comes out on top, John McGraw. Although the combative thirdsacker's major league career included parts of 16 seasons, injuries, suspensions, and refusals to report to his club reduced his number of eligible seasons to only seven. He leads in runs scored per season, batting average, and on-base percentage. He had some spectacular years, leading the league in runs scored and bases on balls twice, and in on-base percentage three times. His OBP of .547 in 1899 established a major league record that stood until Ted Williams's great season in 1941 and was not bested in the National League until Barry Bonds topped it in 2002. Boggs leads in hits per season, Schmidt in home runs, and Al Rosen in runs batted in. Rosen joins McGraw, pioneer Denny Lyons and contemporary star Scott Rolen as leaders in points per season who did not make the top ten in either of the other lists.

Third Base Career (Best Years)

Player	Best years		AB	Runs	Hits	HR	RBI	BA	OBP	Points
1. Wade Boggs	1983–94	10	5727	1015	1972	84	648	.344	.436	1682
2. Mike Schmidt	1974–87	10	5263	991	1486	367	1054	.283	.392	1627
3. Edgar Martinez	1991–2003	10	5202	967	1688	252	996	.324	.434	1592
4. George Brett	1975–90	10	5606	980	1826	201	946	.326	.389	1555
5. Chipper Jones	1995–2006	10	5261	999	1627	313	1000	.309	.413	1514
6. Paul Molitor	1979–96	10	5963	1065	1889	141	787	.317	.393	1508
7. Eddie Mathews	1953–63	10	5475	1043	1569	366	1031	.287	.397	1472
8. Ron Santo	1963–72	10	5703	872	1640	268	1003	.288	.377	1411
9. Stan Hack	1935–45	10	5692	885	1749	50	530	.307	.398	1185
10. Ken Boyer	1956–65	10	5905	910	1715	237	939	.290	.352	1176

Third Base Extended Careers (All Eligible Seasons)

Player	Eligible Years		AB	Runs	Hits	HR	RBI	BA	OBP	Points
1. George Brett	1974–93	20	10309	1581	3149	317	1625	.305	.369	2458
2. Mike Schmidt	1973–88	16	8170	1485	2197	541	1564	.269	.386	2179
3. Wade Boggs	1982–98	17	8888	1473	2922	116	985	.329	.420	2119
4. Paul Molitor	1978–98	19	10089	1653	3055	222	1245	.303	.372	2033
5. Eddie Mathews	1952–67	16	8485	1505	2304	509	1445	.272	.379	1903
6. Edgar Martinez	1990–2004	13	6500	1130	2056	288	1159	.316	.421	1789

Player	Eligible Years		AB	Runs	Hits	HR	RBI	BA	OBP	Points
7. Chipper Jones	1995–2006	12	6382	1186	1942	357	1197	.304	.402	1657
8. Ron Santo	1961–74	14	7796	1094	2167	333	1287	.278	.368	1539
9. Darrell Evans	1972–89	18	8643	1295	2138	402	1343	.247	.379	1287
10. Stan Hack	1934–45	11	6094	1049	1865	51	551	.306	.397	1185

THIRD BASE POINTS PER SEASON

Player	Eligible years		AB	Runs	Hits	HR	RBI	BA	OBP	Points
1. John McGraw	1893–1900	7	431	121	149	2	53	.346	.479	163.4
2. Chipper Jones	1995–2006	12	532	99	162	30	100	.304	.402	138.1
3. Edgar Martinez	1990–2004	13	500	87	158	22	89	.316	.421	137.6
4. Mike Schmidt	1973–88	16	511	93	137	34	98	.269	.386	136.2
5. Denny Lyons	1887–96	8	455	101	145	7	69	.318	.414	127.4
6. Wade Boggs	1982–98	17	523	87	172	7	58	.329	.420	124.6
7. Eddie Mathews	1952–67	16	530	94	144	32	90	.272	.379	118.9
8. George Brett	1974–93	20	515	79	157	16	81	.305	.369	116.6
9. Al Rosen	1950–56	7	525	86	151	27	102	.287	.386	114.3
10. Scott Rolen	1997–2006	9	531	96	153	23	101	.288	.378	111.1

Catcher

Mike Piazza is the best hitting catcher in major league history. He leads all backstops in home runs and has the highest on-base percentage of anyone with ten eligible seasons. Even so, his numbers do not quite measure up to leading hitters at other positions. Mike has never led the league in any major hitting category. Counting his seasons at other positions, Joe Torre leads our list in hits and ranks second among catchers in career hitting. He won the National League batting championship in 1971, but he played exclusively at third base that year. Johnny Bench, the third ranking career hitter, is tops in runs scored and runs batted in. He led the league in home runs twice and in runs batted in three times. He is followed in the rankings by modern day catchers Ted Simmons, Yogi Berra, Gary Carter, and Carlton Fisk, all of whom were good hitters, but not world beaters. A nineteenth-century star, Buck Ewing, ranks eighth. Bill Dickey, who has the highest career batting average of any catcher, is ninth. Tenth place goes to Ernie Lombardi, the only catcher in major league history to win two batting titles.

In extended career rankings Piazza leads in home runs, batting average, and on-base percentage. Fisk leads in runs scored, with one more than Berra. Simmons has the most hits, and Bench the most runs batted in. Torre ranks second, followed by Simmons, Bench, Berra, Fisk, and Carter. In eighth place , famed for his "homer in the gloamin'" that clinched the 1938 pennant for the Chicago Cubs, is Gabby Hartnett. Lombardi ranks ninth, and Ivan Rodriguez is tenth.

The top five places in points per season are identical to those in extended career rankings. Piazza leads in home runs, runs batted in, and batting average. Ewing ranks sixth and leads in runs scored. Thurman Munson, whose career came to a tragic end when he was killed in an airplane crash during the 1979 season, ranks seventh and has the most hits per season. In eighth place is John Clapp, who started his professional career in the National Association. Roger Bresnahan is ninth and the leader in on-base percentage. Gary Carter ranks tenth.

CATCHER CAREER (BEST YEARS)

Player	Best Years		AB	Runs	Hits	HR	RBI	BA	OBP	Points
1. Mike Piazza	1993–2002	10	5047	836	1625	346	1022	.323	.389	1495
2. Joe Torre	1963–74	10	5581	750	1700	202	918	.306	.375	1251

Johnny Bench has the best career ranking of any catcher. One of the leaders of Cincinnati's Big Red Machine, Bench excelled as a batter, as a fielder, and as a handler of pitchers (National Baseball Hall of Fame Library, Cooperstown, New York).

Player	Best Years		AB	Runs	Hits	HR	RBI	BA	OBP	Points
3. Johnny Bench	1968–79	10	5298	899	1464	288	1050	.276	.353	1204
4. Ted Simmons	1971–83	10	5478	723	1657	177	935	.302	.366	1200
5. Yogi Berra	1948–59	10	5200	844	1521	246	1013	.293	.356	1051
6. Gary Carter	1977–86	10	5222	755	1433	247	887	.275	.354	984
7. Carlton Fisk	1972–90	10	4725	814	1325	204	742	.281	.359	962
8. Buck Ewing	1882–95	10	3929	864	1224	57	687	.312	.353	958
9. Bill Dickey	1929–39	10	4443	728	1451	164	921	.327	.387	902
10. Ernie Lombardi	1932–45	10	3787	412	1212	137	680	.320	.374	883

CATCHER EXTENDED CAREER (ALL ELIGIBLE SEASONS)

Player	Eligible years		AB	Runs	Hits	HR	RBI	BA	OBP	Points
1. Mike Piazza	1993–2001	13	6299	975	1953	407	1229	.310	.378	1588
2. Joe Torre	1961–76	15	7601	971	2270	246	1059	.299	.367	1453
3. Ted Simmons	1970–85	16	8252	1032	2366	238	1311	.287	.350	1432
4. Johnny Bench	1968–83	15	7394	1070	1979	380	1344	.268	.342	1407
5. Yogi Berra	1948–61	14	6851	1085	1967	327	1309	.287	.350	1249
6. Carlton Fisk	1972–91	16	7439	1086	1988	306	1087	.267	.339	1161
7. Gary Carter	1975–92	16	7480	975	1985	315	1166	.265	.338	1078
8. Gabby Hartnett	1924–37	15	5893	810	1748	221	1089	.297	.370	1030
9. Ernie Lombardi	1932–45	14	5325	554	1618	170	907	.304	.356	993
10. Buck Ewing	1881–95	11	4201	904	1292	57	712	.308	.348	979

CATCHER POINTS PER SEASON

Player	Eligible years		AB	Runs	Hits	HR	RBI	BA	OBP	Points
1. Mike Piazza	1993–2001	13	485	75	150	31	95	.310	.378	122.2
2. Joe Torre	1961–76	15	507	65	151	16	71	.299	.367	96.9
3. Johnny Bench	1968–83	15	493	71	132	25	90	.268	.342	93.8
4. Ted Simmons	1970–85	16	516	65	148	15	82	.287	.350	89.5
5. Yogi Berra	1948–61	14	489	78	141	23	94	.287	.350	89.2
6. Buck Ewing	1881–95	11	382	82	117	5	65	.308	.348	89.0
7. Thurman Munson	1970–79	10	526	69	154	11	69	.292	.348	84.5
8. John Clapp	1876–81	6	282	46	81	0	29	.287	.326	84.2
9. Roger Bresnahan	1902–14	10	344	55	99	2	42	.288	.395	84.2
10. Gary Carter	1975–92	16	468	61	124	20	73	.265	.338	82.9

Right Field

Babe Ruth is by far the best hitting right fielder in major league history. He leads career rankings in runs scored, home runs, runs batted in, and on-base percentage. The Bambino's accomplishments are legion. He led the American League in slugging 13 times, in home runs 12 times, in bases on balls 11 times, on-base percentage 10 times, runs scored eight times, and runs batted in six times. In every one of these categories he ranks among the top three hitters of all time, regardless of position. He even won one batting championship. Wee Willie Keeler has the most hits, and Harry Heilmann edges Ruth for the best batting average .3652 to .3647. Hank Aaron, Frank Robinson, and Mel Ott rank second through fourth, respectively. For their best ten years Larry Walker ranks fifth, Keeler sixth, King Kelly seventh, Heilmann eighth, Gary Sheffield ninth, and Sammy Sosa tenth.

The Babe is tied with Aaron in points for an extended career. Ruth accumulated 3298 points in 16 seasons, the same number that Aaron amassed in 22 years. Ruth leads in batting average and on-base percentage, but Hammerin' Hank is tops in runs scored, hits, home runs, and runs batted in. Robinson and Ott again rank third and fourth. Of the right fielders ranking fifth through tenth in career hitting, none had more than 14 eligible seasons and only Keeler makes the top ten in extended career hitting. After the top four spots, the leading hitters on an extended career basis are Al Kaline, Dave Winfield, Sam Crawford, Tony Gwynn, Reggie Jackson, and Keeler. Keeler's .3479 batting average nearly matches Ruth's .3481.

In points per season Ruth leads by a wide margin. Two active players— Vladimir Guerrero and Lance Berkman— occupy the next two spots. It will be interesting to see how their numbers hold up over the next few years. Aaron, Robinson, and Ott hold the next three places. Still-active Bobby Abreu is seventh, followed by Walker, Keeler, and Sam Thompson. Ruth leads in runs scored, home runs, runs batted in, batting average, and on-base percentage. Keeler has the most hits per season. There are so many outstanding batsmen among right fielders that several great stars do not make the top ten in any category. Included among these luminaries are Paul Waner and Roberto Clemente, both of the Pittsburgh Pirates, and winners of a combined seven batting championships.

RIGHT FIELD CAREER (BEST YEARS)

Player	Best years		AB	Runs	Hits	HR	RBI	BA	OBP	Points
1. Babe Ruth	1920–32	10	5129	1508	1871	497	1473	.365	.505	2697
2. Hank Aaron	1957–63	10	5852	1117	1888	392	1141	.323	.402	1856
3. Frank Robinson	1956–69	10	5474	1093	1699	354	1076	.310	.402	1797
4. Mel Ott	1928–45	10	5349	1139	1700	316	1145	.318	.431	1730
5. Larry Walker	1990–2003	10	4792	968	1581	283	972	.330	.418	1657
6. Willie Keeler	1894–1906	10	5684	1266	2044	25	587	.360	.407	1609
7. King Kelly	1879–89	10	4191	1039	1355	58	642	.323	.374	1589
8. Harry Heilmann	1919–29	10	5279	970	1928	141	1135	.365	.431	1589
9. Gary Sheffield	1992–2005	10	5303	1013	1644	314	1075	.310	.415	1524
10. Sammy Sosa	1994–2004	10	5488	1022	1599	468	1177	.291	.368	1516

RIGHT FIELD EXTENDED CAREER (ALL ELIGIBLE SEASONS)

Player	Eligible years		AB	Runs	Hits	HR	RBI	BA	OBP	Points
1. Babe Ruth	1918–34	16	7607	2051	2648	674	2077	.348	.480	3298
2. Hank Aaron	1954–75	22	12113	2152	3689	745	2261	.309	.374	3298
3. Frank Robinson	1956–69	19	9821	1805	2900	574	1778	.295	.389	2825
4. Mel Ott	1928–45	18	9161	1827	2802	509	1833	.306	.416	2616
5. Al Kaline	1954–74	20	9778	1573	2921	388	1625	.299	.378	2366
6. Dave Winfield	1974–93	19	10453	1614	2975	450	1774	.285	.355	2072
7. Sam Crawford	1900–16	17	9339	1358	2904	94	1493	.311	.364	2001
8. Tony Gwynn	1984–99	16	8565	1294	2918	131	1050	.341	.391	1987
9. Reggie Jackson	1968–87	20	9769	1538	2563	562	1694	.262	.356	1973
10. Willie Keeler	1894–1907	14	7741	1606	2693	29	742	.348	.395	1970

RIGHT FIELD POINTS PER SEASON

Player	Eligible years		AB	Runs	Hits	HR	RBI	BA	OBP	Points
1. Babe Ruth	1918–34	16	475	128	166	42	130	.348	.480	206.1
2. Vladimir Guerrero	1998–2006	9	563	101	186	35	111	.325	.394	158.0
3. Lance Berkman	2000–06	7	513	97	157	32	105	.305	.417	156.0

For an extended career Hank Aaron ranks with Babe Ruth as baseball's best-hitting rightfielder. Aaron is tops in home runs, hits, runs batted in, and runs scored (National Baseball Hall of Fame Library, Cooperstown, New York).

Player	Eligible years		AB	Runs	Hits	HR	RBI	BA	OBP	Points
4. Hank Aaron	1954–75	22	551	98	168	34	103	.309	.374	149.9
5. Frank Robinson	1956–69	19	517	95	153	30	94	.295	.389	148.7
6. Mel Ott	1928–45	18	509	102	156	28	102	.306	.416	145.3
7. Bobby Abreu	1998–2006	9	563	103	171	22	95	.305	.415	142.7
8. Larry Walker	1990–2003	13	484	95	152	27	92	.315	.416	141.3

Player	Eligible years		AB	Runs	Hits	HR	RBI	BA	OBP	Points
9. Willie Keeler	1894–1907	14	553	115	192	2	53	.348	.395	140.7
10. Sam Thompson	1886–96	10	540	114	181	11	120	.335	.388	138.4

Center Field

Ty Cobb is the best hitting center fielder of all time. His career batting average is the highest ever recorded, and he leads all center fielders in on-base percentage. A ten-time batting champion, he led the American League in hits, on-base percentage, and slugging six times, in runs scored five times, and runs batted in twice. Mickey Mantle is second, Willie Mays third, and Tris Speaker fourth. In fifth place is Sliding Billy Hamilton, whose propensity for getting aboard and stealing bases helped him lead all center fielders in runs scored. George Gore ranks sixth. Joe DiMaggio, in seventh place, leads in hits and runs batted in. Ranking eighth is Ken Griffey, Jr., the home run leader at the position. Old-timers Pete Browning and Jim O'Rourke round out the top ten.

Cobb also tops the field in extended career hitting, leading in runs scored, hits, batting average, and on-base percentage. In second place is Willie Mays, who leads in both home runs and runs batted in over an extended career. Mays is followed in order by Speaker, Mantle, O'Rourke, Hamilton, Griffey, Gore, and DiMaggio. Duke Snider holds down the tenth spot, replacing Browning in the top ten.

In points per year, Cobb again leads, completing a sweep of the top spots for center fielders. The Georgia Peach leads in hits and batting average. Mays is again in second place. Hamilton takes third and is the leader in runs scored and on-base percentage. Speaker is fourth, followed by Mantle, Browning, and Gore. In eighth position is RBI leader DiMaggio. Benny Kauff, with only five eligible seasons, takes down the ninth spot. In tenth place is Griffey, the home run leader.

CENTER FIELD CAREER (BEST YEARS)

Player	Best years		AB	Runs	Hits	HR	RBI	BA	OBP	Points
1. Ty Cobb	1907–21	10	5457	1156	2091	67	1028	.383	.448	2128
2. Mickey Mantle	1954–64	10	5010	1173	1564	382	1017	.312	.440	1959
3. Willie Mays	1954–65	10	5830	1213	1863	416	1124	.320	.396	1849
4. Tris Speaker	1910–25	10	5380	1072	1957	60	858	.364	.448	1787
5. Billy Hamilton	1889–1901	10	4975	1362	1724	32	594	.347	.459	1769
6. George Gore	1880–90	10	4043	1088	1272	42	506	.315	.390	1608
7. Joe DiMaggio	1937–50	10	6549	1322	2120	347	1470	.324	.396	1561
8. Ken Griffey, Jr.	1991–2005	10	5331	1044	1665	418	1179	.312	.385	1553
9. Pete Browning	1882–92	10	4267	875	1482	41	282	.349	.393	1472
10. Jim O'Rourke	1876–90	10	3948	898	1285	30	336	.325	.367	1444

CENTER FIELD EXTENDED CAREER (ALL ELIGIBLE SEASONS)

Player	Eligible years		AB	Runs	Hits	HR	RBI	BA	OBP	Points
1. Ty Cobb	1907–27	19	9998	2009	3723	109	1746	.372	.440	3407
2. Willie Mays	1951–71	19	10301	1986	3148	642	1833	.306	.380	3273
3. Tris Speaker	1909–27	19	9868	1842	3434	108	1530	.348	.431	3183
4. Mickey Mantle	1952–68	16	7589	1576	2270	508	1409	.300	.421	2579
5. Jim O'Rourke	1976–93	18	7434	1445	2303	50	1010	.310	.355	1981
6. Billy Hamilton	1889–1901	11	5502	1503	1903	34	654	.346	.459	1849
7. Ken Griffey, Jr.	1989–2006	14	7175	1315	2176	505	1457	.303	.373	1818

Player	Eligible years		AB	Runs	Hits	HR	RBI	BA	OBP	Points
8. George Gore	1879–91	12	4837	1234	1492	44	586	.308	.382	1738
9. Joe DiMaggio	1936–51	12	6549	1322	2120	347	1470	.324	.396	1675
10. Duke Snider	1949–63	13	6360	1152	1909	377	1204	.300	.381	1545

CENTER FIELD POINTS PER SEASON

Player	Eligible years		AB	Runs	Hits	HR	RBI	BA	OBP	Points
1. Ty Cobb	1907–27	19	526	106	196	6	92	.372	.440	179.2
2. Willie Mays	1951–71	19	543	105	166	34	96	.306	.380	172.3
3. Billy Hamilton	1889–1901	11	500	137	173	4	59	.346	.459	168.1
4. Tris Speaker	1909–27	19	519	97	165	6	81	.348	.431	167.5
5. Mickey Mantle	1952–68	16	474	99	142	32	88	.300	.421	161.2
6. Pete Browning	1882–92	10	427	88	148	4	28	.349	.393	147.2
7. George Gore	1879–91	12	403	103	124	4	49	.308	.382	144.8
8. Joe DiMaggio	1936–51	12	546	110	177	29	123	.324	.391	139.6
9. Benny Kauff	1914–19	5	531	89	166	9	77	.313	.391	136.6
10. Ken Griffey, Jr.	1989–2006	14	513	94	155	36	104	.303	.373	129.9

Left Field

The Splendid Splinter, Ted Williams is the best hitting left fielder, by a slim margin over Barry Bonds. Williams had a .499 on-base percentage for his best ten years. He led the American League in that statistic 12 times. He led the league in bases on balls and in slugging eight times, in runs scored and batting average six times, and in home runs and runs batted in four times each. Almost certainly he would have had many more league-leading seasons had he not lost five seasons due to military service in World War II and Korea. Home run leader Bonds ranks second. Stan Musial, the leader in base hits, is third. Ed Delahanty, who has the highest batting average, is fourth. In fifth place is Manny Ramirez. Jesse Burkett, the leader in runs scored, is sixth, followed by RBI leader Al Simmons. Pete Rose, Carl Yastrzemski, and Rickey Henderson fill positions eight through ten.

For an extended career Bonds moves up to first place, followed by Musial, while Williams drops to third. Bonds is the home run leader, Musial has the most runs batted in, and Williams leads in on-base percentage. Fourth place goes to Pete Rose, who leads in both base hits and runs scored. Positions five through eight are taken by Yastrzemski, Henderson, Burkett, and Ramirez. In ninth spot is Billy Williams, while Delahanty, possessor of the highest batting average, is tenth.

In points per year Williams has a commanding lead. He has the highest on-base percentage among left fielders. Bonds is second. Shoeless Joe Jackson, the leader in hits per year, is third. RBI leader Ramirez is fourth. Mike Donlin is fifth. Musial is sixth. Seventh-ranking Ed Delahanty is the leader in both batting average and runs scored per season. Burkett is eighth. Making the top ten in points per year, but not in the other rankings are Albert Belle and Joe Medwick.

LEFT FIELD CAREER (BEST YEARS)

Player	Best years		AB	Hits	Runs	HR	RBI	BA	OBP	Points
1. Ted Williams	1941–58	10	5647	1196	1798	360	1167	.354	.499	2335
2. Barry Bonds	1992–2004	10	4600	1184	1496	454	1102	.325	.490	2329
3. Stan Musial	1943–57	10	5874	1165	2052	263	1072	.340	.467	1965
4. Ed Delahanty	1893–1902	10	5282	1223	1976	85	1150	.374	.446	1713

Player	Best years		AB	Hits	Runs	HR	RBI	BA	OBP	Points
5. Manny Ramirez	1995–2006	10	5121	1009	1625	392	1251	.317	.414	1707
6. Jesse Burkett	1893–1904	10	5610	1257	2047	53	727	.365	.443	1705
7. Al Simmons	1925–34	10	5590	1078	2005	232	1277	.359	.404	1601
8. Carl Yastrzemski	1962–77	10	5610	965	1699	222	918	.303	.402	1570
9. Pete Rose	1965–81	10	6283	1078	2043	97	614	.325	.400	1568
10. Rickey Henderson	1980–93	10	5249	1158	1548	159	567	.295	.408	1555

LEFT FIELD EXTENDED CAREER (ALL ELIGIBLE SEASONS)

Player	Eligible years		AB	Runs	Hits	HR	RBI	BA	OBP	Points
1. Barry Bonds	1986–2006	20	9465	2144	2829	729	1920	.299	.449	3446
2. Stan Musial	1942–63	21	10925	1941	3610	474	1944	.331	.417	3126
3. Ted Williams	1939–60	15	6951	1620	2393	451	1622	.345	.477	2893
4. Pete Rose	1963–85	23	13816	2150	4204	160	1289	.304	.376	2673
5. Carl Yastrzemski	1961–83	23	11988	1816	3419	452	1844	.285	.379	2593
6. Rickey Henderson	1980–2001	21	9705	2055	2800	264	1011	.289	.407	2497
7. Jesse Burkett	1890–1905	15	8259	1691	2805	75	939	.340	.416	2145
8. Manny Ramirez	1994–2006	13	6522	1253	2057	468	1511	.315	.412	2008
9. Billy Williams	1963–76	16	9270	1406	2693	424	1466	.291	.362	1944
10. Ed Delahanty	1890–1902	13	6815	1701	2407	99	1387	.353	.419	1932

LEFT FIELD POINTS PER SEASON

Player	Eligible years		AB	Runs	Hits	HR	RBI	BA	OBP	Points
1. Ted Williams	1939–60	15	463	108	160	30	108	.345	.477	206.6
2. Barry Bonds	1986–2006	20	473	107	141	36	96	.299	.449	172.3
3. Joe Jackson	1911–20	9	533	94	190	6	83	.357	.424	154.6
4. Manny Ramirez	1994–2006	13	502	96	158	36	121	.315	.414	154.5
5. Mike Donlin	1901–08	5	510	95	175	6	74	.343	.398	151.4
6. Stan Musial	1942–63	21	520	92	172	23	93	.331	.417	148.9
7. Ed Delahanty	1890–1902	13	524	131	185	8	107	.353	.419	148.6
8. Jesse Burkett	1890–1905	15	551	113	187	5	63	.340	.416	143.0
9. Albert Belle	1991–2000	10	561	95	167	37	120	.298	.372	137.2
10. Joe Medwick	1933–44	12	581	94	189	16	107	.326	.362	131.2

Designated Hitters

Edgar Martinez is the all-time best designated hitter. He led the league in on-base percentage three times, and was tops in runs scored and runs batted in one time each. While a designated hitter he won the American League batting championship once; earlier he had won the title while playing third base. The tables below show the records of the players only during the years they were designated hitters. With the exception of David Ortiz and Cliff Johnson, all of them had been position players for several years before turning to DH in the latter part of their careers. Most of them had posted higher numbers as position players than they did as DH. Martinez is an exception to the rule. Only ten players have five or more eligible seasons as DH, a position that did not exist before 1973. Among them Martinez leads in runs scored, home runs, runs batted in. batting average, and on-base percentage. Hal McRae has the most hits as a DH. If the position is continued and more young players become DH early in their careers, it is likely that several changes will occur in these rankings during the next decade. Hitters now ranked eighth, ninth, and tenth will likely fall out of the top ten.

Only two designated hitters—Hal McRae and Harold Baines—have more than ten eligible seasons at the position. Neither of them earned as many Faber System points in their extended careers as Martinez earned in his nine seasons. However, Baines does overtake career leaders in hits, home runs, and RBIs.

In points per year Martinez again tops the list, with David Ortiz and Frank Thomas moving up to second and third place, respectively. The Mariner leads in batting average and OBP. Ortiz leads in home runs and RBIs, while Thomas has scored the most runs per year. Paul Molitor leads in hits per season. Within a few years, Ortiz is likely to move up several places in the career rankings.

DESIGNATED HITTERS CAREER (BEST YEARS)

Hitter	Best years		AB	Runs	Hits	HR	RBI	BA	OBP	Points
1. Edgar Martinez	1995–2004	9	4616	814	1468	232	874	.318	.437	1311
2. Hal McRae	1974–85	10	5051	664	1522	190	809	.301	.358	993
3. Harold Baines	1987–99	10	4716	639	1386	194	846	.294	.376	953
4. Paul Molitor	1991–98	8	4594	729	1449	103	681	.315	.378	873
5. Frank Thomas	1991–2006	7	3747	643	1076	228	707	.287	.402	829
6. Chili Davis	1991–99	8	3798	518	1088	191	704	.286	.382	772
7. David Ortiz	2000–06	6	3016	518	873	203	663	.289	.422	716
8. Don Baylor	1978–87	8	4053	631	1036	193	680	.256	.342	625
9. Cliff Johnson	1979–85	5	1712	233	465	88	329	.272	.360	339
10. Willie Horton	1975–79	5	2578	272	704	94	389	.273	.328	313

DESIGNATED HITTERS EXTENDED CAREER (ALL ELIGIBLE SEASONS)

Hitter	Eligible years		AB	Runs	Hits	HR	RBI	BA	OBP	Points
1. Edgar Martinez	1995–2004	9	4616	814	1468	232	874	.318	.437	1311
2. Harold Baines	1987–99	13	5787	778	1706	235	1024	.295	.374	1101
3. Hal McRae	1974–85	12	5440	702	1628	147	845	.299	.355	1029
4. Paul Molitor	1991–98	8	4594	729	1449	103	681	.315	.378	873
5. Frank Thomas	1991–2006	7	3747	643	1076	228	707	.287	.402	829
6. Chili Davis	1991–99	8	3798	518	1088	191	704	.286	.382	772
7. David Ortiz	2000–06	6	3016	518	873	203	663	.289	.422	716
8. Don Baylor	1978–87	8	4053	631	1036	193	680	.256	.342	625
9. Cliff Johnson	1979–85	5	1712	233	465	88	329	.272	.360	339
10. Willie Horton	1975–79	5	2578	272	704	94	389	.273	.328	313

DESIGNATED HITTERS POINTS PER SEASON

Hitter	Eligible years		AB	Runs	Hits	HR	RBI	BA	OBP	Points
1. Edgar Martinez	1995–2004	9	496	70	163	26	97	.318	.437	145.7
2. David Ortiz	2000–06	6	503	86	146	34	111	.289	.422	119.3
3. Frank Thomas	1991–2006	7	535	92	154	33	101	.287	.402	118.4
4. Paul Molitor	1991–98	8	574	91	181	13	85	.315	.378	109.1
5. Chili Davis	1991–99	8	475	65	136	25	88	.286	.382	96.5
6. Hal McRae	1974–85	12	495	64	148	13	77	.299	.355	93.5
7. Harold Baines	1987–99	13	445	60	131	18	79	.295	.374	84.7
8. Don Baylor	1978–87	8	507	79	130	24	85	.256	.342	78.1
9. Cliff Johnson	1979–85	5	342	47	97	18	66	.272	.360	67.8
10. Willie Horton	1975–79	5	516	54	141	19	78	.273	.328	62.6

GARDNER HARVEY LIBRARY
Miami University-Middletown
Middletown, Ohio

All Positions

When hitters are ranked regardless of position played in the field, Babe Ruth comes out as the best hitter of all time, besting Ted Williams by a comfortable margin. The rankings are dominated by outfielders and corner infielders. No catchers and only two shortstops and three second basemen rank in the top fifty hitters. The best hitters on a career basis also show up well in extended career and points per year rankings. Every one of the top 23 career hitters makes the top 50 in both of the other lists. All but seven of the top 50 are also among the 50 best in at least one of the other rankings. At number 33 Al Simmons is the best career hitter not to make either of the other best 50 lists. Although Simmons had 10 outstanding years, he averaged below the league mean for his other six eligible seasons.

On an extended career basis Barry Bonds edges Ty Cobb for the top spot. Bonds collected 3440 points in 20 years, while Cobb amassed 3407 points in 19 seasons. Ruth and Williams fall out of the top places because they had fewer years in which to acquire points. The Bambino was a pitcher for his first few big league seasons, and Williams lost five years because of military service. Outfielders and corner infielders provide the bulk of the extended career leaders. Most of the extended career leaders also rank among the top 50 in career rankings. The best extended career hitter not to make the top 50 in career rankings is Al Kaline, who ranks 21st when all eligible seasons are counted, moving up from 53rd in rankings for the best 10 years. The Detroit star accomplished this feat by exceeding the league mean in 19 of his 20 eligible seasons.

In hitting points per season Albert Pujols heads the rankings, nosing out Ted Williams and Babe Ruth. The still-active Cardinal slugger will have to maintain a torrid pace to keep that rank. It will be interesting to see whether he can do so. Among the top 50 hitters are several still-active players who will find that keeping their places in the rankings is quite a challenge. Also included are several who for one reason or another were not able to play enough years to make the lists of career leaders. Among the best of these are John McGraw, Shoeless Joe Jackson, Hank Greenberg, and Turkey Mike Donlin. Outfield and corner infield positions again provide most of the leaders in these rankings.

CAREER HITTING LEADERS—ALL POSITIONS

Hitter	Best years		AB	Runs	Hits	HR	RBI	BA	OBP	Points
1. Babe Ruth	1918–34	10	5129	1508	1871	497	1473	.365	.505	2697
2. Ted Williams	1941–58	10	5647	1196	1798	360	1167	.354	.499	2335
3. Barry Bonds	1992–2004	10	4600	1184	1496	454	1102	.325	.490	2329
4. Lou Gehrig	1927–37	10	5797	1428	2056	392	1560	.355	.462	2232
5. Ty Cobb	1907–21	10	5457	1156	2091	67	1028	.383	.448	2128
6. Stan Musial	1943–57	10	5874	1165	2052	263	1072	.340	.467	1965
7. Rogers Hornsby	1917–29	10	5445	1185	2089	248	1126	.384	.459	1959
8. Mickey Mantle	1954–64	10	5010	1173	1564	382	1017	.312	.440	1951
9. Jimmie Foxx	1929–42	10	5448	1269	1879	418	1388	.345	.450	1942
10. Hank Aaron	1957–63	10	5852	1117	1888	497	1141	.323	.402	1856
11. Willie Mays	1954–65	10	5830	1213	1863	416	1124	.320	.396	1849
12. Dan Brouthers	1882–92	10	4651	1078	1622	79	649	.349	.422	1842

Oppposite: **Babe Ruth (left) and John McGraw at the 1923 World Series. Ruth led his Yankees to their world title by hitting three home runs in the Series. The greatest hitter ever, Ruth revolutionized the game with his long-distance drives. McGraw, a former sparkplug at third base for the old Baltimore Orioles, was the most successful manager in National League history. His Giants won the World Series over the Yankees in 1921 and 1922 but never again defeated their crosstown rivals in the fall classic (Library of Congress).**

Hitter	Best years		AB	Runs	Hits	HR	RBI	BA	OBP	Points
13. Cap Anson	1876–90	10	4079	829	1406	61	903	.345	.465	1801
14. Frank Robinson	1956–69	10	5474	1093	1699	354	1076	.310	.402	1797
15. Tris Speaker	1910–25	10	5380	1072	1957	60	858	.364	.448	1787
16. Frank Thomas	1991–2003	10	5343	1057	1690	364	1180	.316	.438	1775
17. Billy Hamilton	1889–1901	10	4975	1362	1724	32	594	.347	.459	1769
18. Honus Wagner	1900–09	10	5263	1019	1844	45	956	.350	.416	1730
19. Mel Ott	1928–45	10	5349	1139	1700	316	1145	.318	.431	1730
20. Jeff Bagwell	1993–2003	10	5537	1148	1690	365	1156	.305	.416	1728
21. Ed Delahanty	1893–1902	10	5282	1223	1976	85	1150	.374	.446	1713
22. Manny Ramirez	1994–2006	10	5121	1009	1625	392	1251	.317	.414	1707
23. Jesse Burkett	1893–1904	10	5610	1257	2047	53	727	.365	.443	1705
24. Todd Helton	1993–2006	9	5013	1005	1674	281	985	.334	.430	1703
25. Johnny Mize	1936–48	10	5183	959	1680	297	1096	.324	.410	1683
26. Wade Boggs	1983–94	10	5727	1015	1972	84	648	.344	.436	1682
27. Larry Walker	1990–2003	10	4792	968	1581	283	972	.330	.418	1657
28. Mike Schmidt	1974–87	10	5263	991	1486	367	1054	.283	.392	1627
29. Eddie Collins	1909–24	10	5435	1093	1893	32	738	.348	.439	1624
30. Willie Keeler	1894–1906	10	5684	1266	2044	25	587	.360	.407	1609
31. George Gore	1880–90	10	4043	1088	1272	42	506	.315	.390	1608
31. Alex Rodriguez	1997–2006	10	5984	1239	1847	436	1242	.309	.381	1608
33. Al Simmons	1925–34	10	5590	1078	2005	232	1277	.359	.404	1601
34. Edgar Martinez	1991–2003	10	5202	967	1688	252	996	.324	.434	1592
35. King Kelly	1879–89	10	4191	1039	1355	58	642	.323	.374	1589
36. Harry Heilmann	1919–29	10	5279	970	1928	141	1135	.365	.431	1589
37. Roger Connor	1880–92	10	4540	974	1498	72	704	.330	.400	1578
38. Harmon Killebrew	1959–71	10	5429	917	1441	431	1155	.265	.387	1576
39. Carl Yastrzemski	1962–77	10	5610	965	1699	222	918	.303	.402	1575
40. Pete Rose	1965–81	10	6283	1078	2043	97	614	.325	.400	1568
41. Nap Lajoie	1897–1912	10	4957	872	1775	47	985	.358	.400	1567
42. Joe DiMaggio	1937–50	10	6549	1322	2120	347	1470	.324	.396	1561
43. George Brett	1975–90	10	5606	980	1826	201	946	.326	.389	1555
44. Mark McGwire	1987–99	10	4897	945	1329	479	1155	.271	.400	1555
45. Rickey Henderson	1980–93	10	5249	1158	1548	159	567	.295	.408	1555
46. Ken Griffey, Jr.	1991–2005	10	5331	1044	1665	418	1179	.312	.385	1553
47. Dick Allen	1964–74	10	5173	921	1544	303	916	.298	.385	1529
48. Gary Sheffield	1992–2005	10	5303	1013	1644	314	1075	.310	.415	1524
49. Billy Williams	1963–72	10	6272	1006	1882	307	1013	.300	.364	1519
50. Willie McCovey	1963–74	10	4627	784	1314	339	946	.284	.401	1516
50. Sammy Sosa	1994–2004	10	5488	1022	1599	468	1177	.291	.368	1516

EXTENDED CAREER HITTING—ALL POSITIONS

Hitter	Eligible years		AB	Runs	Hits	HR	RBI	BA	OBP	Points
1. Barry Bonds	1986–2006	20	9465	2144	2829	729	1920	.299	.449	3440
2. Ty Cobb	1907–27	19	9998	2009	3723	109	1746	.372	.440	3407
3. Babe Ruth	1918–34	16	7607	2051	2648	674	2077	.348	.480	3298
4. Hank Aaron	1954–75	22	12113	2152	3689	745	2261	.309	.374	3298
5. Willie Mays	1951–71	19	10301	1986	3148	642	1833	.306	.380	3273
6. Tris Speaker	1909–27	19	9868	1842	3434	108	1530	.348	.431	3183
7. Stan Musial	1942–63	21	10925	1941	3610	474	1944	.331	.417	3126
8. Ted Williams	1939–60	15	6851	1620	2393	451	1622	.345	.477	2893

Hitter	Eligible years		AB	Runs	Hits	HR	RBI	BA	OBP	Points
9. Frank Robinson	1956–69	19	9821	1805	2900	574	1778	.295	.389	2825
10. Cap Anson	1876–97	20	8534	1597	2807	92	1746	.329	.398	2729
11. Lou Gehrig	1925–38	14	7935	1878	2700	493	1989	.340	.448	2701
12. Pete Rose	1963–85	23	13816	2150	4204	160	1289	.304	.376	2673
13. Mel Ott	1928–45	18	9161	1827	2802	509	1833	.306	.416	2616
14. Jimmie Foxx	1928–42	15	7719	1688	2527	524	1827	.327	.431	2610
15. Carl Yastrzemski	1961–83	23	11988	1816	3419	452	1844	.285	.379	2598
16. Mickey Mantle	1952–68	16	7589	1576	2270	508	1409	.300	.421	2579
17. Honus Wagner	1898–1916	19	9967	1686	3288	97	1670	.330	.393	2549
18. Rogers Hornsby	1916–31	15	7752	1527	2809	294	1434	.362	.449	2503
19. Rickey Henderson	1980–2001	21	9705	2055	2800	264	1011	.289	.407	2497
20. Eddie Collins	1908–26	19	9849	1730	3217	46	1275	.327	.423	2453
21. Al Kaline	1954–74	20	1778	1573	2921	388	1625	.299	.378	2366
22. George Brett	1974–93	20	10309	1581	3149	317	1625	.305	.369	2332
23. Eddie Murray	1977–96	20	11169	1614	3218	501	1899	.288	.363	2257
24. Mike Schmidt	1973–88	16	8170	1485	2197	541	1564	.269	.386	2179
25. Jesse Burkett	1890–1905	15	8259	1691	2805	75	939	.340	.416	2145
26. Rafael Palmeiro	1988–2003	18	10078	166	2941	552	1793	.289	.376	2137
27. Wade Boggs	1982–78	17	8888	1473	2922	116	985	.329	.420	2119
28. Roger Connor	1880–96	17	7714	1607	2448	137	1311	.329	.398	2118
29. Cal Ripken	1982–2001	18	10871	1552	2987	398	1582	.275	.344	2118
30. Dave Winfield	1974–93	19	10453	1614	2975	450	1774	.285	.355	2072
31. Rod Carew	1967–85	17	8795	1355	2890	86	956	.329	.396	2061
32. Paul Molitor	1978–98	19	10089	1653	3055	222	1245	.303	.372	2033
33. Frank Thomas	1991–2006	13	6818	1285	2096	446	1463	.307	.431	2028
34. Harmon Killebrew	1959–74	15	7332	1200	1907	543	1478	.260	.382	2019
35. Manny Ramirez	1994–2006	13	6522	1253	2057	468	1511	.315	.412	2008
36. Sam Crawford	1900–16	17	9339	1358	2904	94	1493	.311	.364	2001
37. Jeff Bagwell	1991–2004	14	7697	1506	2289	446	1510	.297	.412	1988
38. Tony Gwynn	1984–99	16	8565	1294	2918	131	1050	.341	.391	1987
39. Joe Morgan	1965–84	19	9195	1635	2499	268	1170	.272	.391	1986
40. Jim O'Rourke	1876–93	18	7434	1445	2303	50	1010	.310	.355	1981
41. Reggie Jackson	1968–87	20	9769	1538	2563	562	1694	.262	.356	1973
42. Willie Keeler	1894–1907	14	7741	1606	2693	29	742	.348	.395	1970
43. Billy Williams	1963–76	16	9270	1406	2693	424	1466	.291	.362	1944
44. Ed Delahanty	1890–1902	13	6815	1701	2407	99	1387	.353	.419	1932
45. Dan Brouthers	1881–94	13	6188	1449	2137	99	1217	.345	.427	1927
46. Eddie Mathews	1952–67	16	8485	1505	2304	509	1445	.272	.379	1903
47. Harry Heilmann	1916–30	14	7288	1229	2532	176	1479	.348	.413	1898
48. Jim Rice	1975–88	14	7949	1221	2385	378	1409	.301	.356	1873
49. Fred McGriff	1987–2002	16	8383	1309	2402	478	1503	.287	.382	1858
50. Billy Hamilton	1889–1901	11	5502	1503	1903	34	654	.346	.459	1849

HITTING POINTS PER SEASON—ALL POSITIONS

Hitter	Eligible years		AB	Runs	Hits	HR	RBI	BA	OBP	Points
1. Albert Pujols	2001–06	6	582	125	173	42	126	.332	.419	207.2
2. Ted Williams	1939–60	15	463	108	160	30	108	.345	.477	206.6
3. Babe Ruth	1918–34	16	475	128	166	42	130	.348	.480	206.1
4. Lou Gehrig	1925–38	14	567	134	193	35	142	.340	.448	192.9
5. Todd Helton	1998–2006	9	557	112	186	31	109	.334	.434	189.2

Hitter	Eligible years		AB	Runs	Hits	HR	RBI	BA	OBP	Points
6. Ty Cobb	1907–27	19	526	106	196	6	92	.372	.440	179.2
7. Jimmie Foxx	1928–42	15	512	113	168	35	124	.327	.431	174.0
8. Willie Mays	1951–71	19	543	105	166	34	96	.306	.380	172.3
9. Barry Bonds	1986–2006	20	473	107	141	34	96	.299	.449	172.3
10. Billy Hamilton	1889–1901	11	500	137	173	4	59	.346	.459	168.1
11. Rogers Hornsby	1916–31	15	517	102	187	20	96	.362	.449	166.9
12. Tris Speaker	1909–27	19	519	97	165	6	81	.348	.431	167.5
13. John McGraw	1893–1900	7	431	121	149	2	53	.346	.479	163.4
14. Mickey Mantle	1952–68	16	474	99	142	32	88	.300	.421	161.2
15. Vladimir Guerrero	1998–2006	9	563	101	186	35	111	.325	.399	158.0
16. Hank Greenberg	1933–47	9	534	109	157	35	130	.314	.412	156.3
17. Frank Thomas	1991–2006	13	524	99	161	34	113	.307	.431	156.0
18. Joe Jackson	1911–20	9	533	94	190	6	83	.357	.424	154.6
19. Manny Ramirez	1994–2006	13	502	96	158	36	121	.315	.414	154.5
20. Lance Berkman	2000–06	7	513	97	157	32	105	.302	.413	154.1
21. Alex Rodriguez	1996–2006	11	597	122	184	42	121	.308	.388	153.8
22. Mike Donlin	1901–08	5	510	95	175	6	74	.343	.398	151.4
23. Hank Aaron	1954–75	22	551	98	168	34	103	.309	.374	149.0
24. Stan Musial	1942–63	21	520	92	172	23	93	.331	.417	148.9
25. Frank Robinson	1956–69	19	517	95	153	30	94	.295	.389	148.7
26. Ed Delahanty	1890–1902	13	524	131	185	8	107	.353	.419	148.6
27. Dan Brouthers	1881–94	13	476	111	164	8	94	.345	.427	148,2
28. Pete Browning	1882–92	10	427	88	148	4	28	.349	.393	147.2
29. Mel Ott	1928–45	18	509	102	156	28	102	.306	.416	145.3
30. George Gore	1879–91	12	403	103	124	4	49	.308	.382	144.8
31. Mark McGwire	1987–99	11	489	92	130	46	111	.261	.394	144.1
32. Johnny Mize	1936–51	12	492	88	156	27	101	.316	.405	143.8
33. Jesse Burkett	1890–1905	15	551	113	187	5	63	.340	.416	143.0
34. Bobby Abreu	1998–2006	9	563	103	171	22	95	.305	.415	142.7
35. Jeff Bagwell	1991–2004	14	550	108	164	32	108	.297	.412	142.0
36. Larry Walker	1990–2003	13	484	95	152	27	92	.315	.416	141.3
37. Dick Allen	1964–75	11	517	93	154	30	92	.298	.380	141.0
38. Willie Keeler	1894–1907	14	553	115	192	2	53	.348	.395	140.7
39. Joe DiMaggio	1936–51	12	546	110	177	29	123	.324	.391	139.6
40. Sam Thompson	1886–96	10	540	114	181	11	120	.335	.388	138.4
41. Chipper Jones	1995–2006	12	532	99	162	30	100	.304	.402	138.1
42. Edgar Martinez	1990–2004	13	500	87	158	22	89	.316	.421	137.6
43. Jason Giambi	1996–2006	10	518	96	154	33	108	.297	.418	137.4
44. Albert Belle	1991–2000	10	561	95	167	37	120	.298	.372	137.2
45. Benny Kauff	1914–19	5	531	89	166	9	77	.313	.391	136.6
46. Cap Anson	1876–97	20	417	80	140	5	87	.329	.398	136.5
47. Mike Schmidt	1873–88	16	511	93	137	34	98	.269	.386	136.2
48. Harry Heilmann	1916–30	14	521	88	181	13	106	.348	.413	135.5
49. Harmon Killebrew	1959–74	15	489	80	127	36	99	.260	.382	134.6
50. Honus Wagner	1898–1916	19	525	89	173	5	88	.330	.393	134.2

2

FIELDERS

Some people believe that fielding statistics are misleading. They say that statistics never show the true worth of a fielder. That is because they look at the wrong numbers. There is a way that the figures can reflect the real contributions of defensive players. The fundamental purpose of fielding is to get opposing players out. Other things being equal the fielder who gets the most batters out and allows the fewest hitters to be safe when they should have been retired is the best fielder. Unfortunately, other things are not always equal. The Faber system compensates for these inequalities.

One indicator of a defensive player's ability is the amount of ground he covers. The other is the accuracy with which he executes plays. Traditional fielding averages show only the latter data. Fans are now becoming familiar with the former. Called the range factor, this statistic reveals the total number of chances handled per game played. Our system combines the traditional fielding average with a more sophisticated computation of the range factor. For one thing this system includes in the range factor only those chances that are handled successfully — putouts and assists. Errors should not be, and in this system are not, utilized to increase the fielder's range factor. The major change, however, is that putouts and assists are differentiated at three positions—catcher, first base, and outfield.

Assists reflect far more accurately a catcher's defensive accomplishments than do putouts. Catchers compile assists the same way other fielders do — by throwing out base runners. However, they are credited with putouts not only for catching fly balls and tagging out or forcing out runners, but also for strikeouts by the pitcher. In reality the responsibility for striking out a batter lies primarily with the pitcher. Through the pitches he calls for, the catcher may make a contribution. But Nolan Ryan's catcher was not necessarily a better *fielder* just because Ryan was a strikeout pitcher. Therefore, we weight assists by a catcher at a ratio of 10 to 1 over putouts.

The same weighting system is used at first base to compensate for the fact that a majority of the putouts by a first baseman are made by merely catching throws from other fielders. Sometimes the first sacker must dig balls out of the dirt or leap to catch throws slightly off target, but most putouts at first base are relatively easy. Assists are a more reliable indicator of the first baseman's fielding ability than are putouts, for in order to get an assist he must first field the ball, then make an accurate throw to the man covering the bag in time for a putout to be made.

Outfield performance is weighted in the same way. Sometimes outfielders make spectacular diving or leaping catches in order to make a putout. More often an out is achieved by making a routine catch of a fly ball. Assists, however, almost always require extraordinary effort or skill.

The key fielding positions are in the middle of the infield at second base and shortstop. These players must not only be able to field ground balls and make accurate throws, but they must also be able to make the putout at the keystone sack and quickly and accurately throw to first base in double play situations, frequently while eluding or being upset by a sliding base runner. The range factor for middle infielders is greater than that for the corner infielders. Putouts and assists are weighted equally for middle infielders and for third basemen.

Season Ratings

The formula used to compute a fielder's yearly total includes the weighted number of chances successfully handled per 100 games plus a number derived from the fielding percentage (The fielding average is divided by three, then multiplied by 1000 in order to convert it to a whole number.) Because fewer balls are hit to third base and the outfield than to the middle of the infield, points are reduced to one-half for third basemen and one-third for outfielders. A league mean is calculated for each position each year, and each player is scored on how many points he deviates from the mean. In seasons shorter than 154 games, the points are adjusted by applying a multiplier derived by dividing the number of games scheduled by 154.

Some fielders may play at two or more positions in the same year. Thus, it is possible for a person to be a full-time player, yet not be involved in two-thirds of his team's games at any one position. The Faber System recognizes this possibility and provides half credit at their main fielding position for players meeting certain criteria (appearing in a total of 100 or more games with between 75 and 100 games at one position, with the number of games required adjusted appropriately in seasons of fewer than 154 games.) For example, in 1992 Bip Roberts was perhaps the most valuable player for the Cincinnati Reds, appearing in 147 games, filling in for injured players wherever needed. During the course of the season he played three different infield positions and 79 games in the outfield. Although he did not meet the full eligibility requirements at any one position, he receives half-credit as an outfielder. During that same 1992 season Mariano Duncan participated in 142 games for the Philadelphia Phillies with 574 times at bat. Very clearly he was a full-time player and receives full credit for his hitting. However, he appeared in only 65 games in the outfield, 52 at second base, and a scattering at other positions. Unfortunately, he cannot receive any fielding points for that season, for he did not have enough games at any position to be eligible.

Career Ratings

Career totals for fielders are computed in the same way as for batters; that is, by adding the yearly points and counting the best ten years. As with hitting records, since 1901 fifty points per year are allocated to each player when the yearly points are totaled. Because of shorter seasons in the early years of professional baseball, 30 points are added in the years from 1876 through 1893 and 40 points from 1894 through 1900.

One exception to the above rule is that in a season where the player has fewer than four times at bat per minimum number of games required for eligibility, the season may be excluded from the player's ratings if doing so would be to his advantage. The reason for this is to avoid penalizing a player who is inserted late into the game for defensive purposes. Even though he might be an excellent fielder, such a player would not have the opportunity to accept as many chances as a full-time player. For players during the 2006 season, for example, this means a player with fewer than 400 at bats could have the season excluded from his eligible years, regardless of in how many games he actually appeared.

There is another complicating factor with fielders. Some players do not spend their entire careers at the same position. Suppose, for example, that after eight years of excellent fielding at shortstop, a player moves to first base and performs well at that position for another eight years. Ernie Banks is an example of such a player. Was Mr. Cub a shortstop or a first baseman? Since he played an equal number of years at each position, the fair thing seems to be to list him where it is to his advantage. Banks accumulated 583 fielding points at shortstop to 552 at first base. Therefore, he is listed as a shortstop. As a shortstop he is not entitled to the fielding points he earned at first base, so in the list of fielding leaders at that position he is credited with only 583 points. However, when we look at Ernie Banks as a total player, it is not fair to ignore his work at the other position. In the section of the book on Players, he receives the credit he has earned.

Another Hall of Famer, Rod Carew, divided his career between the middle of the infield and first base, as did Banks. Carew had eight eligible seasons at second base and seven years at first base. As he had more than five years at each position, he is listed where it is to his advantage. For Carew that is first base, for he earned more fielding points (362) in his seven years at first than he accrued in his eight years at the keystone sack (231). So a player with a lengthy career is not necessarily listed at the spot where he played the most seasons. However, this option is not available in ranking players with short careers, because no player is listed at a position where he had fewer than five complete seasons if he had five full years at another position. For example, Jorge Orta was not a good fielding second baseman by major league standards. He acquired fewer Faber System points in five seasons at the keystone than he did in two years in the outfield, yet he must be listed as a second baseman because it is the only position where he had five eligible seasons.

In summary, a fielder is ranked at one position only. His primary position is the one at which he played the most years, unless he had five or more full seasons at each of two or more positions, in which case he is listed where it is to his advantage. If he played an equal number of years at two or more positions, he is listed at the one where he compiled the best record.

Leading Fielders by Year

National League—First Base

In 1887 Roger Connor set a National League record for fielding points by a first baseman with 48 points, a mark that stood for over 100 years until Mark Grace tallied 52 points in 1991. The following year Grace eclipsed his own record with 55 points. The number of chances accepted by fielders naturally increased as the number of games played increased during the pioneer era. In 1876 Herman Dehlman led the league with 750 putouts in 64 games. By 1883 three different first basemen posted 1000 or more putouts in a 100 game season. In 1898 Tommy Tucker set the 19th century record with 1552 putouts. The record was broken in turn by Fred Tenney and Ed Konetchy. In 1920 George "Highpockets" Kelly established a new standard with 1759 putouts, which is still the most ever recorded by a National League first sacker.

The assist record follows a similar upward spiral. In 1876 Joe Gerhardt and Charlie Gould were league leaders with 13 assists each. By 1892 Jake Beckley had recorded 132 assists in a single season. In 1905 Tenney raised the record to 152, a mark that stood until Bill Buckner posted 159 assists in 1982. Buckner twice exceeded that number and holds the American League record at 184, set in 1985. Mark Grace holds the National League mark with 180 assists in 1990 while playing for the Chicago Cubs.

Fielding percentage also shows an upward trend. Joe Start led the league in 1876 with .964. an average that would have ranked next to last among the league's first basemen in 1887, when Roger Connor turned in a .993 record. Dan McGann fielded .995 in 1906, as did Ed Konetchy in 1913 and 1914. In 1916 Fritz Mollwitz posted .996. In 1921 Walter Holke fielded at a .997 clip. In 1946 Frank McCormick raised the mark to .999. Steve Garvey became the first to play an error-less season at the position in 1984. That is one record that can never be broken.

During the pioneer era Joe Start and Cap Anson each led the National League first basemen in fielding points four times, a feat that was matched by Ed Konetchy in the 1910s. Then along came Bill Terry, who was the league's best nine times, including six in a row from 1927 through 1932. These records have not been equaled, although Keith Hernandez came close with seven league-leading seasons, and Mark Grace was best at the position six times. Among others leading the league four times were two Hall of Famers whose primary position was not first base — Stan Musial and Ernie Banks.

NATIONAL LEAGUE FIELDING LEADERS — FIRST BASE

Year	First Baseman	G	PO	A	E	Pct.	Total	Mean	Points
1876	Joe Start	56	547	10	21	.964	329	278	21
1877	Al Spalding	45	472	21	21	.959	349	338	4
1878	Chub Sullivan	61	680	23	18	.975	399	327	29
1879	Joe Start	65	779	11	22	.973	380	315	34
1880	Cap Anson	81	833	15	20	.977	378	336	23
1881	Cap Anson	84	892	43	24	.975	407	348	31
1882	Joe Start	82	905	21	25	.974	383	333	28
1883	John Morrill	81	794	20	22	.974	370	341	19
1884	Joe Start	93	939	21	20	.980	391	349	31
1885	Alex McKinnon	100	1102	26	25	.978	396	378	13
1886	Sid Farrar	118	1220	45	26	.980	409	372	30
1887	Roger Connor	127	1325	44	10	.993	449	389	49
1888	Cap Anson	134	1314	65	20	.986	434	404	26
1889	Cap Anson	134	1409	79	27	.982	437	400	32
1890	Dave Foutz	113	1192	39	28	.978	400	388	8
1891	Willard Brown	97	997	48	12	.989	449	413	32
1892	Jake Beckley	151	1523	132	38	.978	448	412	36
1893	Jake Beckley	131	1360	95	21	.986	463	424	33
1894	Tommy Tucker	123	1108	68	18	.985	428	403	22
1895	Roger Connor	103	953	62	14	.986	440	419	18
1896	Patsy Tebeau	122	1341	79	19	.987	465	427	33
1897	Perry Werden	131	1318	116	23	.984	469	428	36
1898	Tommy Tucker	145	1552	85	30	.982	439	409	30
1899	Dan McGann	137	1312	67	17	.988	438	423	15
1900	Dan McGann	121	1212	58	13	.990	448	430	17
1901	John Ganzel	138	1421	77	21	.986	446	419	25
1902	Fred Tenney	134	1251	105	21	.985	455	428	25
1903	Kitty Bransfield	127	1347	88	28	.981	445	423	20
1904	Frank Chance	123	1205	106	13	.990	475	456	19
1905	Fred Tenney	148	1556	152	32	.982	481	445	36
1906	Dan McGann	133	1391	83	8	.995	484	450	34
1907	Frank Chance	109	1129	80	10	.992	484	452	32
1908	Fred Tenney	156	1624	117	18	.990	479	458	21
1909	Kitty Bransfield	138	1377	89	16	.989	461	441	20
1910	Ed Konetchy	144	1499	98	15	.991	475	441	34
1911	Jake Daubert	149	1485	88	18	.989	455	448	7
1912	Fred Luderus	146	1421	104	15	.990	468	449	19

Year	First Baseman	G	PO	A	E	Pct.	Total	Mean	Points
1913	Ed Konetchy	140	1432	91	7	.995	484	444	40
1914	Butch Schmidt	147	1485	88	16	.990	461	434	17
1915	Fred Luderlus	141	1409	99	11	.993	480	454	26
1916	Ed Konetchy	158	1626	96	18	.990	464	442	22
1917	Ed Konetchy	129	1351	70	8	.994	472	450	22
1918	Fred Luderlus	125	1307	98	17	.988	476	470	5
1919	Walter Holke	136	1474	95	11	.993	488	463	23
1920	George Kelly	155	1759	103	11	.994	493	462	31
1921	George Kelly	149	1552	115	17	.990	484	463	21
1922	George Kelly	151	1642	103	13	.883	487	451	36
1923	Jake Daubert	121	1224	77	9	.993	475	453	22
1924	Jake Daubert	102	1128	74	12	.990	483	458	25
1925	Bill Terry	126	1270	77	14	.990	462	444	18
1926	Wally Pipp	155	1710	92	15	.992	477	454	23
1927	Bill Terry	150	1621	105	12	.993	488	459	29
1928	Bill Terry	149	1584	78	12	.993	468	449	19
1929	Bill Terry	149	1576	111	11	.994	494	461	33
1930	Bill Terry	154	1538	128	17	.990	483	454	29
1931	Bill Terry	153	1411	105	16	.990	461	450	11
1932	Bill Terry	154	1493	137	14	.991	489	471	18
1933	Charlie Grimm	104	979	83	4	.996	495	462	33
1934	Bill Terry	153	1592	105	10	.994	486	456	30
1935	Bill Terry	143	1379	99	6	.996	486	449	17
1936	Buck Jordan	136	1307	96	10	.993	477	454	23
1937	Elbie Fletcher	148	1587	108	12	.993	490	468	22
1938	Ripper Collins	135	1264	111	6	.996	496	474	22
1939	Frank McCormick	156	1504	105	7	.996	484	464	20
1940	Elbie Fletcher	147	1512	104	11	.993	483	470	13
1941	Elbie Fletcher	151	1444	118	14	.991	477	456	21
1942	Elbie Fletcher	144	1379	118	12	.992	485	464	21
1943	Elbie Fletcher	154	1541	108	6	.996	490	466	24
1944	Frank McCormick	153	1508	135	13	.992	493	461	32
1945	Frank McCormick	151	1469	118	9	.994	488	469	19
1946	Frank McCormick	134	1185	98	1	.999	492	476	16
1947	Johnny Mize	154	1380	117	6	.996	486	459	27
1948	Eddie Waitkus	116	1064	92	9	.991	474	452	22
1949	Johnny Mize	107	953	68	7	.993	463	448	15
1950	Eddie Waitkus	154	1387	99	10	.993	464	443	21
1951	Gil Hodges	158	1365	126	12	.992	473	460	13
1952	Whitey Lockman	154	1435	111	13	.992	472	455	17
1953	Steve Bilko	154	1446	124	15	.991	477	458	19
1954	Gil Hodges	154	1381	132	7	.995	492	462	30
1955	Stan Musial	110	925	92	8	.992	475	466	9
1956	Stan Musial	103	870	90	7	.993	482	455	27
1957	Stan Musial	130	1167	99	10	.992	478	463	15
1958	Stan Musial	124	1019	100	13	.989	460	453	7
1959	Gil Hodges	113	891	66	8	.992	444	426	18
1960	Ed Bouchee	102	867	71	8	.992	481	457	24
1961	Pancho Herrera	115	1003	96	8	.993	481	450	31
1962	Ernie Banks	149	1458	106	11	.993	479	442	37
1963	Donn Clendennon	151	1450	118	15	.991	478	447	31

Year	First Baseman	G	PO	A	E	Pct.	Total	Mean	Points
1964	Ernie Banks	157	1565	135	10	.994	497	457	40
1965	Wes Parker	154	1434	95	5	.997	478	459	19
1966	Bill White	158	1422	109	9	.994	472	450	22
1967	Ernie Banks	147	1383	91	10	.993	466	459	7
1968	Donn Clendennon	155	1587	127	17	.990	484	463	21
1969	Ernie Banks	153	1419	87	4	.997	473	453	20
1970	Wes Parker	161	1498	125	7	.996	491	464	27
1971	Bob Robertson	126	1089	128	9	.993	498	469	29
1972	Nate Colbert	150	1290	103	6	.996	475	447	28
1973	Bob Robertson	107	957	79	5	.995	480	454	26
1974	Joe Torre	139	1165	102	10	.992	464	450	14
1975	Mike Jorgenson	133	1150	91	7	.994	468	449	19
1976	Keith Hernandez	110	867	107	10	.990	476	456	20
1977	Bob Watson	146	1331	118	9	.994	485	446	39
1978	Bill Buckner	105	1075	83	6	.995	498	456	42
1979	Keith Hernandez	160	1489	146	8	.995	501	464	37
1980	Keith Hernandez	157	1572	115	9	.995	490	476	14
1981	Keith Hernandez	98	1054	86	3	.997	518	474	31
1982	Bill Buckner	161	1547	159	12	.993	505	472	33
1983	Bill Buckner	144	1366	161	13	.992	514	468	46
1984	Keith Hernandez	153	1214	142	8	.994	485	455	30
1985	Keith Hernandez	157	1310	139	4	.997	495	471	24
1986	Keith Hernandez	149	1199	149	5	.996	500	465	35
1987	Keith Hernandez	154	1298	149	10	.993	491	460	31
1988	Sid Bream	138	1118	140	6	.995	499	465	34
1989	Mark Grace	142	1230	126	6	.996	495	463	32
1990	Mark Grace	153	1324	180	12	.992	511	564	47
1991	Mark Grace	160	1520	167	8	.995	516	464	52
1992	Mark Grace	157	1580	141	4	.998	517	462	55
1993	Mark Grace	154	1456	112	5	.997	490	464	26
1994	Jeff Bagwell	109	922	120	9	.991	498	465	24
1995	Jeff Bagwell	114	1004	129	7	.994	514	482	30
1996	Mark Grace	142	1259	107	4	.997	488	467	21
1997	John Olerud	146	1292	120	7	.995	488	468	20
1998	Todd Helton	146	1164	146	7	.995	497	467	30
1999	Rico Brogna	157	1240	123	7	.995	474	443	31
2000	Todd Helton	160	1328	149	7	,995	493	458	35
2001	Todd Helton	157	1302	120	2	.999	489	455	34
2002	Eric Karros	142	1175	106	4	.997	480	449	31
2003	Todd Helton	159	1418	156	11	.993	497	467	30
2004	Todd Helton	153	1356	144	4	.997	506	457	49
2005	Todd Helton	144	1236	118	5	.996	488	465	23
2006	Albert Pujols	143	1345	110	6	.996	491	456	35

American Association—First Base

Eight different first sackers led the Association during its ten year history. Only Dave Orr and Mickey Lehane were able to lead more than once. Orr holds the league record with 37 points in 1889. The ill-fated Orr also holds the league record for single-season putouts. Lehane owns the record for assists, while Dave Foutz has the highest fielding average.

AMERICAN ASSOCIATION FIELDING LEADERS—FIRST BASE

Year	First Baseman	G	PO	A	E	Pct.	Total	Mean	Points
1882	Charlie Householder	74	749	20	23	.971	365	353	6
1883	Harry Stovey	93	984	22	27	.965	346	316	19
1884	John Kerins	87	887	41	27	.972	389	346	28
1885	Milt Scott	93	1017	34	23	.979	409	353	36
1886	Dave Orr	136	1445	34	28	.981	401	383	17
1887	Bill Phillips	132	1299	46	24	.982	406	396	9
1888	Dave Foutz	120	1171	39	13	.989	427	405	20
1889	Dave Orr	134	1291	61	23	.983	419	378	37
1890	Mickey Lehane	140	1430	73	27	.982	427	398	26
1891	Mickey Lehane	137	1362	71	28	.981	421	401	18

Players Association—First Base

Roger Connor was the Association's best fielder at the initial sack, with a very impressive 52 points. Connor holds the AA record for putouts, assists, and fielding average.

PLAYERS ASSOCIATION FIELDING LEADERS—FIRST BASE

Year	Fist Baseman	G	PO	A	E	Pct.	Total	Mean	Points
1890	Roger Connor	123	1335	80	34	.985	457	397	52

American League—First Base

Jiggs Donahue, the first baseman of the Chicago White Sox's famed Hitless Wonders, was the best fielder at his position in the early days of the American League. For three consecutive seasons he led the league in putouts, assists, total chances, and fielding average, as well as Faber System points. His 1846 putouts in 1907 remains a major league high 100 years after the fact. His 76 points amassed in 1907 also is the highest ever recorded in the majors. He might well have become the greatest fielding first baseman to ever play the game, but his career ended too soon. He had only four eligible seasons. Another White Sox first sacker whose career ended prematurely, Chick Gandil of Black Sox fame, became the first to lead the league four times. Stuffy McInnis and Phil Todt also accomplished that feat. Vic Power topped that mark with five league-leading seasons. Donahue's putout record still stands, of course, but his assists mark has been bettered several times, with Bill Buckner holding the record with 184 during the 1985 season, an all-time major league high. In 1921 McInnis set an American League record with a fielding average of .999. At least four other players have posted a .999 average, but when carried out to another decimal point Stuffy's record remains intact.

AMERICAN LEAGUE FIELDING LEADERS—FIRST BASE

Year	First Baseman	G	PO	A	E	Pct.	Total	Mean	Points
1901	Frank Isbell	137	1387	101	31	.980	438	420	16
1902	Frank Isbell	133	1401	93	21	.986	462	442	18
1903	John Ganzel	129	1385	94	18	.988	473	436	33
1904	Tom Jones	134	1443	92	19	.988	469	450	19
1905	Jiggs Donahue	149	1645	114	31	.986	480	452	28
1906	Jiggs Donahue	154	1697	118	22	.988	480	438	42
1907	Jiggs Donahue	157	1846	140	12	.994	520	444	76

Year	First Baseman	G	PO	A	E	Pct.	Total	Mean	Points
1908	George Stovall	132	1508	86	16	.990	479	442	37
1909	Frank Isbell	101	1204	66	8	.994	498	454	44
1910	George Stovall	128	1404	91	18	.985	458	434	24
1911	George Stovall	118	1073	87	17	.986	452	432	20
1912	Chick Gandil	117	1106	68	12	.990	454	431	23
1913	Chick Gandil	145	1422	106	15	.990	471	450	21
1914	Chick Gandil	145	1214	143	13	.991	490	463	27
1915	Wally Pipp	134	1396	85	12	.992	475	453	22
1916	Chick Gandil	145	1557	105	9	.995	496	461	35
1917	Stuffy McInnis	150	1658	95	12	.993	484	464	20
1918	George Sisler	114	1244	97	13	.990	494	471	19
1919	Stuffy McInnis	118	1236	82	7	.995	491	458	30
1920	Stuffy McInnis	148	1586	91	7	.996	489	465	24
1921	Stuffy McInnis	152	1549	102	1	.999	499	464	35
1922	Joe Judge	148	1378	101	6	.996	481	474	7
1923	Joe Judge	112	1070	88	8	.993	484	464	20
1924	Joe Harris	137	1288	103	10	.993	484	467	17
1925	Phil Todt	140	1408	100	13	.991	475	449	26
1926	Phil Todt	154	1755	126	22	.988	489	458	31
1927	Phil Todt	139	1401	112	13	.991	484	465	19
1928	Phil Todt	144	1486	94	5	.997	491	468	23
1929	Lew Fonseca	147	1486	107	8	.995	491	466	25
1930	Joe Judge	117	1050	67	2	.998	474	449	25
1931	Jack Burns	143	1346	125	11	.993	492	448	44
1932	Dale Alexander	103	1055	67	9	.992	474	454	20
1933	Harley Boss	110	1062	71	7	.994	474	450	24
1934	Zeke Bonura	127	1239	77	5	.996	478	452	26
1935	Jimmie Foxx	121	1109	77	3	.997	478	458	20
1936	Zeke Bonura	146	1500	107	7	.996	495	455	40
1937	Jimmie Foxx	150	1297	106	8	.994	478	458	20
1938	Hank Greenberg	155	1484	120	14	.991	476	459	17
1939	George McQuinn	154	1377	118	11	.993	475	461	14
1940	George McQuinn	150	1436	124	13	.992	485	453	32
1941	George McQuinn	125	1138	109	6	.995	495	472	23
1942	Rudy York	152	1413	146	19	.988	482	461	21
1943	Tony Lupien	153	1487	118	12	.993	484	467	17
1944	Mickey Rocco	155	1467	138	11	.993	494	461	33
1945	Dick Siebert	147	1427	135	14	.991	492	466	26
1946	Rudy York	154	1327	116	8	.994	474	462	12
1947	Roy Cullenbine	138	1184	139	15	.989	484	460	24
1948	Eddie Robinson	131	1213	79	7	.995	470	460	10
1949	Mickey Vernon	153	1438	155	14	.991	498	457	41
1950	Mickey Vernon	110	959	78	9	.991	461	450	11
1951	Ferris Fain	108	931	113	11	.990	491	440	51
1952	Ferris Fain	144	1245	150	22	.984	471	453	18
1953	Walt Dropo	150	1260	127	14	.990	469	449	20
1954	Harry Agganis	119	1064	89	12	.990	464	446	18
1955	Vic Power	144	1281	130	10	.993	475	456	19
1956	Bill Skowron	120	968	80	7	.993	457	439	18
1957	Vic Power	113	968	99	2	.998	500	451	49

Year	First Baseman	G	PO	A	E	Pct.	Total	Mean	Points
1958	Dick Gernert	114	1101	93	11	.991	481	458	23
1959	Vic Power	121	1039	110	6	.995	494	429	65
1960	Vic Power	147	1177	145	5	.996	499	456	43
1961	Vic Power	141	1154	142	8	.994	496	455	41
1962	Vic Power	142	1191	134	10	.993	481	462	19
1963	Lee Thomas	104	961	84	4	.996	493	463	30
1964	Norm Cash	137	1105	92	4	.997	479	452	18
1965	Joe Pepitone	115	1036	71	3	.997	475	445	30
1966	Joe Pepitone	119	1044	92	6	.995	482	448	34
1967	Tim McCraw	123	1167	110	11	.991	487	450	37
1968	Norm Cash	117	924	88	8	.992	461	442	39
1969	Don Mincher	122	1033	93	6	.994	474	454	20
1970	Mike Hegan	139	1097	113	7	.994	473	451	20
1971	Jim Spencer	145	1296	93	5	.996	474	449	25
1972	John Mayberry	146	1338	82	7	.995	465	446	19
1973	George Scott	157	1388	118	9	.994	477	455	22
1974	George Scott	148	1345	114	12	.992	475	447	28
1975	Lee May	144	1312	106	10	.993	475	450	25
1976	Jim Spencer	143	1206	112	2	.998	490	465	25
1977	Rod Carew	151	1459	121	10	.994	490	464	26
1978	Chris Chambliss	155	1366	111	4	.997	483	457	26
1979	Ron Jackson	157	1447	137	9	.994	492	462	30
1980	Cecil Cooper	142	1336	106	5	.997	492	459	33
1981	Eddie Murray	99	899	91	1	.999	513	468	32
1982	Mike Hargrove	153	1293	123	5	.996	485	460	25
1983	Pete O'Brien	133	1144	120	9	.993	486	456	30
1984	Don Mattingly	133	1107	124	5	.996	496	456	40
1985	Bill Buckner	162	1384	184	12	.992	506	463	41
1986	Darrell Evans	105	808	108	2	.998	507	468	39
1987	Darrell Evans	105	810	100	3	.997	495	469	26
1988	Wally Joyner	156	1369	143	8	.995	496	470	26
1989	George Brett	104	896	80	2	.998	490	469	21
1990	Fred McGriff	147	1246	126	6	.996	492	457	35
1991	Wally Joyner	141	1335	98	8	.994	477	467	10
1992	Wally Joyner	145	1236	137	10	.993	490	468	22
1993	Rafael Palmeiro	160	1388	147	5	.997	502	460	42
1994	Cecil Fielder	102	887	108	7	.993	503	465	28
1995	Wally Joyner	126	1111	118	3	.998	509	471	36
1996	Rafael Palmeiro	159	1383	119	8	.995	479	452	27
1997	Jeff King	150	1217	147	5	.996	499	455	44
1998	David Segui	131	1045	116	1	.999	495	460	35
1999	Lee Stevens	133	1296	128	8	.994	507	480	27
2000	John Olerud	158	1271	132	5	.986	484	454	30
2001	Scott Spiezio	105	819	74	1	.999	478	460	18
2002	Mike Sweeney	102	838	105	9	.991	488	457	31
2003	John Olerud	152	1096	125	3	.998	496	470	26
2004	Carlos Delgado	120	1041	88	5	.996	480	459	21
2005	Mark Teixera	155	1377	101	3	.998	481	456	25
2006	Richie Sexson	150	1233	110	4	.997	479	462	17

Players' League—First Base

Two veterans from the more established leagues—George Stovall and Ed Konetchy—were the Federal League's top fielders at first base during its brief existence. Each led the league in Faber System points once. Harry Swacina holds the loop's record for putouts and assists, while Konetchy has the highest fielding average

FEDERAL LEAGUE FIELDING LEADERS—FIRST BASE

Year	First Baseman	G	PO	A	E	Pct.	Total	Mean	Points
1914	George Stovall	116	1201	70	14	.989	461	449	12
1915	Ed Konetchy	152	1536	81	10	.994	467	447	20

National League—Second Base

In 1878 Jack Burdock set a record for Faber System fielding points by a second baseman. The Boston second sacker led the infant National League in put outs, assists, total chances, double plays, and fielding average. However, his record lasted only six years. It was broken, successively, by Fred Pfeffer, Bid McPhee, Heinie Reitz, George Cutshaw, and Frankie Frisch. The record 154 points amassed by the Fordham Flash in 1927 has stood for 80 years and is the second-most points ever attained by a National League fielder at any position, trailing only the 166 points garnered by shortstop Ozzie Smith in 1982. Burdock led the circuit in points four times. McPhee, one of the last major leaguers to field without a glove, led the NL five times, after having led the American Association four times, giving him a total of nine league-leading seasons. Counting only seasons in the senior circuit, Red Schoendienst set a record by leading for seven years, including six in a row in the 1940s and 1950s. The Redhead's record was soon broken by Bill Mazeroski of the Pittsburgh Pirates, who led the loop eleven times, including nine consecutively.

Fred Pfeffer set an early standard for putouts by a National League second baseman with 452 in 1889. That mark was surpassed by Billy Herman, who tallied 466 outs at the keystone for the Chicago Cubs in 1933. During the 19th century, the most assists in a season by a senior circuit second baseman were made by Heinie Reitz with 499 in 1897. This mark was exceeded several times in the 1920s, with Frankie Frisch establishing a major league record of 641 for the St. Louis Cardinals in 1927, a record that has never been seriously threatened. As is the case with all positions, the record for the highest fielding percentage for NL second basemen has risen dramatically over the years. In 1876 Ross Barnes led the league with a .915 average. By 1896 McPhee had raised the record to .982. Sparky Adams fielded at a .985 clip in 1925. In 1951 Schoendienst became the first points leader to post a .990 percentage, a mark that has since been exceeded several times. Bret Boone holds the current record at .997.

LEADING NATIONAL LEAGUE FIELDERS—SECOND BASE

Year	Second Baseman	G	PO	A	E	Pct.	Total	Mean	Points
1876	Ed Somerville	64	210	251	69	.870	620	548	30
1877	Jack Burdock	60	185	189	40	.903	686	650	14
1878	Jack Burdock	60	245	212	41	.918	822	578	98
1879	Joe Quest	83	263	331	48	.925	799	707	48
1880	Jack Burdock	83	223	256	35	.932	778	617	89
1881	Joe Quest	77	238	249	37	.929	729	635	51
1882	Jack Burdock	83	223	256	35	.932	684	628	31
1883	Jack Farrell	95	258	365	51	.924	736	621	74
1884	Fred Pfeffer	112	395	422	88	.903	739	596	106

Year	Second Baseman	G	PO	A	E	Pct.	Total	Mean	Points
1885	Fred Dunlap	106	314	374	49	.934	762	625	99
1886	Fred Dunlap	122	333	393	58	.926	682	600	66
1887	Charley Bassett	119	273	444	53	.931	706	683	19
1888	Fred Pfeffer	135	421	457	65	.931	753	653	88
1889	Fred Pfeffer	134	452	483	56	.943	841	729	96
1890	Bid McPhee	115	404	431	51	.942	773	695	69
1891	Danny Richardson	114	323	429	46	.952	833	720	102
1892	Bid McPhee	144	451	471	51	.948	800	692	108
1893	Bid McPhee	127	396	455	41	.954	850	733	99
1894	Heinie Reitz	97	264	336	25	.968	846	701	125
1895	Bid McPhee	115	355	366	34	.955	810	700	95
1896	Bid McPhee	116	299	358	12	.982	839	721	101
1897	Heinie Reitz	128	280	499	29	.962	777	718	52
1898	Bobby Lowe	145	397	457	37	.958	782	719	63
1899	Kid Gleason	146	403	465	50	.946	748	688	60
1900	Nap Lajoie	102	287	341	30	.954	796	668	118
1901	Dick Padden	115	281	336	33	.950	708	690	16
1902	Bobby Lowe	117	326	406	33	.957	816	714	94
1903	Claude Ritchey	137	281	400	30	.961	744	675	63
1904	Fred Raymer	114	272	351	27	.958	739	709	30
1905	Miller Huggins	149	346	525	51	.945	735	689	46
1906	Claude Ritchey	151	326	439	27	.966	720	666	54
1907	Claude Ritchey	144	340	460	24	.971	793	735	58
1908	Claude Ritchey	120	325	368	24	.967	801	712	89
1909	Dick Egan	116	271	376	34	.950	725	640	85
1910	Dave Shean	148	408	493	44	.953	786	678	108
1911	John Hummel	127	296	352	19	.972	750	682	68
1912	Bill Sweeney	153	459	475	40	.959	807	719	88
1913	Miller Huggins	113	266	339	14	.977	792	711	81
1914	George Cutshaw	153	455	444	38	.959	785	684	101
1915	George Cutshaw	154	397	473	26	.971	802	667	135
1916	Albert Betzel	113	275	366	27	.960	769	756	13
1917	Dave Shean	131	332	412	30	.961	769	719	50
1918	George Cutshaw	126	323	366	26	.964	760	753	6
1919	Morrie Rath	138	345	452	21	.974	822	752	64
1920	Morrie Rath	126	319	399	17	.977	820	785	35
1921	Hod Ford	119	297	427	20	.972	834	801	33
1922	Frank Parkinson	139	323	562	34	.963	847	779	68
1923	Frankie Frisch	135	307	451	21	.973	803	773	30
1924	Frankie Frisch	143	391	537	27	.972	889	806	83
1925	Sparky Adams	144	354	551	16	.983	905	834	71
1926	Hughie Critz	155	357	588	18	.984	850	810	40
1927	Frankie Frisch	153	396	641	22	.979	941	787	154
1928	Freddie Maguire	138	410	524	23	.976	930	828	102
1929	Hughie Critz	106	210	395	16	.984	850	810	40
1930	Frankie Frisch	123	307	473	25	.969	864	812	52
1931	Freddie Maguire	148	372	478	21	.976	827	801	26
1932	Rabbit Maranville	149	402	473	22	.975	837	799	38
1933	Hughie Critz	133	316	541	16	.982	917	840	77
1934	Hughie Critz	137	353	510	19	.978	890	846	44
1935	Billy Herman	154	416	520	35	.964	821	758	63

Year	Second Baseman	G	PO	A	E	Pct.	Total	Mean	Points
1936	Burgess Whitehead	153	442	552	42	.969	880	829	51
1937	Burgess Whitehead	152	394	514	24	.974	844	748	96
1938	Billy Herman	151	404	517	18	.981	880	798	82
1939	Lonnie Frey	124	324	412	18	.976	847	786	61
1940	Billy Herman	135	366	448	22	.974	857	790	67
1941	Lou Stringer	137	356	455	34	.960	792	740	52
1942	Mickey Witek	147	371	441	19	.978	812	758	54
1943	Lonnie Frey	144	399	461	13	.985	880	784	96
1944	Woody Williams	155	377	542	27	.971	830	750	80
1945	Don Johnson	138	309	440	19	.975	793	775	18
1946	Red Schoendienst	128	340	354	11	.984	822	767	55
1947	Emil Verban	155	450	453	17	.982	856	793	63
1948	Jackie Robinson	116	308	314	13	.980	804	762	42
1949	Red Schoendienst	138	399	424	11	.987	886	823	63
1950	Red Schoendienst	143	393	403	12	.985	840	796	44
1951	Red Schoendienst	123	339	386	7	.990	885	822	63
1952	Red Schoendiesnt	142	399	424	19	.977	837	777	60
1953	Red Schoendienst	140	365	430	14	.983	845	775	70
1954	Red Schoendienst	144	394	477	18	.980	872	799	73
1955	Danny O'Connell	114	309	357	13	.981	854	798	56
1956	Jim Gilliam	102	233	326	11	.981	818	793	35
1957	Don Blasingame	154	372	512	14	.984	854	782	72
1958	Bill Mazeroski	152	344	496	17	.980	820	782	38
1959	Charlie Neal	151	386	413	9	.989	826	773	53
1960	Bill Mazeroski	151	413	449	10	.989	868	747	121
1961	Bill Mazeroski	152	410	505	23	.975	852	770	82
1962	Bill Mazeroski	159	425	509	14	.985	870	731	139
1963	Bill Mazeroski	138	340	506	14	.984	893	755	138
1964	Bill Mazeroski	152	346	543	23	.975	799	732	67
1965	Bill Mazeroski	127	290	439	9	.988	867	761	106
1966	Bill Mazeroski	162	411	538	8	.992	893	774	119
1967	Bill Mazeroski	163	417	498	18	.981	831	751	80
1968	Bill Mazeroski	142	319	467	15	.981	823	775	48
1969	Ted Sizemore	118	283	331	13	.979	783	745	38
1970	Bill Mazeroski	102	227	325	7	.987	831	779	52
1971	Tommy Helms	149	395	468	9	.990	879	787	92
1972	Joe Morgan	149	370	436	8	.990	841	790	51
1973	Joe Morgan	154	417	440	9	.990	856	802	54
1974	Rennie Stennett	154	441	475	19	.980	862	791	71
1975	Rennie Stennett	144	379	463	18	.979	848	787	61
1976	Rennie Stennett	157	430	502	18	.981	864	782	82
1977	Dave Cash	153	343	443	11	.986	801	759	42
1978	Manny Trillo	149	354	505	19	.978	837	743	94
1979	Manny Trillo	118	270	368	10	.985	824	739	85
1980	Manny Trillo	140	360	467	11	.987	881	793	88
1981	Tom Herr	103	211	374	5	.992	875	813	43
1982	Glenn Hubbard	144	312	505	14	.983	844	782	62
1983	Ryne Sandberg	157	330	571	13	.986	861	768	93
1984	Ryne Sandberg	153	309	492	5	.994	837	756	81
1985	Glenn Hubbard	140	339	539	10	.989	924	792	132

Year	Second Baseman	G	PO	A	E	Pct.	Total	Mean	Points
1986	Ryne Sandberg	153	309	492	5	.994	837	756	81
1987	Glenn Hubbard	139	284	478	11	.986	835	762	73
1988	Ryne Sandberg	153	291	522	11	.987	821	771	50
1989	Jose Oquendo	156	346	500	5	.994	855	754	101
1990	Jose Lind	152	330	449	7	.991	816	748	68
1991	Ryne Sandberg	157	267	515	4	.995	879	753	126
1992	Jose Lind	134	311	428	6	.992	859	754	105
1993	Jody Reed	132	280	413	5	.993	835	757	78
1994	Carlos Garcia	98	225	315	12	.978	811	751	44
1995	Mike Lansing	127	306	373	6	.991	838	787	47
1996	Eric Young	139	340	431	12	.985	838	746	92
1997	Craig Biggio	160	341	509	18	.979	791	747	44
1998	Fernando Vina	158	404	468	12	.986	839	767	72
1999	Pokey Reese	146	325	409	7	.991	806	742	64
2000	Warren Morris	134	291	414	15	.979	789	752	37
2001	Edgardo Alfonso	122	211	301	7	.987	803	744	59
2002	Pokey Reese	117	283	363	8	.988	845	736	109
2003	Marcus Giles	139	278	471	14	.982	812	746	66
2004	Placido Polanco	109	264	304	3	.995	838	750	88
2005	Craig Counsell	143	304	458	8	.990	833	765	68
2006	Jamey Carroll	101	187	396	3	.995	852	767	85

American Association—Second Base

During four of its ten seasons as a major league, Bid McPhee led the American Association second basemen in Faber System fielding points. He holds the circuit's record for single season putouts and assists. Jack Crooks has the loop's best fielding percentage and highest single season points. The 185 points amassed by the Columbus Buckeyes' second sacker is the most ever attained by any major leaguer at any fielding position. McPhee and Lou Bierbauer also had seasons in which they racked up an exceptional number of points.

AMERICAN ASSOCIATION FIELDING LEADERS—SECOND BASE

Year	Second Baseman	G	PO	A	E	Pct.	Total	Mean	Points
1882	Cub Stricker	72	237	251	52	.904	694	590	53
1883	Joe Gerhardt	78	278	263	56	.906	714	581	84
1884	Bid McPhee	112	415	365	64	.924	776	628	96
1885	Pop Smith	106	372	384	64	.922	786	661	90
1886	Bid McPhee	140	529	464	65	.939	839	666	159
1887	Bid McPhee	129	442	434	72	.924	759	642	104
1888	Bid McPhee	109	369	365	47	.940	806	627	159
1889	Lou Bierbauer	130	472	406	55	.941	812	635	161
1990	Joe Gerhardt	119	409	403	52	.940	815	661	136
1991	Jack Crooks	138	399	404	36	.957	772	566	185

Players' League—Second Base

Joe Quinn was the best fielding second baseman in the Players' League's one season as a major league. He led the league in fielding percentage, as well as in points. Fred Pfeffer led in putouts, while Lou Bierbauer had the most assists.

PLAYERS' LEAGUE FIELDING LEADER—SECOND BASE

Year	Second Baseman	G	PO	A	E	Pct.	Total	Mean	Points
1890	Joe Quinn	130	431	395	51	.942	775	627	127

American League—Second Base

Nap Lajoie was the best fielding second baseman during the American League's infancy. In 1906 he set a league fielding record of 124 Faber System points, which was first broken by Eddie Collins in 1910 with 125 and then by Damion Easley in 1998 with 126 points. Lajoie and Collins each led the league six times. Bobby Doerr topped them with eight seasons as the loop's top second sacker. The league record for the most putouts in a season was set in 1974 by the vastly underrated Bobby Grich. His 484 putouts that year ranks second in all of major league history to Bid McPhee's 1886 record. Grich was also the last leading AL second baseman to make more putouts than assists in a season. Oscar Melillo set the league record for assists with 572 in 1930, a mark that has stood for more than three-quarters of a century. The highest fielding average posted by an AL second sacker is .997, a mark set by Grich in 1985 and tied by Mark Ellis in 2006. By carrying the average out to another decimal point, we find that Ellis holds the record by a margin of .0001.

AMERICAN LEAGUE FIELDING LEADERS—SECOND BASE

Year	Second Baseman	G	PO	A	E	Pct.	Total	Mean	Points
1901	Nap Lajoie	117	395	381	32	.960	747	685	64
1902	Dick Padden	117	388	363	22	.967	779	726	48
1903	Nap Lajoie	123	366	402	36	.955	807	710	87
1904	Hobe Ferris	156	366	460	33	.962	736	688	48
1905	Gus Dundon	104	218	321	12	.978	778	718	60
1906	Nap Lajoie	130	354	415	21	.973	835	711	124
1907	Hobe Ferris	143	424	459	30	.967	840	774	66
1908	Nap Lajoie	156	450	538	37	.964	846	728	118
1909	Nap Lajoie	120	282	373	28	.959	745	689	56
1910	Eddie Collins	153	402	451	25	.970	791	666	125
1911	Eddie Collins	132	348	349	24	.966	748	699	49
1912	Morrie Rath	157	353	463	31	.963	730	665	65
1913	Nap Lajoie	136	289	363	20	.970	750	682	68
1914	Eddie Collins	152	354	387	23	.970	721	653	68
1915	Eddie Collins	155	344	487	22	.974	783	746	37
1916	Del Pratt	158	438	491	33	.966	808	749	59
1917	Del Pratt	119	324	353	29	.959	766	719	47
1918	Joe Gedeon	123	309	409	17	.977	841	793	39
1919	Del Pratt	140	315	491	26	.969	806	777	26
1920	Eddie Collins	155	449	471	28	.976	847	786	61
1921	Eddie Collins	136	376	458	20	.968	831	755	76
1922	Bucky Harris	154	479	483	30	.970	851	784	67
1923	Aaron Ward	152	307	493	18	.980	846	796	50
1924	Bill Wambsganss	156	463	494	37	.963	823	789	34
1925	Frank O'Rourke	118	309	382	21	.971	823	768	55
1926	Max Bishop	119	235	365	8	.987	794	759	35
1927	Charlie Gehringer	131	304	438	27	.965	830	755	75
1928	Charlie Gehringer	154	377	507	35	.962	788	759	29

Year	Second Baseman	G	PO	A	E	Pct.	Total	Mean	Points
1929	John Kerr	122	307	459	23	.971	861	821	40
1930	Oscar Melillo	148	384	572	21	.979	909	811	98
1931	Oscar Melillo	151	428	543	32	.968	869	823	46
1932	Oscar Melillo	153	393	526	18	.981	890	841	49
1933	Oscar Melillo	130	362	451	7	.991	928	840	88
1934	Oscar Melillo	141	412	462	17	.981	890	841	49
1935	Buddy Myer	151	460	473	20	.979	881	823	58
1936	Charlie Gehringer	154	397	524	25	.974	845	804	41
1937	Jackie Hayes	143	353	490	14	.984	890	798	92
1938	Buddy Myer	121	308	355	12	.982	821	777	44
1939	Bobby Doerr	126	336	432	19	.976	862	795	67
1940	Bobby Doerr	151	401	480	21	.977	847	756	91
1941	Jimmy Bloodworth	132	380	426	24	.971	855	767	88
1942	Bobby Doerr	142	376	453	21	.975	834	796	38
1943	Bobby Doerr	151	415	490	9	.990	884	798	86
1944	George Stirnweiss	143	433	481	17	.982	867	786	81
1945	Irv Hall	151	422	498	21	.978	869	813	56
1946	Bobby Doerr	151	420	483	13	.986	885	822	63
1947	Bobby Doerr	146	366	430	16	.981	847	796	51
1948	Bobby Doerr	138	366	430	6	.992	884	814	70
1949	Bobby Doerr	139	395	439	17	.980	867	770	97
1950	Gerry Priddy	157	440	542	19	.981	895	810	85
1951	Pete Suder	103	274	313	8	.987	860	817	43
1952	Billy Goodman	103	284	340	15	.975	856	812	44
1953	Bobby Avila	140	346	445	11	.986	852	806	46
1954	Nellie Fox	155	400	392	9	.989	808	749	59
1955	Gil McDougald	126	352	348	11	.985	838	783	55
1956	Nellie Fox	154	478	396	12	.986	855	759	96
1957	Nellie Fox	155	453	453	13	.986	854	782	72
1958	Nellie Fox	155	444	399	13	.985	827	790	37
1959	Nellie Fox	156	364	453	10	.986	817	785	32
1960	Nellie Fox	149	412	447	13	.985	860	795	65
1961	Chuck Schilling	158	397	449	8	.991	838	745	93
1962	Billy Moran	160	422	477	13	.986	849	797	52
1963	Jerry Lumpe	155	341	452	10	.988	806	756	49
1964	Jerry Adair	153	395	422	5	.994	847	741	106
1965	Jerry Adair	157	395	446	12	.986	813	738	75
1966	Bobby Knoop	161	381	488	17	.981	810	758	52
1967	Horace Clarke	140	348	410	8	.990	841	719	122
1968	Horace Clarke	139	357	444	13	.984	856	760	94
1969	Bobby Knoop	131	335	386	12	.984	830	736	94
1970	Bobby Knoop	126	276	403	11	.984	819	771	48
1971	Sandy Alomar	137	350	432	9	.989	868	789	79
1972	Davey Johnson	116	286	307	8	.990	811	757	54
1973	Bobby Grich	162	431	509	5	.995	897	779	118
1974	Bobby Grich	160	484	453	20	.979	849	761	88
1975	Bobby Grich	150	423	484	21	.977	862	768	94
1976	Bobby Grich	140	389	400	12	.985	847	758	89
1977	Bump Wills	150	321	492	15	.982	815	773	42
1978	Bump Wills	156	350	526	17	.981	832	781	51

Year	Second Baseman	G	PO	A	E	Pct.	Total	Mean	Points
1979	Julio Cruz	107	258	361	13	.979	834	780	54
1980	Julio Cruz	115	269	365	11	.983	861	822	39
1981	Bump Wills	101	268	326	10	.983	865	813	36
1982	Tony Bernazard	137	353	443	12	.985	864	793	71
1983	Frank White	145	390	442	8	.990	874	782	92
1984	Frank White	129	299	425	11	.985	845	768	77
1985	Bobby Grich	116	234	380	2	.997	844	775	69
1986	Harold Reynolds	126	278	415	16	.977	807	763	37
1987	Marty Barrett	137	320	438	9	.988	846	752	94
1988	Willie Randolph	110	254	339	7	.988	832	763	69
1989	Jim Gantner	114	241	363	8	.987	819	777	42
1990	Johnny Ray	100	241	295	7	.987	826	786	40
1991	Luis Sojo	107	228	326	11	.981	788	751	37
1992	Jody Reed	142	304	472	14	.982	820	779	41
1993	Carlos Baerga	150	347	445	17	.979	791	753	38
1994	Jody Reed	106	231	353	3	.995	868	751	87
1995	Roberto Alomar	128	272	367	4	.994	812	736	71
1996	Mark McLemore	147	313	473	12	.985	818	747	71
1997	Scott Spiezio	146	280	415	7	.990	769	729	40
1998	Damion Easley	140	312	480	12	.985	849	723	126
1999	Miguel Cairo	117	251	377	9	.986	815	755	60
2000	Randy Velarde	122	243	399	12	.982	799	754	45
2001	Damion Easley	153	279	496	14	.982	780	733	47
2002	Jerry Hairston	119	232	365	11	.982	775	727	48
2003	Orlando Hudson	139	267	477	12	.984	815	752	63
2004	Orlando Hudson	133	276	449	12	.984	825	735	90
2005	Orlando Hudson	130	302	390	6	.991	830	750	80
2006	Mark Ellis	123	273	357	2	.997	835	758	77

Federal League—Second Base

Even though he had a very short major league career Bill Kenworthy was the Players' League's best fielding second baseman. He set the circuit's single-season record for putouts and is tied with Frank LaPorte for the most Faber System points. Jack Farrell holds the loop's record for assists, and Steve Yerkes has the highest fielding percentage.

FEDERAL LEAGUE FIELDING LEADERS—SECOND BASE

Year	Second Baseman	G	PO	A	E	Pct.	Total	Mean	Points
1914	Bill Kenworthy	145	437	407	43	.952	755	699	56
1915	Frank LaPorte	146	330	431	32	.960	721	665	56

National League—Shortstop

In 1883 Jack Glasscock compiled a remarkable 121 Faber System fielding points, which stood as the league record for shortstops until Hughie Jennings amassed 186 points in 1895, which is still the NL record. Ozzie Smith holds the record for the most points earned in a 20th century season with 166 compiled in 1982. No other fielder at any position in any major league earned that many points in a season in this century. Glasscock led the league seven times. Only Smith, with 12 league-leading seasons has surpassed that mark. In 1895 Jennings set a league record that has never been broken with 425 putouts. (For many years Bob Allen was credited with 433 putouts during the 1892 season, but this record has been shown by modern researchers to have been in error. Allen is now credited with 331 putouts in 1892.) The major league mark for assists by a shortstop is held by Smith, who threw out 621 runners in 1980. The improvement in fielding averages by shortstops has been impressive. In 1876 Davy Force was the league's best fielding shortstop even though his average was only .894. In 2000 Rey Ordonez set a league record by fielding .994.

NATIONAL LEAGUE FIELDING LEADERS—SHORTSTOP

Year	Shortstop	G	PO	A	E	Pct.	Total	Mean	Points
1876	Davy Force	63	112	242	42	.894	543	368	74
1877	Davy Force	50	75	160	22	.914	517	390	50
1878	George Wright	59	72	197	15	.947	613	460	61
1879	George Wright	85	96	319	34	.924	568	403	86
1880	Arthur Irwin	82	95	339	51	.895	512	455	31
1881	Jack Glasscock	79	105	274	37	.911	517	388	71
1882	Jack Glasscock	83	111	311	47	.900	508	457	28
1883	Jack Glasscock	93	134	313	38	.922	554	365	121
1884	Davy Force	105	110	312	48	.898	396	348	36
1885	Jack Glasscock	110	156	397	50	.917	560	467	67
1886	Jack Glasscock	120	156	392	57	.906	477	373	83
1887	Monte Ward	129	226	469	61	.919	602	477	103
1888	Jack Glasscock	110	201	334	59	.901	489	372	103
1889	Jack Glasscock	132	246	478	67	.915	598	508	82
1890	Bob Allen	133	337	500	69	.924	709	581	113
1891	Herman Long	139	345	441	85	.902	572	536	32
1892	Germany Smith	139	239	561	70	.920	643	547	86
1893	Germany Smith	130	250	500	53	.934	690	561	110
1894	Hughie Jennings	128	307	499	63	.928	723	583	120
1895	Hughie Jennings	131	425	457	56	.940	806	590	186
1896	Hughie Jennings	129	377	476	66	.926	751	622	111
1897	Hughie Jennings	116	335	425	55	.933	765	620	128
1898	George Davis	121	349	421	57	.933	746	649	67
1899	Bones Ely	132	274	472	58	.928	773	621	152
1900	George Davis	114	279	450	43	.944	786	712	68
1901	Bobby Wallace	134	326	542	66	.929	745	634	101
1902	Herman Long	105	279	360	37	.945	759	612	135
1903	Honus Wagner	111	303	397	50	.933	741	641	91
1904	Tommy Corcoran	150	353	471	56	.936	669	628	41
1905	Tommy Corcoran	151	344	531	44	.919	752	675	77
1906	Honus Wagner	137	334	473	51	.941	741	641	100
1907	Al Bridwell	140	325	437	47	.942	684	643	41
1908	Bill Dahlen	144	291	533	43	.952	759	682	77
1909	Mickey Doolan	147	352	484	54	.939	729	639	91
1910	Tony Smith	100	254	318	36	.941	709	631	78
1911	Joe Tinker	143	333	486	55	.937	696	611	85
1912	Honus Wagner	143	341	462	32	.962	769	693	76
1913	Honus Wagner	105	289	323	24	.962	790	680	110
1914	Rabbit Maranville	156	407	574	65	.938	746	704	42
1915	Buck Herzog	153	391	513	53	.945	741	640	101

Year	Shortstop	G	PO	A	E	Pct.	Total	Mean	Points
1916	Rabbit Maranville	155	386	515	50	.947	738	681	57
1917	Art Fletcher	151	276	565	39	.956	744	659	85
1918	Art Fletcher	124	268	484	32	.959	803	696	88
1919	Rabbit Maranville	131	361	488	53	.941	785	715	64
1920	Dave Bancroft	150	362	598	45	.955	823	729	94
1921	Dave Bancroft	153	396	546	39	.960	816	764	52
1922	Rabbit Maranville	138	359	453	33	.961	791	737	54
1923	Rabbit Maranville	141	332	505	30	.965	811	738	73
1924	Heinie Sand	137	333	460	34	.959	776	747	29
1925	Dave Bancroft	125	300	459	44	.945	757	671	86
1926	Jimmy Cooney	141	344	492	24	.972	833	747	86
1927	Jimmy Cooney	107	230	340	13	.978	793	722	71
1928	Hod Ford	149	355	508	25	.972	819	728	91
1929	Travis Jackson	149	329	552	28	.969	821	759	62
1930	Rabbit Maranville	138	343	445	29	.965	788	752	36
1931	Travis Jackson	145	303	396	26	.970	784	739	45
1932	Dick Bartell	154	359	529	34	.963	787	714	73
1933	Dick Bartell	152	381	493	45	.951	745	717	28
1934	Dick Bartell	146	350	483	40	.954	751	717	34
1935	Billy Jurges	146	348	484	31	.964	783	684	99
1936	Dick Bartell	144	317	559	40	.956	795	693	103
1937	Dick Bartell	128	281	476	33	.958	784	694	90
1938	Arky Vaughan	147	306	507	33	.961	756	699	57
1939	Billy Jurges	137	295	482	28	.965	784	729	55
1940	Eddie Miller	151	405	487	28	.970	824	700	124
1941	Eddie Miller	154	336	485	29	.966	753	677	76
1942	Eddie Miller	142	285	450	13	.983	795	690	105
1943	Eddie Miller	154	335	543	19	.979	833	743	90
1944	Eddie Miller	155	357	544	27	.971	810	708	102
1945	Eddie Miller	115	245	382	16	.975	795	669	126
1946	Buddy Kerr	126	240	400	12	.982	781	695	86
1947	Marty Marion	141	329	452	15	.981	824	737	87
1948	Marty Marion	142	263	445	19	.974	746	688	56
1949	Marty Marion	134	242	441	17	.976	763	721	42
1950	Marty Marion	101	180	313	11	.978	748	712	36
1951	Solly Hemus	105	181	344	19	.965	717	661	56
1952	Johnny Logan	117	247	385	18	.972	780	711	69
1953	Johnny Logan	150	295	481	20	.975	767	731	36
1954	Johnny Logan	154	324	489	26	.969	758	705	53
1955	Roy McMillan	150	290	495	25	.969	753	709	44
1956	Roy McMillan	150	319	511	21	.975	803	683	120
1957	Johnny Logan	129	263	440	29	.960	745	683	59
1958	Don Zimmer	114	265	372	23	.965	776	729	47
1959	Ernie Banks	154	271	519	12	.986	796	728	68
1960	Ernie Banks	156	283	488	18	.977	751	657	94
1961	Roy McMillan	154	257	496	19	.975	738	685	53
1962	Roy McMillan	135	243	424	19	.972	734	692	42
1963	Dick Schofield	117	232	366	21	.966	731	666	65
1964	Roy McMillan	119	217	353	15	.975	741	672	69
1965	Maury Wills	155	267	535	25	.970	750	691	51

Year	Shortstop	G	PO	A	E	Pct.	Total	Mean	Points
1966	Dick Groat	139	260	454	19	.974	761	695	66
1967	Gene Alley	146	257	500	26	.967	751	693	58
1968	Hal Lanier	150	282	496	17	.979	782	700	82
1969	Don Kessinger	157	266	542	20	.976	768	694	74
1970	Gene Alley	108	202	381	15	.975	790	700	90
1971	Larry Bowa	157	272	560	11	.987	820	711	109
1972	Larry Bowa	150	212	494	9	.987	761	707	54
1973	Tim Foli	123	245	396	27	.960	721	689	32
1974	Tim Foli	120	220	412	19	.971	764	664	100
1975	Dave Concepcion	130	238	445	16	.977	382	693	89
1976	Dave Concepcion	150	304	506	27	.968	767	704	63
1977	Dave Concepcion	156	280	490	11	.986	781	713	68
1978	Larry Bowa	156	224	502	10	.986	752	680	72
1979	Ozzie Smith	155	256	555	20	.976	776	704	72
1980	Ozzie Smith	158	288	621	24	.974	822	693	129
1981	Ozzie Smith	110	220	422	16	.976	837	694	100
1982	Ozzie Smith	139	279	535	13	.984	866	700	166
1983	Ozzie Smith	158	245	516	10	.987	772	658	83
1984	Ozzie Smith	124	233	437	12	.982	814	675	139
1985	Ozzie Smith	158	264	549	14	.983	792	676	116
1986	Ozzie Smith	144	229	453	15	.978	734	662	72
1987	Ozzie Smith	158	245	516	10	.987	772	658	114
1988	Ozzie Smith	150	234	519	22	.972	742	657	85
1989	Ozzie Smith	153	209	483	17	.976	705	658	47
1990	Barry Larkin	156	254	469	17	.977	721	657	84
1991	Barry Larkin	119	226	372	15	.976	756	688	68
1992	Ozzie Smith	132	232	420	10	.985	777	657	120
1993	Jay Bell	154	256	527	11	.986	795	651	144
1994	Jay Bell	110	152	381	15	.973	728	645	61
1995	Jose Vizcaino	134	189	410	10	.984	727	642	79
1996	Jay Bell	151	215	478	10	.986	746	668	78
1997	Walt Weiss	119	191	372	10	.983	750	664	86
1998	Neifi Perez	162	272	516	20	.975	737	654	83
1999	Neifi Perez	157	260	481	14	.981	742	634	108
2000	Neifi Perez	162	288	523	18	.978	761	644	117
2001	Orlando Cabrera	162	246	514	11	.986	756	653	103
2002	Jimmy Rollins	152	226	455	14	.980	715	663	52
2003	Jack Wilson	149	218	454	17	.975	701	672	29
2004	Royce Clayton	144	213	418	9	.986	725	676	49
2005	Rafael Furcal	152	255	504	15	.981	769	686	83
2006	Omar Vizquel	152	205	389	4	.993	703	668	35

American Association — Shortstop

Chick Fulmer led the Association with 107 fielding points in 1882, a mark that was first surpassed by Pop Smith in 1886 with 136 points and then by Germany Smith a year later with 143 points, the best mark in the circuit's history. In 1889 Shorty Fuller posted the highest fielding average with a .913 mark. Tommy Corcoran set the league's record for putouts with 300 in 1891, while Ollie Beard had the most assists in a season with 537 in 1889. Germany Smith was the league's best fielder twice; no one else led more than once.

Year	Shortstop	G	PO	A	E	Pct.	Total	Mean	Points
1882	Chick Fulmer	79	130	243	43	.897	462	252	107
1883	John Richmond	91	123	304	60	.877	391	245	92
1884	Tom McLaughlin	93	121	330	55	.891	455	320	88
1885	Germany Smith	108	161	455	81	.884	517	417	72
1886	Pop Smith	98	132	356	57	.895	481	333	136
1887	Germany Smith	101	157	387	70	.886	492	331	143
1888	Henry Easterday	115	120	459	73	.888	463	358	96
1889	Shorty Fuller	140	240	459	67	.913	542	474	62
1890	Phil Tomney	108	180	406	64	.902	550	460	79
1891	Tommy Corcoran	133	300	434	72	.911	589	470	107

Players' League — Shortstop

Monte Ward, one of the founders of the Players' League, was the circuit's best shortstop. As playing manager of the Brooklyn Wonders, he led his league in putouts, assists, and Faber System points. Jack Rowe led the loop in fielding average.

Year	Shortstop	G	PO	A	E	Pct.	Total	Mean	Points
1890	Monte Ward	128	303	450	105	.878	515	457	50

American League — Shortstop

In 1921 Everett "Deacon" Scott set an American League record for fielding points, not only by a shortstop, but by a fielder at any position. His 165 points is second only to Ozzie Smith's 166 as the most ever posted during the 20th century. Scott and George McBride each led the league in five different seasons, a record until Lou Boudreau led six times. Later, Luis Aparicio extended the mark to seven seasons. Donie Bush holds the record for putouts by an AL second sacker with 425 in 1925. Cal Ripken, Jr., tops the short fielders in assists with 583 collected in 1984. The highest fielding average ever recorded by a major league shortstop is the amazing .998 posted by Mike Bordick in 2002. Mike made only one error while handling 569 chances successfully at this demanding position.

Year	Fielder	G	PO	A	E	Pct.	Total	Mean	Points
1901	Wid Conroy	118	285	408	59	.922	660	553	95
1902	Bobby Wallace	131	299	474	42	.948	750	677	66
1903	Kid Elberfield	124	285	404	61	.928	649	588	55
1904	Bobby Wallace	139	303	482	44	.947	722	654	68
1905	George Davis	151	330	501	46	.948	710	625	85
1906	Terry Turner	147	287	570	36	.960	783	669	114
1907	Charley O'Leary	138	353	448	48	.948	740	709	31
1908	George McBride	155	372	568	52	.948	766	661	105
1909	Heinie Wagner	123	282	413	50	.933	675	627	48
1910	George McBride	154	370	518	58	.939	707	635	72
1911	Lee Tannehill	106	262	380	29	.951	776	669	107

Year	Fielder	G	PO	A	E	Pct.	Total	Mean	Points
1912	Donie Bush	144	317	547	66	.929	697	621	76
1913	George McBride	150	315	485	33	.961	736	674	62
1914	Donie Bush	157	425	544	58	.944	769	701	68
1915	George McBride	146	326	422	25	.968	739	666	73
1916	Doc Lavan	106	217	386	32	.950	736	652	84
1917	Ray Chapman	156	360	528	59	.938	696	611	85
1918	Everett Scott	126	270	419	17	.976	800	692	89
1919	Everett Scott	132	270	426	17	.976	780	701	72
1920	Everett Scott	154	330	496	23	.973	779	690	89
1921	Everett Scott	154	380	528	26	.972	830	665	165
1922	Everett Scott	154	302	538	30	.966	765	687	78
1923	Roger Peckinpaugh	154	311	510	45	.948	693	643	50
1924	Joe Sewell	153	349	514	36	.960	764	721	43
1925	Joe Sewell	153	314	529	29	.967	774	671	103
1926	Topper Rigney	146	286	492	25	.967	756	634	122
1927	Joe Sewell	153	361	489	33	.962	757	677	80
1928	Joe Sewell	137	297	438	28	.963	746	634	112
1929	Red Kress	146	312	441	43	.946	669	624	45
1930	Joe Cronin	154	336	509	35	.960	749	646	103
1931	Hal Rhyne	147	295	502	31	.963	752	666	86
1932	Joe Cronin	141	306	448	32	.959	732	665	67
1933	Joe Cronin	152	297	528	34	.960	743	674	69
1934	Joe Cronin	127	246	486	38	.951	746	702	44
1935	Luke Appling	153	335	556	39	.958	775	729	46
1936	Skeeter Newsome	123	273	417	31	.957	751	720	31
1937	Billy Rogell	146	323	451	26	.968	757	707	50
1938	Billy Rogell	134	291	431	31	.959	735	676	59
1939	Frankie Crosetti	152	323	460	26	.968	742	700	42
1940	Lou Boudreau	155	277	454	24	.968	700	647	53
1941	Lou Boudreau	147	296	444	26	.966	723	648	75
1942	Phil Rizzuto	144	324	445	30	.962	741	689	52
1943	Lou Boudreau	152	328	488	25	.970	770	675	95
1944	Lou Boudreau	149	339	516	29	.978	834	686	148
1945	Skeeter Webb	104	215	343	25	.957	726	685	41
1946	Lou Boudreau	139	315	405	22	.970	751	686	65
1947	Lou Boudreau	148	305	475	14	.982	800	720	80
1948	Eddie Joost	135	325	409	20	.973	787	738	49
1949	Eddie Joost	144	352	442	25	969	782	729	53
1950	Phil Rizzuto	155	301	452	14	.982	759	679	80
1951	Eddie Joost	140	326	422	20	.974	781	722	59
1952	Phil Rizzuto	152	308	450	18	.976	757	725	32
1953	George Strickland	122	238	400	17	.974	770	701	69
1954	Chico Carrasquel	155	280	492	20	.975	745	661	84
1955	George Strickland	128	221	360	14	.976	707	680	27
1956	Don Buddin	113	213	370	29	.953	693	665	28
1957	Rocky Bridges	108	226	382	18	.971	800	711	89
1958	Luis Aparicio	145	289	463	21	.973	762	702	60
1959	Luis Aparicio	152	282	460	23	.970	721	636	85
1960	Luis Aparicio	153	305	551	18	.979	822	678	144
1961	Luis Aparicio	156	264	487	30	.962	688	655	33
1962	Zoilo Versalles	160	335	501	26	.970	756	685	71

Year	Fielder	G	PO	A	E	Pct.	Total	Mean	Points
1963	Ron Hansen	144	247	483	12	.983	784	705	79
1964	Ron Hansen	158	292	514	21	.975	760	691	69
1965	Ron Hansen	161	287	527	26	.969	736	658	78
1966	Luis Aparicio	151	303	441	17	.978	753	672	81
1967	Ruben Amaro	123	212	374	16	.973	719	656	63
1968	Luis Aparicio	154	269	535	19	.977	779	675	104
1969	Luis Aparicio	157	248	563	20	.976	778	702	76
1970	Ed Brinkman	157	301	569	23	.974	801	701	100
1971	Gene Michael	136	243	474	20	.973	770	701	69
1972	Bert Campaneris	148	283	494	18	.977	782	715	67
1973	Frank Duffy	115	198	377	8	.986	787	718	69
1974	Mark Belanger	155	243	552	13	.984	793	709	84
1975	Bucky Dent	157	279	543	16	.981	794	674	120
1976	Mark Belanger	153	239	545	14	.982	785	696	89
1977	Mark Belanger	142	244	417	10	.985	748	664	84
1978	Rick Burleson	144	285	482	15	.981	802	701	101
1979	Rick Burleson	153	272	523	16	.980	787	670	117
1980	Rick Burleson	155	301	528	22	.974	782	669	113
1981	Robin Yount	93	162	370	8	.985	854	706	104
1982	Tim Foli	139	235	432	10	.985	763	680	83
1983	Cal Ripken, Jr.	162	272	534	25	.970	731	644	87
1984	Cal Ripken, Jr.	162	297	583	26	.971	780	661	119
1985	Spike Owen	117	196	361	14	.975	726	641	85
1986	Tony Fernandez	163	294	445	13	.983	730	664	66
1987	Ozzie Guillen	149	266	475	19	.975	747	666	81
1988	Ozzie Guillen	156	273	570	20	.977	797	699	98
1989	Tony Fernandez	140	260	475	6	.992	832	726	106
1990	Tony Fernandez	161	297	480	9	.989	780	681	99
1991	Cal Ripken, Jr.	162	267	528	11	.986	778	670	108
1992	Omar Vizquel	136	223	403	7	.989	758	686	72
1993	Tony Fernandez	142	278	410	13	.981	755	691	64
1994	Gary DiSarcina	110	159	358	9	.983	747	674	54
1995	Mike Bordick	126	245	338	10	.983	740	705	33
1996	Alex Gonzalez	147	279	465	21	.973	749	691	58
1997	Jay Bell	149	227	443	10	.985	732	686	46
1998	Omar Vizquel	151	273	442	5	.993	784	699	85
1999	Mike Bordick	159	277	511	9	.989	783	697	86
2000	Rey Sanchez	143	224	446	4	.994	782	696	86
2001	Alex Gonzalez	154	249	509	10	.987	782	683	99
2002	Mike Bordick	117	197	372	1	.998	818	702	116
2003	Alex Rodriguez	158	226	464	8	.989	734	677	57
2004	Bobby Crosby	151	242	505	19	.975	745	691	54
2005	Derek Jeter	157	262	454	15	.979	719	669	50
2006	Michael Young	155	241	493	14	.981	744	679	65

Federal League—Shortstop

Mickey Doolan was the Federal League's best fielding shortstop. He led the circuit in Faber System points both years and posted the highest fielding average. Jimmy Esmond holds the league record for single season putouts and assists. In 1915 he made four more putouts and one more assist than did Doolan.

FEDERAL LEAGUE FIELDING LEADERS—SHORTSTOP

Year	Shortstop	G	PO	A	E	Pct.	Total	Mean	Points
1914	Mickey Doolan	145	305	476	42	.949	702	645	57
1915	Mickey Doolan	143	349	481	52	.941	717	624	93

National League—Third Base

For third basemen Faber System points are one half of the difference between the player's total and the league mean, adjusted for length of season The National League record for fielding points by a third baseman was set by Lafayette Napoleon "Lave" Cross with 110 points way back in 1895, a record that seems destined to last forever. The 71 points compiled by Terry Pendleton in 1989 in the most attained in the 20th century. Cross led the National League in Faber System fielding points four times, moved to the fledgling American League and topped that circuit's third sackers in 1907 at the age of 40. Ned Williamson also led five times, all in the National League. Heinie Groh and Willie Jones both surpassed them in league-leading seasons with six. Jones and Ron Santo each led five consecutive seasons. Jimmie Williams and Jimmie Collins share the NL record for single-season putouts with 251 each, accomplished in 1899 and 1900, respectively. Mike Schmidt holds the record for assists with 404 runners thrown out in 1974. In 1876 Joe Battin was the league's best fielding third baseman despite an average of only .869. That mark was surpassed year after year. By 1897 Billy Clingman was the league's best with a .947 average, and the standard continued to be raised. In 1907 Harry Steinfeldt was the first league leader to top the .960 level, and Hans Lobert exceeded .970 in 1913. Groh raised the record for the highest fielding average with .983 in 1924, a mark that stood for 70 years until Tony Fernandez fielded .991 in 1994.

NATIONAL LEAGUE FIELDING LEADERS—THIRD BASE

Year	Third Baseman	G	PO	A	E	Pct.	Total	Mean	Points
1876	Joe Battin	63	115	145	40	.869	303	139	34
1877	Cap Anson	40	74	77	20	.883	321	261	12
1878	Bill Hague	62	81	177	21	.925	499	272	46
1879	Ned Williamson	70	84	193	41	.871	299	206	24
1880	Ned Williamson	63	83	143	27	.893	336	221	32
1881	Ned Williamson	76	117	194	31	.909	439	250	52
1882	Ned Williamson	83	108	210	43	.881	320	224	26
1883	Joe Farrell	101	111	248	66	.845	436	237	64
1884	Ezra Sutton	110	119	186	31	.908	304	169	50
1885	Ned Williamson	113	113	258	45	.892	301	248	19
1886	Jerry Denny	117	182	270	53	.895	369	241	51
1887	Art Whitney	119	166	237	33	.924	419	287	49
1888	Billy Nash	105	139	250	37	.913	413	290	55
1889	Jerry Denny	123	199	276	45	.913	429	345	36
1890	Chippy McGarr	115	151	228	27	.933	440	342	48
1891	Charley Bassett	121	143	270	47	.908	368	318	23
1892	Billy Nash	135	197	351	62	.898	399	316	42
1893	Billy Nash	128	189	300	41	.923	459	391	28
1894	Lave Cross	100	177	234	28	.919	474	334	60
1895	Lave Cross	125	191	308	32	.940	532	276	110
1896	Charlie Irwin	127	200	262	34	.931	467	348	52
1897	Billy Clingman	113	176	269	25	.947	557	348	92

Year	Third Baseman	G	PO	A	E	Pct.	Total	Mean	Points
1898	Lave Cross	149	215	351	33	.945	530	397	67
1899	Jimmy Collins	151	217	376	36	.943	536	423	57
1900	Lave Cross	133	173	321	29	.945	521	370	68
1901	Charlie Irwin	132	175	245	36	.921	388	348	18
1902	Ed Grimminger	140	222	282	26	.951	530	431	46
1903	Ed Grimminger	140	217	300	36	.935	486	397	41
1904	Tommy Leach	146	212	371	60	.907	422	352	35
1905	Doc Casey	142	160	252	22	.949	453	398	28
1906	Art Devlin	148	171	355	31	.944	502	411	46
1907	Harry Steinfeldt	151	161	307	36	.967	533	469	32
1908	Art Devlin	157	203	331	30	.947	497	447	25
1909	Eddie Grant	154	184	310	22	.957	511	422	45
1910	Harry Steinfeldt	128	137	246	22	.946	452	420	16
1911	Eddie Zimmerman	122	167	229	16	.961	528	456	36
1912	Buck Herzog	140	159	308	29	.942	473	425	24
1913	Hans Lobert	135	181	225	11	.974	524	446	39
1914	Red Smith	150	220	332	37	.937	491	412	40
1915	Heinie Groh	131	153	280	14	.969	561	473	44
1916	Heinie Groh	110	123	252	17	.957	531	441	45
1917	Heinie Groh	154	178	331	18	.966	551	436	58
1918	Heinie Groh	126	180	253	13	.969	574	487	36
1919	Charlie Deal	116	157	233	11	.973	579	514	30
1920	Charlie Deal	128	129	268	11	.973	553	488	33
1921	Charlie Deal	112	122	239	10	.972	565	437	64
1922	Babe Pinelli	156	204	350	32	.945	505	466	20
1923	Heinie Groh	118	117	333	9	.975	547	438	55
1924	Heinie Groh	145	121	286	7	.983	558	491	34
1925	Pie Traynor	150	226	303	24	.957	543	431	56
1926	Charlie Dressen	123	108	284	14	.966	539	466	37
1927	Pie Traynor	143	212	265	19	.962	541	464	39
1928	Freddie Lindstrom	153	145	340	21	.958	510	478	16
1929	Pinky Whitney	154	168	333	17	.967	548	487	31
1930	Pinky Whitney	148	186	313	18	.965	554	447	54
1931	Sparky Adams	138	118	223	13	.963	457	419	19
1932	Pinky Whitney	151	177	276	19	.960	500	419	40
1933	Joe Stripp	140	170	264	15	.967	533	470	32
1934	Pinky Whitney	111	105	227	11	.968	526	441	43
1935	Johnny Vergez	148	188	222	30	.953	454	395	30
1936	Joe Stripp	106	132	174	10	.968	526	441	43
1937	Pinky Whitney	130	136	238	7	.982	561	505	28
1938	Joe Stripp	109	114	187	9	.971	522	468	27
1939	Merrill May	132	154	263	19	.956	503	432	36
1940	Merrill May	135	139	297	20	.956	510	466	22
1941	Jimmy Brown	123	135	276	15	.965	551	481	35
1942	Merrill May	107	109	227	13	.963	524	460	31
1943	Merrill May	132	142	280	16	.963	530	487	22
1944	Whitey Kurowski	146	188	281	17	.965	536	494	21
1945	Stan Hack	146	195	312	13	.975	597	501	48
1946	Lee Handley	102	107	237	15	.958	530	485	23
1947	Frankie Gustine	156	198	330	31	.945	488	445	22

Year	Third Baseman	G	PO	A	E	Pct.	Total	Mean	Points
1948	Frankie Gustine	118	119	256	21	.947	475	449	13
1949	Grady Hatton	136	143	290	11	.975	568	521	24
1950	Willie Jones	158	190	323	25	.954	505	477	14
1951	Billy Johnson	124	99	316	10	.976	588	523	33
1952	Willie Jones	147	216	281	16	.969	568	510	29
1953	Willie Jones	147	176	253	11	.975	542	466	38
1954	Willie Jones	141	184	277	15	.968	554	405	69
1955	Willie Jones	146	202	235	18	.960	499	460	20
1956	Willie Jones	149	202	264	13	.973	549	457	46
1957	Don Hoak	149	193	269	14	.971	547	503	22
1958	Ken Boyer	144	156	350	20	.962	558	480	39
1959	Don Hoak	155	169	322	20	.961	520	465	55
1960	Ken Boyer	146	140	300	19	.959	498	463	18
1961	Jimmy Davenport	132	119	235	13	.965	561	473	44
1962	Eddie Mathews	140	141	283	16	.964	516	465	26
1963	Eddie Mathews	121	113	176	13	.968	548	452	48
1964	Ron Santo	161	156	367	20	.963	535	457	39
1965	Ron Santo	164	155	373	24	.957	506	426	40
1966	Ron Santo	152	150	391	25	.956	543	473	35
1967	Ron Santo	161	187	393	26	.957	550	447	52
1968	Ron Santo	162	130	378	15	.971	551	483	34
1969	Ken Boyer	141	139	275	15	.965	511	440	26
1970	Doug Rader	154	147	357	18	.966	547	444	52
1971	Tony Perez	148	113	304	18	.959	479	429	25
1972	Don Money	151	139	316	10	.978	561	464	49
1973	Ron Cey	146	111	328	18	.961	504	443	31
1974	Doug Rader	152	128	347	17	.965	529	461	34
1975	Doug Rader	124	111	257	11	.971	534	447	44
1976	Ron Cey	144	111	334	16	.965	526	474	26
1977	Phil Garner	107	98	240	10	.971	553	473	40
1978	Ken Reitz	150	111	314	12	.973	526	471	28
1979	Ron Cey	150	123	265	9	.977	516	453	32
1980	Ron Cey	157	127	317	13	.972	523	441	41
1981	Ken Reitz	81	57	157	5	.977	521	443	28
1982	Ken Oberkfell	135	78	304	11	.972	523	433	45
1983	Mike Schmidt	153	107	332	19	.959	484	425	30
1984	Ron Cey	144	97	230	11	.967	450	377	37
1985	Tim Wallach	154	148	383	18	.967	568	438	65
1986	Terry Pendleton	156	133	371	20	.962	520	424	48
1987	Mike Schmidt	138	87	315	12	.971	533	456	39
1988	Terry Pendleton	101	75	239	12	.963	525	434	41
1989	Terry Pendleton	161	113	392	15	.971	551	409	71
1990	Charlie Hayes	146	121	324	20	.957	495	428	67
1991	Tim Wallach	149	107	310	14	.968	507	428	40
1992	Terry Pendleton	158	133	325	19	.960	490	456	17
1993	Matt Williams	144	117	266	12	.970	499	411	44
1994	Tony Fernandez	91	54	166	3	.991	540	459	30
1995	Charlie Hayes	141	104	264	14	.963	471	409	29
1996	Vinny Castilla	160	97	389	20	.960	504	433	36
1997	Kevin Orie	112	91	212	9	.971	508	404	52

Year	Third Baseman	G	PO	A	E	Pct.	Total	Mean	Points
1998	Jeff Cirillo	149	99	339	11	.976	547	473	37
1999	Robin Ventura	160	123	320	9	.980	544	436	54
2000	Scott Rolen	128	89	245	10	.971	498	444	27
2001	Jeff Cirillo	137	78	308	7	.982	555	435	60
2002	Placido Polanco	131	90	272	8	.978	536	476	45
2003	Chris Stynes	119	92	225	9	.972	506	459	24
2004	Vinny Castilla	148	124	316	6	.987	587	471	58
2005	Mike Lowell	135	107	243	6	.983	536	461	38
2006	Pedro Feliz	159	117	330	21	.955	539	433	53

American Association—Third Base

Bill Shindle has the Association record for the most points in a season. Art Whitney and George Pinckney each led the league twice. Among the league leaders Shindle had the most putouts in a season, and Charley Reilly had the most assists. Shindle also holds the league record for the highest fielding average.

AMERICAN ASSOCIATION FIELDING LEADER—THIRD BASE

Year	Third Baseman	G	PO	A	E	Pct.	Total	Mean	Points
1882	Hick Carpenter	80	137	167	60	.835	163	93	18
1883	Arlie Latham	98	120	256	58	.866	271	194	25
1884	Joe Battin	78	101	178	33	.894	338	249	29
1885	Frank Hankinson	94	106	212	33	.906	358	222	49
1886	Art Whitney	95	120	209	34	.906	366	213	68
1887	George Pinckney	136	196	290	60	.890	324	232	36
1888	Bill Shindle	135	218	340	47	.922	486	311	78
1889	George Pinckney	138	183	278	52	.897	331	260	33
1890	Charlie Reilly	136	205	354	67	.893	388	318	31
1891	Art Whitney	96	129	198	35	.903	351	299	23

Players' League—Third Base

Patsy Tebeau was the league's best fielder at the hot corner. In addition to leading in Faber System points, he also topped the circuit in putouts and fielding average. Billy Nash was the league's best assist man.

PLAYERS' LEAGUE LEADING FIELDERS—THIRD BASE

Year	Third Baseman	G	PO	A	E	Pct.	Total	Mean	Points
1890	Patsy Tebeau	110	204	246	66	.872	316	212	52

American League—Third Base

In its initial season as a major league, Bill Bradley was the AL's top fielding third sacker. Bradley topped performers at the hot corner three times, as did Jimmy "Pepper" Austin and Frank "Home Run" Baker. Their marks were eclipsed by Willie Kamm, who led six consecutive seasons and two more for a total of twelve. Brooks Robinson fell one shy of this feat by logging eleven league-leading seasons. In 1901 Bradley attained 27 Faber System points, a number that was doubled by Collins the very next year. The venerable Lave Cross raised the mark to 61 points in 1906, and Austin pushed it to 66 in 1913. Ossie Vitt established a new standard with 70 points in 1915, a record that stood for 76 years until it was surpassed by Buddy Bell with 80 points in 1982.

Kamm holds the AL record for putouts by an AL third baseman, with 243 in 1928. With 412 assists in 1971, Graig Nettles holds the league record in that category. Don Money is usually credited with the highest single-season fielding average by an American League third sacker with the .989 mark he posted in 1974. However, some sources give that honor to Steve Buechele, who fielded .991 in his AL games in 1991, but Steve split his playing time between the two major leagues that year. In the 31 games he played for Pittsburgh in the National League he committed four errors, one more than he was charged with in 111 games for Texas in the junior circuit. His total major league fielding average was .983.

AMERICAN LEAGUE FIELDING LEADERS—THIRD BASE

Year	Third Baseman	G	PO	A	E	Pct.	Total	Mean	Points
1901	Bill Bradley	133	192	298	37	.930	468	408	27
1902	Jimmie Collins	107	143	255	19	.954	552	425	58
1903	Jimmie Collins	130	178	260	22	.952	510	415	43
1904	Lee Tannehill	153	180	369	31	.947	516	423	47
1905	Bill Bradley	145	187	312	29	.944	491	400	46
1906	Lave Cross	130	157	242	20	.952	480	358	61
1907	Bill Bradley	139	164	278	29	.938	445	368	39
1908	Hobe Ferris	148	222	316	27	.952	536	437	50
1909	Harry Lord	134	180	268	34	.929	506	459	24
1910	Jimmy Austin	133	204	284	30	.942	507	438	35
1911	Jimmy Austin	148	228	337	42	.931	485	448	19
1912	Frank Baker	149	217	321	34	.941	494	409	43
1913	Jimmy Austin	142	215	288	30	.944	501	370	66
1914	Terry Turner	103	138	229	14	.963	566	475	46
1915	Ossie Vitt	151	191	324	19	.964	553	441	56
1916	Ossie Vitt	151	208	385	22	.964	606	467	70
1917	Frank Baker	146	202	317	28	.949	518	467	25
1918	Frank Baker	126	175	282	13	.972	604	544	25
1919	Ossie Vitt	133	129	254	13	.967	511	474	17
1920	Aaron Ward	114	132	303	16	.965	599	546	27
1921	Howard Shanks	154	218	330	23	.960	556	514	21
1922	Bob Jones	119	161	267	17	.962	567	509	29
1923	Joe Dugan	146	155	300	12	.974	559	486	37
1924	Willie Kamm	145	185	312	15	.971	559	484	38
1925	Willie Kamm	152	182	310	22	.957	514	474	20
1926	Willie Kamm	142	177	323	11	.978	612	521	46
1927	Willie Kamm	146	236	279	15	.972	593	511	41
1928	Willie Kamm	155	243	278	12	.977	593	533	30
1929	Willie Kamm	145	221	270	11	.978	599	500	50
1930	Marty McManus	130	152	241	14	.966	527	489	19
1931	Ossie Bluege	152	151	286	18	.960	488	470	9
1932	Jimmy Dykes	141	142	251	8	.980	546	509	19
1933	Willie Kamm	131	153	221	6	.984	565	473	46
1934	Willie Kamm	118	109	248	8	.978	568	448	60
1935	Cecil Travis	114	136	254	15	.963	552	474	39
1936	Red Rolfe	133	162	265	19	.957	511	455	28

Year	Third Baseman	G	PO	A	E	Pct.	Total	Mean	Points
1937	Harlond Clift	155	198	405	34	.947	546	486	30
1938	Harlond Clift	149	176	206	19	.962	530	449	41
1939	Ken Keltner	154	187	297	13	.974	561	449	56
1940	Harlond Clift	147	161	329	21	.959	530	459	36
1941	Ken Keltner	149	181	346	16	.971	591	480	56
1942	Ken Keltner	151	166	353	30	.945	494	416	39
1943	Eddie Mayo	123	176	223	10	.976	577	510	34
1944	Ken Keltner	149	168	369	18	.968	587	530	29
1945	George Kell	147	186	345	20	.964	574	450	62
1946	George Kell	131	141	267	7	.983	589	540	25
1947	Hank Majeski	134	160	263	5	.988	609	526	42
1948	Hank Majeski	142	163	268	11	.975	554	498	28
1949	Johnny Pesky	148	184	333	16	.970	582	518	32
1950	Johnny Pesky	116	160	257	11	.974	606	536	35
1951	George Kell	147	175	310	20	.960	530	469	31
1952	Gil McDougald	117	124	273	13	.968	566	511	28
1953	Al Rosen	154	174	338	19	.964	545	519	13
1954	Andy Carey	120	154	283	15	.967	587	546	21
1955	Grady Hatton	111	97	225	8	.976	543	496	24
1956	Eddie Yost	135	164	303	18	.963	556	485	36
1957	Frank Malzone	153	151	370	25	.954	521	474	24
1958	Frank Malzone	155	139	378	27	.950	501	470	18
1959	Eddie Yost	146	168	259	17	.962	499	472	14
1960	Brooks Robinson	152	171	328	12	.977	585	470	58
1961	Clete Boyer	141	151	353	17	.967	580	520	30
1962	Clete Boyer	157	187	396	22	.964	578	522	28
1963	Brooks Robinson	160	153	330	12	.976	555	462	47
1964	Clete Boyer	123	118	278	13	.968	549	479	35
1965	Don Wert	161	163	331	12	.976	560	517	22
1966	Brooks Robinson	157	174	313	12	.976	563	480	42
1967	Brooks Robinson	158	147	405	11	.980	616	499	59
1968	Brooks Robinson	162	168	353	16	.970	555	490	33
1969	Ken McMullen	154	185	347	13	.976	598	495	52
1970	Graig Nettles	154	134	358	17	.967	542	484	29
1971	Graig Nettles	158	159	412	16	.973	604	512	46
1972	Brooks Robinson	152	129	333	11	.977	561	486	38
1973	Buddy Bell	154	144	363	22	.958	552	471	41
1974	Don Money	157	111	336	5	.989	694	507	44
1975	Brooks Robinson	143	96	326	9	.979	558	498	30
1976	Aurelio Rodriguez	128	120	280	9	.978	573	463	55
1977	Graig Nettles	156	132	321	12	.974	537	474	32
1978	Buddy Bell	139	125	355	15	.970	578	447	66
1979	Buddy Bell	147	112	364	15	.969	554	462	46
1980	Buddy Bell	120	125	282	8	.981	609	486	62
1981	John Castino	98	86	224	8	.975	566	465	36
1982	Buddy Bell	145	131	396	13	.976	616	456	80
1983	Gary Gaetti	154	131	360	17	.967	542	462	40
1984	Gary Gaetti	154	142	334	20	.960	509	420	45
1985	George Brett	152	107	339	15	.967	516	438	39
1986	Carney Lansford	100	67	147	4	.982	487	436	26

Year	Third Baseman	G	PO	A	E	Pct.	Total	Mean	Points
1987	Carney Lansford	142	98	249	7	.980	511	449	35
1988	Kelly Gruber	156	114	349	14	.971	534	434	50
1989	Jack Howell	142	95	322	11	.974	541	455	43
1990	Gary Gaetti	151	102	318	18	.959	475	405	35
1991	Steve Buechele	142	109	303	7	.983	567	501	33
1992	Robin Ventura	157	141	372	23	.957	517	434	42
1993	Wade Boggs	134	75	311	12	.970	521	421	50
1994	Gary Gaetti	85	61	162	4	.982	535	422	42
1995	Travis Fryman	144	107	337	14	.969	538	411	60
1996	Travis Fryman	128	96	291	8	.979	550	445	53
1997	Travis Fryman	153	126	312	10	.978	546	434	56
1998	Joe Randa	118	102	252	7	.976	553	395	79
1999	Scott Brosius	132	87	239	13	.962	454	406	24
2000	Tony Batista	154	120	318	17	.963	495	424	36
2001	Eric Chavez	149	100	321	12	.972	523	448	38
2002	Joe Randa	129	108	234	10	.972	525	443	41
2003	Eric Chavez	154	125	343	14	.971	541	454	44
2004	Eric Chavez	125	113	276	13	.968	538	449	45
2005	Brandon Inge	160	128	378	23	.957	506	480	13
2006	Mike Lowell	153	143	313	6	.987	588	488	50

Federal League—Third Base

In 1914 the Federal League was led in fielding at the hot corner by a rookie, Tex Wisterzill. The young Texan led the league in all fielding categories and will forever hold the loop record for putouts, assists, and points in a season. Despite this auspicious beginning, he never was never able to repeat his success. In 1915 George Perring closed out an undistinguished career by leading the league. Neither he nor Wisterzill remained in the major leagues following the demise of the Federal League at the end of the 1915 season. Of the loop leaders, the only one to enjoy prolonged major league success was Mike Mowrey, who posted the highest fielding average with a .959 mark in 915.

FEDERAL LEAGUE FIELDING LEADERS—THIRD BASE

Year	Third Baseman	G	PO	A	E	Pct.	Total	Mean	Points
1914	Tex Wisterzil	149	207	294	23	.956	523	438	43
1915	George Perring	102	135	226	16	.958	547	494	27

National League—Catcher

Charlie Bennett was the National League's best defensive catcher during the league's early years. He not only led in Faber System points five times, but also set a single-season records with 93 points, a mark tied by Chief Zimmer. This still stands as the major league record. In the 1920s and 1930s Gabby Hartnett led the circuit's backstops in points six times, topping Bennett's achievement. The 20th century record for the most points in a season was set by Pat Moran with 80 in 1905 and tied by Bill Bergen four years later. The league record for the highest fielding average has increased dramatically over the years. Doug Allison's record of .881 lasted only one year. In 1877 Pop Snyder fielded .910 and broke his own mark each of the next two seasons. By 1881 Bennett had raised the standard to .962. In 1897 Heinie Peitz posted the highest mark of the 19th century with .979. In 1901 Malachi Kittredge topped the .980 mark, and in 1912 George Gibson reached .990. The first National League catcher to field 1.000 was Spud Davis in 1939. This record has since been tied, but it can never be broken.

The record for putouts in a season has also increased over the years. No NL backstop posted as many as 600 putouts in a season during the 19th century. In 1911 Chief Meyers made 729 putouts, which stood as a record for many years. In 1959 Johnny Roseboro recorded 848 outs. The 1000 mark was topped for the first time by Johnny Edwards in 1963. In 1969 Edwards broke his own record with 1135, which still stands as the major league record. Catching for Houston in a year when the Astros' pitching staff racked up 1221 strikeouts, it is obvious that most of Johnny's putouts came on held third strikes. The 1000 mark has been exceeded at least a half dozen times since then.

On the other hand, the single season record for assists by catchers peaked in the early 1900s and has since declined. Pat Moran set the National League standard in 1903 with 214 assists, and that record still stands. Between 1900 and 1915 the 200 assists mark was surpassed at least ten times. This was an era where bunting was a common strategy and base-stealing was rife. Most of the catcher assists were attained by throwing out bunters or would-be base stealers. Since the early 1920s very few catchers have made as many as 100 assists in a season.

NATIONAL LEAGUE FIELDING LEADERS—CATCHER

Year	Catcher	G	PO	A	E	Pct.	Total	Mean	Points
1876	Doug Allison	40	201	43	33	.881	95	−51	18
1877	Pop Snyder	61	292	102	39	.910	248	146	40
1878	Pop Snyder	58	344	92	42	.912	258	202	22
1879	Pop Snyder	80	398	142	44	.925	310	176	70
1880	Silver Flint	67	388	117	37	.932	340	218	62
1881	Charlie Bennett	70	418	85	20	.962	388	241	81
1882	Pat Deasley	56	357	54	18	.958	353	277	46
1883	Charlie Bennett	72	333	88	25	.944	315	206	51
1884	Fatty Briody	64	437	112	41	.931	346	281	48
1885	Silver Flint	68	356	100	36	.927	289	232	41
1886	Charlie Bennett	69	425	84	24	.955	366	321	36
1887	Tom Daly	64	354	148	35	.937	331	280	42
1888	Charlie Bennett	73	424	94	18	.966	407	301	93
1889	Buck Ewing	97	524	149	45	.937	331	252	68
1890	Charlie Bennett	85	448	90	23	.959	356	297	52
1891	Dick Buckley	74	446	83	23	.958	365	284	73
1892	Connie Mack	92	404	143	28	.951	369	284	85
1893	Farmer Vaughn	80	270	77	11	.969	360	291	60
1894	Chief Zimmer	89	289	100	15	.963	355	247	93
1895	Wilbert Robinson	75	243	78	7	.979	399	304	82
1896	Heinie Peitz	67	201	42	8	.968	320	214	81
1897	Heinie Peitz	71	260	67	7	.979	423	319	92
1898	Jack Warner	109	536	139	22	.968	404	339	65
1899	Chief Zimmer	82	242	107	8	.978	420	350	70
1900	Heinie Peitz	80	310	125	19	.958	388	348	37
1901	Malachi Kittredge	111	581	136	12	.984	452	407	32
1902	Johnny Kling	112	471	158	17	.974	430	391	36
1903	Jack Warner	85	450	123	8	.986	485	432	48
1904	Jack Warner	86	427	115	10	.982	456	393	63
1905	Pat Moran	78	389	113	7	.986	482	402	80
1906	Johnny Kling	96	520	126	12	.982	458	406	52

Year	Catcher	G	PO	A	E	Pct.	Total	Mean	Points
1907	Johnny Kling	98	499	109	8	.987	454	406	48
1908	Bill Bergen	99	470	137	7	.989	483	416	67
1909	Bill Bergen	112	436	202	18	.973	462	382	80
1910	Bill Bergen	89	373	151	10	.981	482	424	58
1911	Bill Bergen	84	346	121	9	.981	455	401	54
1912	George Gibson	94	484	101	6	.990	459	418	41
1913	Bill Killefer	120	570	166	9	.988	479	421	58
1914	Bill Killefer	90	464	154	14	.978	483	415	58
1915	Pancho Snyder	142	592	201	14	.983	462	421	41
1916	Mike Gonzales	93	367	136	10	.981	456	426	30
1917	Bill Killefer	120	615	138	12	.984	446	402	44
1918	Walter Schmidt	104	273	120	8	.986	453	408	37
1919	Bill Killefer	100	478	124	8	.987	452	437	15
1920	Otto Miller	89	418	65	7	.986	407	379	28
1921	Walter Schmidt	111	438	153	10	.981	435	359	76
1922	Bob O'Farrell	125	446	143	14	.977	407	369	38
1923	Pancho Snyder	112	428	90	5	.990	419	391	28
1924	Zach Taylor	93	388	96	6	.988	438	388	50
1925	Pancho Snyder	96	336	71	8	.985	391	343	48
1926	Zach Taylor	123	394	123	6	.985	415	342	73
1927	Bubbles Hargrave	92	261	57	4	.987	380	360	20
1928	Gabby Hartnett	118	455	103	6	.989	423	369	54
1929	Walt Lerian	103	271	69	5	.986	380	331	49
1930	Jimmie Wilson	99	456	67	7	.987	404	345	59
1931	Spud Davis	114	420	78	3	.994	418	367	51
1932	Al Spohrer	100	374	62	4	.991	402	372	30
1933	Shanty Hogan	95	280	56	1	.997	411	368	43
1934	Gabby Hartnett	129	605	86	3	.996	434	362	72
1935	Gabby Hartnett	110	477	77	9	.984	393	345	48
1936	Gabby Hartnett	114	504	75	5	.991	413	366	47
1937	Gabby Hartnett	103	436	65	2	.996	425	371	54
1938	Gabby Hartnett	83	358	40	2	.995	408	378	30
1939	Spud Davis	85	260	40	0	1.000	411	365	46
1940	Al Lopez	95	343	62	4	.990	401	362	39
1941	Harry Danning	116	530	77	4	.993	422	378	44
1942	Al Lopez	99	327	53	2	.995	404	362	42
1943	Ray Mueller	140	579	100	8	.988	406	367	39
1944	Dewey Williams	77	317	50	7	.981	376	351	25
1945	Ken O'Dea	91	321	58	2	.995	407	372	35
1946	Ray Mueller	100	405	65	3	.994	419	376	43
1947	Ray Lamanno	109	556	62	9	.986	395	365	30
1948	Del Rice	99	447	46	2	.996	412	351	61
1949	Phil Masi	81	291	34	2	.994	391	369	22
1950	Wes Westrum	139	608	71	1	.999	425	360	65
1951	Clyde McCullough	87	364	52	5	.988	394	379	15
1952	Roy Campanella	122	662	55	4	.994	412	370	42
1953	Del Crandall	108	566	62	9	.986	397	379	20
1954	Del Crandall	136	665	79	8	.989	404	372	32
1955	Andy Seminick	93	461	45	3	.994	411	381	30
1956	Del Crandall	109	448	44	2	.996	418	379	39

Year	Catcher	G	PO	A	E	Pct.	Total	Mean	Points
1957	Cal Neeman	118	703	56	8	.990	407	384	23
1958	Del Crandall	124	659	64	7	.990	405	383	22
1959	Johnny Roseboro	117	848	54	8	.991	422	393	29
1960	Johnny Roseboro	87	640	48	5	.993	439	395	44
1961	Johnny Roseboro	125	877	56	13	.986	402	371	31
1962	Johnny Edwards	130	807	92	12	.987	423	399	24
1963	Johnny Edwards	148	1008	87	6	.995	444	406	38
1964	Johnny Edwards	120	890	73	8	.992	442	398	44
1965	Clay Dalrymple	102	657	70	5	.993	443	406	37
1966	Johnny Roseboro	138	904	65	7	.993	423	398	25
1967	Tim McCarver	130	819	67	3	.997	438	402	36
1968	Tom Haller	139	863	81	6	.994	433	408	25
1969	Johnny Edwards	151	1135	79	7	.994	441	413	28
1970	Johnny Edwards	139	854	74	5	.995	432	392	40
1971	Manny Sanguillen	135	712	72	5	.994	419	388	31
1972	Duffy Dyer	91	690	61	5	.993	453	400	53
1973	Joe Ferguson	122	757	57	3	.996	429	386	43
1974	Steve Yeager	93	552	58	5	.992	429	394	35
1975	Jerry Grote	111	706	55	4	.995	431	383	48
1976	Jerry Grote	95	617	49	5	.993	427	391	36
1977	Biff Pocaroba	100	542	78	7	.989	479	401	78
1978	Biff Pocaroba	78	454	43	5	.990	412	386	26
1979	Gene Tenace	94	413	51	1	.998	425	395	30
1980	Gary Carter	149	822	108	7	.994	438	388	50
1981	Gary Carter	100	509	58	4	.993	419	386	25
1982	Gary Carter	153	954	104	10	.991	433	397	36
1983	Gary Carter	144	847	107	5	.995	450	400	50
1984	Tony Pena	146	895	95	9	.991	430	398	32
1985	Tony Pena	146	922	100	12	.988	425	394	31
1986	Jody Davis	145	885	105	8	.992	440	402	38
1987	Bob Melvin	78	407	43	1	.998	434	407	27
1988	Tony Pena	142	777	70	5	.994	417	401	16
1989	Tony Pena	134	674	70	2	.997	426	390	36
1990	Joe Oliver	118	686	59	6	.992	415	385	30
1991	Mike LaValliere	105	565	46	1	.998	425	396	29
1992	Kirt Manwaring	108	564	68	4	.994	429	412	17
1993	Rick Wilkins	133	717	89	3	.996	441	410	31
1994	Darrin Daulton	68	435	42	3	.994	439	416	17
1995	Charles Johnson	97	641	63	6	.992	438	415	22
1996	Javier Lopez	135	1000	80	6	.994	446	408	38
1997	Charles Johnson	123	900	73	0	1.000	466	416	50
1998	Javier Lopez	128	978	68	5	.995	447	405	42
1999	Henry Blanco	86	552	58	5	.992	440	408	32
2000	Mike Matheny	124	803	75	5	.994	438	408	30
2001	Damian Miller	134	959	81	7	.993	457	419	38
2002	Brad Ausmus	129	942	65	3	.997	444	417	27
2003	Damian Miller	114	940	73	3	.997	469	417	52
2004	Chad Moeller	100	718	46	1	.999	448	422	26
2005	Brad Ausmus	134	884	65	1	.999	444	414	30
2006	Brad Ausmus	138	933	61	2	.995	439	415	24

American Association—Catcher

In 1883 Bill Holbert led American Association backstops with 101 Faber System points, the only catcher in major league history to go over the century mark. Jack O'Connor was the only AA catcher to lead the league more than once. Doc Bushong has the circuit's record for single-season putouts, while Kid Baldwin had the most assists, and O'Connor posted the highest fielding average.

AMERICAN ASSOCIATION FIELDING LEADERS—CATCHER

Year	Catcher	G	PO	A	E	Pct.	Total	Mean	Points
1882	Jack O'Brien	45	205	66	22	.925	275	160	59
1883	Bill Holbert	68	527	138	58	.920	347	186	101
1884	Jocko Milligan	65	474	100	37	.939	357	271	56
1885	Bill Traffley	61	357	105	28	.943	374	290	60
1886	Doc Bushong	106	647	134	48	.942	327	221	98
1887	Sam Trott	69	373	102	44	.915	252	172	71
1888	Jim Keenan	69	356	114	29	.942	357	315	37
1889	Jack O'Connor	84	423	128	26	.955	386	345	37
1890	Jack O'Connor	106	539	146	27	.962	396	348	41
1891	Morg Murphy	104	532	118	31	.954	345	276	62

Players' League—Catcher

Buck Ewing, who spent most of his long career in the National League, was the best catcher in the Players' League, leading the circuit in Faber System points and fielding average. Connie Mack, who later spent more than half a century at the helm of the Philadelphia Athletics, led the loop in both putouts and assists.

PLAYERS' LEAGUE FIELDING LEADER—CATCHER

Year	Catcher	G	PO	A	E	Pct.	Total	Mean	Points
1890	Buck Ewing	81	372	107	31	.949	341	250	78

American League—Catcher

Billy Sullivan led American League catchers in defense in the circuit's first major league season in 1901 and repeated ten years later. In 1938 the league leader was another Billy Sullivan — the son of the loop's first premier backstop. Bill Dickey was the league's best catcher six times in the 1930s and 1940s. The often-overlooked Jim Sundberg surpassed that total with seven league-leading seasons in the 1970s and 1980s. Ossee Schreckengost, playing in 1907 under the name Ossie Schreck, set the league standard with 94 Faber System points, one of the few records that has lasted for 100 years. In 1948 Buddy Rosar became the first American Leaguer to field 1.000, a mark that has been matched several times since then. Dan Wilson holds the circuit's record for the most putouts in a season. The 212 assists racked up by Oscar Stanage in 1911 has stood as a league record for 95 years and may never be broken. Despite his record setting performance, Stanage was the loop's poorest defensive catcher that year. His 41 errors were more than twice the number committed by any other backstop and over five times the number charged to Sullivan.

AMERICAN LEAGUE FIELDING LEADERS—CATCHER

Year	Catcher	G	PO	A	E	Pct.	Total	Mean	Points
1901	Billy Sullivan	97	396	104	17	.967	371	340	28
1902	Lou Criger	80	330	117	16	.965	405	365	36
1903	Ossie Schreck	77	514	106	16	.975	455	403	47
1904	Joe Sugden	79	370	94	5	.989	463	405	58
1905	Joe Sugden	85	420	112	7	.983	458	429	29
1906	Jack Warner	81	348	136	13	.974	458	401	57
1907	Ossie Schreck	99	640	145	12	.985	495	401	94
1908	Lou Criger	84	280	120	10	.980	455	399	56
1909	Gabby Street	137	714	210	18	.981	475	414	61
1910	Gabby Street	86	417	151	11	.978	484	425	59
1911	Billy Sullivan	89	447	114	8	.986	465	422	43
1912	Walt Kuhn	75	318	104	15	.966	414	364	50
1913	Bill Carrigan	81	393	126	11	.979	467	413	54
1914	Ed Sweeney	78	369	120	10	.980	468	421	47
1915	Ray Schalk	134	655	159	13	.984	448	391	57
1916	Ray Schalk	124	653	166	10	.988	480	418	62
1917	Dorf Ainsmith	119	580	154	22	.977	435	396	39
1918	Steve O'Neill	113	409	154	10	.983	449	430	16
1919	Cy Perkins	87	340	134	14	.971	430	391	35
1920	Roxy Walters	85	351	94	9	.980	419	380	39
1921	Ray Schalk	126	453	129	9	.985	421	378	43
1922	Ray Schalk	142	591	150	8	.989	444	395	49
1923	Hank Severeid	116	471	88	4	.993	426	376	50
1924	Hank Severeid	130	443	134	6	.980	434	379	55
1925	Benny Bengough	94	325	83	3	.993	433	372	61
1926	Muddy Ruel	117	452	81	6	.989	405	368	37
1927	Larry Woodall	86	265	72	1	.997	438	369	69
1928	Muddy Ruel	101	397	83	5	.989	409	354	55
1929	Wally Schang	85	268	56	4	.988	390	370	20
1930	Mickey Cochrane	137	654	69	5	.993	426	364	62
1931	Bill Dickey	125	670	78	3	.996	436	379	57
1932	Mickey Cochrane	137	652	94	5	.993	426	364	62
1933	Bill Dickey	127	721	82	6	.993	431	398	33
1934	Rick Ferrell	128	531	72	6	.990	398	361	37
1935	Bill Dickey	118	536	62	3	.995	415	373	42
1936	Luke Sewell	126	461	87	9	.984	386	355	31
1937	Bill Dickey	137	692	80	7	.991	412	381	31
1938	Billy Sullivan	99	441	65	5	.990	410	375	35
1939	Bill Dickey	126	571	57	7	.989	388	352	36
1940	Rollie Hemsley	117	591	65	4	.994	419	376	43
1941	Bill Dickey	104	422	45	3	.994	397	373	20
1942	Jake Early	98	392	71	9	.981	386	367	21
1943	Paul Richards	100	537	86	9	.986	427	381	46
1944	Buddy Rosar	98	409	59	5	.989	399	361	38
1945	Rick Ferrell	83	331	64	4	.990	417	397	20
1946	Buddy Rosar	117	532	73	0	1.000	441	373	68
1947	Buddy Rosar	102	406	70	2	.996	428	381	47
1948	Buddy Rosar	90	335	39	1	.997	404	378	26
1949	Yogi Berra	109	544	60	7	.989	402	367	35

Year	Catcher	G	PO	A	E	Pct.	Total	Mean	Points
1950	Jim Hegan	129	656	64	5	.993	410	379	31
1951	Sherman Lollar	85	361	48	2	.995	416	361	55
1952	Clint Courtney	113	487	60	2	.996	416	382	34
1953	Sherman Lollar	107	470	51	3	.994	405	379	26
1954	Frank House	107	534	56	4	.993	412	383	29
1955	Jim Hegan	111	583	34	2	.997	416	381	35
1956	Hal Smith	108	496	55	5	.991	400	382	18
1957	Lou Berberet	77	349	48	0	1.000	441	409	32
1958	Yogi Berra	88	509	41	0	1.000	437	397	40
1959	Yogi Berra	116	698	61	2	.997	436	393	43
1960	Sherman Lollar	123	555	54	3	.995	406	385	21
1961	Earl Battey	131	812	60	6	.993	418	386	32
1962	Earl Battey	147	872	82	9	.991	433	403	30
1963	Gus Triandos	90	535	29	1	.998	419	393	26
1964	Elston Howard	110	939	67	2	.998	473	404	69
1965	Bill Freehan	129	869	57	4	.996	430	392	38
1966	Bill Freehan	132	898	56	4	.996	430	404	26
1967	Joe Azcue	88	636	57	1	.999	470	407	63
1968	Joe Azcue	97	699	50	3	.996	444	407	37
1969	Ellie Hendricks	87	479	40	1	.998	428	393	35
1970	George Mitterwald	117	740	62	3	.996	436	396	40
1971	Ed Hermann	97	556	56	3	.995	432	400	32
1972	Ed Hermann	112	641	69	8	.989	416	394	22
1973	Bill Freehan	98	584	50	3	.995	428	388	40
1974	Ellie Rodriguez	137	782	75	7	.992	419	371	48
1975	Brian Downing	137	730	84	8	.990	415	380	35
1976	Jim Sundberg	140	719	96	7	.991	423	373	50
1977	Jim Sundberg	149	801	103	5	.994	436	377	59
1978	Jim Sundberg	148	769	91	3	.997	436	386	50
1979	Jim Sundberg	150	754	75	4	.995	417	367	50
1980	Jim Sundberg	151	853	76	7	.993	417	376	41
1981	Jim Sundberg	98	464	52	2	.996	420	379	29
1982	Carlton Fisk	133	639	62	4	.994	408	380	28
1983	Lance Parrish	131	695	73	4	.995	426	371	55
1984	Jim Sundberg	109	556	55	3	.995	410	380	30
1985	Bob Boone	147	670	71	10	.987	417	388	29
1986	Lance Parrish	85	483	48	6	.989	420	385	35
1987	Ernie Whitt	131	803	55	5	.994	416	386	30
1988	Rick Cerone	83	471	28	0	1.000	423	390	33
1989	Dave Valle	104	631	44	3	.997	426	397	29
1990	Lance Parrish	131	760	88	6	.993	435	397	38
1991	Lance Parrish	111	658	57	2	.997	434	407	27
1992	Pat Borders	137	784	88	8	.991	425	403	22
1993	Dave Valle	135	888	71	5	.995	439	402	37
1994	Terry Steinbach	93	569	58	1	.998	451	410	30
1995	Dan Wilson	119	895	52	5	.995	436	398	36
1996	Dan Wilson	135	834	58	4	.996	425	398	27
1997	Dan Wilson	144	1051	72	6	.995	440	408	32
1998	Joe Girardi	78	978	38	3	.995	435	402	33
1999	John Flaherty	115	726	87	6	.993	449	414	35

Year	Catcher	G	PO	A	E	Pct.	Total	Mean	Points
2000	Ivan Rodriguez	87	507	34	2	.996	417	403	14
2001	Einar Diaz	134	959	92	8	.992	447	399	48
2002	Bengie Molina	121	797	60	1	.999	448	416	32
2003	Jorge Posada	137	933	75	6	.994	436	404	32
2004	Bengie Molina	89	597	56	3	.995	447	411	36
2005	Jorge Posada	133	718	76	3	.996	431	412	19
2006	Bengie Molina	99	615	47	2	.997	433	408	25

Federal League—Catcher

Bill Rariden was the Federal League's best defensive catcher. He holds the league record for Faber System points, putouts, and assists. Fred Jacklitsch has the mark for the highest fielding average with .988. Rariden not only holds the FL record for single season assists, but in his two seasons in the league he racked up the two highest assist totals ever accomplished by any major league player. His record is the only significant major league record held by a Federal League player at any position.

FEDERAL LEAGUE FIELDING LEADERS—CATCHER

Year	Catcher	G	PO	A	E	Pct.	Total	Mean	Points
1914	Mike Simon	78	433	132	9	.984	505	463	42
1915	Bill Rariden	142	709	238	21	.978	478	427	51

Reporting Outfield Data

Throughout baseball history, fielding records for outfielders have usually been reported generically. That is, all outer gardeners are considered simply as outfielders, with no distinction among right fielders, center fielders, and left fielders. There is good reason for this. Although some outfielders may patrol the same segment throughout their careers, others may roam all three sectors during their career, a season, or even during a single game. In this book we follow the standard practice and combine an outfielder's performance at all outfield positions into one statistical line, and list him at the position at which he played the most games. For example, in 1953 Minnie Minoso appeared in 70 games in left field, 63 games in center field, 10 games in right field, nine games at third base, and one game at shortstop. We combine all his outfield data and list him as a left fielder. We do not include data from his infield play as it is incompatible with outfielding. Had Minoso played more games in right than in left one season, he would have been listed as a right fielder that particular season. He did not do this, but many players did. For example, Al Kaline in some seasons is listed as a right fielder and in others as a center fielder, depending on which position he more often played during the year in question.

Because the league mean is computed by combining all outfield positions, it is possible for a fielder to be the best at his particular place and yet be below the mean. In fact, this has happened several times. For example, in the early 1930s the National League's best outfielders apparently were concentrated in center field and right field with the result being that the leading left fielders had negative points every year from 1929 through 1932.

National League—Right Field

In 1882 Jake Evans recorded the most Faber System points ever amassed in a season by a National League right fielder with 75, one more than Jim Fogarty acquired in 1887. The record for putouts in a season by an NL right fielder is held by Dave Parker, who retired 389 batters in 1977. Orator Shaffer set a major league record for assists with an amazing 50 in 1879. He did this in only 72 games. The most anyone got during the 20th century was 44 by Chuck Klein in 1930 in 156 games, more than twice as many games as Shaffer played during his record-setting season. The best fielding average turned in by a 19th century right fielder was Sam Thompson's .977 in 1894. In 1914 Owen "Chief" Wilson became the first to top the .980 mark, and only two years later Max Flack pushed the standard above .990. Pete Rose holds the present record for National League right fielders with .997 in 1970.

In the league's pioneer era Orator Shaffer, Jake Evans, and Sam Thompson each led the circuit in points four times. In 1961 Roberto Clemente became the first to match this total, just before Johnny Callison led for four consecutive seasons. Clemente and Callison now share the record with five league-leading seasons apiece.

NATIONAL LEAGUE FIELDING LEADERS—RIGHT FIELD

Year	Right Fielder	G	PO	A	E	Pct.	Totals	Mean	Points
1876	Joe Blong	62	64	13	9	.895	296	230	9
1877	Orator Shaffer	60	121	21	28	.835	335	144	25
1878	Orator Shaffer	63	105	28	25	.842	418	247	23
1879	Jake Evans	72	153	30	24	.884	576	330	43
1880	Orator Shaffer	83	128	35	18	.901	579	330	46
1881	Jake Evans	83	145	31	14	.926	635	421	39
1882	Jake Evans	68	131	31	16	.910	681	271	75
1883	Orator Shaffer	95	182	41	36	.861	493	324	36
1884	Jake Evans	76	136	19	14	.917	486	305	60
1885	Jack Manning	107	134	21	18	.896	309	338	−7
1886	Sam Thompson	122	194	29	13	.945	547	358	50
1887	Jim Fogarty	123	273	39	27	.920	606	335	74
1888	Jim Fogarty	117	239	26	20	.930	526	401	31
1889	Jack McGeachy	131	189	36	20	.918	479	400	22
1890	Steve Brodie	132	225	19	12	.953	493	454	11
1891	Sam Thompson	133	234	32	18	.937	540	406	41
1892	Bug Holliday	152	271	20	21	.933	483	400	28
1893	Tommy Dowd	132	225	21	15	.944	524	447	22
1894	Sam Thompson	102	159	12	4	.977	531	471	17
1895	Willie Keeler	131	244	21	10	.964	574	458	34
1896	Sam Thompson	119	235	28	8	.970	666	482	52
1897	Jimmy Ryan	135	211	28	14	.940	511	464	14
1898	Harry Blake	136	234	25	13	.952	529	476	18
1899	Jimmy Sheckard	146	298	33	20	.943	573	479	31
1900	Honus Wagner	118	181	11	7	.965	464	466	−1
1901	Patsy Donovan	124	215	19	5	.979	577	477	30
1902	Patsy Donovan	126	179	30	9	.959	577	488	27
1903	Bill Keister	100	133	22	10	.939	483	455	8
1904	Jimmy Sebring	136	234	27	7	.974	618	482	45
1905	Jack Dunleavy	118	177	25	8	.962	569	502	22
1906	John Titus	142	218	23	7	.974	563	513	17
1907	Mike Mitchell	143	256	39	11	.964	665	532	44
1908	Mike Donlin	127	197	20	5	.977	570	534	12
1909	John Titus	149	241	23	8	.971	553	556	−1
1910	Owen Wilson	146	255	23	8	.972	572	528	15
1911	Mike Mitchell	140	280	23	9	.971	601	551	17

Year	Right Fielder	G	PO	A	E	Pct.	Totals	Mean	Points
1912	Gavvy Cravath	113	200	26	8	.966	667	534	44
1913	Gavvy Cravath	141	208	20	10	.958	483	556	−24
1914	Owen Wilson	154	312	34	6	.983	700	523	59
1915	Bill Hinchman	156	261	17	9	.969	506	520	−5
1916	Max Flack	136	193	22	2	.991	607	533	25
1917	Tommy Griffith	100	165	19	5	.974	602	527	25
1918	Max Flack	121	199	20	5	.978	590	565	7
1919	Max Flack	116	194	18	3	.986	610	581	9
1920	Greasy Neale	150	347	19	5	.987	648	564	28
1921	Possum Whitted	102	247	9	3	.988	632	595	13
1922	Curt Walker	147	295	24	15	.955	547	573	−9
1923	Cliff Heathcote	118	231	14	5	.980	599	551	16
1924	George Harper	131	270	16	4	.986	615	543	24
1925	Jimmy Welsh	116	237	27	11	.960	637	558	26
1926	Cliff Heathcote	133	306	22	5	.985	679	552	42
1927	Max Carey	141	331	19	11	.970	602	593	3
1928	George Harper	102	196	17	4	.982	632	556	25
1929	Mel Ott	149	335	26	10	.973	642	565	26
1930	Chuck Klein	156	362	44	17	.960	714	543	57
1931	Paul Waner	138	342	28	9	.976	704	570	45
1932	Chuck Klein	154	331	29	15	.960	695	590	35
1933	Chuck Klein	152	339	21	5	.986	648	570	26
1934	Johnny Moore	125	267	18	5	.983	635	563	24
1935	Mel Ott	137	285	17	3	.990	632	562	23
1936	Gene Moore	151	314	32	8	.977	677	545	44
1937	Gene Moore	148	340	21	8	.978	632	550	27
1938	Goody Rosen	113	263	19	3	.989	698	561	46
1939	Paul Waner	106	206	12	5	.978	602	571	10
1940	Max West	102	230	16	6	.976	635	551	28
1941	Dixie Walker	146	309	19	8	.976	595	553	14
1942	Bill Nicholson	151	327	18	5	.986	622	566	19
1943	Chuck Workman	149	310	22	4	.988	652	596	19
1944	Stan Musial	146	353	16	5	.987	642	587	18
1945	Dixie Walker	153	346	18	3	.992	651	599	21
1946	Tommy Holmes	146	294	17	4	.987	608	569	13
1947	Frankie Baumholtz	150	282	18	7	.977	565	551	5
1948	Tommy Holmes	137	283	8	5	.983	542	555	−4
1949	Stan Musial	156	326	19	3	.991	626	572	18
1950	Gus Bell	104	203	10	5	.977	549	554	−2
1951	Carl Furillo	157	330	24	5	.986	650	591	20
1952	Johnny Wyrostek	117	272	16	6	.980	636	563	24
1953	Carl Furillo	131	232	11	3	.988	554	548	35
1954	Don Mueller	153	263	14	6	.979	533	542	−3
1955	Roberto Clemente	118	253	18	6	.978	627	555	24
1956	Walt Moryn	141	268	18	5	.983	595	543	14
1957	Roberto Clemente	109	272	9	6	.979	595	550	15
1958	Roberto Clemente	135	312	22	6	.982	667	576	30
1959	Gus Bell	145	269	15	1	.996	609	569	13
1960	Ken Walters	119	220	17	3	.988	621	557	21
1961	Roberto Clemente	144	256	27	9	.969	596	537	20
1962	Johnny Callison	152	327	24	7	.980	640	515	42

Year	Right Fielder	G	PO	A	E	Pct.	Totals	Mean	Points
1963	Johnny Callison	157	298	26	2	.994	668	517	50
1964	Johnny Callison	162	319	19	4	.988	608	498	37
1965	Johnny Callison	159	313	21	6	.982	602	504	33
1966	Hank Aaron	158	315	12	4	.988	568	505	21
1967	Tommy Harper	100	208	6	1	.995	585	502	28
1968	Pete Rose	148	268	20	3	.990	617	522	31
1969	Johnny Callison	129	273	12	3	.990	605	494	37
1970	Pete Rose	159	309	8	1	.997	569	509	20
1971	Roberto Clemente	124	267	11	2	.993	614	540	25
1972	Bobby Bonds	153	345	8	8	.978	538	534	1
1973	Cesar Geronimo	130	243	9	2	.992	563	531	11
1974	Cesar Geronimo	145	355	13	5	.987	625	532	31
1975	Bake McBride	107	289	4	3	.990	608	547	20
1976	Jay Johnstone	122	266	8	5	.982	557	533	8
1977	Dave Parker	158	389	26	15	.965	628	532	32
1978	Ellis Valentine	146	296	24	10	.970	600	534	22
1979	George Hendrick	138	254	20	2	.993	639	538	34
1980	Terry Puhl	135	311	14	3	.991	637	574	21
1981	Jack Clark	98	193	14	4	.981	610	579	9
1982	Sixto Lezcano	134	275	16	3	.990	623	533	30
1983	Warren Cromartie	101	208	12	6	.973	568	527	14
1984	Lee Lacy	127	268	15	1	.996	649	525	41
1985	Tony Gwynn	152	337	14	4	.989	611	541	23
1986	Glenn Wilson	154	331	20	4	.989	642	523	40
1987	Dale Murphy	159	325	14	8	.977	550	533	6
1988	Dale Murphy	156	340	15	3	.992	622	536	29
1989	Tony Gwynn	157	353	13	6	.984	588	530	19
1990	Tony Gwynn	141	327	11	5	.985	593	545	16
1991	Paul O'Neill	150	301	13	2	.994	600	533	22
1992	Larry Walker	139	269	16	2	.993	619	559	20
1993	Larry Walker	132	273	13	6	.979	569	550	6
1994	Reggie Sanders	104	218	12	6	.975	575	531	11
1995	Raul Mondesi	138	282	16	6	.980	586	523	21
1996	Orlando Merced	115	241	14	3	.988	611	507	35
1997	Raul Mondesi	159	338	10	4	.989	516	526	-3
1998	Mark Kotsay	145	346	20	6	.984	657	520	46
1999	Mark Kotsay	129	245	19	5	.981	608	535	24
2000	Bobby Abreu	152	337	13	4	.989	604	524	27
2001	Brian Jordan	144	321	11	3	.991	603	536	22
2002	Larry Walker	123	229	14	4	.984	580	521	20
2003	Jose Cruz, Jr.	157	336	18	2	.994	642	543	33
2004	Ruben Rivera	104	192	14	3	.986	606	516	30
2005	Austin Kearns	107	238	8	3	.988	589	514	25
2006	Brad Hawpe	145	280	16	4	.987	593	526	22

American Association — Right Field

Chicken Wolf was the American Association's best right fielder. Born in Louisville, Wolf played for his home town team through the entire major league existence of the Association. Four times he led the circuit in Faber System points, but Pop Corkhill acquired the most points in a season with 92 in 1885, the most ever amassed by a major league outfielder. Of the league leaders Tommy McCarthy had the most putouts, Hugh Nichol the most assists, and Orator Shaffer the highest fielding average.

AMERICAN ASSOCIATION FIELDING LEADERS—RIGHT FIELD

Year	Right Fielder	G	PO	A	E	Pct.	Totals	Mean	Points
1882	Chicken Wolf	70	71	21	10	.902	408	190	37
1883	Hugh Nichol	84	133	31	15	.916	580	130	74
1884	Hugh Nichol	87	144	48	28	.873	628	218	89
1885	Pop Corkhill	110	208	38	16	.939	665	281	92
1886	Chicken Wolf	122	197	28	16	.934	504	280	69
1887	Chicken Wolf	128	207	27	15	.940	506	389	35
1888	Tommy McCarthy	131	243	44	21	.932	627	405	66
1889	Joe Sommer	105	172	24	15	.929	492	410	25
1890	Orator Shaffer	98	143	17	7	.958	512	399	33
1891	Chicken Wolf	133	185	28	19	.918	409	391	5

Players' League—Right Field

Jim Fogarty led Players' League right fielders with 57 points. Hugh Duffy led in putouts and assists. Fogarty had the best fielding average. His .963 was one of the highest percentages ever recorded by a major league outfielder up until that time.

PLAYERS' LEAGUE FIELDING LEADER—RIGHT FIELD

Year	Right Fielder	G	PO	A	E	Pct.	Total	Mean	Points
1890	Jim Fogarty	91	192	17	8	.963	608	409	57

American League Right Field

Harry Hooper's reputation as one of baseball's greatest right fielders is confirmed by the statistics. He led the junior circuit right fielders in Faber System points a record six times. William "Baby Doll" Jacobson had the most single-season putouts of any league leading right fielder, but his 401 putouts recorded in 1917 included several made while he was playing centerfield. In 1906, his rookie year with the St. Louis Browns, Harry Niles threw out 34 baserunners, the most ever by a league-leading AL right fielder. In 1907 Ed Hahn became the first right fielder to lead the league with a .990 average, a mark that stood until Pete Fox fielded .994 in 1938. In 1965 Rocky Colavito became the first American League right fielder to play a full season of errorless ball. Three years later Ken Harrelson became the first to lead the league in points while fielding 1.000.

AMERICAN LEAGUE FIELDING LEADERS—RIGHT FIELD

Year	Right Fielder	G	PO	A	E	Pct.	Total	Mean	Points
1901	Cy Seymour	155	271	23	17	.945	525	472	16
1902	Ducky Holmes	92	155	16	9	.950	509	472	11
1903	Charlie Hemphill	104	155	17	7	.961	501	471	9
1904	Patsy Donovan	122	217	15	9	.963	511	458	18
1905	Sam Crawford	103	152	18	2	.988	598	452	49
1906	Harry Niles	111	145	34	6	.968	696	513	61
1907	Ed Hahn	156	182	24	2	.990	570	504	22

Year	Right Fielder	G	PO	A	E	Pct.	Total	Mean	Points
1908	Ty Cobb	150	212	23	14	.944	442	460	−6
1909	Danny Murphy	149	191	17	5	.976	496	479	6
1910	Danny Murphy	151	209	15	6	.974	484	437	16
1911	Joe Jackson	147	242	32	12	.958	575	528	16
1912	Joe Jackson	152	273	30	16	.950	544	486	19
1913	Harry Hooper	148	248	25	9	.968	563	501	21
1914	Harry Hooper	140	231	23	7	.973	558	509	16
1915	Harry Hooper	149	255	23	8	.972	566	507	20
1916	Harry Hooper	151	266	19	10	.966	522	541	−6
1917	Baby Doll Jacobson	141	401	25	5	.988	755	550	68
1918	Shano Collins	93	230	20	7	.973	706	582	34
1919	Harry Hooper	128	262	19	6	.979	631	547	25
1920	Nemo Leibold	106	190	18	5	.977	606	561	15
1921	Jack Tobin	150	277	28	14	.956	558	548	3
1922	Bob Meusel	121	202	24	12	.950	533	534	0
1923	Ira Flagstead	102	218	33	10	.962	744	570	58
1924	Harry Hooper	123	251	22	4	.986	670	576	31
1925	Sam Rice	132	281	18	9	.971	587	563	8
1926	Harry Rice	133	300	22	10	.970	624	553	24
1927	Bill Barrett	147	289	22	12	.963	547	520	9
1928	Earl McNeely	120	229	19	4	.984	630	576	18
1929	Beauty McGowan	117	257	16	7	.975	606	559	16
1930	Bing Miller	154	309	10	8	.976	518	517	0
1931	Roy Johnson	150	332	25	15	.960	588	546	14
1932	Earl Webb	134	237	15	11	.958	482	528	−15
1933	Ben Chapman	147	288	24	8	.975	609	538	24
1934	Pete Fox	121	245	13	7	.974	557	526	10
1935	Pete Fox	125	244	9	3	.988	545	559	−3
1936	Beau Bell	142	291	11	8	.974	541	555	−5
1937	Beau Bell	131	222	22	4	.984	617	563	18
1938	Pete Fox	155	301	13	2	.994	591	543	16
1939	Pete Fox	126	275	12	9	.970	546	546	0
1940	Wally Moses	133	295	10	8	.974	544	535	3
1941	Tommy Henrich	139	280	13	6	.980	562	573	−3
1942	Wally Moses	145	323	14	7	.980	586	557	10
1943	Roy Cullenbine	121	245	14	5	.981	621	569	17
1944	Roy Cullenbine	151	275	15	10	.967	597	592	2
1945	Roy Cullenbine	150	326	23	7	.980	638	573	22
1946	Tommy Henrich	111	224	10	2	.992	599	552	16
1947	Tommy Henrich	132	278	13	5	.983	606	572	11
1948	Taft Wright	114	227	9	3	.987	568	566	1
1949	Dick Kokos	138	290	16	6	.981	596	590	2
1950	Bud Stewart	100	202	10	2	.991	605	580	8
1951	Sam Mele	116	265	5	2	.993	568	574	−2
1952	Jackie Jensen	148	291	17	7	.978	571	571	0
1953	Hank Bauer	126	230	13	2	.992	592	588	1
1954	Tom Umphlett	101	169	13	2	.989	593	585	3
1955	Jim Rivera	143	288	22	6	.981	625	561	15
1956	Al Kaline	153	343	18	6	.984	622	543	26
1957	Al Kaline	145	319	13	5	.985	583	546	12

Year	Right Fielder	G	PO	A	E	Pct.	Total	Mean	Points
1958	Al Kaline	145	316	23	2	.994	690	522	56
1959	Jackie Jensen	146	311	12	6	.982	568	536	11
1960	Roger Maris	131	263	6	4	.985	529	537	−3
1961	Al Kaline	147	378	9	4	.990	618	527	30
1962	Al Kaline	100	225	8	4	.983	579	519	20
1963	Willie Kirkland	112	234	11	4	.984	587	533	18
1964	Lu Clinton	121	182	18	2	.990	606	523	28
1965	Mike Hershberger	144	238	14	3	.988	556	499	19
1966	Mike Hershberger	143	285	14	7	.977	554	512	14
1967	Mike Hershberger	130	206	17	4	.982	562	513	16
1968	Ken Harrelson	132	241	8	0	1.000	577	525	17
1969	Pat Kelly	107	237	12	5	.980	601	529	24
1970	Roger Repoz	110	203	6	1	.995	556	528	9
1971	Del Unser	152	394	10	8	.981	594	545	16
1972	Buddy Bell	123	274	10	3	.990	604	548	19
1973	Bob Coluccio	108	236	12	2	.992	637	539	33
1974	Dwight Evans	122	294	8	3	.990	607	572	12
1975	Dwight Evans	115	281	15	4	.987	665	552	38
1976	Dwight Evans	145	324	15	2	.994	640	581	20
1977	Sixto Lezcano	108	238	11	3	.988	616	557	20
1978	Sixto Lezcano	127	262	18	6	.979	611	560	17
1979	Bob Bailor	118	218	16	3	.987	604	571	11
1980	Tony Armas	158	374	17	10	.975	594	565	10
1981	Dwight Evans	108	259	9	2	.993	632	578	13
1982	Tom Brunansky	127	343	8	5	.986	620	559	20
1983	Tom Brunansky	146	375	16	6	.985	650	558	31
1984	George Vukovich	130	316	13	2	.994	656	568	29
1985	Jesse Barfield	154	349	22	4	.989	669	555	38
1986	Jesse Barfield	157	368	20	3	.992	669	541	43
1987	Mike Kingery	114	226	15	2	.992	636	536	33
1988	Jesse Barfield	136	325	12	4	.988	619	539	27
1989	Cory Snyder	125	291	18	1	.997	700	544	52
1990	Joe Orsulak	109	267	5	3	.989	588	546	14
1991	Dante Bichette	127	270	14	7	.976	577	579	−1
1992	Jay Buhner	150	314	14	2	.994	616	584	11
1993	Wayne Kirby	123	273	19	5	.983	578	506	24
1994	Jay Buhner	96	178	11	2	.990	600	566	8
1995	Bobby Higginson	123	247	13	4	.985	590	548	13
1996	Matt Mieske	122	250	7	1	.996	583	543	13
1997	Dave Martinez	107	229	6	1	.996	595	559	12
1998	Matt Lawton	151	398	12	4	.990	644	573	24
1999	Jermaine Dye	157	362	17	6	.984	619	553	22
2000	Dave Martinez	110	229	15	2	.992	652	526	42
2001	Tim Salmon	125	254	13	3	.989	605	550	18
2002	Michael Tucker	108	224	9	2	.991	594	567	9
2003	Ichiro Suzuki	159	337	12	2	.994	600	548	17
2004	Ichiro Suzuki	158	372	12	3	.992	618	559	20
2005	Ichiro Suzuki	158	381	10	2	.995	641	537	35
2006	Ichiro Suzuki	121	250	8	2	.992	580	568	4

Federal League—Right Field

Not only was Benny Kauff the Federal League's best hitter, but he was also the best outfielder. In 1914 he played more games in right field than any of the other outfield positions, so we list him as the league leader at that position. In 1915 he moved full time to center field. No other right fielder matched Kauff's 1914 putout and assist totals, but these were not all achieved when he was in right field. The record for the league's highest fielding average by a right fielder is held by Grover Gilmore.

FEDERAL LEAGUE FIELDING LEADERS—RIGHT FIELD

Year	Right Fielder	G	PO	A	E	Pct.	Total	Mean	Points
1914	Benny Kauff	154	310	31	17	.953	580	495	28
1915	Max Flack	138	226	24	8	.969	568	532	12

National League—Center Field

In 1889 Jim Fogarty of the Philadelphia Quakers became the only outfielder in major league history to earn 100 Faber System fielding points in a season. The following year he played for and managed the Philadelphia entry in the upstart Players' League. After that circuit folded Fogarty never again played in the majors. Fogarty, Paul Hines, and Mike Griffin each led the league in points three times. In the early 1900s Roy Thomas outdid them with five league-leading seasons, a record that stood until Richie Ashburn was the league's best eight times in the 1940s and 1950s. Griffin held the 19th century record for the most putouts by a center fielder. In 1916 Max Carey became the first to compile more than 400 in a season. In 1928 Taylor Douthit established the all-time record for outfielders with 547 putouts. Ashburn is the only other NLer to top the 500 mark. Richie did it six times for the Phillies. In 1881 Hardy Richardson set the record for assists by a senior circuit center fielder with 45, a mark that has not been matched in 125 years. The highest fielding average turned in by a 19th century center fielder was .983 by Steve Brodie in 1897. During the 1900s the bar was raised several times until Tony Gonzalez fielded a perfect 1.000 in 1962.

NATIONAL LEAGUE FIELDING LEADERS—CENTER FIELD

Year	Center Fielder	G	PO	A	E	Pct.	Total	Mean	Points
1876	Paul Hines	64	159	8	14	.923	450	230	31
1877	Bill Crowley	58	109	20	23	.849	362	144	28
1878	Jack Remsen	56	103	14	7	.944	581	247	40
1879	Dave Eggler	78	114	11	11	.919	350	330	4
1880	Paul Hines	75	148	17	13	.905	442	324	21
1881	Hardy Richardson	79	179	45	21	.914	844	421	78
1882	John Richmond	59	94	16	11	.907	453	286	31
1883	Paul Hines	89	169	21	13	.905	442	324	25
1884	Jim Fogarty	78	193	12	19	.915	451	336	28
1885	Jim Fogarty	88	227	26	16	.941	691	338	85
1886	Dick Johnston	109	243	29	33	.892	462	358	28
1887	Dick Johnston	127	339	34	27	.933	645	335	84
1888	Billy Sunday	120	297	27	21	.939	603	401	59
1889	Jim Fogarty	128	302	42	14	.961	767	400	105
1890	George Davis	133	282	35	18	.946	628	454	51
1891	Mike Griffin	134	353	31	16	.960	595	406	57

Year	Center Fielder	G	PO	A	E	Pct.	Total	Mean	Points
1892	Ed Delahanty	121	261	25	17	.944	569	400	56
1893	Tom Brown	122	339	39	29	.929	720	447	77
1894	Mike Griffin	131	349	14	10	.969	642	371	49
1895	Mike Griffin	131	349	23	12	.969	672	458	61
1896	Jiggs Parrott	112	278	21	12	.961	639	482	45
1897	Steve Brodie	100	218	11	4	.983	606	464	41
1898	Bill Lange	111	269	19	9	.970	645	476	56
1899	Steve Brodie	137	310	15	7	.979	599	479	40
1900	George Van Haltren	141	325	28	23	.939	559	466	29
1901	Roy Thomas	129	283	9	10	.967	512	477	11
1902	Roy Thomas	138	277	23	8	.979	614	488	39
1903	Davy Jones	130	249	14	8	.970	532	455	23
1904	Roy Thomas	139	321	21	9	.974	629	482	49
1905	Roy Thomas	147	373	27	7	.983	721	502	73
1906	Roy Thomas	142	340	12	5	.988	617	513	35
1907	Tommy Leach	109	278	15	6	.980	660	532	43
1908	John Kane	120	292	15	6	.980	636	534	34
1909	Bill O'Hara	111	202	19	5	.977	610	556	18
1910	Dode Paskert	139	355	25	17	.957	625	528	32
1911	Fred Snodgrass	149	293	31	9	.973	647	551	32
1912	Herbie Moran	129	273	24	12	.961	600	534	22
1913	Dode Paskert	120	330	19	10	.972	.674	556	39
1914	Les Mann	123	273	24	15	.952	590	523	22
1915	Owen Wilson	105	234	20	4	.984	692	520	57
1916	Max Carey	157	419	32	8	.983	757	533	75
1917	Max Carey	153	440	28	10	.979	734	527	36
1918	Hy Myers	107	294	17	8	.975	684	565	33
1919	Edd Roush	133	335	22	4	.989	714	581	40
1920	Edd Roush	139	410	18	11	.975	675	564	37
1921	Cy Williams	146	382	29	9	.979	724	595	43
1922	Ray Powell	136	377	18	8	.980	676	573	34
1923	Jigger Statz	154	438	26	12	.975	703	551	51
1924	Jigger Statz	131	373	22	16	.961	656	543	28
1925	Gus Felix	114	328	15	10	.972	659	558	34
1926	Fred Leach	123	313	15	7	.979	640	552	28
1927	Fred Leach	140	385	26	8	.981	731	593	46
1928	Taylor Douthit	154	547	10	9	.984	700	556	48
1929	Lloyd Waner	151	450	22	6	.987	734	565	56
1930	Johnny Frederick	142	394	12	4	.990	640	542	33
1931	Lloyd Waner	153	484	20	11	.979	710	570	47
1932	Wally Berger	134	396	10	3	.993	686	590	32
1933	Chick Hafey	144	364	16	5	.987	654	570	28
1934	Kiddo Davis	109	327	14	4	.988	722	563	53
1935	Ethan Allen	156	412	26	9	.980	698	562	45
1936	Terry Moore	133	418	14	10	.977	677	545	44
1937	Vince DiMaggio	130	351	21	7	.982	704	550	51
1938	Harry Craft	151	436	15	8	.983	665	561	35
1939	Terry Moore	121	291	16	2	.994	686	571	38
1940	Terry Moore	133	383	11	5	.987	660	551	36
1941	Johnny Cooney	111	274	9	1	.996	648	553	32
1942	Vince DiMaggio	138	383	20	9	.978	682	566	39

Year	Center Fielder	G	PO	A	E	Pct.	Total	Mean	Points
1943	Tommy Holmes	152	408	18	3	.993	697	596	34
1944	Andy Pafko	123	333	24	6	.983	743	587	53
1945	Carden Gillenwater	140	451	24	10	.979	756	599	52
1946	Johnny Wyrostek	142	388	18	8	.981	670	569	34
1947	Bobby Thomson	127	330	12	7	.980	621	551	23
1948	Richie Ashburn	116	344	14	7	.981	685	555	43
1949	Richie Ashburn	154	514	13	11	.980	685	572	31
1950	Bobby Thomson	149	394	15	9	.978	625	554	24
1951	Richie Ashburn	154	538	15	7	.988	727	591	45
1952	Richie Ashburn	154	428	23	9	.980	694	563	34
1953	Richie Ashburn	156	496	18	5	.990	733	548	62
1954	Richie Ashburn	153	483	12	8	.984	675	542	44
1955	Willie Mays	152	407	23	8	.982	692	555	46
1956	Richie Ashburn	154	503	11	9	.983	675	543	44
1957	Richie Ashburn	156	502	18	7	.987	727	550	59
1958	Curt Flood	120	346	18	8	.978	698	576	41
1959	Bill Virdon	144	404	16	9	.979	655	569	29
1960	Bill Virdon	109	272	10	5	.983	619	557	21
1961	Vada Pinson	153	391	19	10	.976	633	537	32
1962	Tony Gonzalez	114	268	8	0	1.000	638	515	41
1963	Curt Flood	158	401	12	5	.988	623	517	35
1964	Willie Davis	155	400	16	7	.983	638	498	47
1965	Willie Mays	151	337	19	6	.983	626	504	41
1966	Adolfo Phillips	112	260	14	6	.979	621	505	39
1967	Adolfo Phillips	141	340	13	7	.981	603	502	34
1968	Curt Flood	149	386	11	7	.983	609	522	29
1969	Curt Flood	152	362	14	4	.989	627	494	44
1970	Willie Davis	143	342	12	3	.992	631	509	41
1971	George Foster	132	315	9	5	.985	589	540	16
1972	Willie Montanez	130	318	15	5	.985	643	534	36
1973	Del Unser	132	329	14	4	.988	648	531	39
1974	Cesar Cedeno	157	446	11	3	.993	664	532	44
1975	Garry Maddox	110	325	13	5	.985	696	547	50
1976	Garry Maddox	144	441	10	5	.989	673	533	47
1977	Cesar Cedeno	137	335	14	1	.997	670	532	46
1978	Andre Dawson	153	411	17	5	.988	673	534	46
1979	Garry Maddox	140	433	13	2	.996	723	538	62
1980	Omar Moreno	162	479	15	5	.990	688	574	38
1981	Ruppert Jones	104	295	9	2	.993	692	579	26
1982	Mookie Wilson	156	415	12	5	.988	636	533	34
1983	Eddie Milner	139	392	9	4	.990	646	527	40
1984	Keith McReynolds	143	422	10	4	.991	669	525	48
1985	Keith McReynolds	150	430	12	3	.993	677	541	45
1986	Willie McGee	121	325	9	3	.991	646	523	41
1987	Eric Davis	128	380	10	4	.990	675	533	47
1988	Andy Van Slyke	152	406	12	4	.991	648	536	37
1989	Gerald Young	143	412	15	1	.998	720	530	63
1990	Joe Carter	150	385	13	5	.988	637	545	31
1991	Marquis Grissom	138	350	15	6	.984	642	533	36
1992	Darrin Jackson	153	436	18	2	.996	723	559	55
1993	Chuck Carr	139	393	7	6	.985	636	550	29

Year	Center Fielder	G	PO	A	E	Pct.	Total	Mean	Points
1994	Marquis Grissom	109	321	7	5	.985	642	531	27
1995	Marquis Grissom	136	309	9	2	.994	606	523	28
1996	Ray Lankford	144	356	9	1	.997	630	507	41
1997	Steve Finley	140	338	10	4	.989	610	526	28
1998	Andruw Jones	159	413	20	2	.995	702	520	61
1999	Andruw Jones	162	492	13	10	.981	654	535	40
2000	Andruw Jones	161	438	9	2	.996	648	524	41
2001	Preston Wilson	121	287	12	2	.993	646	536	37
2002	Jim Edmonds	132	347	11	5	.986	620	521	33
2003	Mark Kotsay	126	323	13	3	.991	664	543	40
2004	Jay Payton	128	341	11	4	.989	649	516	44
2005	Brady Clark	145	399	5	2	.995	627	514	38
2006	Carlos Beltran	136	357	13	2	.995	675	526	50

American Association—Center Field

No one individual was the dominant center fielder in the American Association. Curt Welch led in Faber System points three times. Charlie Duffee and Farmer Weaver tied for the most points in a season. Welch has the loop record for the most putouts in a campaign, while Duffee has the most assists and Weaver the highest average.

AMERICAN ASSOCIATION FIELDING LEADERS—CENTER FIELD

Year	Center Fielder	G	PO	A	E	Pct.	Total	Mean	Points
1882	Jimmy Macullar	79	141	13	13	.922	416	160	44
1883	Charley Jones	90	172	12	26	.876	244	230	3
1884	Monk Cline	90	143	25	24	.875	354	218	29
1885	Charley Jones	112	214	22	29	.891	358	281	19
1886	Curt Welch	138	297	19	16	.952	526	280	75
1887	Curt Welch	123	336	29	23	.941	646	589	77
1888	Pop Corkhill	135	316	26	13	.963	636	405	69
1889	Charlie Duffee	132	296	43	23	.936	670	410	81
1890	Curt Welch	120	269	28	23	.928	551	399	45
1891	Farmer Weaver	132	294	33	15	.956	660	391	81

Players' League—Center Field

Mike Griffin was the Players' League's best center fielder, based on Faber System points. He topped patrollers of the middle garden in assists and fielding average and was second to Ned Hanlon in putouts.

PLAYERS' LEAGUE FIELDING LEADER—CENTER FIELD

Year	Center Fielder	G	PO	A	E	Pct.	Total	Mean	Points
1890	Mike Griffin	115	278	33	15	.954	708	409	86

American League—Center Field

Tris Speaker led American League center fielders in Faber System points eight times. His closest competitor is Sam West with six league-leading seasons. Speaker holds the AL record for the most points in a season with 78 in 1909. The Grey Eagle also holds the junior circuit record for assists with 35, a number he reached twice. He was the first American League outfielder to make 400 putouts in a season, but his record of 425 was broken successively by Happy Felsch, Baby Doll Jacobson, and Jim Busby. Chet Lemon currently holds the record with 512 outs made in 1977. For many years the aptly named Fielder Jones held the league record for fielding average by a center fielder. His .988 average set in 1906 prevailed until broken by West with .990 in 1931. In 1946 Walt Judnich fielded .995. In 1968 Mickey Stanley became the first AL center fielder to field a perfect 1.000. Since then this feat has been accomplished several times.

AMERICAN LEAGUE FIELDING LEADERS—CENTER FIELD

Year	Center Fielder	G	PO	A	E	Pct.	Total	Mean	Points
1901	Dummy Hoy	132	178	16	13	.958	631	472	47
1902	Fielder Jones	135	323	25	10	.972	664	472	58
1903	Fielder Jones	136	324	11	5	.985	602	471	39
1904	Jimmy Barrett	162	339	29	11	.979	625	458	56
1905	Ben Koehler	124	227	24	8	.969	606	452	51
1906	Fielder Jones	144	312	23	4	.988	670	513	52
1907	Sam Crawford	144	311	22	12	.965	586	504	27
1908	Joe Birmingham	121	250	20	12	.957	562	460	34
1909	Tris Speaker	142	319	35	10	.973	714	479	78
1910	Joe Birmingham	103	223	24	10	.961	653	437	72
1911	Joe Birmingham	102	231	19	7	.973	656	528	43
1912	Tris Speaker	153	372	35	18	.958	665	486	60
1913	Tris Speaker	139	374	30	24	.944	632	501	44
1914	Tris Speaker	157	425	30	15	.968	689	509	60
1915	Amos Strunk	143	291	20	7	.978	603	541	21
1916	Armando Marsans	150	351	25	9	.976	654	541	38
1917	Happy Felsch	152	440	24	7	.985	730	550	60
1918	Tris Speaker	127	352	15	10	.973	638	582	46
1919	Tris Speaker	134	375	25	7	.983	744	547	66
1920	Happy Felsch	142	385	25	8	.981	717	561	52
1921	Ty Cobb	121	301	27	10	.970	705	548	52
1922	Tris Speaker	110	285	13	5	.983	654	534	40
1923	Johnny Mostil	143	422	21	12	.974	689	570	40
1924	Baby Doll Jacobson	152	488	7	7	.986	654	576	26
1925	Ira Flagstead	144	429	24	11	.976	718	563	52
1926	Tris Speaker	149	394	28	8	.981	669	553	39
1927	Ira Flagstead	129	326	19	5	.986	685	520	55
1928	Johnny Mostil	131	394	18	10	.976	692	576	39
1929	Sam West	139	376	25	9	.978	710	559	50
1930	Tom Oliver	154	477	9	9	.982	642	517	42
1931	Sam West	127	402	13	4	.990	718	546	57
1932	Sam West	143	450	15	10	.979	682	528	51
1933	Sam West	127	329	14	4	.988	662	538	41
1934	Doc Cramer	152	385	12	6	.985	615	526	30
1935	Sam West	135	449	7	5	.989	682	559	41
1936	Doc Cramer	154	443	20	12	.975	668	555	38
1937	Sam West	105	298	17	4	.987	736	563	58
1938	Doc Cramer	148	417	15	6	.986	670	543	42
1939	Mike Kreevich	123	419	18	11	.975	737	546	63
1940	Mike Kreevich	144	428	12	8	.982	654	535	40

Year	Center Fielder	G	PO	A	E	Pct.	Total	Mean	Points
1941	Sam Chapman	141	416	21	15	.967	667	573	31
1942	Dom DiMaggio	151	439	19	6	.987	706	557	50
1943	Thurman Tucker	132	399	14	5	.988	701	569	44
1944	Stan Spence	150	434	29	5	.989	780	592	63
1945	George Case	123	316	17	7	.979	658	573	28
1946	Walt Judnich	137	409	6	2	.995	659	552	36
1947	Dom DiMaggio	134	413	19	10	.977	707	572	35
1948	Dave Philley	128	381	22	9	.978	730	566	55
1949	Dom DiMaggio	144	425	13	10	.977	651	590	20
1950	Irv Noren	121	357	20	6	.984	741	580	54
1951	Irv Noren	126	420	15	10	.978	712	574	46
1952	Dave Philley	149	442	13	4	.991	699	571	43
1953	Johnny Groth	141	425	18	4	.991	732	588	48
1954	Chuck Diering	119	330	17	6	.983	698	585	38
1955	Jimmy Piersall	147	426	7	3	.993	650	561	30
1956	Jimmy Piersall	155	455	10	4	.991	661	543	39
1957	Jimmy Piersall	151	397	12	4	.990	643	546	32
1958	Harvey Kuenn	138	358	9	6	.984	605	522	28
1959	Bill Tuttle	121	294	17	5	.984	663	536	42
1960	Bill Tuttle	148	381	16	5	.988	658	537	40
1961	Jimmy Piersall	120	328	9	3	.991	652	527	42
1962	Lenny Green	156	361	8	2	.995	600	519	27
1963	Don Lock	147	377	14	8	.980	619	533	29
1964	Vic Davalillo	143	346	11	5	.986	606	522	28
1965	Vic Davalillo	134	320	5	4	.988	570	499	24
1966	Jose Cardinal	146	351	10	3	.992	618	512	35
1967	Paul Blair	146	369	13	6	.985	625	513	38
1968	Del Unser	156	388	22	5	.988	683	525	53
1969	Paul Blair	150	407	14	5	.988	658	529	43
1970	Paul Blair	128	368	10	4	.990	665	528	46
1971	Amos Otis	144	404	10	4	.990	650	545	35
1972	Ken Berry	116	272	13	0	1.000	680	548	44
1973	Billy North	138	429	14	9	.980	679	539	47
1974	Billy North	138	437	9	4	.991	685	572	38
1975	Ken Henderson	137	394	7	4	.990	639	552	29
1976	Juan Beniquez	131	410	18	6	.986	706	581	42
1977	Chet Lemon	149	512	12	12	.978	684	557	42
1978	Rick Bosetti	135	417	17	6	.986	721	560	54
1979	Ruppert Jones	161	453	13	5	.989	659	571	29
1980	Dwayne Murphy	158	507	13	5	.990	703	565	46
1981	Mickey Rivers	97	225	12	1	.996	675	578	23
1982	Dwayne Murphy	147	452	14	8	.983	680	559	40
1983	Dave Henderson	133	304	17	6	.982	637	558	26
1984	Kirby Puckett	128	438	16	3	.993	778	568	70
1985	Brett Butler	150	437	19	1	.996	745	555	63
1986	Gary Pettis	153	462	9	7	.985	644	541	34
1987	Ellis Burks	132	320	15	4	.988	649	536	38
1988	Robin Yount	158	444	12	2	.996	609	539	23
1989	Kirby Puckett	157	438	13	4	.991	665	544	40
1990	Kirby Puckett	141	354	9	4	.989	611	546	22
1991	Devon White	156	439	8	1	.998	660	579	27

Year	Center Fielder	G	PO	A	E	Pct.	Total	Mean	Points
1992	Kenny Lofton	143	420	14	8	.982	665	584	27
1993	Robin Yount	114	299	6	1	.997	637	506	44
1994	Kenny Lofton	112	276	13	2	.993	672	566	26
1995	Jim Edmonds	139	401	8	1	.998	673	548	39
1996	Daryl Hamilton	147	387	2	0	1.000	610	543	22
1997	Jim Edmonds	115	312	9	5	.985	633	559	25
1998	Brian L. Hunter	139	386	11	5	.988	650	573	26
1999	Chris Singleton	127	376	9	4	.990	667	553	38
2000	Chris Singleton	145	373	9	3	.992	647	526	40
2001	Torii Hunter	147	460	14	4	.992	715	550	55
2002	Darin Erstad	143	452	11	1	.998	721	567	51
2003	Rocco Baldelli	154	436	15	5	.989	678	548	43
2004	Rocco Baldelli	124	342	11	8	.978	625	559	22
2005	Jeremy Reed	137	383	7	3	.992	638	537	34
2006	Grady Sizemore	160	409	7	3	.993	609	568	14

Federal League—Center Field

Benny Kauff, who was the Federal League's top right fielder in 1914, was the loop's best center fielder in 1915. Dutch Zwilling holds the league record for putouts, Kauff has the mark for assists by a center fielder, and Chet Chatbourne has the best fielding average in league annals.

FEDERAL LEAGUE FIELDING LEADERS—CENTER FIELD

Year	Center Fielder	G	PO	A	E	Pct.	Total	Mean	Points
1914	Charlie Hanford	155	331	24	10	.973	615	495	40
1915	Benny Kauff	136	317	32	15	.959	665	532	44

National League—Left Field

Joe Hornung, Ed Delahanty, Jimmie Sheckard, and Barry Bonds all led senior circuit left fielders in Faber System points five times, with Big Ed getting his five in consecutive seasons. Delahanty also led the American League once. His 71 points in 1893 is an all-time NL high. He was the first left fielder to make as many as 300 putouts in a season and the first to field as high as .970. Among those who led the league in Faber System points, Fred Clarke holds the record for putouts with 362, and Sheckard is tops in assists with 36. Clarke's .986 average in 1909 was the best until Zack Wheat fielded .991 in 1922. In 1942 Danny Litwhiler fielded a perfect 1.000. Since then Luis Gonzales, Eric Owens, and Geoff Jenkins have all played errorless ball for a full season. In 1978 Warren Cromartie joined center fielder Andre Dawson and right fielder Ellis Valentine to give the Montreal Expos the best fielder at all three outfield positions. Of the trio only Valentine was awarded a Golden Glove. In 2006 a former second baseman, Alfonso Soriano, reluctantly switched positions and became the first National League outfielder in a quarter of a century to lead in Faber System points while making more than ten errors. He accomplished this feat by topping all NL left fielders in both putouts and assists.

NATIONAL LEAGUE FIELDING LEADERS—LEFT FIELD

Year	Left Fielder	G	PO	A	E	Pct.	Total	Mean	Points
1876	Tom York	67	153	8	18	.899	344	230	16
1877	Charley Jones	48	133	14	28	.840	369	144	33

Year	Left Fielder	G	PO	A	E	Pct.	Total	Mean	Points
1878	Charley Jones	61	120	9	15	.896	331	247	11
1879	Charley Jones	83	162	20	13	.933	546	330	37
1880	Pete Gillespie	82	185	14	21	.905	414	330	15
1881	Joe Hornung	83	198	19	12	.948	627	421	38
1882	Joe Hornung	84	191	14	15	.932	505	286	40
1883	Joe Hornung	98	175	15	13	.936	452	324	28
1884	Joe Hornung	110	182	14	18	.916	346	336	2
1885	Ed Andrews	99	175	11	16	.921	412	338	15
1886	Abner Dalrymple	82	126	15	7	.953	514	358	42
1887	Joe Hornung	98	192	23	15	.935	547	335	58
1888	Emmett Seery	133	258	19	18	.939	467	401	22
1889	Walt Wilmot	108	232	22	20	.927	508	400	36
1890	Cliff Carroll	136	265	28	20	.936	520	454	19
1891	Darby O'Brien	103	203	11	11	.951	474	406	21
1892	Charlie Duffee	125	230	34	25	.913	499	400	33
1893	Ed Delahanty	117	318	31	19	.948	696	447	71
1894	Ed Delahanty	88	212	23	19	.925	585	471	33
1895	Ed Delahanty	103	237	20	15	.945	575	458	34
1896	Ed Delahanty	100	269	16	16	.947	586	482	30
1897	Ed Delahanty	127	266	23	9	.970	567	464	31
1898	Kip Selbach	131	320	24	19	.948	588	476	37
1899	Joe Kelley	143	307	26	8	.977	654	479	58
1900	Chick Stahl	135	277	22	10	.968	596	466	40
1901	Fred Clarke	129	282	13	9	.970	553	477	23
1902	John Dobbs	122	268	19	9	.970	608	488	37
1903	Jimmy Sheckard	130	314	36	18	.951	655	455	61
1904	Fred Odwell	126	284	18	14	.956	536	482	18
1905	Jimmy Sheckard	129	266	24	10	.967	615	502	38
1906	Jimmy Sheckard	149	264	13	4	.986	582	513	23
1907	Fred Clarke	144	298	15	4	.987	601	532	23
1908	Al Burch	116	242	24	8	.971	652	534	39
1909	Fred Clarke	152	362	17	5	.987	634	556	26
1910	Bill Collins	151	355	23	9	.977	644	528	39
1911	Jimmy Sheckard	156	332	32	14	.963	628	551	26
1912	Jimmy Sheckard	146	332	26	14	.962	612	534	26
1913	Lee Magee	108	250	21	5	.982	699	556	48
1914	Zack Wheat	144	331	21	14	.962	582	523	20
1915	Max Carey	139	307	21	6	.982	645	520	42
1916	Greasy Neale	133	307	20	9	.973	623	533	30
1917	Casey Stengel	150	256	30	9	.969	601	527	25
1918	Greasy Neale	102	249	11	5	.981	622	565	47
1919	Austin McHenry	103	183	20	3	.985	675	581	31
1920	Carson Bigbee	133	289	16	9	.971	574	564	3
1921	Carson Bigbee	146	357	27	9	.977	682	595	29
1922	Zack Wheat	152	317	14	3	.991	604	573	10
1923	Carson Bigbee	122	283	12	3	.990	627	551	25
1924	Bill Cunningham	109	243	16	8	.970	603	543	20
1925	Ray Blades	114	266	13	6	.979	611	558	18
1926	Kiki Cuyler	157	405	19	14	.968	606	552	18
1927	Dick Spalding	113	250	7	2	.992	590	593	−1

Year	Left Fielder	G	PO	A	E	Pct.	Total	Mean	Points
1928	Fred Leach	120	296	11	7	.978	599	566	11
1929	Riggs Stephenson	130	245	9	4	.984	537	565	−9
1930	Adam Comorosky	152	337	12	11	.969	531	542	−4
1931	Red Worthington	124	242	8	3	.988	553	570	−6
1932	Red Worthington	104	216	8	3	.987	574	590	−5
1933	Johnny Moore	132	329	12	9	.974	587	570	6
1934	Ethan Allen	145	337	19	8	.978	624	563	20
1935	Augie Galan	154	351	12	8	.978	566	562	1
1936	Joe Moore	149	291	25	6	.981	633	545	29
1937	Woody Jensen	120	353	10	10	.973	583	550	11
1938	Morrie Arnovich	133	327	18	6	.983	658	561	32
1939	Morrie Arnovich	132	335	10	6	.983	615	571	15
1940	Mike McCormick	107	265	9	4	.986	619	551	23
1941	Max West	132	302	13	6	.981	598	553	15
1942	Danny Litwhiler	151	308	9	0	1.000	598	566	11
1943	Danny Litwhiler	104	225	12	1	.996	652	596	19
1944	Jim Russell	149	345	20	5	.986	654	587	22
1945	Peanuts Lowrey	138	280	17	4	.987	613	599	5
1946	Tommy Holmes	146	294	17	4	.987	608	569	13
1947	Enos Slaughter	142	306	16	6	.982	594	551	14
1948	Peanuts Lowrey	103	225	9	4	.983	583	555	9
1949	Peanuts Lowrey	109	258	8	3	.989	607	572	12
1950	Whitey Lockman	128	305	11	7	.978	584	554	10
1951	Andy Pafko	154	263	14	2	.993	635	591	15
1952	Hank Sauer	151	327	17	6	.983	604	563	14
1953	Frank Thomas	118	306	17	8	.976	657	548	36
1954	Monte Irvin	128	274	7	7	.976	521	542	−4
1955	Frank Thomas	139	307	8	5	.984	559	555	1
1956	Jackie Brandt	122	198	9	2	.990	537	543	−2
1957	Frank Robinson	136	336	11	4	.989	626	550	25
1958	Frank Robinson	138	310	12	3	.991	614	576	13
1959	Bobby Thomson	116	223	9	3	.987	560	569	−3
1960	Bob Skinner	141	250	13	5	.981	540	557	−6
1961	Stan Musial	103	149	9	1	.994	545	537	3
1962	Billy Williams	159	273	18	10	.967	508	515	−2
1963	Billy Williams	160	298	13	4	.987	557	517	13
1964	George Altman	109	202	12	7	.968	522	498	8
1965	Tommy Harper	159	277	6	5	.983	489	504	−5
1966	Tony Gonzalez	121	206	7	3	.986	515	505	3
1967	Tony Gonzalez	143	260	10	2	.993	562	502	20
1968	Jimmy Wynn	153	298	20	4	.988	619	522	32
1969	Cleon Jones	122	223	4	2	.991	519	494	8
1970	Willie Stargell	125	184	16	5	.976	528	509	6
1971	Ralph Garr	153	315	15	11	.968	541	540	0
1972	Pete Rose	154	330	15	2	.994	625	534	30
1973	Pete Rose	159	343	15	3	.992	617	531	29
1974	Pete Rose	163	346	11	1	.997	604	532	24
1975	George Foster	125	299	11	3	.990	627	547	27
1976	George Foster	142	332	9	2	.994	610	533	26
1977	George Foster	158	352	12	3	.992	605	532	24

Year	Left Fielder	G	PO	A	E	Pct.	Total	Mean	Points
1978	Warren Cromartie	158	340	24	8	.978	627	534	31
1979	Dave Winfield	157	344	14	5	.986	595	538	19
1980	Gene Richards	156	307	21	7	.979	594	574	7
1981	Mike Easler	90	188	13	4	.980	620	579	10
1982	Tim Raines	120	232	7	2	.992	560	533	9
1983	Tim Raines	153	307	21	4	.988	629	527	34
1984	Carmelo Martinez	142	312	15	8	.976	579	525	18
1985	Vince Coleman	150	306	16	7	.979	573	541	11
1986	Tim Raines	147	270	13	6	.979	536	523	4
1987	Barry Bonds	145	330	15	5	.986	618	533	28
1988	Phil Bradley	153	298	14	3	.990	586	536	17
1989	Barry Bonds	156	365	14	6	.984	604	530	25
1990	Billy Hatcher	131	308	10	1	.997	635	545	30
1991	Barry Bonds	150	321	13	3	.991	604	533	24
1992	Luis Gonzales	111	261	5	2	.993	591	559	11
1993	Phil Plantier	134	272	14	3	.990	607	550	19
1994	Barry Bonds	112	198	10	3	.986	553	531	5
1995	Barry Bonds	143	279	12	6	.980	546	523	7
1996	Bernard Gilkey	151	310	18	6	.982	597	507	30
1997	Bernard Gilkey	136	251	17	3	.989	607	526	27
1998	Bernard Gilkey	104	170	12	2	.989	576	520	18
1999	Richard Hidalgo	108	214	15	2	.991	640	535	35
2000	Eric Owens	144	315	6	0	1.000	594	524	23
2001	Luis Gonzalez	161	280	8	0	1.000	557	536	7
2002	Brian Jordan	125	213	10	4	.982	523	521	1
2003	Geoff Jenkins	123	222	11	0	1.000	603	543	20
2004	Geoff Jenkins	156	261	10	1	.996	552	516	12
2005	Cliff Floyd	150	283	15	2	.993	599	514	28
2006	Alfonso Soriano	158	326	22	11	.969	576	526	17

American Association—Left Field

Joe Sommer is the only left fielder to lead the Association in Faber System points more than once. Leech Maskrey has the most points in a season. Of the league-leaders Harry Stovey has both the most putouts and the most assists. Blondie Purcell logged the highest fielding average.

AMERICAN ASSOCIATION FIELDING LEADERS—LEFT FIELD

Year	Left Fielder	G	PO	A	E	Pct.	Total	Mean	Points
1882	Joe Sommer	89	188	9	16	.925	430	190	41
1883	Leech Maskrey	96	193	19	20	.914	446	230	45
1884	Ed Kennedy	100	138	13	14	.915	318	218	21
1885	Joe Sommer	107	230	14	16	.921	416	281	37
1886	Tip O'Neill	138	279	14	23	.927	393	280	35
1887	Darby O'Brien	121	244	20	25	.913	410	389	6
1888	Mike Griffin	137	274	27	20	.938	484	405	23
1889	Harry Stovey	137	287	38	37	.898	480	410	21
1890	Blondie Purcell	110	170	17	10	.949	472	399	21
1891	Charlie Duffee	128	235	33	21	.927	531	391	42

Players' League—Left Field

Hardy Richardson, who played every position on the diamond but mostly at second base during his National League career, was the Players' League's leading left fielder. He led the loop in Faber System points and fielding average. George Wood led in both putouts and assists.

PLAYERS' LEAGUE FIELDING LEADER—LEFT FIELD

Year	Left Fielder	G	PO	A	E	Pct.	Total	Mean	Points
1890	Hardy Richardson	124	235	13	13	.950	461	409	23

American League—Left Field

During the American League's first decade Matty McIntyre was the circuit's best left fielder. He led the loop in Faber System points five times, and set the loop record for most points in a season, highest fielding average, and most putouts in a campaign. Eventually these marks fell by the wayside. Amos Strunk amassed 60 points in 1912, a record that fell to Babe Ruth with 67 in 1919. The Bambino's record still stands as the most ever attained by an AL left fielder. In 1916 future big league manager Burt Shotten tallied 357 putouts. This mark was topped by Bobby Veach in 1921 and by Joe Vosmik in 1932. Gary Ward presently holds the record with 474 putouts in 1982. (Willie Wilson's 1980 mark includes outs made while playing centerfield as well as left.) In 1919 Ruth fielded .992, in 1941 Indian Bob Johnson fielded .994, and Gene Woodling topped them all with .996 in 1952. Five years later Charlie Maxwell raised the mark to .997. In 1977 Carl Yastrzemski was perfect, playing errorless ball for the entire season. This feat gave Yaz five league-leading seasons in Faber System points, tying him for honors with McIntyre and Al Simmons. The one record that survived intact all these years was the remarkable 35 assists logged by Sam Mertes in 1902. It still stands not only as the most by an AL left fielder, but also as the record at any outfield position in the junior circuit.

AMERICAN LEAGUE FIELDING LEADERS—LEFT FIELD

Year	Left Fielders	G	PO	A	E	Pct.	Total	Mean	Points
1901	Tommy Dowd	137	288	11	20	.937	541	472	20
1902	Ed Delahanty	111	236	11	10	.961	515	472	13
1903	Billy Lush	101	227	17	8	.968	620	471	40
1904	Matty McIntyre	152	334	16	15	.959	522	458	21
1905	Matty McIntyre	131	286	18	10	.968	583	452	44
1906	Matty McIntyre	133	254	25	5	.982	652	513	46
1907	Davy Jones	125	282	15	9	.971	583	504	26
1908	Matty McIntyre	151	329	17	8	.977	587	460	49
1909	Matty McIntyre	122	217	14	6	.975	542	479	21
1910	Bris Lord	126	219	30	7	.972	573	437	45
1911	Bris Lord	132	271	17	11	.963	544	528	5
1912	Amos Strunk	120	278	16	3	.990	665	486	60
1913	Johnny Johnston	109	222	23	9	.966	635	501	25
1914	Tilly Walker	145	311	10	10	.972	661	509	51
1915	Jack Graney	115	227	17	7	.972	585	507	26
1916	Burt Shotten	157	357	25	20	.950	553	541	4
1917	Joe Jackson	145	341	18	6	.984	640	550	30
1918	Ping Bodie	90	181	17	6	.971	683	582	28
1919	Babe Ruth	111	230	26	2	.992	749	547	67

Year	Left Fielders	G	PO	A	E	Pct.	Total	Mean	Points
1920	Bobby Veach	154	357	26	13	.967	623	561	21
1921	Bobby Veach	149	384	21	11	.974	646	548	33
1922	Bobby Veach	154	375	16	7	.982	621	534	29
1923	Ken Williams	145	333	23	12	.967	612	570	15
1924	Bibb Falk	138	292	26	10	.970	633	576	19
1925	Goose Goslin	140	337	19	10	.973	619	563	19
1926	Goose Goslin	147	373	25	15	.964	638	553	28
1927	Bibb Falk	145	372	22	9	.978	669	520	50
1928	Charlie Jamieson	111	282	22	5	.984	732	576	52
1929	Al Simmons	142	349	19	4	.989	676	559	19
1930	Al Simmons	136	275	10	3	.990	576	517	20
1931	Al Simmons	128	287	10	4	.987	594	546	16
1932	Joe Vosmik	153	432	12	5	.989	658	528	43
1933	Al Simmons	145	372	15	4	.990	660	538	41
1934	Al Simmons	138	286	14	4	.987	598	526	24
1935	Julius Solters	148	382	20	6	.985	677	559	39
1936	John Stone	114	249	12	9	.967	547	555	−3
1937	Bob Johnson	133	313	14	8	.976	594	563	10
1938	Joe Vosmik	146	302	14	7	.978	562	543	6
1939	Bob Johnson	150	369	15	13	.967	569	546	8
1940	Bob Johnson	136	310	15	13	.962	545	535	3
1941	Bob Johnson	122	287	17	3	.994	645	573	24
1942	Ted Williams	150	313	15	4	.988	602	557	15
1943	Charlie Keller	141	338	8	2	.994	609	569	13
1944	Bob Johnson	142	270	23	7	.977	609	592	6
1945	George Case	123	316	17	7	.979	658	573	28
1946	Sam Chapman	145	369	13	12	.970	577	552	8
1947	Barney McCoskey	136	346	8	6	.983	590	572	6
1948	Dale Mitchell	140	307	12	3	.991	608	566	14
1949	Hoot Evers	123	319	12	2	.994	669	590	26
1950	Gene Woodling	118	263	16	2	.993	668	580	29
1951	Gil Coan	132	374	17	14	.965	641	574	22
1952	Gene Woodling	118	241	12	1	.996	627	571	19
1953	Gus Zernial	141	300	17	9	.972	574	588	−5
1954	Vic Power	101	256	13	4	.985	659	585	25
1955	Minnie Minoso	138	287	19	9	.971	583	561	7
1956	Whitey Herzog	103	240	9	5	.980	588	543	15
1957	Charlie Maxwell	137	317	6	1	.997	698	546	51
1958	Bob Cerv	136	311	13	5	.985	607	522	28
1959	Minnie Minoso	148	314	14	5	.985	590	536	18
1960	Charlie Maxwell	120	254	5	1	.996	574	537	12
1961	Rocky Colavito	161	329	16	9	.975	553	527	9
1962	Rocky Colavito	161	359	10	3	.992	592	519	24
1963	Chuck Hinton	125	274	8	3	.989	581	533	16
1964	Tom Tresh	146	259	7	1	.996	545	523	7
1965	Carl Yastrzemski	130	222	11	3	.987	545	499	15
1966	Carl Yastrzemski	158	310	15	5	.985	584	512	9
1967	Rick Reichardt	138	254	10	7	.974	529	513	5
1968	Roy White	154	283	14	1	.997	598	525	24
1969	Carl Yastrzemski	143	246	17	4	.985	574	529	15

Year	Left Fielders	G	PO	A	E	Pct.	Total	Mean	Points
1970	Don Buford	130	221	13	3	.987	560	528	11
1971	Carl Yastrzemski	146	281	16	2	.993	612	545	22
1972	Roy White	155	323	8	2	.994	600	548	17
1973	Tommy Harper	143	251	13	4	.985	559	539	7
1974	Cesar Tovar	135	331	13	7	.980	609	572	12
1975	Roy White	135	303	11	5	.984	586	552	11
1976	Larry Hisle	154	361	16	6	.984	619	581	13
1977	Carl Yastrzemski	140	287	16	0	1.000	652	557	32
1978	Jim Rice	114	245	13	3	.989	659	560	33
1979	Willie Wilson	152	384	12	6	.985	615	571	15
1980	Willie Wilson	159	482	9	6	.988	653	565	29
1981	Willie Wilson	102	299	14	4	.987	721	578	33
1982	Gary Ward	150	343	13	4	.989	612	559	17
1983	Gary Ward	152	474	24	9	.978	664	558	35
1984	Mickey Hatcher	100	249	11	7	.974	606	568	13
1985	Joe Carter	135	278	11	5	.983	564	555	3
1986	Gary Ward	104	237	8	1	.996	621	541	17
1987	Devon White	159	424	10	9	.980	635	536	33
1988	Dan Gladden	140	319	12	3	.991	610	539	24
1989	Rickey Henderson	137	335	6	4	.988	562	544	6
1990	Candy Maldonado	134	293	9	2	.993	595	546	16
1991	Joe Orsulak	132	273	22	1	.997	696	579	39
1992	Tim Raines	129	312	12	2	.994	649	584	22
1993	Albert Belle	150	338	16	5	.986	619	506	38
1994	Juan Gonzalez	107	223	9	2	.991	622	566	19
1995	Marty Cordova	137	345	12	5	.986	626	548	26
1996	Tony Phillips	150	345	13	7	.981	583	543	13
1997	Marty Cordova	101	217	12	2	.991	637	559	26
1998	Troy O'Leary	155	303	9	3	.990	553	573	−7
1999	Brian L. Hunter	139	301	15	4	.988	655	553	34
2000	Darin Erstad	136	350	9	3	.992	631	526	35
2001	Garret Anderson	149	313	9	2	.994	583	550	11
2002	Melvin Mora	104	251	9	3	.989	635	567	23
2003	Garret Anderson	144	326	14	1	.997	647	548	33
2004	Carl Crawford	140	350	5	2	.994	599	559	13
2005	Carl Crawford	154	361	3	2	.995	571	537	11
2006	Melky Cabrera	116	217	12	1	.996	611	568	14

Federal League—Left Field

Chet Chadbourne holds the Federal League record for Faber System points and also for the most assists in a season. Max Flack has the highest seasonal average at .973, and Wade Miller leads in putouts with 299. Of these leaders only Flack enjoyed a long and distinguished major league career.

FEDERAL LEAGUE FIELDING LEADERS—LEFT FIELD

Year	Left Fielder	G	PO	A	E	Pct.	Total	Mean	Points
1914	Chet Chadbourne	146	238	34	10	.965	613	495	39
1915	Claude Cooper	121	274	26	13	.958	634	532	34

Leading Fielders by Career

The ten best fielders at each position are ranked in three different tables, according to their Faber System points in their best ten years, their points in all eligible seasons, and their average points per year.

First Base

Three different first sackers can lay claim to being the best fielder of all time at their position. Based on a career consisting of his best ten seasons, Keith Hernandez is tops. When all eligible seasons are taken into account Eddie Murray moves to first place. In points per year Todd Helton is the cream of the crop. Hernandez ranks no worse than third in any of the computations. Mark Grace is the only other first baseman to appear in all three tables, ranking second in both of the career lists and ninth in points per season. Although Murray ranks third and first in the two career rankings, he does not make the top ten in points per season. With only nine eligible seasons so far, Helton is not included in the extended career listing. Seven of the top ten in career rankings also make the extended career list. Of the three who do not make it — Terry, Helton, and Fred Tenney — none have more than ten eligible seasons. They are replaced by Rafael Palmeiro, Jake Daubert, and Charlie Grimm, each of whom has at least 14 seasons. As expected, the points per season list contains names of some players who are not on the other rankings, primarily because of short careers. They are Frank McCormick, George Kelly, Dan McGann, and Richie Sexson.

Tenney and McGann both started their big league careers before 1900. Grace, Bagwell, and Palmeiro all ended their careers after 2000. In addition to Helton, one other currently active player is among the leaders. Richie Sexson is currently in seventh place in points per year. Where he will rank when his career is completed remains to be seen. The other leaders were all strictly 20th century players.

Among the career leaders Terry has the most putouts, Hernandez the most assists, and Helton the best fielding average. In an extended career Murray has the most putouts and assists, while Grace has the highest percentage. Terry has the most putouts per season, Hernandez the most assists, and Helton the best fielding average.

BEST FIELDING FIRST BASEMEN (BEST TEN YEARS)

First Baseman	Best Years		G	PO	A	E	Pct.	Points
1. Keith Hernandez	1976–87	10	1440	13002	1315	81	.994	816
2. Mark Grace	1989–2000	10	1458	12929	1227	64	.995	784
3. Eddie Murray	1978–91	10	1448	12822	1219	86	.994	747
4. Bill Terry	1925–35	10	1448	14709	1021	123	.992	740
5. Todd Helton	1999–2006	9	1376	11774	1133	56	.996	714
6. Stuffy McInnis	1912–24	10	1423	14451	908	108	.993	691
7. Ed Konetchy	1908–19	10	1461	14970	905	146	.991	694
8. Chris Chambliss	1973–84	10	1396	12876	913	85	.994	688
9. Jeff Bagwell	1992–2002	10	1460	12248	1237	86	.994	678
10. Fred Tenney	1897–1908	10	1343	13335	1040	229	.984	669

BEST FIELDING FIRST BASEMEN (EXTENDED CAREER)

First Baseman	Eligible Seasons		G	PO	A	E	Pct.	Points
1. Eddie Murray	1978–93	17	2326	20474	1811	158	.993	1038
2. Mark Grace	1988–2002	15	2123	18245	1656	108	.995	951
3. Keith Hernandez	1976–87	12	1756	15891	1517	103	.994	925

First Baseman	Eligible Seasons		G	PO	A	E	Pct.	Points
4. Ed Konetchy	1908–21	14	1982	20439	1221	199	.991	914
5. Rafael Palmeiro	1989–2002	16	2088	16894	1512	107	.994	913
6. Jake Daubert	1910–24	15	2002	19634	1126	181	.991	867
7. Chris Chambliss	1971–84	14	1903	17331	1320	128	.993	866
8. Jeff Bagwell	1991–2004	14	2087	17332	1689	129	.993	865
9. Stuffy McInnis	1911–24	14	1908	19284	1197	156	.992	858
10. Charlie Grimm	1920–33	14	1965	19201	1119	133	.993	803

BEST FIELDING FIRST BASEMEN POINTS PER YEAR

First Baseman	Eligible Seasons		G	PO	A	E	Pct.	Points
1. Todd Helton	1999–2006	9	153	1308	126	6	.996	79.33
2. Keith Hernandez	1978–87	12	146	1324	126	9	.994	77.08
3. Bill Terry	1925–35	10	145	1471	102	12	.992	74.00
4. Frank McCormick	1938–46	9	147	1413	103	8	.995	66.56
5. George Kelly	1920–29	8	136	1436	87	12	.993	65.88
6. Ed Konetchy	1908–21	14	142	1460	87	14	.991	65.29
7. Richie Sexson	1999–2006	6	144	1165	116	7	.994	65.16
8. Dan McGann	1898–1908	10	130	1289	74	16	.988	64.60
9. Mark Grace	1988–2002	15	142	1216	110	7	.995	63.40
10. Fred Tenney	1897–1908	10	134	1334	104	23	.984	62.42

JOHN McPHEE, 2d B. Cincinnati
COPYRIGHTED BY GOODWIN & CO. 1888
OLD JUDGE
CIGARETTES.
GOODWIN & CO., New York.

Second Base

Bid McPhee, one of the last major leaguers to play without a glove, was the best fielding second baseman of all time. The Hall of Famer tops all three of our lists. Bill Mazeroski is second in career fielding and in points per season, dropping to third in extended career rankings. Nap Lajoie is second in extended career fielding and third in the other two categories. No one other than the big three of McPhee, Mazeroski, and Lajoie ranks in the top three in any of the lists. Ryne Sandberg is fourth in career fielding and seventh in each of the other rankings. Bobby Doerr and Bobby Grich, who ranked fifth and sixth for their best ten years also rank in the top ten in the other lists. Thus, we see that all the top six in career fielding are in the top ten across the board.

Among the career leaders Fox has the most putouts, while Sandberg the most assists and highest fielding average. For an extended career

John Alexander "Bid" McPhee was baseball's all-time best-fielding second baseman. He was one of the last to field barehanded. McPhee spent his entire career with Cincinnati teams—first in the American Association and later in the National League (Library of Congress).

Eddie Collins, with his 18 eligible seasons, leads in both putouts and assists; Sandberg again is best in fielding percentage. Among the leaders McPhee has the most putouts per season, and Sandberg leads in assists per year and, of course, in highest fielding average.

BEST FIELDING SECOND BASEMEN (BEST TEN YEARS)

Second Baseman	Best Years		G	PO	A	E	Pct.	Points
1. Bid McPhee	1883–96	10	1283	4085	4264	548	.944	1587
2. Bill Mazeroski	1960–70	10	1458	3598	4779	141	.983	1452
3. Nap Lajoie	1900–13	10	1258	3368	4018	273	.964	1329
4. Ryne Sandberg	1982–92	10	1526	3013	4999	83	.990	1165
5. Bobby Doerr	1939–50	10	1429	3818	4492	153	.982	1160
6. Bobby Grich	1973–85	10	1378	3440	4322	125	.984	1081
7. Eddie Collins	1909–26	10	1498	3845	4337	257	.970	1066
8. Red Schoendienst	1946–58	10	1334	3539	3955	115	.985	1029
9. Nellie Fox	1951–61	10	1538	4144	4305	141	.984	995
10. Glenn Hubbard	1980–89	9	1149	2418	3914	100	.983	939

BEST FIELDING SECOND BASEMEN (EXTENDED CAREERS)

Second Baseman	Best Years		G	PO	A	E	Pct.	Points
1. Bid McPhee	1881–96	17	2044	6340	6642	778	.943	2241
2. Nap Lajoie	1898–1916	15	1786	4761	5475	401	.962	1712
3. Bill Mazeroski	1957–70	13	1887	4553	6091	188	.983	1641
4. Eddie Collins	1909–26	18	2606	6463	7519	439	.970	1497
5. Bobby Doerr	1938–51	13	1805	4834	5586	208	.980	1368
6. Nellie Fox	1950–64	15	2213	5885	6169	201	.984	1321
7. Ryne Sandberg	1983–97	13	1913	3653	6264	104	.990	1254
8. Bobby Grich	1946–58	12	1622	3962	5009	147	.982	1128
9. Red Schoendienst	1946–58	13	1714	4422	5009	147	.982	1087
10. Willie Randolph	1976–91	16	2059	4676	6099	223	.80	1007

BEST FIELDING SECOND BASEMEN (POINTS PER YEAR)

Second Baseman	Best Years		G	PO	A	E	Pct.	Points
1. Bid McPhee	1882–96	17	120	373	391	46	.943	131.82
2. Bill Mazeroski	1957–70	13	145	350	469	14	.983	126.23
3. Nap Lajoie	1898–1916	15	119	317	365	27	.962	114.13
4. Horace Clarke	1967–73	7	148	367	437	14	.983	108.71
5. Bobby Doerr	1938–51	13	139	372	430	16	.980	105.23
6. Glenn Hubbard	1980–89	9	128	269	435	11	.983	104.33
7. Ryne Sandberg	1983–97	13	147	281	482	8	.990	96.46
8. Jose Lind	1988–94	7	137	293	406	9	.988	95.29
9. Bobby Grich	1946–58	12	135	330	417	12	.984	94.00
10. Manny Trillo	1975–85	10	135	310	416	14	.981	91.90

Shortstop

By whatever method one chooses to use, Ozzie Smith emerges as baseball's best fielding shortstop. The Wizard of Oz tops the lists in career fielding, extended career, and points per season. Luis Aparicio is second in both career and extended career standings. Cal Ripken, Jr., Everett

Ozzie Smith is the best fielder in the history of the game. Smith sits atop not only the shortstop rankings but all glove men, regardless of position (National Baseball Hall of Fame Library, Cooperstown, New York).

Scott, and Honus Wagner make the top ten in all three lists. For their best ten years Rabbit Maranville has the most putouts, Aparicio the most assists, and Smith the highest fielding percentage. For an extended career Maranville leads in putouts, Smith in assists, and Omar Vizquel has the best average. Among the leaders in points per season Hughie Jennings leads in putouts per year, and Smith is first in both assists and fielding percentage.

BEST FIELDING SHORTSTOPS (BEST TEN YEARS)

Shortstop	Best Ten Years		G	PO	A	E	Pct.	Points
1. Ozzie Smith	1979–94	10	1362	2424	4726	149	.980	1680
2. Luis Aparicio	1958–70	10	1486	2966	5224	203	.976	1230
3. Jack Glasscock	1881–93	10	1102	1840	3922	550	.913	1151

Shortstop	Best Ten Years		G	PO	A	E	Pct.	Points
4. Cal Ripken, Jr.	1983–95	10	1617	2691	4972	165	.979	1135
5. Everett Scott	1915–24	10	1403	2849	4396	245	.967	1126
6. Honus Wagner	1903–15	10	1278	3142	4146	434	.934	1120
7. Bobby Wallace	1899–1911	10	1321	3035	4693	510	.938	1094
8. Rabbit Maranville	1913–30	10	1426	3591	4877	449	.950	1069
9. George Davis	1897–1907	10	1284	3024	4515	468	.942	1054
10. Tommy Corcoran	1891–1905	10	1350	2042	4686	589	.929	1030

BEST FIELDING SHORTSTOPS (EXTENDED CAREER)

Shortstop	Eligible Seasons		G	PO	A	E	Pct.	Points
1. Ozzie Smith	1978–94	17	2438	4099	8085	266	.979	2405
2. Luis Aparicio	1956–73	18	2581	4548	8016	366	.972	1556
3. Cal Ripken, Jr.	1982–96	15	1987	3638	6953	223	.979	1462
4. Honus Wagner	1903–16	13	1748	4084	5410	582	.942	1305
5. Rabbit Maranville	1913–31	14	1959	4720	6613	578	.951	1262
6. Bobby Wallace	1897–1911	13	1654	3824	5833	624	.939	1260
7. Jack Glasscock	1880–91	14	1505	2549	5243	770	.910	1236
8. Omar Vizquel	1989–2006	15	2282	3411	6483	158	.984	1180
9. Everett Scott	1914–24	11	1486	3173	4404	284	.964	1150
10. Alan Trammell	1978–94	15	1925	3113	5619	220	.975	1139

BEST FIELDING SHORTSTOPS (POINTS PER SEASON)

Shortstop	Eligible Seasons		G	PO	A	E	Pct.	Points
1. Ozzie Smith	1978–94	17	143	241	476	16	.979	141.47
2. Eddie Miller	1940–48	8	143	311	460	22	.973	127.88
3. Hughie Jennings	1892–98	6	129	346	307	64	.926	113.33
4. Lou Boudreau	1940–49	9	142	291	441	20	.973	112.11
5. Jay Bell	1990–98	9	146	209	457	16	.977	108.78
6. Buddy Kerr	1944–50	6	143	296	473	26	.967	105.85
7. George Davis	1897–1907	10	128	302	452	47	.942	105.40
8. Everett Scott	1914–24	11	135	289	437	26	.964	104.55
9. Honus Wagner	1903–16	13	134	314	416	45	.942	100.38
10. Cal Ripken, Jr.	1982–96	15	153	243	464	15	.979	97.46

Third Base

For his best ten years Buddy Bell was the top fielding third baseman. However, on an extended career basis, Brooks Robinson ranks first, and Lave Cross tops the rankings in points per season. The greatly underrated Bell is second in extended career rankings and third in points per year. The more heralded Robinson is third in career rankings and fourth in points per season. Oldtimer Cross is second on the career list and seventh for an extended career. Willie Kamm, Gary Gaetti, Terry Pendleton, and Mike Schmidt make the top ten in all three rankings. Two currently active players, Scott Rolen and Eric Chavez, are in the top ten in points per season. Barring injury, both have a good chance to enter the other rankings within a few years.

Among the career leaders Cross has the most putouts, Nettles the most assists, and Robinson the highest fielding percentage. Over an extended career Robinson leads in all three categories. Of the leaders in points per season, Cross has the most putouts per year, while Robinson is tops in both assists and fielding average.

BEST FIELDING THIRD BASEMEN (BEST TEN YEARS)

Third Baseman	Best Ten Years		G	PO	A	E	Pct.	Points
1. Buddy Bell	1973–87	10	1395	1153	3278	141	.970	969
2. Lave Cross	1894–1906	10	1403	1943	2488	282	.940	938
3. Brooks Robinson	1960–75	10	1547	1445	3503	129	.975	914
4. Willie Kamm	1923–34	10	1442	1843	2892	138	.972	875
5. Gary Gaetti	1983–97	10	1464	1068	2655	133	.966	857
6. Terry Pendleton	1985–95	10	1438	1126	3223	190	.958	832
7. Jimmie Collins	1897–1908	10	1355	1921	2947	348	.934	848
8. Graig Nettles	1970–85	10	1514	1233	3648	171	.968	816
9. Mike Schmidt	1974–87	10	1455	939	3424	190	.958	806
10. Heinie Groh	1913–24	9	1159	1322	2320	115	.969	779

BEST FIELDING THIRD BASEMEN (EXTENDED CAREER)

Third Baseman	Eligible Seasons		G	PO	A	E	Pct.	Points
1. Brooks Robinson	1958–75	17	2630	2495	5746	237	.972	1370
2. Buddy Bell	1973–87	15	2089	1750	4762	241	.965	1240
3. Gary Gaetti	1982–98	16	2249	1607	4211	214	.965	1205
4. Mike Schmidt	1973–88	15	2138	1435	4954	299	.956	1098
5. Graig Nettles	1970–86	16	2266	1896	5138	282	.964	1079
6. Wade Boggs	1983–97	15	2018	1425	3906	215	.961	996
7. Lave Cross	1894–1906	11	1558	2107	2735	310	.940	969
8. Willie Kamm	1923–34	12	1668	2148	3341	184	.968	951
9. Terry Pendleton	1985–96	12	1664	1296	3668	220	.958	933
10. Ron Cey	1973–85	13	1895	1451	3877	212	.962	900

BEST FIELDING THIRD BASEMEN (POINTS PER SEASON)

Third Baseman	Eligible Seasons		G	PO	A	E	Pct.	Points
1. Lave Cross	1894–1906	11	142	192	249	28	.940	88.09
2. Heinie Groh	1915–24	9	129	147	258	13	.969	86.56
3. Buddy Bell	1973–87	15	139	117	317	16	.965	82.67
4. Brooks Robinson	1958–75	17	155	147	338	14	.972	80.59
5. Scott Rolen	1997–2006	9	144	112	298	14	.967	79.89
6. Willie Kamm	1923–34	12	139	179	278	15	.968	79.25
7. Terry Pendleton	1985–96	12	139	108	306	18	.958	77.75
8. Gary Gaetti	1982–98	16	141	100	263	13	.965	75.31
9. Eric Chavez	1999–2006	8	139	106	279	13	.968	75.13
10. Mike Schmidt	1973–88	15	143	96	330	20	.956	73.20

Catcher

For his best ten years and for an extended career Gabby Hartnett was baseball's best fielding catcher. On a points per season basis Buck Ewing leads the rankings. That baseball pioneer had a long and illustrious career but only seven eligible seasons as a catcher. He found time to play all four infield positions and all three outfield positions, not as a one-time publicity stunt, but on a fairly regular basis. He even pitched four complete games. Jim Sundberg ranks second in career and extended career fielding and third in points per season. Sundberg and Hartnett are the only backstops to make the top ten in all three lists.

Among the career leaders Gary Carter has the most putouts, Ray Schalk the most assists, and Bill Freehan the highest fielding average. Over an extended career Ivan Rodriguez has the most putouts, while Schalk again leads in assists, and Brad Ausmus has the highest percentage. Of the leaders in points per season Freehan has the most putouts, Bill Bergen the most assists, and Damian Miller the highest fielding average.

Best Fielding Catchers (Best Ten Years)

Catcher	Best Ten Years		G	PO	A	E	Pct.	Points
1. Gabby Hartnett	1926–39	10	1107	4674	724	54	.990	965
2. Jim Sundberg	1974–84	10	1340	6863	742	50	.993	903
3. Charlie Bennett	1880–91	10	703	3989	813	280	.945	843
3. Ray Schalk	1913–25	10	1315	5788	1449	124	.983	843
5. Bill Dickey	1931–41	10	1177	5721	635	57	.991	831
6. Chief Zimmer	1889–1900	10	930	3510	984	260	.945	826
7. Lance Parrish	1979–91	10	1222	6540	670	58	.994	820
8. Gary Carter	1977–87	10	1382	8174	848	79	.992	786
9. Bill Bergen	1901–11	9	934	2797	1292	146	.972	778
10. Bill Freehan	1964–75	10	1234	7952	560	51	.994	769

Best Fielding Catchers (Extended Career)

Catcher	Eligible Seasons		G	PO	A	E	Pct.	Points
1. Gabby Hartnett	1924–39	15	1669	6859	1177	131	.984	1171
2. Jim Sundberg	1974–86	13	1741	8912	930	76	.992	1084
3. Gary Carter	1977–92	14	1809	10547	1050	103	.991	1012
4. Bill Dickey	1929–42	14	1592	7436	916	103	.988	975
5. Ray Schalk	1913–26	13	1630	7012	1738	156	.982	965
6. Bob Boone	1972–89	17	2171	10951	1148	169	.987	955
7. Ivan Rodriguez	1991–2006	16	1934	11676	989	117	.991	923
8. Brad Ausmus	1994–2006	13	1647	11010	824	64	.995	893
9. Tony Pena	1981–95	14	1799	10438	985	111	.990	887
10. Lance Parrish	1978–91	14	1635	8663	888	84	.991	842

Best Fielding Catchers Points Per Season

Catcher	Eligible Seasons		G	PO	A	E	Pct.	Points
1. Buck Ewing	1881–90	7	72	377	116	35	.934	91.00
2. Bill Bergen	1901–11	9	104	311	144	16	.972	86.44
3. Jim Sundberg	1974–86	13	134	686	72	6	.984	83.88
4. Chief Zimmer	1889–1900	10	93	351	94	26	.945	82.60
5. John Warner	1897–1906	8	89	412	122	17	.968	80.63
6. Damian Miller	1999–2006	8	105	750	57	4	.995	79.38
7. Ossee Schreck	1901–07	7	87	529	109	18	.973	79.14
8. Gabby Hartnett	1921–39	15	111	457	78	9	.984	78.07
9. Frank Snyder	1914–25	10	101	364	108	8	.983	75.10
10. Bill Freehan	1964–75	11	126	809	57	5	.994	75.09

Right Field

Included in the point totals of right fielders are the records of their games in which they played centerfield and leftfield. Very few outfielders played every game in the same outfield spot during their entire career. Al Kaline leads the list of best fielding right fielders, both for a ten-year career and an extended career. Baseball pioneer Uriah "Bloody Jake" Evans has the most points per year, but he had only five eligible seasons. Johnny Callison is second in the career rankings, tenth in extended career, and third in points per season. He is the only right fielder to make all three lists. Roberto Clemente is third in career points and second in the extended career rankings. The points per season list is dominated by players with shorter careers. No one in the top ten had more than ten eligible seasons. Included in the top ten are three nineteenth century players and one, Ichiro Suzuki, who is still active.

Among the career leaders Al Kaline has the most putouts, oldtimer William "Chicken" Wolf, the most assists, and George Hendrick the highest fielding average. For an extended career Hank Aaron has the most putouts, Harry Hooper leads in assists, and Kaline has the best average. Of the leaders in points per season, Ichiro has the most putouts and the highest percentage, while Evans has the most assists per year.

BEST FIELDING RIGHT FIELDERS (BEST TEN YEARS)

Right Fielder	Ten Best Years		G	PO	A	E	Pct.	Points
1. Al Kaline	1956–66	10	1589	3474	110	46	.987	723
2. Johnny Callison	1961–70	10	1437	2780	153	49	.984	720
3. Roberto Clemente	1955–74	10	1482	2712	220	72	.976	685
4. Hank Aaron	1957–68	10	1502	3185	116	54	.984	662
5. Harry Hooper	1912–24	10	1399	3016	221	90	.973	648
6. Willie Keeler	1894–1906	10	1331	2133	177	73	.967	643
7. Tony Gwynn	1984–95	10	1449	3067	114	44	.986	639
8. Paul Waner	1926–39	10	1462	3127	167	67	.980	632
9. George Hendrick	1973–84	10	1312	2913	95	36	.988	607
10. Chicken Wolf	1882–91	10	1039	1641	229	168	.918	605

BEST FIELDING RIGHT FIELDERS (EXTENDED CAREER)

Right Fielder	Eligible Seasons		G	PO	A	E	Pct.	Points
1. Al Kaline	1954–72	18	2331	4791	167	70	.990	1015
2. Roberto Clemente	1955–72	18	2370	4696	266	140	.973	1004
3. Hank Aaron	1954–72	19	2681	5404	195	117	.980	998
4. Harry Hooper	1910–25	16	2208	3857	330	144	.967	881
5. Tony Gwynn	1984–99	16	2150	4191	147	60	.986	877
6. Mel Ott	1928–45	17	2218	4353	246	95	.980	820
7. Paul Waner	1926–42	16	2227	4640	231	125	.975	802
8. Willie Keeler	1894–1906	14	1844	2888	260	118	.964	762 tie
8. Dave Winfield	1974–92	16	2401	4846	164	92	.982	762 tie
10. Johnny Callison	1961–71	11	1526	2907	157	50	.984	736

BEST FIELDING RIGHT FIELDERS (POINTS PER SEASON)

Right Fielder	Eligible Seasons		G	PO	A	E	Pct.	Points
1. Jake Evans	1879–84	5	77	137	28	17	.907	78.60
2. Bake McBride	1974–80	6	126	288	8	2	.991	67.17
3. Johnny Callison	1961–71	11	139	264	14	5	.984	66.91
4. Ichiro Suzuki	2001–06	6	157	354	9	2	.994	65.33
5. Brian Jordan	1995–2002	7	139	282	9	9	.988	63.14
6. Tommy Holmes	1942–50	9	136	313	13	4	.989	61.44
7. Chicken Wolf	1882–91	10	104	164	23	17	.918	60.50
8. Jesse Barfield	1982–90	9	139	294	16	7	.979	59.56

Right Fielder	Eligible Seasons		G	PO	A	E	Pct.	Points
9. Owen Wilson	1908–16	9	141	270	20	9	.968	59.33
10. Sam Thompson	1886–96	10	127	196	25	14	.939	58.60

Center Field

Tris Speaker leads center fielders in both the ten-year and extended career rankings and is fourth in points per season. Old timer Jim Fogarty leads in points per season. All three of the fielders ranking ahead of Speaker in this list were nineteenth century players with relatively short careers. Mike Griffin ranks second in career fielding, eighth in extended career, and sixth in points per season. Richie Ashburn is third in the career rankings and fifth for an extended career. Willie Mays is second in extended career fielding and ninth for his best ten years. Pop Corkhill, who ranks second in points per season, is tenth in the career rankings. Speaker and Griffin are the only center fielders to make all three lists.

For a ten-year career Ashburn has the most putouts, Speaker the most assists, and Andruw Jones the highest fielding average. Among the top ten in extended career fielding Ashburn and Speaker lead in putouts and assists, respectively, while Steve Finley boasts the highest percentage. Of the leaders in points per season, Jones has the most putouts and best average, while old timer Curt Welch has the most assists.

BEST FIELDING CENTER FIELDERS (BEST TEN YEARS)

Center Fielder	Best Ten Years		G	PO	A	E	Pct.	Points
1. Tris Speaker	1909–22	10	1392	3610	232	97	.975	1034
2. Mike Griffin	1888–98	10	1233	3033	213	125	.963	943

Tris Speaker was the best-fielding outfielder in the history of baseball. He was also an outstanding hitter, interrupting Ty Cobb's streak of titles to take the American League batting championship in 1916. The Grey Eagle's lifetime batting average of .245 is the fifth best of all time (Library of Congress).

Center Fielder	Best Ten Years		G	PO	A	E	Pct.	Points
3. Richie Ashburn	1948–58	10	1596	4708	140	76	.985	936
4. Sam West	1928–37	10	1278	3569	136	63	.983	890
5. Max Carey	1913–24	10	1443	3942	202	127	.970	874
6. Roy Thomas	1899–1908	10	1328	3084	174	96	.972	851
7. Andruw Jones	1997–2006	10	1566	4027	104	40	.990	826
8. Curt Flood	1958–69	10	1462	3617	100	44	.988	821
9. Willie Mays	1954–66	10	1530	4024	131	73	.983	818
10. Pop Corkhill	1883–91	8	925	1588	215	123	.936	808

BEST FIELDING CENTER FIELDERS (EXTENDED CAREER)

Center Fielder	Eligible Seasons		G	PO	A	E	Pct.	Points
1. Tris Speaker	1909–26	18	2615	6619	430	154	.979	1649
2. Willie Mays	1951–71	19	2701	6745	190	136	.981	1258
3. Max Carey	1911–28	17	2353	6173	333	225	.967	1215
4. Ty Cobb	1907–28	18	2560	5628	392	236	.962	1170
5. Richie Ashburn	1948–62	15	2104	7091	178	113	.985	1106
6. Steve Finley	1990–2006	17	2383	5473	132	70	.988	1095
7. Andre Dawson	1977–92	16	2214	4976	153	82	.984	1046
8. Mike Griffin	1887–98	12	1478	3535	316	183	.952	1029
9. Willie Davis	1961–76	16	2294	5389	142	126	.978	988
10. Vada Pinson	1959–74	16	2376	5057	168	101	.981	928

BEST FIELDING CENTER FIELDERS (POINTS PER SEASON)

Center Fielder	Eligible Seasons		G	PO	A	E	Pct.	Points
1. Jim Fogarty	1884–90	6	104	238	27	17	.939	105.67
2. Pop Corkhill	1883–91	8	116	236	26	15	.944	101.00
3. Curt Welch	1884–91	8	122	270	29	22	.932	93.75
4. Tris Speaker	1909–26	18	145	368	24	9	.979	91.61
5. Happy Felsch	1915–20	5	137	354	22	5	.976	88.40
6. Mike Griffin	1887–98	12	123	295	26	15	.952	85.75
7. Roy Thomas	1899–1908	10	133	308	17	10	.972	85.10
8. Andruw Jones	1997–2006	10	157	403	10	4	.990	82.60
9. Sam West	1928–37	12	124	345	12	6	.981	82.08
10. Jimmy McAleer	1889–98	7	125	293	19	17	.949	81.44

Left Field

Ed Delahanty leads left fielders in career fielding and points per season. He ranks seventh in the extended career standings and undoubtedly would have ranked higher in this category had not his career ended so tragically that night at Niagara Falls. Barry Bonds leads the extended career rankings and is fifth in the ten-year career list. Jimmy Sheckard is second in career fielding and third in both extended career and points per year, the only center fielder to rank in the top three in all the lists. Al Simmons joins Delahanty and Sheckard in making the top ten in all three rankings with a rank of second in career fielding, second in extended career, and seventh in points per season, as does Kip Selbach who comes in tenth in each category. Matty McIntyre, who with Ty Cobb and Sam Crawford, comprised one of the all-time great outfields for the Detroit Tigers in the early years of the twentieth century, ranks second in points per year. Also noteworthy is the fact that Warren Cromartie, who ranks ninth on the points per season list, combined with Andre Dawson and Ellis Valentine to give the Montreal Expos the top fielder at each of the three outfield positions in 1978 (Gil Coan, Irv Noren, and Sam Mele had done the same thing for the Washington Senators in 1951.)

Among the leaders in career fielding Rickey Henderson has the most putouts, Sheckard leads by a large margin in assists, and Tim Raines has the highest fielding average. All three retain their leads in the extended career rankings, which does not happen at any position except left field. A couple of changes occur in the points per season list, however. Although Sheckard repeats as the assist leader, Carson Bigbee moves in front in putouts and Charlie Maxwell takes over the lead in fielding percentage.

BEST FIELDING LEFT FIELDERS (BEST TEN YEARS)

Left Fielder	Best Ten Years		G	PO	A	E	Pct.	Points
1. Ed Delahanty	1891–1902	10	1154	2477	215	147	.948	793
2. Jimmy Sheckard	1898–1912	10	1361	2889	288	168	.950	768
3. Al Simmons	1924–37	10	1333	2959	112	49	.984	717
4. Fred Clarke	1895–1910	10	1317	3176	151	120	.965	675
5. Barry Bonds	1986–2004	10	1376	2872	111	47	.984	648
6. Carl Yastrzemski	1962–77	10	1492	2928	152	52	.983	646
7. Tim Raines	1982–92	10	1376	2944	102	32	.990	640
8. Rickey Henderson	1980–93	10	1328	3440	70	61	.983	628
9. Sherry Magee	1905–17	10	1349	2803	132	79	.974	612
10. Kip Selbach	1895–1905	10	1305	2915	172	181	.945	609

BEST FIELDING LEFT FIELDERS (EXTENDED CAREERS)

Left Fielder	Eligible Seasons		G	PO	A	E	Pct.	Points
1. Barry Bonds	1986–2006	20	2754	5458	172	93	.984	1040
2. Al Simmons	1924–38	16	2084	4680	165	91	.982	993
3. Jimmy Sheckard	1898–1912	14	1907	3894	348	208	.953	983
4. Fred Clarke	1895–1911	16	2042	4491	235	230	.954	935
5. Rickey Henderson	1980–2001	19	2661	5959	118	125	.980	925
6. Tim Raines	1981–95	15	1895	3940	126	50	.988	835
7. Ed Delahanty	1891–1902	11	1238	2656	224	157	.948	823
8. Sherry Magee	1905–17	12	1615	3322	150	96	.973	798
9. Zach Wheat	1910–26	16	2175	4702	215	164	.968	758
10. Kip Selbach	1894–1905	12	1510	3283	191	210	.943	714

BEST FIELDING LEFT FIELDERS (POINTS PER SEASON)

Left Fielder	Eligible Seasons		G	PO	A	E	Pct.	Points
1. Ed Delahanty	1891–1911	11	113	241	20	14	.948	74.82
2. Matty McIntyre	1904–11	6	139	176	18	10	.968	74.33
3. Jimmy Sheckard	1898–1912	14	136	278	25	15	.953	70.21
4. Sherry Magee	1905–17	12	135	277	13	8	.973	66.50
5. Charlie Maxwell	1956–60	5	129	268	7	3	.991	63.60
6. Greasy Neale	1916–20	5	128	281	16	7	.976	62.80
7. Al Simmons	1924–38	16	130	293	10	6	.982	62.06
8. Carson Bigbee	1917–23	7	127	310	19	11	.968	61.00
9. Warren Cromartie	1977–83	5	142	197	18	7	.977	61.00
10. Kip Selbach	1894–1905	12	126	274	16	18	.943	59.50

3

PLAYERS (HITTING AND FIELDING)

In previous sections of this book batting and fielding have been discussed separately. Playing the game of baseball, however, involves just more than hitting *or* fielding. It includes both hitting *and* fielding. The best player is the one who contributes most to his team's winning. This contribution and, hence, the player's value is likely to be greatest if the player excels at *both* producing runs for his team and by limiting the productivity of the opposing team. Offensive performance *plus* defensive performance is the measure of a player. Therefore, a player's rating is determined in the Faber System by adding his points for hitting and his points for fielding to get a total point score.

Producing one run for your team is of exactly equal value as preventing the opponents from scoring a run. Thus, defensive performance and offensive performance are of equal value. Therefore, no weighting in favor of either is appropriate. Weighting of the various defensive positions has already been explained in the section on fielders.

In the case of catchers one factor in addition to hitting and fielding might be considered. That is the intangible known as the ability to handle pitchers. No objective measure of this quality is available, so in all computations of Player of the Year catchers are rated exactly the same as everyone else, i.e., hitting plus fielding. However, for ratings of catchers in comparison with other catchers a surrogate figure is used to estimate the backstop's success in working with pitchers. In baseball, success is measured by winning. So the winning record of a team's pitching staff may reflect, in part, the catcher's skill. The Faber System awards bonus points to catchers who handle a pitching staff that has a winning record. The formula is $B = g \times (pct. - .500)/2$, where B is bonus, g is games caught, pct. is the team's winning percentage. If the formula yields a negative number, no points are subtracted. Bonus points are just that — *bonus* points are can only be added.

The fact that some players participate at more than one position during their careers (or even during a single season) has been discussed in the section on fielding. In order to insure that all multiposition players are treated the same way a rather rigid set of rules has been constructed to determine which years are counted in a player's career total.

1. *If a player has ten or more eligible seasons at his primary position, nothing else is counted.*
2. *If a player has five or fewer eligible seasons, everything must be counted.*
3. *If a player has more than five but fewer than ten seasons in his primary position, all years in which he played two thirds of his team's games at the primary position must be counted first, then other seasons are selected in a way to maximize his total points, except that no season with*

fewer than two thirds of the games at any position may be counted until all seasons of more than two thirds of the games have been included.. (With catchers, substitute one-half for two-thirds in the above rule.)

Player of the Year by Position

First Base

National League. In the senior circuit's pioneer era Cap Anson and Dan Brouthers were the outstanding first basemen. Anson was the league's best eight times, while Brouthers led five times. In the 1920s and 1930s Bill Terry led eight times, including seven years in a row. In 1881 Anson compiled 207 Faber System points, a record that stood for well over 100 years until Jeff Bagwell posted 215 points in 1994. Bagwell's standard was short-lived, however, as Todd Helton compiled 233 points in 2000, the first of four 200 plus seasons for the Colorado star.

NATIONAL LEAGUE LEADING FIRST BASEMEN, 1877–2006

Year	First Baseman	Bat	Field	Total
1876	Cal McVey	93	11	104
1877	Joe Start	45	4	49
1878	Joe Start	103	1	104
1879	Joe Start	75	34	109
1880	Cap Anson	120	23	143
1881	Cap Anson	176	31	207
1882	Dan Brouthers	131	23	154
1883	Dan Brouthers	129	3	132
1884	Cap Anson	136	−13	123
1885	Roger Connor	151	12	163
1886	Cap Anson	182	−11	171
1887	Roger Connor	63	49	112
1888	Cap Anson	137	26	163
1889	Dan Brouthers	136	−7	129
1890	Cap Anson	98	7	105
1891	Cap Anson	77	17	94
1892	Dan Brouthers	124	29	153
1893	Jake Beckley	27	33	60
1894	Dan Brouthers	61	−1	60
1895	Roger Connor	−10	18	8
1896	Cap Anson	25	−4	21
1897	Fred Tenney	37	23	60
1898	Dan McGann	64	13	77
1899	Fred Tenney	76	40	116
1900	Jake Beckley	43	3	46
1901	Dan McGann	-3	9	6
1902	Fred Tenney	90	25	115
1903	Jack Doyle	74	7	81
1904	Frank Chance	78	19	97
1905	Frank Chance	104	21	125
1906	Frank Chance	116	8	124
1907	Frank Chance	66	32	98

Year	First Baseman	Bat	Field	Total
1908	Fred Tenney	62	21	83
1909	Ed Konetchy	62	10	72
1910	Ed Konetchy	64	34	98
1911	Ed Konetchy	49	5	54
1912	Ed Konetchy	42	15	57
1913	Jake Daubert	64	9	73
1914	Jake Daubert	46	1	47
1915	Fred Luderlus	58	26	84
1916	Jake Daubert	69	15	84
1917	Fred Luderlus	31	16	47
1918	Fred Luderlus	43	5	48
1919	Fred Luderlus	32	−1	31
1920	George Kelly	9	31	40
1921	George Kelly	71	21	92
1922	Jake Daubert	68	17	85
1923	Jack Fournier	81	−8	73
1924	George Kelly	100	5	105
1925	Jack Fournier	127	0	127
1926	Jim Bottomley	68	−18	50
1927	Bill Terry	87	29	116
1928	Jim Bottomley	115	−26	89
1929	Bill Terry	110	33	143
1930	Bill Terry	135	29	164
1931	Bill Terry	90	11	101
1932	Bill Terry	116	18	134
1933	Bill Terry	41	16	57
1934	Bill Terry	98	30	128
1935	Bill Terry	60	37	97
1936	Dolf Camilli	107	−12	95
1937	Dolf Camilli	129	16	145
1938	Johnny Mize	123	−24	99
1939	Frank McCormick	100	20	120
1940	Johnny Mize	152	−15	137
1941	Dolf Camilli	117	0	117
1942	Johnny Mize	113	8	121
1943	Elbie Fletcher	65	24	89
1944	Frank McCormick	74	32	106
1945	Phil Cavarretta	117	1	118
1946	Stan Musial	166	−29	137
1947	Johnny Mize	122	27	149
1948	Johnny Mize	120	13	133
1949	Gil Hodges	63	6	69
1950	Earl Torgeson	76	2	78
1951	Gil Hodges	55	13	68
1952	Gil Hodges	68	14	82
1953	Gil Hodges	96	8	104
1954	Ted Kluzewski	147	9	156
1955	Stan Musial	101	9	110
1956	Stan Musial	101	27	128
1957	Stan Musial	132	15	147

Year	First Baseman	Bat	Field	Total
1958	Stan Musial	72	7	79
1959	Frank Robinson	121	−6	115
1960	Joe Adcock	63	20	83
1961	Joe Adcock	62	22	84
1962	Bill White	83	16	99
1963	Bill White	107	7	114
1964	Bill White	80	21	101
1965	Bill White	72	15	87
1966	Bill White	59	22	81
1967	Orlando Cepeda	131	−3	128
1968	Willie McCovey	122	−20	102
1969	Willie McCovey	184	1	185
1970	Willie McCovey	140	8	148
1971	Bob Robertson	49	29	78
1972	Nate Colbert	73	28	101
1973	Tony Perez	100	−7	93
1974	Steve Garvey	90	5	95
1975	Steve Garvey	60	10	70
1976	Bob Watson	92	−4	88
1977	Bob Watson	66	39	105
1978	Steve Garvey	117	−2	115
1979	Keith Hernandez	123	37	160
1980	Keith Hernandez	120	21	141
1981	Keith Hernandez	75	31	106
1982	Bill Buckner	64	33	97
1983	Keith Hernandez	54	40	94
1984	Keith Hernandez	91	30	121
1985	Keith Hernandez	71	24	95
1986	Keith Hernandez	101	35	136
1987	Jack Clark	121	−11	110
1988	Will Clark	101	5	106
1989	Will Clark	141	12	153
1990	Eddie Murray	112	−3	109
1991	Will Clark	103	24	127
1992	Mark Grace	62	55	117
1993	Andres Galarraga	113	8	121
1994	Jeff Bagwell	191	24	215
1995	Jeff Bagwell	59	34	93
1996	Andres Galarraga	132	9	141
1997	Jeff Bagwell	126	17	143
1998	Mark McGwire	203	−9	194
1999	Jeff Bagwell	153	−1	152
2000	Todd Helton	198	35	233
2001	Todd Helton	176	34	210
2002	Todd Helton	128	28	156
2003	Todd Helton	182	30	212
2004	Todd Helton	164	49	213
2005	Derrek Lee	164	19	183
2006	Albert Pujols	165	35	200

American Association. Although Dan Brouthers played in the league one season, the American Association did not have a dominant first baseman. Long John Reilly led first sackers twice and holds the league mark with 146 Faber System points, but he was hardly in a class with Brouthers or Cap Anson and Roger Connor.

AMERICAN ASSOCIATION LEADING FIRST BASEMEN, 1882–91

Year	First Baseman	Bat	Field	Total
1882	Juice Latham	26	5	31
1883	Harry Stovey	107	19	126
1884	Long John Reilly	138	8	146
1885	Bill Phillips	50	19	69
1886	Dave Orr	75	17	92
1887	Charlie Comiskey	70	−1	69
1888	Long John Reilly	103	−4	99
1889	Tommy Tucker	70	−38	32
1890	Harry Taylor	48	25	73
1891	Dan Brouthers	132	−13	119

Players' League. Roger Connor was the league's top first baseman with 179 points in 1890. He was good enough to lead the National League three times when he played in the senior circuit.

PLAYERS' LEAGUE LEADING FIRST BASEMAN, 1890

Year	First Baseman	Bat	Field	Total
1890	Roger Connor	127	52	179

American League. Although Stuffy McInnis led the American League first basemen four times in a row from 1912 through 1915, he was soon overshadowed by George Sisler, who led eight times, including seven consecutive years from 1916 through 1922. Then came the Lou Gehrig era. The Iron Horse led the league seven times. His chief rival was Jimmie Foxx, who topped the circuit six times. Sisler was the first American League first baseman to reach 100 Faber System points in a season with 119 in 1916. He upped his mark to 164 points in 1920. In 1927 Gehrig set a new record with 232 points, a mark that was tied by Foxx in 1932. The only other American League first sackers to top the 200 mark were Norm Cash with 201 points in 1961 and Rod Carew with 202 in 1977.

AMERICAN LEAGUE — LEADING FIRST BASEMEN, 1901–2006

Year	First Baseman	Bat	Field	Total
1901	Buck Freeman	92	−27	65
1902	Charlie Hickman	88	−28	60
1903	John Ganzel	17	33	50
1904	Harry Davis	56	−18	38
1905	Jiggs Donahue	33	27	60
1906	Hal Chase	59	−11	48
1907	Jiggs Donahue	3	76	79
1908	George Stovall	38	37	75
1909	Jake Stahl	56	−20	36
1910	Jake Stahl	24	−4	20
1911	Germany Schaefer	38	−2	36

Year	First Baseman	Bat	Field	Total
1912	Stuffy McInnis	66	15	81
1913	Stuffy McInnis	76	12	88
1914	Stuffy McInnis	61	7	68
1915	Stuffy McInnis	6	8	14
1916	George Sisler	129	−10	119
1917	George Sisler	78	−1	77
1918	George Sisler	83	21	104
1919	George Sisler	88	22	110
1920	George Sisler	168	−4	164
1921	George Sisler	107	16	123
1922	George Sisler	163	−1	162
1923	Lu Blue	30	18	48
1924	Joe Hauser	41	8	49
1925	George Sisler	36	5	41
	Earl Sheeley	33	8	41 tie
1926	Lou Gehrig	118	−7	111
1927	Lou Gehrig	226	6	232
1928	Lou Gehrig	171	−23	158
1929	Jimmie Foxx	139	−11	128
1930	Lou Gehrig	207	−9	198
1931	Lou Gehrig	202	−20	182
1932	Jimmie Foxx	223	9	232
1933	Jimmie Foxx	191	7	198
1934	Lou Gehrig	195	−3	192
1935	Hank Greenberg	150	9	159
1936	Lou Gehrig	174	0	174
1937	Hank Greenberg	178	14	192
1938	Jimmie Foxx	173	−3	170
1939	Jimmie Foxx	154	9	163
1940	Rudy York	113	6	119
1941	Jimmie Foxx	68	18	86
1942	Rudy York	17	21	38
1943	Rudy York	96	16	112
1944	Nick Etten	71	−5	66
1945	Nick Etten	91	−15	76
1946	Rudy York	70	12	82
1947	George McQuinn	55	3	58
1948	Ferris Fain	33	8	41
1949	Mickey Vernon	19	41	60
1950	Walt Dropo	106	−14	94
1951	Ferris Fain	62	51	113
1952	Ferris Fain	85	18	103
1953	Mickey Vernon	109	12	121
1954	Mickey Vernon	64	5	69
1955	Vic Power	54	19	73
1956	Bill Skowron	44	18	62
1957	Bill Skowron	47	20	67
1958	Dick Gernert	−3	23	20
1959	Vic Power	44	65	109
1960	Roy Sievers	85	4	89
1961	Norm Cash	190	11	201

Year	First Baseman	Bat	Field	Total
1962	Norm Siebern	112	16	128
1963	Norm Cash	67	1	68
1964	Norm Cash	38	18	56
	Norm Siebern	44	12	56 tie
1965	Joe Pepitone	61	30	91
1966	Boog Powell	84	−21	63
1967	Harmon Killebrew	149	−9	140
1968	Norm Cash	42	19	61
1969	Boog Powell	129	0	129
1970	Boog Powell	127	1	128
1971	Norm Cash	84	−7	77
1972	Dick Allen	162	4	166
1973	George Scott	97	22	119
1974	George Scott	49	20	69
1975	John Mayberry	123	11	134
1976	Rod Carew	100	−5	95
1977	Rod Carew	176	26	202
1978	Andre Thornton	83	25	108
1979	Cecil Cooper	85	4	89
1980	Cecil Cooper	140	33	173
1981	Eddie Murray	66	32	95
1982	Cecil Cooper	95	19	114
1983	Eddie Murray	116	20	136
1984	Don Mattingly	124	40	164
1985	Don Mattingly	135	−8	127
1986	Don Mattingly	145	1	146
1987	Don Mattingly	104	5	109
1988	Fred McGriff	87	2	89
1989	Fred McGriff	96	−8	88
1990	Fred McGriff	105	35	140
	Cecil Fielder	139	1	140 tie
1991	Cecil Fielder	99	8	107
1992	Frank Thomas	146	−12	134
1993	John Olerud	158	2	160
1994	Frank Thomas	179	−19	160
1995	Rafael Palmeiro	82	18	100
1996	Frank Thomas	155	−8	147
1997	Tino Martinez	104	15	119
1998	Rafael Palmeiro	99	21	120
1999	Jason Giambi	105	19	124
2000	Jason Giambi	167	−1	166
2001	Jason Giambi	158	−7	151
2002	Mike Sweeney	79	31	110
2003	Carlos Delgado	150	2	152
2004	Mark Teixeira	70	8	78
2005	Mark Teixeira	131	25	156
2006	Justin Morneau	96	8	104

Federal League. The Federal league's best first baseman was Ed Konetchy, who had already led the National League four times before he switched circuits.

FEDERAL LEAGUE LEADING FIRST BASEMEN, 1914–15

Year	First Baseman	Bat	Field	Total
1914	George Stovall	9	16	25
1915	Ed Konetchy	75	20	95

Second Base

National League. In the National League's first season Ross Barnes set a record for second sackers with 201 Faber System points, a mark that endured for nearly half a century. Bid McPhee led six consecutive years in the 1890s and Miller Huggins was tops for seven seasons after the turn of the century, but neither could match Barnes's best single season mark. Breaking that record was Rogers Hornsby with 210 points in 1922. Five years later Frankie Frisch raised the standard to 233 points, a mark that has stood for 80 years and counting. Hornsby and Joe Morgan each led the league's second basemen seven times, while Ryne Sandberg was on top eight times. Sandberg is the only senior circuit second sacker since Frisch to tally 200 points in a season, with 219 in 1992.

NATIONAL LEAGUE LEADING SECOND BASEMEN, 1876–2006

Year	Second Baseman	Bat	Field	Total
1876	Ross Barnes	184	17	201
1877	Joe Gerhardt	2	12	14
1878	Joe Gerhardt	45	20	65
1879	Chick Fulmer	−22	34	12
1880	Jack Burdock	16	89	105
1881	Fred Dunlap	77	24	101
1882	Hardy Richardson	13	19	32
1883	Jack Farrell	61	74	135
1884	Fred Pfeffer	90	106	196
1885	Fred Dunlap	20	99	119
1886	Fred Dunlap	20	66	86
1887	Fred Pfeffer	8	15	23
1888	Fred Pfeffer	24	88	112
1889	Fred Pfeffer	−50	96	46
1890	Bid McPhee	43	69	112
1891	Bid McPhee	28	88	116
1892	Bid McPhee	50	108	158
1893	Bid McPhee	14	99	113
1894	Bid McPhee	16	96	112
1895	Bid McPhee	−10	85	95
1896	Cupid Childs	82	52	134
1897	Cupid Childs	52	40	92
1898	Nap Lajoie	74	25	99
1899	Tom Daly	38	−2	36
1900	Nap Lajoie	32	118	150
1901	Tom Daly	44	4	48
1902	Bobby Lowe	−40	94	54
1903	Claude Ritchey	−2	63	61
1904	Miller Huggins	36	2	38
1905	Miller Huggins	78	46	124
1906	Miller Huggins	56	41	97

Year	Second Baseman	Bat	Field	Total
1907	Miller Huggins	25	41	66
1908	Claude Ritchey	23	89	112
1909	Dick Egan	9	85	94
1910	Miller Huggins	58	47	105
1911	Bill Sweeney	70	30	100
1912	Bill Sweeney	81	88	169
1913	Miller Huggins	41	81	122
1914	Miller Huggins	38	43	81
1915	George Cutshaw	−19	135	116
1916	Larry Doyle	12	5	17
1917	George Cutshaw	−22	10	−12
1918	George Cutshaw	30	−4	26
1919	Morrie Rath	20	64	84
1920	Rogers Hornsby	127	−3	124
1921	Rogers Hornsby	174	−20	154
1922	Rogers Hornsby	200	10	210
1923	Frankie Frisch	76	30	106
1924	Rogers Hornsby	207	−17	190
1925	Rogers Hornsby	205	−37	168
1926	Hughie Critz	−11	80	69
1927	Frankie Frisch	79	154	233
1928	Rogers Hornsby	147	−53	94
1929	Rogers Hornsby	199	−33	166
1930	Frankie Frisch	59	52	111
1931	Frankie Frisch	27	−1	26
1932	Billy Herman	59	7	66
1933	Hughie Critz	−49	77	28
1934	Billy Herman	8	1	9
1935	Billy Herman	83	63	146
1936	Billy Herman	70	41	111
1937	Billy Herman	88	54	142
1938	Billy Herman	11	82	93
1939	Lonnie Frey	47	61	108
1940	Lonnie Frey	37	52	89
1941	Creepy Crespi	23	21	44
1942	Mickey Witek	−6	54	48
1943	Lonnie Frey	11	96	107
1944	Woody Williams	−47	80	33
1945	Eddie Stanky	79	1	80
1946	Red Schoendienst	22	55	77
1947	Eddie Stanky	3	43	46
1948	Jackie Robinson	65	42	107
1949	Jackie Robinson	129	−30	99
1950	Eddie Stanky	85	3	86
1951	Jackie Robinson	103	35	138
1952	Jackie Robinson	111	−14	97
	Red Schoendienst	37	60	97 tie
1953	Red Schoendienst	91	70	160
1954	Red Schoendienst	33	73	106
1955	Johnny Temple	13	−12	1
1956	Jim Gilliam	75	35	110

Year	Second Baseman	Bat	Field	Total
1957	Don Blasingame	37	72	109
1958	Johnny Temple	52	11	63
1959	Charlie Neal	43	53	96
1960	Bill Mazeroski	−7	121	114
1961	Frank Bolling	−4	74	70
1962	Bill Mazeroski	−6	139	133
1963	Bill Mazeroski	−35	138	103
1964	Ron Hunt	23	46	69
1965	Pete Rose	114	−26	88
	Bill Mazeroski	−18	106	88 tie
1966	Bill Mazeroski	−3	119	116
1967	Bill Mazeroski	−4	80	76
1968	Glenn Beckert	57	9	66
1969	Felix Millan	19	26	45
1970	Joe Morgan	44	33	77
1971	Glenn Beckert	74	9	83
1972	Joe Morgan	125	51	176
1973	Joe Morgan	108	54	162
1974	Joe Morgan	120	−5	115
1975	Joe Morgan	138	50	188
1976	Joe Morgan	151	−3	148
1977	Joe Morgan	97	21	118
1978	Davey Lopes	57	22	79
1979	Davey Lopes	71	7	78
1980	Manny Trillo	16	88	104
1981	Tommy Herr	−3	43	40
1982	Joe Morgan	47	30	77
1983	Ryne Sandberg	9	93	102
1984	Ryne Sandberg	96	82	178
1985	Ryne Sandberg	97	52	149
1986	Steve Sax	90	30	120
1987	Glenn Hubbard	2	73	75
1988	Ryne Sandberg	18	50	68
1989	Ryne Sandberg	94	43	137
1990	Ryne Sandberg	104	35	139
1991	Ryne Sandberg	93	126	219
1992	Ryne Sandberg	81	70	151
1993	Robby Thompson	54	49	103
1994	Craig Biggio	85	30	115
1995	Craig Biggio	104	8	112
1996	Eric Young	84	92	176
1997	Craig Biggio	122	44	166
1998	Fernando Vina	58	72	130
1999	Craig Biggio	69	50	119
2000	Jeff Kent	126	−1	125
2001	Jeff Kent	59	17	76
2002	Jose Vidro	82	52	134
2003	Marcus Giles	81	66	147
2004	Mark Loretta	102	27	129
2005	Marcus Giles	68	29	97
2006	Jamey Carroll	57	90	147

American Association. Bid McPhee was the Association's best second baseman. He holds the single season record with 234 points and led the league five times. Counting the six times he led the National League, McPhee had eleven seasons as the best player at his position in his league. Jack Crooks with 207 points in 1891 is the only other Association second baseman to secure 200 points.

AMERICAN ASSOCIATION LEADING SECOND BASEMEN, 1882–91

Year	Second Baseman	Bat	Field	Total
1882	Bid McPhee	−32	43	11
1883	Joe Gerhardt	−7	84	77
1884	Bid McPhee	75	96	171
1885	Pop Smith	5	90	95
1886	Bid McPhee	75	159	234
1887	Bid McPhee	36	104	141
1888	Bid McPhee	5	159	164
1889	Lou Bierbauer	−13	161	148
1890	Cupid Childs	89	82	171
1891	Jack Crooks	22	185	207

Players' League. Lou Bierbauer was the Players' League's best second sacker. At one time he had also led the American Association at the keystone position.

PLAYERS' LEAGUE LEADING SECOND BASEMAN, 1890

Year	Second Baseman	Bat	Field	Total
1890	Lou Bierbauer	59	93	152

American League. In the circuit's first season as a major league, Nap Lajoie led all second basemen with 253 points, a mark that has never been equaled. After twice having been the National League's top second sacker, Lajoie led the junior circuit eight times. Eddie Collins outdid him with 14 league leading seasons. Bobby Doerr led ten times, and Charlie Gehringer was best eight times. Lajoie topped the 200 mark three times, while Collins did it once. Nine of the ten best seasons by American League second basemen were turned in by either Lajoie or Collins. With 189 points in 1937 Gehringer was the only other junior circuit keystone guardian to break into the top ten.

A star both in the field and at the plate, Eddie Collins led American League second basemen in Faber System points 14 times. During the league's first quarter century either Collins or Nap Lajoie led the league in overall value for all but four seasons (Library of Congress).

American League Leading Second Basemen, 1901–2006

Year	Second Baseman	Bat	Field	Total
1901	Nap Lajoie	198	55	253
1902	Jimmy Williams	27	−16	11
1903	Nap Lajoie	94	89	183
1904	Nap Lajoie	157	32	189
1905	Jimmy Williams	−26	20	−6
1906	Nap Lajoie	109	124	233
1907	Nap Lajoie	36	61	92
1908	Nap Lajoie	59	118	177
1909	Eddie Collins	140	46	186
1910	Nap Lajoie	146	95	241
1911	Eddie Collins	95	49	144
1912	Eddie Collins	142	49	191
1913	Nap Lajoie	54	68	122
1914	Eddie Collins	159	68	227
1915	Eddie Collins	148	37	185
1916	Del Pratt	30	59	89
1917	Eddie Collins	75	−14	61
1918	Eddie Collins	38	30	68
1919	Eddie Collins	62	4	66
1920	Eddie Collins	107	61	168
1921	Eddie Collins	30	76	106
1922	Eddie Collins	33	25	58
1923	Eddie Collins	88	1	89
1924	Eddie Collins	85	22	107
1925	Marty McManus	12	52	64
1926	Eddie Collins	58	14	72
1927	Charlie Gehringer	44	75	121
1928	Max Bishop	67	25	92
1929	Charlie Gehringer	91	17	108
1930	Charlie Gehringer	115	−5	110
1931	Max Bishop	58	17	75
1932	Tony Lazzeri	87	22	109
1933	Charlie Gehringer	53	11	62
1934	Charlie Gehringer	115	−5	110
1935	Buddy Myer	88	59	147
1936	Charlie Gehringer	93	41	134
1937	Charlie Gehringer	130	59	189
1938	Charlie Gehringer	76	34	110
1939	Bobby Doerr	6	67	73
1940	Bobby Doerr	32	91	123
1941	Bobby Doerr	8	84	92
1942	Bobby Doerr	51	38	89
1943	Bobby Doerr	23	86	109
1944	George Stirnweiss	99	81	180
1945	George Stirnweiss	90	28	118
1946	Bobby Doerr	53	63	116
1947	Bobby Doerr	21	51	72
1948	Bobby Doerr	65	70	135
1949	Bobby Doerr	73	97	170

Year	Second Baseman	Bat	Field	Total
1950	Bobby Doerr	56	67	123
1951	Nellie Fox	35	39	74
1952	Billy Goodman	39	44	83
1953	Bobby Avila	24	46	70
1954	Bobby Avila	122	44	166
1955	Nellie Fox	51	37	88
1956	Nellie Fox	71	96	167
1957	Nellie Fox	93	46	137
1958	Pete Runnels	110	47	158
1959	Pete Runnels	86	28	114
1960	Nellie Fox	26	65	91
1961	Jerry Lumpe	4	82	86
1962	Billy Moran	20	52	72
1963	Jerry Lumpe	16	49	65
1964	Jerry Adair	−42	106	64
1965	Don Buford	55	23	78
1966	Bobby Knoop	−9	52	43
1967	Horace Clarke	27	122	149
1968	Mike Andrews	62	0	62
1969	Dick Green	17	81	98
1970	Davey Johnson	22	45	67
1971	Sandy Alomar	−10	79	69
1972	Rod Carew	52	13	65
1973	Rod Carew	112	42	154
1974	Bobby Grich	68	88	156
1975	Bobby Grich	47	94	141
1976	Bobby Grich	60	89	149
1977	Bump Wills	35	42	77
1978	Jerry Remy	14	47	61
1979	Willie Randolph	44	47	91
1980	Willie Randolph	90	−17	73
1981	Bobby Grich	64	30	94
1982	Tony Bernazard	12	71	83
1983	Frank White	−23	90	67
1984	Willie Randolph	49	39	88
1985	Bobby Grich	−2	69	67
1986	Tony Bernazard	62	36	98
1987	Marty Barrett	3	94	97
1988	Julio Franco	54	3	57
1989	Harold Reynolds	45	31	76
1990	Jody Reed	34	9	43
1991	Julio Franco	116	−32	84
1992	Carlos Baerga	84	31	115
1993	Carlos Baerga	80	38	118
1994	Jody Reed	−18	87	69
1995	Chuck Knoblauch	91	24	115
1996	Roberto Alomar	101	49	150
1997	Chuck Knoblauch	66	43	109
1998	Damion Easley	25	126	151
1999	Roberto Alomar	115	24	139

Year	Second Baseman	Bat	Field	Total
2000	Roberto Alomar	56	−16	40
2001	Bret Boone	130	0	130
2002	Ray Durham	51	−9	42
2003	Bret Boone	81	13	68
2004	Orlando Hudson	−15	90	75
2005	Brian Roberts	65	10	75
2006	Robinson Cano	31	−1	30

Federal League. No outstanding second basemen were attracted to the Federal League. Although Bill Kenworthy had a fine year in 1914, it was the only good year he had in the majors.

FEDERAL LEAGUE LEADING SECOND BASEMEN, 1914–15

Year	Second Baseman	Bat	Field	Total
1914	Bill Kenworthy	75	56	131
1915	Steve Yerkes	−5	53	48

Shortstop

National League. Playing first for the Cleveland Blues then for several other teams, Jack Glasscock was the best shortstop of the early pioneer era. He led the National League in Faber System points ten times and set a mark with 175 points in 1889. Then along came Hughie Jennings, who led five consecutive seasons from 1894 through 1898, setting a record with an incredible 320 points in 1895 and going over the 200 mark two other times. Around the turn of the century Honus Wagner emerged as the league's top shortstop and one of the best of all time, leading the league 12 times and topping the 200 point mark twice. The only other NL second sacker to reach that plateau was Ernie Banks with 204 points in 1959. The modern fielding wizard Ozzie Smith led the league nine times but his bat was not potent enough to enable him to reach 200 points in a season.

NATIONAL LEAGUE LEADING SHORTSTOPS, 1876–2006

Year	Second Baseman	Bat	Field	Total
1876	Johnny Peters	46	41	85
1877	Johnny Peters	34	23	57
1878	Bob Ferguson	54	−1	53
1879	George Wright	45	86	131
1880	Art Irwin	19	31	50
1881	Jack Glasscock	−6	65	59
1882	Jack Glasscock	42	28	70
1883	Jack Glasscock	15	121	136
1884	Bill McClellan	7	5	12
1885	Jack Glasscock	15	94	109
1886	Jack Glasscock	72	83	155
1887	Monte Ward	66	103	169
1888	Jack Glasscock	8	103	111
1889	Jack Glasscock	100	75	175
1890	Jack Glasscock	64	33	97
1891	Herman Long	82	32	114
1892	Jack Glasscock	6	47	53

Year	Second Baseman	Bat	Field	Total
1893	Jack Glasscock	24	65	89
1894	Hughie Jennings	39	120	159
1895	Hughie Jennings	134	186	320
1896	Hughie Jennings	126	107	233
1897	Hughie Jennings	106	128	234
1898	Hughie Jennings	128	39	167
1899	George Davis	21	171	192
1900	George Davis	−1	69	68
1901	Bobby Wallace	37	97	134
1902	Herman Long	−63	141	78
1903	Honus Wagner	99	121	220
1904	Honus Wagner	124	−1	123
1905	Honus Wagner	143	42	185
1906	Honus Wagner	128	54	182
1907	Honus Wagner	144	22	166
1908	Honus Wagner	163	9	172
1909	Honus Wagner	130	73	203
1910	Honus Wagner	73	33	106
1911	Honus Wagner	87	34	121
1912	Honus Wagner	69	76	145
1913	Honus Wagner	−4	110	106
1914	Rabbit Maranville	−20	42	22
1915	Honus Wagner	23	49	72
1916	Rabbit Maranville	−5	59	54
1917	Art Fletcher	21	85	106
1918	Art Fletcher	−11	70	59
1919	Rabbit Maranville	−20	58	38
1920	Dave Bancroft	26	94	120
1921	Dave Bancroft	65	52	117
1922	Dave Bancroft	57	31	88
1923	Rabbit Maranville	−43	73	30
1924	Glenn Wright	16	1	17
1925	Glenn Wright	41	33	74
1926	Dave Bancroft	23	21	44
1927	Travis Jackson	47	4	51
1928	Travis Jackson	−20	50	30
1929	Travis Jackson	−5	62	57
1930	Glenn Wright	38	27	65
1931	Woody English	72	31	103
1932	Dick Bartell	61	73	134
1933	Arky Vaughan	75	−43	32
1934	Arky Vaughan	107	−1	106
1935	Arky Vaughan	117	−27	90
1936	Arky Vaughan	2	102	104
1937	Dick Bartell	50	90	140
1938	Arky Vaughan	87	63	150
1939	Arky Vaughan	47	44	91
1940	Eddie Miller	1	124	125
1941	Eddie Miller	−47	76	39
1942	PeeWee Reese	27	49	76

Year	Second Baseman	Bat	Field	Total
1943	Eddie Miller	−53	90	37
1944	Eddie Miller	−88	110	22
1945	Buddy Kerr	−64	115	51
1946	PeeWee Reese	39	17	56
1947	Marty Marion	−20	87	67
1948	PeeWee Reese	36	48	84
1949	PeeWee Reese	88	33	121
1950	PeeWee Reese	6	5	11
1951	Solly Hemus	3	56	59
1952	Alvin Dark	49	4	53
1953	Alvin Dark	62	3	65
1954	PeeWee Reese	54	9	63
1955	Ernie Banks	78	32	110
1956	Roy McMillan	−4	120	116
1957	Ernie Banks	92	−4	88
1958	Ernie Banks	127	−32	95
1959	Ernie Banks	136	68	204
1960	Ernie Banks	90	94	184
1961	Ernie Banks	30	43	73
1962	Leo Cardenas	11	29	40
1963	Dick Groat	78	−7	71
1964	Denis Menke	53	20	73
1965	Maury Wills	40	59	99
1966	Gene Alley	32	63	95
1967	Gene Alley	11	58	69
1968	Gene Alley	−27	57	30
1969	Don Kessinger	48	74	122
1970	Don Kessinger	12	32	44
1971	Larry Bowa	−18	109	91
1972	Chris Speier	37	47	84
1973	Don Kessinger	−36	30	−6
1974	Larry Bowa	16	59	75
1975	Dave Concepcion	−16	89	73
1976	Dave Concepcion	20	63	83
1977	Larry Bowa	3	45	48
1978	Larry Bowa	18	72	90
1979	Garry Templeton	52	41	93
1980	Garry Templeton	46	90	136
1981	Ozzie Smith	−41	100	59
1982	Ozzie Smith	−26	166	140
1983	Dickie Thon	33	46	79
1984	Ozzie Smith	−9	139	130
1985	Ozzie Smith	15	116	131
1986	Ozzie Smith	27	72	99
1987	Ozzie Smith	59	114	173
1988	Ozzie Smith	22	85	107
1989	Ozzie Smith	25	47	72
1990	Barry Larkin	40	64	104
1991	Barry Larkin	76	68	144
1992	Ozzie Smith	1	120	121

Year	Second Baseman	Bat	Field	Total
1993	Jay Bell	21	144	165
1994	Jay Bell	18	61	79
1995	Barry Larkin	75	33	108
1996	Barry Larkin	109	16	125
1997	Walt Weiss	−29	86	57
1998	Barry Larkin	72	9	81
1999	Neifi Perez	3	108	111
2000	Neifi Perez	−9	117	108
2001	Rich Aurelia	95	46	141
2002	Jose Hernandez	33	46	79
2003	Edgar Renteria	81	−18	63
2004	Jack Wilson	29	47	76
2005	Rafael Furcal	50	83	133
2006	Rafael Furcal	61	40	101

American Association. In its 10 seasons, the American Association was led by 10 different second basemen. The best single season was turned in by Sadie Houck with 135 points in 1884.

AMERICAN ASSOCIATION LEADING SHORTSTOPS, 1882–91

Year	Shortstop	Bat	Field	Points
1882	Chick Fulmer	29	48	77
1883	John Richmond	27	22	119
1884	Sadie Houck	56	79	135
1885	Candy Nelson	52	17	69
1886	Pop Smith	−47	116	69
1887	Germany Smith	−45	123	78
1888	Frank Fennelly	−32	31	−1
1889	Ollie Beard	−46	42	−4
1890	Phil Tomney	−22	79	57
1891	Paul Radford	28	64	92

Players' League. The outstanding shortstop in the Players' League was the remarkable John Montgomery "Monte" Ward, who was also at various times a successful pitcher, second baseman, outfielder, manager, and club executive.

PLAYERS' LEAGUE—LEADING SHORTSTOP, 1890

Year	Shortstop	Bat	Field	Points
1890	Monte Ward	79	50	129

American League. In its early years the American League had no shortstop who could rival the NL's Honus Wagner. Donie Bush was the league leader in five times and Ray Chapman led four times. Chapman's 167 Faber System points in 1917 was a league record. After Chapman was fatally struck by a pitch from fellow Kentuckian Carl Mays, the Cleveland Indians brought up young Joe Sewell from New Orleans as a replacement. Sewell helped lead the Indians to the 1920 pennant and for six consecutive years was the league's best shortstop. In the 1930s Joe Cronin was the leader seven times and raised the record for single season points to 188. In the war year of 1944 Lou Boudreau became the first American League shortstop to top the 200 mark with 221 points. The former Illinois basketball star led the league five times. Luis Aparicio led seven times between 1958 and 1970. Then came Cal Ripken, Jr. The Baltimore star led the league nine times and twice topped the 200 mark, with 217 points in 1984 and a record 228 points in 1991. More recently Alex Rodriguez led the league six times before the New York Yankees tried to convert him into a third baseman.

AMERICAN LEAGUE LEADING SHORTSTOPS, 1901–2006

Year	Second Baseman	Bat	Field	Points
1901	Kid Elberfield	28	85	113
1902	George Davis	53	43	96
1903	Fred Parent	34	48	82
1904	Bobby Wallace	28	68	96
1905	George Davis	68	85	153
1906	Terry Turner	46	114	160
1907	Charley O'Leary	42	31	73
1908	Bobby Wallace	11	90	101
1909	Donie Bush	94	13	107
1910	Donie Bush	41	63	104
1911	Lee Tannehill	−72	107	35
1912	Donie Bush	19	76	95
1913	Donie Bush	15	20	35
1914	Donie Bush	38	68	106
1915	Ray Chapman	32	31	63
1916	Doc Lavan	75	84	159
1917	Ray Chapman	82	85	167
1918	Ray Chapman	50	32	82
1919	Roger Peckinpaugh	48	23	71
1920	Ray Chapman	41	60	101
1921	Everett Scott	−82	165	83
1922	Chick Galloway	12	11	23
1923	Joe Sewell	103	−24	79
1924	Joe Sewell	37	43	80
1925	Joe Sewell	29	103	132
1926	Joe Sewell	34	61	95
1927	Joe Sewell	22	80	102
1928	Joe Sewell	21	110	131
1929	Red Kress	27	45	72
1930	Joe Cronin	85	103	188
1931	Joe Cronin	64	24	88
1932	Joe Cronin	57	67	124
1933	Joe Cronin	54	69	123
1934	Joe Cronin	−7	44	37
1935	Luke Appling	42	46	88
1936	Luke Appling	107	27	134
1937	Lyn Lary	20	25	45
1938	Joe Cronin	49	34	83
1939	Joe Cronin	61	20	81
1940	Lou Boudreau	26	53	79
1941	Cecil Travis	86	55	141
1942	Johnny Pesky	75	28	103
1943	Lou Boudreau	34	95	129
1944	Lou Boudreau	73	148	221

Year	Second Baseman	Bat	Field	Points
1945	Eddie Lake	64	32	96
1946	Johnny Pesky	96	49	145
1947	Lou Boudreau	33	80	113
1948	Lou Boudreau	129	29	158
1949	Eddie Joost	92	52	144
1950	Phil Rizzuto	82	80	162
1951	Eddie Joost	70	59	129
1952	Phil Rizzuto	4	32	36
1953	Harvey Kuenn	37	25	62
1954	Chico Carrasquel	43	84	127
1955	Chico Carrasquel	−4	22	18
1956	Harvey Kuenn	54	−8	46
1957	Gil McDougald	42	43	85
1958	Luis Aparicio	−9	60	51
1959	Luis Aparicio	11	85	96
1960	Luis Aparicio	7	144	151
1961	Luis Aparicio	−12	33	21
1962	Tom Tresh	47	10	57
1963	Wayne Causey	27	50	67
1964	Ron Hansen	37	69	106
1965	Jim Fregosi	19	65	84
1966	Luis Aparicio	41	57	98
1967	Jim Fregosi	57	20	77
1968	Luis Aparicio	0	104	104
1969	Rico Petrocelli	115	48	163
1970	Luis Aparicio	57	55	112
1971	Leo Cardenas	13	47	60
1972	Bert Campaneris	0	67	67
1973	Frank Duffy	−23	69	46
1974	Mark Belanger	−40	84	44
1975	Toby Harrah	90	22	112
1976	Mark Belanger	5	89	94
1977	Mark Belanger	14	67	81
1978	Roy Smalley	42	50	92
1979	Roy Smalley	50	96	146
1980	Rick Burleson	29	113	142
1981	Rick Burleson	29	79	108
1982	Robin Yount	128	32	160
1983	Cal Ripken, Jr.	111	87	198
1984	Cal Ripken, Jr.	98	119	217
1985	Cal Ripken, Jr.	69	54	123
1986	Cal Ripken, Jr.	67	55	122
1987	Alan Trammell	116	3	119
1988	Cal Ripken, Jr.	52	19	71
1989	Cal Ripken, Jr.	29	72	101
1990	Tony Fernandez	30	99	129
1991	Cal Ripken, Jr.	120	108	228
1992	Omar Vizquel	−9	72	63
1993	Tony Fernandez	−10	64	54
1994	Cal Ripken, Jr.	42	10	52

Year	Second Baseman	Bat	Field	Points
1995	John Valentin	78	12	90
1996	Alex Rodriguez	140	6	146
1997	Jay Bell	28	47	75
1998	Derek Jeter	97	4	101
1999	Alex Rodriguez	93	21	114
2000	Alex Rodriguez	124	51	175
2001	Alex Rodriguez	146	24	170
2002	Alex Rodriguez	136	39	175
2003	Alex Rodriguez	117	57	174
2004	Miguel Tejada	114	34	148
2005	Derek Jeter	99	50	149
2006	Michael Young	36	65	101

Federal League. Neither of the two men who led Federal League shortstops had distinguished major league careers.

FEDERAL LEAGUE LEADING SHORTSTOPS, 1914–15

Year	Shortstop	Bat	Field	Total
1914	Baldy Loudon	53	−34	19
1915	Jimmy Esmond	17	45	62

Third Base

National League. In the first major league season Cap Anson, better known as a first baseman, was the top third sacker in the NL with 142 points. After Ned Williamson had led for four consecutive years, Ezra Sutton set a new record with 168 points. In 1899 this record was obliterated by John McGraw, who amassed 231 points—a mark that still stands as the best in National League annals. In some years in the early part of the 20th century (1901 and 1905, for example), no National League third sacker exceeded the league mean in both hitting and fielding, so the league leader had an exceptional low point total. From 1918 to 1924 Heinie Groh had eight league-leading seasons. Eddie Mathews went him one better with nine years on top, and Mike Schmidt outdid them all with ten seasons as the best hot corner denizen in the senior circuit. In 2004 Adrian Beltre compiled 194 points, the best single season in the league in over 100 years. This was quite an anomaly. As of this writing 2004 was Beltre's only league-leading season.

NATIONAL LEAGUE LEADING THIRD BASEMEN, 1876–2006

Year	Third Baseman	Bat	Field	Total
1876	Cap Anson	112	25	142
1877	Cap Anson	50	12	62
1878	Frank Hankinson	10	10	20
1879	Ned Williamson	64	24	88
1880	Ned Williamson	28	32	60
1881	Ned Williamson	17	52	69
1882	Ned Williamson	45	15	60
1883	Joe Farrell	9	63	72
1884	Ezra Sutton	125	43	168
1885	Ezra Sutton	54	0	54
1886	Tom Burns	20	32	52

Year	Third Baseman	Bat	Field	Total
1887	Jack Denny	22	37	59
1888	Billy Nash	47	55	102
1889	Jack Denny	22	37	59
1890	George Pinckney	88	40	128
1891	Arlie Latham	60	8	68
1892	Billy Nash	9	37	46
1893	Billy Nash	47	29	76
1894	Lave Cross	64	60	124
1895	John McGraw	85	3	88
1896	Bill Everett	40	0	40
1897	Jimmy Collins	71	46	117
1898	Jimmy Collins	83	44	127
1899	John McGraw	191	40	231
1900	John McGraw	155	−8	147
1901	Tommy Leach	0	2	2
1902	Tommy Leach	45	6	51
1903	Harry Steinfeldt	19	25	44
1904	Art Devlin	45	−4	41
	Tommy Leach	18	23	41 tie
1905	Art Devlin	−2	3	1
1906	Art Devlin	67	46	113
1907	Harry Steinfeldt	29	32	61
1908	Tommy Leach	49	2	51
1909	Eddie Grant	14	45	59
1910	Bobby Byrne	58	−7	51
1911	Hans Lobert	40	3	43
1912	Heinie Zimmerman	109	−26	83
1913	Hans Lobert	44	39	83
1914	Red Smith	24	40	64
1915	Heinie Groh	39	44	83
1916	Heinie Groh	54	45	99
1917	Heinie Groh	86	58	144
1918	Heinie Groh	96	25	121
1919	Heinie Groh	73	23	96
1920	Heinie Groh	34	21	55
1921	Tony Boeckel	38	−13	25
1922	Babe Pinelli	−10	20	10
1923	Heinie Groh	6	55	61
1924	Heinie Groh	−3	34	31
1925	Pie Traynor	45	100	145
1926	Pie Traynor	36	9	45
1927	Pie Traynor	61	39	100
1928	Freddie Lindstrom	76	16	92
1929	Pinky Whitney	32	31	63
1930	Freddie Lindstrom	103	7	110
1931	Sparky Adams	2	19	21
1932	Pinky Whitney	52	41	93
1933	Pepper Martin	100	−22	78
1934	Pinky Whitney	−35	43	8
1935	Stan Hack	39	19	58

Year	Third Baseman	Bat	Field	Total
1936	Stan Hack	51	−26	25
1937	Pinky Whitney	63	28	91
1938	Mel Ott	143	10	153
1939	Stan Hack	52	24	76
1940	Stan Hack	79	18	97
1941	Stan Hack	102	−6	96
1942	Stan Hack	82	28	110
1943	Bob Elliott	80	−15	65
1944	Bob Elliott	73	−12	62
1945	Stan Hack	86	48	134
1946	Whitey Kurowski	66	21	87
1947	Bob Elliott	93	17	110
1948	Sid Gordon	95	6	101
1949	Bob Elliott	33	18	51
1950	Bob Elliott	60	−7	53
1951	Willie Jones	19	11	30
1952	Bobby Adams	15	12	27
1953	Eddie Mathews	131	−20	111
1954	Eddie Mathews	88	12	100
1955	Eddie Mathews	97	10	107
1956	Willie Jones	53	46	99
1957	Eddie Mathews	95	2	97
1958	Ken Boyer	69	39	108
1959	Eddie Mathews	121	21	142
1960	Eddie Mathews	122	−11	111
1961	Eddie Mathews	98	14	112
1962	Eddie Mathews	65	26	91
1963	Eddie Mathews	77	48	125
1964	Ron Santo	128	39	167
1965	Ron Santo	100	40	140
1966	Ron Santo	106	35	141
1967	Ron Santo	119	52	171
1968	Ron Santo	70	34	104
1969	Ron Santo	115	8	123
1970	Tony Perez	136	−47	89
1971	Joe Torre	190	−3	187
1972	Ron Santo	70	−4	66
1973	Darrell Evans	116	21	137
1974	Mike Schmidt	122	26	148
1975	Pete Rose	98	4	102
1976	Pete Rose	133	7	140
1977	Mike Schmidt	95	39	134
1978	Ron Cey	62	18	80
1979	Mike Schmidt	102	15	117
1980	Mike Schmidt	133	14	147
1981	Mike Schmidt	146	22	168
1982	Mike Schmidt	105	14	119
1983	Mike Schmidt	94	30	124
1984	Mike Schmidt	95	23	118
1985	Tim Wallach	11	65	76

Year	Third Baseman	Bat	Field	Total
1986	Mike Schmidt	128	42	170
1987	Mike Schmidt	96	39	133
1988	Tim Wallach	77	−2	75
1989	Terry Pendleton	22	71	93
1990	Matt Williams	72	21	93
1991	Terry Pendleton	85	24	109
1992	Gary Sheffield	121	12	133
1993	Matt Williams	62	44	106
1994	Matt Williams	59	13	62
1995	Vinny Castilla	55	15	70
1996	Ken Caminiti	142	16	158
1997	Vinny Castilla	75	20	95
1998	Vinny Castilla	139	12	151
1999	Matt Williams	90	49	139
2000	Jeff Cirillo	74	13	87
2001	Scott Rolen	63	38	101
2002	Scott Rolen	64	25	89
2003	Scott Rolen	72	19	91
2004	Adrian Beltre	144	37	191
2005	David Wright	84	14	98
2006	Scott Rolen	48	37	85

American Association. Hick Carpenter and Denny Lyons each led American Association third basemen three times, with Carpenter's 131 points in 1882 being the circuit's single season best.

AMERICAN ASSOCIATION—LEADING THIRD BASEMEN

Year	Third Baseman	Bat	Field	Total
1882	Hick Carpenter	113	18	131
1883	Hick Carpenter	74	12	86
1884	Dude Esterbrook	8	1	9
1885	Hick Carpenter	26	−27	−1
1886	Arlie Latham	112	−29	53
1887	Denny Lyons	101	−1	100
1888	George Pinckney	74	−2	72
1889	Denny Lyons	110	−6	104
1890	Jimmy Knowles	−1	−1	−2
1891	Denny Lyons	116	−29	87

Players' League. Billy Nash was the Players' League's best third baseman. On three different occasions he also led the National League third sackers.

PLAYERS' LEAGUE—LEADING THIRD BASEMAN

Year	Third Baseman	Bat	Field	Total
1890	Billy Nash	15	28	43

American League. During its first quarter century as a major league, Frank "Home Run" Baker was the American League's premier third baseman. He led the circuit in Faber System points seven times, and his mark of 165 points compiled in 1912 remained a league record for 42 years until broken by Al Rosen with 174 points in 1954. This mark, in turn, fell to George Brett with 196 points in 1980. In 1988 Wade Boggs became the first, and so far the only, third baseman to collect more than 200 points, exceeding that total by a margin of two points. Slick fielding Brooks Robinson was best at the hot corner nine times, and Wade Boggs was the league's best third baseman ten times.

AMERICAN LEAGUE—LEADING THIRD BASEMEN

Year	Third Baseman	Bat	Field	Total
1901	Jimmy Collins	65	11	76
1902	Lave Cross	65	29	94
1903	Jimmy Collins	27	33	60
1904	Bill Bradley	73	38	111
1905	Bill Bradley	11	46	57
1906	Lave Cross	−17	61	47
1907	Bill Coughlin	2	15	17
1908	Hobe Ferris	16	50	66
1909	Harry Lord	66	24	90
1910	Frank Baker	26	−7	19
1911	Frank Baker	73	12	85
1912	Frank Baker	122	43	165
1913	Frank Baker	122	17	139
1914	Frank Baker	84	26	110
1915	Oscar Vitt	47	56	103
1916	Oscar Vitt	20	70	90
1917	Frank Baker	35	25	60
1918	Frank Baker	39	25	64
1919	Buck Weaver	61	14	75
1920	Larry Gardner	44	22	66
1921	Larry Gardner	47	−4	43
1922	Joe Dugan	−25	−4	−29
1923	Willie Kamm	8	33	41
1924	Joe Dugan	6	6	12
1925	Willie Kamm	−15	20	5
1926	Willie Kamm	9	46	55
1927	Willie Kamm	−24	41	17
1928	Willie Kamm	16	30	46
1929	Joe Sewell	15	39	54
1930	Marty McManus	22	19	41
1931	Joe Sewell	32	−1	31
1932	Jimmie Dykes	−12	19	7
1933	Willie Kamm	−2	46	44
1934	Billy Werber	66	22	88
1935	Cecil Travis	7	39	46
1936	Harlond Clift	70	8	78
1937	Harlond Clift	75	30	105
1938	Harlond Clift	67	41	108
1939	Red Rolfe	97	15	112
1940	Harlond Clift	28	41	69
1941	Ken Keltner	−6	56	50

Year	Third Baseman	Bat	Field	Total
1942	Harlond Clift	59	19	78
1943	Billy Johnson	37	19	56
1944	Ken Keltner	42	29	71
1945	George Kell	−25	62	37
1946	George Kell	32	25	57
1947	George Kell	64	6	70
1948	Ken Keltner	88	8	96
1949	George Kell	78	25	103
1950	Johnny Pesky	60	35	95
1951	Eddie Yost	79	−1	78
1952	Al Rosen	90	−19	71
1953	Al Rosen	161	13	174
1954	Al Rosen	101	10	111
1955	Ray Boone	58	−6	52
1956	Ray Boone	48	8	56
1957	Frank Malzone	42	24	66
1958	Frank Malzone	41	16	57
1959	Eddie Yost	113	14	127
1960	Brooks Robinson	32	58	90
1961	Brooks Robinson	6	8	14
1962	Brooks Robinson	42	26	68
1963	Frank Malzone	29	18	47
1964	Brooks Robinson	117	26	143
1965	Brooks Robinson	49	7	56
1966	Brooks Robinson	69	42	111
1967	Brooks Robinson	62	59	121
1968	Brooks Robinson	19	33	52
1969	Sal Bando	112	−4	108
1970	Tommy Harper	95	−15	80
1971	Graig Nettles	47	46	93
1972	Brooks Robinson	−4	38	34
1973	Buddy Bell	24	41	65
1974	Don Money	52	44	96
1975	Eric Soderholm	31	30	61
1976	Graig Nettles	50	42	92
1977	George Brett	85	21	104
1978	Sal Bando	60	46	106
	Graig Nettles	55	51	106 tie
1979	George Brett	113	11	124
1980	George Brett	187	9	196
1981	Buddy Bell	43	35	78
1982	Doug DeCinces	77	41	118
1983	Wade Boggs	126	7	133
1984	Wade Boggs	110	40	150
1985	George Brett	140	39	179
1986	Wade Boggs	145	1	146
1987	Wade Boggs	150	15	165
1988	Wade Boggs	177	25	202
1989	Wade Boggs	124	29	153
1990	Kelly Gruber	82	28	110

Year	Third Baseman	Bat	Field	Total
1991	Wade Boggs	97	−7	90
1992	Edgar Martinez	117	−9	108
1993	Wade Boggs	32	50	82
1994	Wade Boggs	74	21	95
1995	Wade Boggs	44	35	79
1996	Jim Thome	118	−20	98
1997	Travis Fryman	10	56	66
1998	Travis Fryman	45	25	70
1999	Joe Randa	27	36	63
2000	Troy Glaus	143	−10	133
2001	Eric Chavez	59	38	97
2002	Eric Chavez	45	27	72
2003	Eric Chavez	45	49	94
2004	Manny Mora	112	−6	106
2005	Alex Rodriguez	153	4	157
2006	Mike Lowell	−4	50	46

Federal League. Deacon Bill McKechnie is best remembered today as a pennant winning manager of the Pirates, Cardinals, and Reds, but he was also the best third baseman in the short life of the Federal League.

FEDERAL LEAGUE LEADING THIRD BASEMEN, 1914–15

Year	Third Baseman	Bat	Field	Total
1914	Bill McKechnie	67	21	88
1915	George Perring	1	27	28

Catcher

National League. In its early years several catchers vied for the title of the best backstop in the National League. Charlie Bennett won the honors five times, while Buck Ewing came out on top four times. Ewing posted the most points during the pioneer era with 212 points in 1888. This mark was bested by George Gibson with 225 points in 1909. Roy Campanella amassed a very impressive 275 points in 1953, a mark that has stood for more than half a century. Gabby Hartnett was the league's best catcher on eight occasions, as was Johnny Bench. Gary Carter topped them both with nine league-leading seasons. In addition to Ewing, Gibson, and Campanellas, 200 point seasons have been recorded by Hartnett, Bench, and oldtimer Johnny Kling.

NATIONAL LEAGUE LEADING CATCHERS

Year	Catcher	Bat	Field	Bonus	Total
1876	John Clapp	42	46	62	150
1877	Pop Snyder	−38	40	25	27
1878	Deacon White	59	8	28	95
1879	Pop Snyder	3	70	57	130
1880	Silver Flint	−106	67	100	61
1881	Charlie Bennett	64	81	0	145
1882	Charlie Bennett	45	28	2	75
1883	Buck Ewing	70	50	0	120
1884	Jack Rowe	76	9	25	110

Year	Catcher	Bat	Field	Bonus	Total
1885	Buck Ewing	50	31	82	163
1886	Charlie Bennett	−35	36	71	72
1887	Tom Daly	−120	102	28	10
1888	Buck Ewing	68	89	55	212
1889	Buck Ewing	44	68	77	189
1890	Jack Clements	41	5	0	46
	Charlie Bennett	−36	52	30	46 tie
1891	Charlie Bennett	−68	60	49	41
1892	Jack Clements	−4	32	38	66
1893	Farmer Vaughn	24	59	3	86
1894	Wilbert Robinson	14	9	106	129
1895	Jack Clements	63	31	42	136
1896	Wilbert Robinson	−25	48	54	77
1897	Heinie Peitz	−77	93	23	39
1898	Marty Bergen	−36	4	102	70
1899	Ed McFarland	9	42	60	111
1900	Ed McFarland	−39	36	20	17
1901	Ed McFarland	−52	5	34	−13
1902	Johnny Kling	2	36	0	34
1903	Johnny Kling	−8	0	62	70
1904	Frank Bowerman	−63	34	76	47
1905	Roger Bresnahan	42	19	81	142
1906	Johnny Kling	24	52	126	202
1907	Johnny Kling	22	46	100	168
1908	Roger Bresnahan	72	15	95	192
1909	George Gibson	−10	67	168	225
1910	Chief Meyers	23	−8	53	68
1911	Chief Meyers	34	−3	94	125
1912	Chief Meyers	66	−37	111	140
1913	Chief Meyers	12	−25	95	82
1914	Roger Bresnahan	4	21	3	28
1915	Frank Snyder	6	41	0	47
1916	Hank Gowdy	−36	23	50	37
1917	Bill Killefer	−30	44	43	47
1918	Bill Killefer	−67	15	79	27
1919	Ivy Wingo	−41	−19	70	10
1920	Otto Miller	−50	28	47	25
1921	Verne Clemons	−6	52	37	83
1922	Bob O'Farrell	29	38	12	79
1923	Bubbles Hargrave	41	22	50	113
1924	Frank Snyder	−17	2	60	45
1925	Earl Smith	−8	−3	58	47
1926	Bubbles Hargrave	45	34	30	109
1927	Gabby Hartnett	12	−1	35	46
1928	Gabby Hartnett	13	54	54	121
1929	Jimmie Wilson	−16	11	9	4
1930	Gabby Hartnett	82	50	57	189
1931	Jimmie Wilson	−49	29	86	66
1932	Spud Davis	50	−3	4	51
1933	Gabby Hartnett	23	23	41	87

Year	Catcher	Bat	Field	Bonus	Total
1934	Gabby Hartnett	38	72	45	155
1935	Gabby Hartnett	80	48	82	210
1936	Gabby Hartnett	2	47	37	86
1937	Gabby Hartnett	91	54	53	198
1938	Ernie Lombardi	95	6	28	130
1939	Ernie Lombardi	21	12	78	111
1940	Ernie Lombardi	52	20	78	150
1941	Ernie Lombardi	−19	2	41	24
1942	Mickey Owen	−19	22	117	120
1943	Walker Cooper	50	−28	102	124
1944	Walker Cooper	34	3	89	126
1945	Ernie Lombardi	39	0	6	45
1946	Clyde McCullough	−20	16	16	12
1947	Bruce Edwards	9	4	71	84
1948	Bob Scheffing	−11	35	0	24
1949	Roy Campanella	−8	11	83	86
1950	Roy Campanella	26	22	49	97
1951	Roy Campanella	94	11	83	188
1952	Roy Campanella	44	42	78	164
1953	Roy Campanella	131	16	128	275
1954	Del Crandall	−55	32	54	31
1955	Roy Campanella	92	26	88	206
1956	Ed Bailey	63	−2	48	109
1957	Del Crandall	−44	4	60	20
1958	Del Crandall	2	22	61	85
1959	Del Crandall	−11	22	34	45
1960	Del Crandall	36	2	37	75
1961	Johnny Roseboro	−16	31	49	64
1962	Tom Haller	20	2	57	79
1963	Johnny Roseboro	−9	18	75	84
1964	Joe Torre	100	21	21	142
1965	Joe Torre	78	−1	16	93
1966	Joe Torre	106	−6	15	115
1967	Tim McCarver	49	36	41	126
1968	Johnny Bench	36	22	9	77
1969	Johnny Bench	65	0	36	101
1970	Johnny Bench	120	1	91	212
1971	Manny Sanguillen	68	31	67	166
1972	Johnny Bench	122	10	76	208
1973	Johnny Bench	47	28	85	160
1974	Johnny Bench	115	21	72	208
1975	Johnny Bench	77	3	101	181
1976	Johnny Bench	10	30	83	123
1977	Bob Boone	−1	7	81	87
1978	Ted Simmons	64	23	0	87
1979	Gary Carter	23	20	65	108
1980	Gary Carter	56	50	42	148
1981	Gary Carter	14	33	28	75
1982	Gary Carter	84	36	24	144
1983	Gary Carter	16	50	4	70

Year	Catcher	Bat	Field	Bonus	Total
1984	Gary Carter	86	11	0	97
1985	Gary Carter	78	27	75	180
1986	Gary Carter	57	23	102	182
1987	Gary Carter	−27	13	46	32
1988	Mike Sciosia	−45	14	52	21
1989	Craig Biggio	11	13	20	44
1990	Mike Sciosia	4	16	21	41
1991	Craig Biggio	39	14	0	53
1992	Darren Daulton	94	−19	0	75
1993	Darren Daulton	60	6	73	139
1994	Mike Piazza	82	−26	5	61
1995	Mike Piazza	108	3	23	134
1996	Mike Piazza	125	19	40	184
1997	Mike Piazza	153	−1	30	182
1998	Javier Lopez	54	22	99	175
1999	Mike Piazza	86	−7	65	144
2000	Mike Piazza	101	−15	50	166
2001	Paul Lo Duca	60	2	15	77
2002	Paul Lo Duca	3	16	47	66
2003	Javier Lopez	111	0	74	185
2004	Paul Lo Duca	19	25	28	72
2005	Brad Ausmus	−24	30	33	39
2006	Paul Lo Duca	20	−7	58	71

American Association. In the Association's inaugural season Pop Snyder set a league record for catchers with 176 Faber System points. Jocko Milligan, Doc Bushong, and Jack O'Connor each led the circuit twice, but none of them compiled a single season mark that matched Snyder's feat.

AMERICAN ASSOCIATION LEADING CATCHERS

Year	Catcher	Bat	Field	Bonus	Total
1882	Pop Snyder	34	39	66	176
1883	Bill Holbert	−65	89	21	98
1884	Jocko Milligan	0	56	24	110
1885	Doc Bushong	−27	8	87	71
1886	Doc Bushong	−67	98	90	129
1887	Sam Trott	−94	71	23	0
1888	Jack Boyle	−65	20	63	20
1889	Jack O'Connor	−39	37	0	−2
1890	Jack O'Connor	39	42	48	135
1891	Jocko Milligan	67	22	11	102

Players' League. Buck Ewing, who led the National League four times, was the Players' League's best catcher.

PLAYERS' LEAGUE LEADING CATCHER

Year	Catcher	Bat	Field	Bonus	Total
1890	Buck Ewing	59	78	26	176

American League. No catcher dominated the American League in its early years. Ossee Schreck led the backstops four times between 1903 and 1907 and Ray Schalk led an equal number of times from 1915 to 1919, but it was not until Mickey Cochrane took charge in the 1920s that one man stood out above all others. Black Mike led eight times, and was followed by Bill Dickey who was tops seven times. Schreck's early mark of 119 points set in 1907 was eclipsed by Schalk with 120 in 1915. By 1930 Cochrane had raised the standard to 225 points. With 223 points in 1939 Dickey fell only one point short of Cochrane's mark, which finally fell to Yogi Berra, who compiled 241 points in 1954. Berra also set the record for the most years leading the league at 11, all of them consecutively. Cochrane amassed over 200 points on three occasions, Dickey did it twice, and Berra and Bill Freehan once apiece.

American League Leading Catchers

Year	Catcher	Bat	Field	Bonus	Total
1901	Billy Maloney	−51	41	0	−19
1902	Harry Bemis	−19	24	3	8
1903	Ossee Schreck	−66	52	22	9
1904	Joe Sugden	−18	58	0	40
1905	Ossee Schreck	−26	23	68	65
1906	Ossee Schreck	−19	19	17	17
1907	Ossee Schreck	−24	94	49	119
1908	Nig Clarke	−2	−23	38	13
1909	Bill Carrigan	8	14	32	54
1910	Gabby Street	−111	59	0	−52
1911	Ira Thomas	−63	19	87	43
1912	Bill Carrigan	−49	34	83	68
1913	Steve O'Neill	−41	28	26	13
1914	Wally Schang	14	−30	76	60
1915	Ray Schalk	−7	57	70	120
1916	Ray Schalk	−65	62	48	45
1917	Ray Schalk	−23	25	104	106
1918	Steve O'Neill	−36	16	43	23
1919	Ray Schalk	−7	13	83	89
1920	Steve O'Neill	16	−2	100	114
1921	Wally Schang	26	−34	93	85
1922	Hank Severeid	−21	21	69	69
1923	Muddy Ruel	4	50	0	54
1924	Johnny Bassler	30	2	36	68
1925	Muddy Ruel	−26	16	86	76
1926	Muddy Ruel	6	37	24	67
1927	Mickey Cochrane	48	33	56	137
1928	Mickey Cochrane	27	−30	92	89
1929	Mickey Cochrane	66	13	130	209
1930	Mickey Cochrane	69	50	106	225
1931	Mickey Cochrane	65	10	120	195
1932	Mickey Cochrane	64	62	76	202
1933	Bill Dickey	38	24	57	119
1934	Mickey Cochrane	38	29	97	164
1935	Mickey Cochrane	38	15	64	117
1936	Bill Dickey	66	2	80	148
1937	Bill Dickey	105	31	111	219

Year	Catcher	Bat	Field	Bonus	Total
1938	Bill Dickey	62	15	95	172
1939	Bill Dickey	59	36	128	223
1940	Rollie Hemsley	−82	43	46	7
1941	Bill Dickey	−7	26	81	100
1942	Bill Dickey	−52	−19	68	−3
1943	Buddy Rosar	−9	18	21	30
1944	Frankie Hayes	−15	10	0	−5
1945	Rick Ferrell	−19	20	54	55
1946	Aaron Robinson	33	0	31	64
1947	Buddy Rosar	−55	47	3	−5
1948	Jim Hegan	−52	20	90	58
1949	Yogi Berra	6	35	71	112
1950	Yogi Berra	83	0	102	185
1951	Yogi Berra	36	8	126	170
1952	Yogi Berra	61	27	41	129
1953	Yogi Berra	73	−1	103	175
1954	Yogi Berra	107	8	126	241
1955	Yogi Berra	53	−14	89	126
1956	Yogi Berra	60	0	88	148
1957	Yogi Berra	13	17	83	113
1958	Yogi Berra	25	40	41	106
1959	Yogi Berra	29	43	7	79
1960	Sherman Lollar	−40	40	21	21
1961	Elston Howard	65	20	96	181
1962	Elston Howard	20	3	68	91
1963	Earl Battey	71	24	78	143
1964	Elston Howard	69	18	81	168
1965	Earl Battey	32	−10	83	105
1966	Andy Etchebarren	−38	13	64	39
1967	Bill Freehan	83	7	46	136
1968	Bill Freehan	82	30	94	206
1969	Ellie Hendricks	−35	35	76	76
1970	Thurman Munson	32	15	16	63
	Bill Freehan	34	29	0	63 tie
1971	Bill Freehan	35	18	45	98
1972	Carlton Fisk	76	6	31	113
1973	Thurman Munson	59	−4	0	55
1974	Ellie Rodriguez	30	48	0	78
1975	Gene Tenace	71	6	66	143
1976	Thurman Munson	76	6	67	149
1977	Thurman Munson	64	5	80	149
1978	Carlton Fisk	64	−11	82	135
1979	Brian Downing	90	−5	28	113
1980	Rick Cerone	21	20	110	151
1981	Jim Sundberg	14	29	21	64
1982	Ted Simmons	24	35	52	111
1983	Lance Parrish	51	55	45	151
1984	Lance Parrish	22	32	90	144
1985	Lance Parrish	37	24	13	74
1986	Lance Parrish	8	35	16	59

Year	Catcher	Bat	Field	Bonus	Total
1987	Matt Nokes	42	5	57	104
1988	Terry Steinbach	−17	2	60	45
1989	Mickey Tettleton	40	22	14	76
1990	Carlton Fisk	47	27	46	120
1991	Mickey Tettleton	63	−18	12	57
1992	Mickey Tettleton	49	1	0	50
1993	Chris Hoiles	81	16	16	113
1994	Mike Stanley	7	−1	43	49
1995	Dan Wilson	−39	36	27	24
1996	Ivan Rodriguez	33	13	40	86
1997	Chris Hoiles	−19	26	46	53
1998	Jorge Posada	−14	17	101	104
	Ivan Rodriguez	48	25	31	104 tie
1999	Ivan Rodiguez	76	15	61	152
2000	Jorge Posada	54	9	28	91
2001	Jorge Posada	37	17	62	116
2002	Jorge Posada	27	−5	97	119
2003	Jorge Posada	73	52	84	189
2004	Jorge Posada	32	9	82	105
	Jason Varitek	28	21	56	105 tie
2005	Victor Martinez	46	39	10	95
2006	Joe Mauer	71	19	56	146

Federal League. Art Wilson was the Federal League's best catcher, leading the league in Faber System points during both years of the circuit's existence.

FEDERAL LEAGUE LEADING CATCHERS, 1914–15

Year	Catcher	Bat	Field	Bonus	Total
1914	Art Wilson	53	−4	43	92
1915	Art Wilson	58	−5	29	82

Right Field

National League. In 1878 Orator Shaffer led National League right fielders with 111 Faber System points. In 1884 King Kelly bettered that mark with 149 points. Three years later Big Sam Thompson upped the record to 179 points, a standard that was unmatched for over forty years until Chuck Klein set a new record with 230 points in 1930. More than three-quarters of a century later Klein's record still stands. In 2001 Sammy Sosa became the only other National League right fielder to tally 200 points. In the 1880s and 1890s Thompson led the league seven times, a number that was matched by Wee Willie Keeler around the turn of the century. In the 1950s and 1960s Hank Aaron was the league's best right fielder nine times.

NATIONAL LEAGUE LEADING RIGHT FIELDERS

Year	Catcher	Bat	Field	Points
1876	Dick Higham	68	5	73
1877	John Cassidy	95	−51	44
1878	Orator Shaffer	88	23	111
1879	Orator Shaffer	41	30	71

Year	Catcher	Bat	Field	Points
1880	Orator Shaffer	46	46	92
1881	King Kelly	96	−13	83
1882	Jake Evans	−78	125	47
1883	Orator Shaffer	30	36	76
1884	King Kelly	172	−23	149
1885	Mike Dorgan	42	−8	34
1886	Sam Thompson	65	−7	58
1887	Sam Thompson	164	15	179
1888	Mike Tiernan	64	28	92
1889	Mike Tiernan	142	−33	109
1890	Sam Thompson	68	8	76
1891	Sam Thompson	59	41	100
1892	Sam Thompson	51	18	69
1893	Sam Thompson	107	−21	86
1894	Willie Keeler	130	6	136
1895	Sam Thompson	121	46	167
1896	Willie Keeler	130	33	163
1897	Willie Keeler	149	12	161
1898	Willie Keeler	127	0	127
1899	Willie Keeler	122	29	151
1900	Honus Wagner	95	−1	94
1901	Willie Keeler	96	26	122
1902	Willie Keeler	71	11	82
1903	Patsy Donovan	21	2	23
1904	Spike Shannon	37	33	70
1905	John Titus	81	14	95
1906	Harry Lumley	77	−22	55
1907	Mike Mitchell	51	44	95
1908	Mike Donlin	115	12	127
1909	Mike Mitchell	79	−10	69
1910	Frank Schulte	51	−11	41
1911	Frank Schulte	81	−10	71
1912	Gavvy Cravath	3	31	34
1913	Gavvy Cravath	134	−24	110
1914	Gavvy Cravath	92	−14	78
1915	Gavvy Cravath	121	−8	113
1916	Dave Robertson	64	−14	50
1917	Casey Stengel	25	25	50
1918	Max Flack	27	21	48
1919	Max Flack	35	26	61
1920	Max Flack	49	−19	30
1921	Austin McHenry	85	−16	69
1922	Curt Walker	59	−9	50
1923	Ross Youngs	75	−8	67
1924	Ross Youngs	116	−17	99
1925	Kiki Cuyler	128	13	141
1926	Paul Waner	81	24	105
1927	Paul Waner	143	14	157
1928	Paul Waner	141	10	151
1929	Mel Ott	132	26	158

Year	Catcher	Bat	Field	Points
1930	Chuck Klein	173	57	230
1931	Paul Waner	44	45	89
1932	Chuck Klein	164	35	199
1933	Chuck Klein	161	26	187
1934	Paul Waner	129	1	130
1935	Mel Ott	111	23	134
1936	Mel Ott	152	21	173
1937	Frank Demeree	93	4	97
1938	Ival Goodman	77	6	83
1939	Ival Goodman	55	9	64
1940	Mel Ott	95	−3	92
1941	Dixie Walker	65	14	79
1942	Mel Ott	137	3	140
1943	Stan Musial	138	5	143
1944	Stan Musial	132	18	150
1945	Tommy Holmes	142	8	150
1946	Enos Slaughter	111	10	121
1947	Willard Marshall	66	9	75
1948	Enos Slaughter	80	−6	74
1949	Stan Musial	154	1	155
1950	Del Ennis	81	−22	59
1951	Carl Furillo	23	20	43
1952	Enos Slaughter	69	−1	68
1953	Carl Furillo	76	0	76
1954	Stan Musial	129	−12	117
1955	Wally Post	93	−6	87
1956	Hank Aaron	96	5	101
1957	Hank Aaron	136	4	140
1958	Hank Aaron	106	−6	100
1959	Hank Aaron	149	−15	134
1960	Hank Aaron	110	3	113
1961	Frank Robinson	134	14	148
1962	Frank Robinson	163	19	182
1963	Hank Aaron	168	−9	159
1964	Hank Aaron	116	22	138
1965	Hank Aaron	124	16	140
1966	Hank Aaron	109	21	130
1967	Roberto Clemente	145	13	158
1968	Pete Rose	112	32	144
1969	Pete Rose	150	22	172
1970	Pete Rose	94	20	114
1971	Bobby Bonds	102	17	119
1972	Jimmy Wynn	104	−1	103
1973	Ken Singleton	108	14	122
1974	Richie Zisk	98	12	110
1975	Rusty Staub	68	4	72
1976	Ken Griffey	115	−4	111
1977	Dave Parker	105	32	137
1978	Dave Parker	141	−16	125
1979	Dave Parker	95	−9	86

Year	Catcher	Bat	Field	Points
1980	George Hendrick	85	7	92
1981	Ken Griffey	54	49	103
1982	Pedro Guerrero	94	−1	93
1983	Jack Clark	35	4	39
1984	Tony Gwynn	96	20	116
1985	Dave Parker	121	−14	107
1986	Tony Gwynn	107	35	142
1987	Tony Gwynn	142	4	146
1988	Darryl Strawberry	87	−25	62
1989	Tony Gwynn	86	19	105
1990	Darryl Strawberry	83	1	84
1991	Bobby Bonilla	83	−1	82
1992	Larry Walker	73	20	93
1993	David Justice	80	−1	79
1994	Tony Gwynn	142	−3	139
1995	Larry Walker	86	14	100
1996	Gary Sheffield	106	−34	72
1997	Larry Walker	193	5	198
1998	Sammy Sosa	175	10	185
1999	Larry Walker	160	10	170
2000	Sammy Sosa	140	−23	117
2001	Sammy Sosa	202	2	200
2002	Larry Walker	122	20	142
2003	Gary Sheffield	151	−8	143
2004	J. D. Drew	134	28	142
2005	Brian Giles	90	3	93
2006	Bobby Abreu	117	11	128*

includes games in American League

American Association. William "Chicken" Wolf and Hugh Nichol each led the Association's right fielders three times. The 136 Faber System points garnered by Nichol in 1883 was the highest total in league annals.

AMERICAN ASSOCIATION LEADING RIGHT FIELDERS

Year	Right Fielder	Bat	Field	Total
1882	Chicken Wolf	38	34	72
1883	Hugh Nichol	76	60	136
1884	Hugh Nichol	21	89	100
1885	Pop Corkhill	−23	92	69
1886	Chicken Wolf	11	69	80
1887	Chicken Wolf	−18	35	17
1888	Hugh Nichol	35	22	57
1889	Oyster Burns	46	−5	41
1890	Tommy McCarthy	121	−23	98
1891	Hugh Duffy	114	−5	109

Players' League. Hugh Duffy was the short-lived circuit's best right fielder. Duffy also starred in the American Association and the National League. His .440 batting average compiled in 1894 is usually recognized as the highest ever recorded in the major leagues.

PLAYERS' LEAGUE LEADING RIGHT FIELDER

Year	Right Fielder	Bat	Field	Total
1890	Hugh Duffy	101	24	125

American League. Although he played most of his career in center field, Ty Cobb was three times the league's best right fielder and set a record with 171 Faber System points in 1909. Cobb's mark was broken two years later by Shoeless Joe Jackson, who tallied 178 points in 1911. Jackson led AL right fielders three times before moving to left field. In 1920 Babe Ruth set a record for right fielders with 210 points and raised the standard to 269 points in 1923. The Bambino led the circuit ten times and exceeded the 200 mark in half of those seasons. No other American League right fielder has come close to the 200 level, with Frank Robinson's 168 points in 1966 being the best mark attained since the retirement of the Sultan of Swat.

AMERICAN LEAGUE LEADING RIGHT FIELDERS

Year	Right Fielder	Bat	Field	Total
1901	Fielder Jones	83	−11	72
1902	Buck Freeman	64	−18	46
1903	Sam Crawford	76	3	79
1904	Elmer Flick	94	6	100
1905	Sam Crawford	52	49	101
1906	Sam Crawford	36	49	85
1907	Ty Cobb	139	19	158
1908	Ty Cobb	117	−6	111
1909	Ty Cobb	181	−10	171
1910	Sam Crawford	70	−5	65
1911	Joe Jackson	162	16	178
1912	Joe Jackson	157	19	176
1913	Joe Jackson	162	−28	134
1914	Sam Crawford	110	−5	105
1915	Sam Crawford	80	23	57
1916	Harry Hooper	14	−7	7
1917	Sam Rice	52	−4	48
1918	Harry Hooper	63	−23	40
1919	Sam Rice	43	−3	40
1920	Babe Ruth	245	−35	210
1921	Harry Heilmann	148	−38	110
1922	Harry Hooper	41	−2	39
1923	Babe Ruth	248	21	269
1924	Babe Ruth	211	−10	201
1925	Harry Heilmann	133	−27	106
1926	Babe Ruth	244	−3	241
1927	Babe Ruth	225	−1	224
1928	Babe Ruth	191	−25	166
1929	Babe Ruth	162	−19	143
1930	Babe Ruth	194	−15	179
1931	Babe Ruth	221	−31	190
1932	Babe Ruth	173	−25	148
1933	Babe Ruth	96	−49	47
1934	John Stone	6	9	15
1935	Pete Fox	57	−15	42

Year	Right Fielder	Bat	Field	Total
1936	Beau Bell	50	−5	45
1937	Beau Bell	65	18	83
1938	Tommy Henrich	19	10	29
1939	Ted Williams	135	−55	80
1940	Charlie Keller	55	−14	41
1941	Jeff Heath	103	−35	68
1942	Tommy Henrich	5	−3	2
1943	Roy Cullenbine	47	17	64
1944	Roy Cullenbine	59	2	61
1945	Roy Cullenbine	74	22	96
1946	Tommy Henrich	26	14	40
1947	Tommy Henrich	62	11	73
1948	Tommy Henrich	104	−5	99
1949	Vic Wertz	92	−2	90
1950	Vic Wertz	82	−42	40
1951	Vic Wertz	50	−33	17
1952	Hank Bauer	45	−3	42
1953	Hank Bauer	45	2	47
1954	Hank Bauer	35	−22	13
1955	Al Kaline	136	−1	135
1956	Al Kaline	90	26	116
1957	Al Kaline	49	12	61
1958	Rocky Colavito	133	15	118
1959	Al Kaline	110	19	129
1960	Roger Maris	96	−3	93
1961	Rocky Colavito	131	9	140
1962	Rocky Colavito	71	24	95
1963	Harvey Kuenn	106	−24	82
1964	Rocky Colavito	84	−14	70
1965	Rocky Colavito	100	18	118
1966	Frank Robinson	179	−11	168
1967	Al Kaline	132	13	145
1968	Ken Harrelson	118	17	135
1969	Frank Robinson	132	0	132
1970	Tony Oliva	98	0	98
1971	Merv Rettenmund	90	−6	84
1972	Cesar Tovar	33	3	36
1973	Reggie Smith	79	26	105
1974	Jeff Burroughs	129	−37	92
1975	Ken Singleton	95	−4	91
1976	Rusty Staub	88	−39	49
1977	Ken Singleton	116	−7	109
1978	Leon Roberts	72	0	72
1979	Sixto Lezcano	116	0	116
1980	Tony Armas	62	10	72
1981	Dwight Evans	101	13	114
1982	Dwight Evans	116	−15	101
1983	Harold Baines	44	4	48
1984	Dwight Evans	124	−2	122
1985	Jesse Barfield	57	38	95
1986	Jesse Barfield	97	43	140

Year	Right Fielder	Bat	Field	Total
1987	Danny Tartabull	91	−19	72
1988	Jose Canseco	139	3	142
1989	Ruben Sierra	102	−9	93
1990	Jesse Barfield	35	−12	23
1991	Ruben Sierra	91	−11	80
1992	Darryl Hamilton	25	19	44
1993	Tim Salmon	66	29	95
1994	Paul O'Neill	129	7	136
1995	Tim Salmon	119	6	125
1996	Juan Gonzalez	109	−10	99
1997	Tim Salmon	93	−18	75
	Paul O'Neill	85	−10	75 tie
1998	Juan Gonzalez	126	−15	111
1999	Manny Ramirez	181	−25	156
2000	Tim Salmon	71	18	89
2001	Juan Gonzalez	123	1	124
2002	Magglio Ordonez	114	−13	101
2003	Magglio Ordonez	76	5	81
2004	Vladimir Guerrero	123	−3	120
2005	Vladimir Guerrero	90	8	98
2006	Vladimir Guerrero	91	−13	78

Federal League. Benny Kauff, the Federal league's best player, led the circuit's right fielders with 188 Faber System points in his terrific 1914 season before switching to center field the following year.

FEDERAL LEAGUE LEADING RIGHT FIELDERS

Year	Right Fielder	Bat	Field	Total
1914	Benny Kauff	160	28	188
1915	Max Flack	64	12	76

Center Field

National League. In the beginning Paul Hines was the National League's best center fielder, but he was soon challenged for supremacy by George Gore. In 1879 Hines raised his own loop record to 125 Faber System points, only to see it broken by Gore with 144 the very next year. Gore's mark was upstaged by Jimmy Ryan with 177 points in 1889. Then along came Sliding Billy Hamilton. In 1894 the Phillies speedster smashed Ryan's record with a resounding 230 point performance, a mark that has remained intact for over 110 years. Willie Mays with 208 points in 1965 is the only other senior circuit center fielder to cross the 200 point threshold. Hines led the league three times, Gore five times, and the two men tied once. At the turn of the century Roy Thomas was best seven times, a mark that has been exceeded only by Mays, who was the league's best center fielder eleven times.

NATIONAL LEAGUE LEADING CENTER FIELDERS

Year	Center Fielder	Bat	Field	Total
1876	Paul Hines	76	31	107
1877	Jim O'Rourke	123	2	125

Year	Center Fielder	Bat	Field	Total
1878	Paul Hines	106	1	109
1879	Paul Hines	123	2	125
1880	George Gore	147	−3	144
1881	Hardy Richardson	41	78	119
1882	George Gore	114	6	120
1883	George Gore	98	−13	85
	Paul Hines	60	25	85 tie
1884	George Gore	123	3	126
1885	George Gore	125	9	134
1886	George Gore	148	−30	118
1887	Ed Andrews	50	19	69
1888	Jimmy Ryan	138	−11	127
1889	Jimmy Ryan	98	79	177
1890	Walter Wilmot	50	27	77
1891	George Davis	59	36	95
1892	Mike Griffin	44	98	142
1893	Hugh Duffy	53	25	78
1894	Billy Hamilton	190	40	230
1895	Billy Hamilton	141	−21	120
1896	Billy Hamilton	140	−28	112
1897	Billy Hamilton	117	15	132
1898	Joe Kelley	70	30	100
1899	Roy Thomas	57	30	87
1900	Roy Thomas	95	24	119
1901	Roy Thomas	84	11	95
1902	Ginger Beaumont	115	24	139
1903	Roy Thomas	88	45	133
1904	Roy Thomas	85	49	134
1905	Roy Thomas	106	73	179
1906	Roy Thomas	46	35	81
1907	Tommy Leach	92	43	135
1908	Cy Seymour	44	28	72
1909	Tommy Leach	77	1	78
1910	Fred Snodgrass	76	12	88
1911	Johnny Bates	54	17	71
1912	Dode Paskert	72	21	93
1913	Dode Paskert	10	39	49
1914	Tommy Leach	18	20	38
1915	Sherry Magee	47	42	89
1916	Max Carey	40	75	115
1917	Edd Roush	93	14	107
1918	Edd Roush	68	28	96
1919	Edd Roush	66	40	106
1920	Edd Roush	68	37	103
1921	Cy Williams	20	43	63
1922	Max Carey	95	30	125
1923	Max Carey	51	44	95
1924	Cy Williams	86	4	90
1925	Max Carey	71	14	85
1926	Hack Wilson	91	6	97

Year	Center Fielder	Bat	Field	Total
1927	Hack Wilson	113	−2	111
1928	Lloyd Waner	62	28	90
1929	Hack Wilson	134	5	139
1930	Hack Wilson	203	−28	175
1931	Mel Ott	73	30	103
1932	Lloyd Waner	42	30	72
1933	Wally Berger	90	4	94
1934	Wally Berger	78	−2	76
1935	Wally Berger	91	5	96
1936	Kiki Cuyler	53	−1	52
1937	Lloyd Waner	39	21	60
1938	Lloyd Waner	26	22	48
1939	Terry Moore	24	38	62
1940	Terry Moore	53	36	89
1941	Pete Reiser	123	30	153
1942	Pete Reiser	76	−14	62
1943	Augie Galan	68	17	85
1944	Johnny Hopp	101	−3	98
1945	Goody Rosen	102	11	113
1946	Johnny Wyrostek	29	34	63
1947	Harry Walker	72	13	85
1948	Richie Ashburn	64	43	107
1949	Bobby Thomson	70	26	96
1950	Duke Snider	71	26	97
1951	Richie Ashburn	59	45	104
1952	Duke Snider	64	26	90
1953	Duke Snider	147	15	162
1954	Willie Mays	127	41	168
1955	Willie Mays	134	46	180
1956	Duke Snider	118	16	134
1957	Willie Mays	127	31	158
1958	Willie Mays	144	29	173
1959	Vada Pinson	104	19	123
1960	Willie Mays	108	17	125
1961	Willie Mays	126	9	135
1962	Willie Mays	141	31	172
1963	Willie Mays	139	17	156
1964	Willie Mays	127	32	159
1965	Willie Mays	167	41	208
1966	Willie Mays	86	23	109
1967	Matty Alou	78	12	90
1968	Jimmy Wynn	79	32	111
1969	Jimmy Wynn	124	21	145
1970	Bobby Tolan	86	10	96
1971	Willie Davis	51	11	62
1972	Cesar Cedeno	110	18	128
1973	Cesar Cedeno	78	25	103
1974	Jimmy Wynn	100	31	131
1975	Van Joshua	38	29	67
1976	Garry Maddox	60	47	107
1977	George Hendrick	59	32	91

Year	Center Fielder	Bat	Field	Total
1978	Lee Mazzili	37	27	64
1979	Lee Mazzili	59	31	90
1980	Andre Dawson	75	29	104
1981	Andre Dawson	77	71	148
1982	Dale Murphy	99	6	105
1983	Dale Murphy	133	17	150
1984	Tim Raines	87	27	114
1985	Dale Murphy	117	−6	111
1986	Len Dykstra	53	13	66
1987	Eric Davis	111	47	158
1988	Brett Butler	84	10	94
1989	Eric Davis	96	1	97
1990	Len Dykstra	105	29	134
1991	Brett Butler	91	27	118
1992	Andy Van Slyke	100	28	128
1993	Len Dykstra	131	6	137
1994	Brett Butler	102	21	123
1995	Steve Finley	51	1	52
1996	Steve Finley	87	17	104
1997	Kenny Lofton	58	10	68
1998	Ray Lankford	86	16	102
1999	Brian Giles	110	12	122
2000	Jim Edmonds	113	28	141
2001	Jim Edmonds	95	10	105
2002	Jim Edmonds	103	33	136
2003	Jim Edmonds	64	33	97
2004	Jim Edmonds	131	24	155
2005	Andruw Jones	106	34	140
2006	Carlos Beltran	98	50	138

American Association. The Louisville slugger, Pete Browning, holds the American Association center fielders record of 154 Faber System points set in 1885. The Gladiator led the league only once, while the less heralded Curt Welch topped the circuit four times.

AMERICAN ASSOCIATION LEADING CENTER FIELDERS

Year	Center Fielder	Bat	Field	Total
1881	Jimmy Macullar	−22	36	14
1883	Charley Jones	65	3	68
1884	Monk Cline	69	29	98
1885	Pete Browning	134	20	154
1886	Curt Welch	47	75	122
1887	Curt Welch	−22	76	54
1888	Curt Welch	82	42	124
1889	Jim McTamany	75	36	111
1890	Jim McTamany	61	16	77
1891	Curt Welch	59	63	122

Players' League. Mike Griffin, who also starred in both the American Association and the National League, was the Players' League's best center fielder.

PLAYERS' LEAGUE LEADING CENTER FIELDER

Year	Center Fielder	Bat	Field	Total
1890	Mike Griffin	46	86	132

American League. Some of baseball's all-time greats have roamed American League center-field pastures. Dummy Hoy, Fielder Jones, and Sam Crawford set the early league records for Faber System points. In 1909 Tris Speaker broke Crawford's record, only to see his mark demolished by Ty Cobb with 206 points the following year. For the next 16 years the Grey Eagle and the Georgia Peach battled for supremacy with each man coming out on top eight times. In 1912 Speaker broke Cobb's record with 235 points and then, in 1920, set an all-time league record with 278 points. Cobb topped the 200 mark four times and Speaker had two such seasons. In the 87 years since Speaker posted his 278 point total, only one man, Mickey Mantle, has exceeded 200 points in a season. The Mick did it twice, with 202 in 1956 and 208 the following year. Joe DiMaggio led the circuit's center fielders eight times, and his brother Dom did it thrice. Mantle led ten times. Kirby Puckett, whose 179 points in 1988 was the best since Mantle's retirement was the loop's top center fielder six times, and Ken Griffey, Jr. was best five times. Sam Crawford, Al Simmons, and Al Kaline are among the Hall of Famers who usually patrolled a different sector of the outer garden but led the center fielders at least once.

AMERICAN LEAGUE LEADING CENTER FIELDERS

Year	Center Fielder	Bat	Field	Total
1901	Dummy Hoy	61	53	114
1902	Fielder Jones	52	64	116
1903	Jimmy Barrett	90	25	115
1904	Jimmy Barrett	47	56	103
1905	Harry Bay	58	29	87
1906	Elmer Flick	85	3	88
1907	Sam Crawford	101	27	128
1908	Sam Crawford	101	6	107
1909	Tris Speaker	70	78	148
1910	Ty Cobb	169	37	206
1911	Ty Cobb	190	16	206
1912	Tris Speaker	175	60	235
1913	Tris Speaker	117	44	161
1914	Tris Speaker	121	60	181
1915	Ty Cobb	206	5	211
1916	Tris Speaker	155	33	188
1917	Ty Cobb	172	39	211
1918	Ty Cobb	135	38	173
1919	Ty Cobb	111	18	129
1920	Tris Speaker	165	113	278
1921	Ty Cobb	128	53	181
1922	Tris Speaker	100	40	140
1923	Tris Speaker	161	25	186
1924	Ty Cobb	73	21	94
1925	Tris Speaker	95	31	126
1926	Johnny Mostil	96	35	131
1927	Al Simmons	117	31	148
1928	Earle Combs	80	16	96

Year	Center Fielder	Bat	Field	Total
1929	Earle Combs	76	−5	71
1930	Earl Averill	73	−5	68
1931	Earl Averill	122	7	129
1932	Earl Combs	95	24	119
1933	Sam West	18	41	59
1934	Earl Averill	90	17	107
1935	Sam West	21	41	62
1936	Earl Averill	114	−2	112
1937	Joe DiMaggio	160	28	188
1938	Joe DiMaggio	84	19	103
1939	Joe DiMaggio	148	46	194
1940	Joe DiMaggio	136	13	149
1941	Joe DiMaggio	142	26	168
1942	Dom DiMaggio	55	50	105
1943	Stan Spence	42	16	58
1944	Stan Spence	84	63	147
1945	George Case	26	28	54
1946	Joe DiMaggio	59	25	84
1947	Joe DiMaggio	78	−2	76
1948	Joe DiMaggio	146	4	150
1949	Dom DiMaggio	87	20	107
1950	Dom DiMaggio	73	27	100
1951	Larry Doby	61	6	67
1952	Larry Doby	83	30	113
1953	Mickey Mantle	76	13	89
1954	Mickey Mantle	133	10	143
1955	Mickey Mantle	135	29	164
1956	Mickey Mantle	174	28	202
1957	Mickey Mantle	210	−2	208
1958	Mickey Mantle	168	−4	164
1959	Al Kaline	110	19	129
1960	Mickey Mantle	115	14	129
1961	Mickey Mantle	168	8	176
1962	Mickey Mantle	130	−14	116
1963	Albie Pearson	85	14	99
1964	Mickey Mantle	137	−26	111
1965	Tom Tresh	65	−4	61
1966	Al Kaline	102	15	117
1967	Paul Blair	60	37	97
1968	Reggie Smith	55	20	75
1969	Paul Blair	62	43	105
1970	Reggie Smith	55	20	113
1971	Bobby Murcer	126	10	136
1972	Bobby Murcer	110	28	138
1973	Billy North	63	47	110
1974	Ken Henderson	78	16	94
1975	Fred Lynn	122	27	149
1976	Fred Lynn	61	29	90
1977	Lyman Bostock	96	14	110
1978	Amos Otis	78	35	113

Year	Center Fielder	Bat	Field	Total
1979	Fred Lynn	158	18	176
1980	Al Bumbry	105	28	133
1981	Dwayne Murphy	24	26	50
1982	Gorman Thomas	60	29	89
1983	Lloyd Moseby	86	19	105
1984	Lloyd Moseby	68	29	97
1985	Rickey Henderson	144	24	168
1986	Kirby Puckett	122	24	146
	Robin Yount	124	22	146 tie
1987	Kirby Puckett	82	12	94
1988	Kirby Puckett	134	45	179
1989	Kirby Puckett	82	40	122
1990	Kirby Puckett	55	22	77
1991	Ken Griffey, Jr.	103	28	131
1992	Kirby Puckett	106	16	122
1993	Ken Griffey, Jr.	123	27	150
1994	Kenny Lofton	116	26	142
1995	Jim Edmonds	69	39	108
1996	Ken Griffey, Jr.	114	35	149
1997	Ken Griffey, Jr.	132	12	144
1998	Ken Griffey, Jr.	123	16	139
1999	Bernie Williams	110	1	111
2000	Johnny Damon	86	30	116
2001	Carlos Beltran	65	34	99
2002	Bernie Williams	86	−10	76
2003	Carlos Beltran	74	35	109
2004	Carlos Beltran	90	29	119*
2005	Johnny Damon	72	20	92
2006	Grady Sizemore	108	14	122

*includes games played in National League

Federal League. Dutch Zwilling, whose name is last in any alphabetical listing of major league players, was first among Federal League center fielders in 1914 with 81 Faber System points. The following season Benny Kauff played centerfield and outshone Zwilling with a very impressive 195 points.

FEDERAL LEAGUE LEADING CENTER FIELDERS, 1914–15

Year	Center Fielder	Bat	Field	Total
1914	Dutch Zwilling	71	10	91
1915	Benny Kauff	153	44	197

Left Field

National League. Charley Jones was the National League's best left fielder during the league's infancy. His record of 150 Faber System points stood until Ed Delahanty posted a 201 mark in 1893. Six years later Delahanty raised the standard to 206 points. That mark endured for over 100 years until Barry Bonds amassed 212 points in 2001. The Giant slugger twice raised that record, to 224 points in 2002 and to 275 points in 2204. The only other senior circuit left fielder to compile 200 points in a season was Stan Musial in 1948 with 201. Delahanty led National

League left fielders five times. In the 1930s and 1940s Joe Medwick was on top eight times. Musial was the leading left fielder five times, the best right fielder four times, and led first basemen five times for a total of 14 years as the league's best performer at his position. Bonds matched that total and at a single position; from 1990 to 2004 Bonds was the league's best left fielder 14 times.

NATIONAL LEAGUE LEADING LEFT FIELDERS

Year	Left Fielder	Bat	Field	Total
1876	George Hall	110	−27	73
1877	Charley Jones	58	29	87
1878	Abner Dalrymple	104	−11	93
1879	Charley Jones	113	37	150
1880	Abner Dalrymple	119	−12	107
1881	Buttercup Dickerson	60	17	77
1882	Joe Hornung	40	40	80
1883	Joe Hornung	49	27	76
1884	Jim O'Rourke	142	−29	113
1885	Abner Dalrymple	76	−26	50
1886	Joe Hornung	−24	34	10
1887	Joe Hornung	9	58	49
1888	Emmett Seery	12	19	31
1889	Emmett Seery	82	−12	70
1890	Cliff Carroll	66	20	86
1891	Billy Hamilton	154	−12	142
1892	Billy Hamilton	123	20	143
1893	Ed Delahanty	130	71	201
1894	Joe Kelley	147	11	158
1895	Ed Delahanty	140	34	174
1896	Ed Delahanty	143	30	173
1897	Jesse Burkett	116	3	119
1898	Ed Delahanty	99	28	127
1899	Ed Delahanty	163	44	207
1900	Kip Selbach	64	38	102
1901	Jesse Burkett	170	−20	150
1902	Fred Clarke	100	3	103
1903	Jimmy Sheckard	95	61	156
1904	Fred Odwell	22	18	40
1905	Sherry Magee	59	17	76
1906	Fred Clarke	51	20	71
1907	Sherry Magee	114	12	126
1908	Sherry Magee	61	0	61
1909	Fred Clarke	80	26	106
1910	Sherry Magee	141	−12	129
1911	Jimmy Sheckard	86	26	112
1912	Max Carey	102	22	124
1913	Max Carey	20	22	42
1914	Zach Wheat	68	20	88
1915	Max Carey	12	42	54
1916	Zach Wheat	72	12	84
1917	George Burns	98	13	111
1918	George Burns	57	−9	48

Year	Left Fielder	Bat	Field	Total
1919	George Burns	76	32	108
1920	George Burns	59	1	60
1921	Austin McHenry	35	29	64
1922	Carson Bigbee	72	8	80
1923	Pat Duncan	20	11	31
1924	Zach Wheat	103	−8	95
1925	Ray Blades	84	48	132
1926	Kiki Cuyler	69	18	87
1927	Riggs Stephenson	82	−5	77
1928	Chick Hafey	64	−8	56
1929	Lefty O'Doul	166	−9	157
1930	Lefty O'Doul	114	−47	67
1931	Chuck Klein	107	−16	91
1932	Lefty O'Doul	107	−27	80
1933	Joe Medwick	55	10	65
1934	Johnny Moore	63	24	87
1935	Joe Medwick	126	−22	104
1936	Joe Medwick	121	26	147
1937	Joe Medwick	187	2	189
1938	Joe Medwick	98	0	98
1939	Joe Medwick	88	−14	74
1940	Joe Medwick	36	3	39
1941	Joe Medwick	76	5	81
1942	Stan Musial	87	−4	83
1943	Eric Tipton	59	−15	44
1944	Jim Russell	87	22	109
1945	Luis Olmo	67	−25	42
1946	Del Ennis	55	10	65
1947	Ralph Kiner	138	12	150
1948	Stan Musial	200	1	201
1949	Ralph Kiner	154	−8	146
1950	Sid Gordon	67	3	70
1951	Monte Irvin	103	−17	86
1952	Hank Sauer	88	14	102
1953	Stan Musial	139	−8	131
1954	Monte Irvin	16	−7	9
1955	Del Ennis	67	1	68
1956	Frank Robinson	112	−15	97
1957	Frank Robinson	89	25	114
1958	Frank Robinson	42	13	55
1959	Wally Moon	69	−16	53
1960	Wally Moon	49	−14	35
1961	Stan Musial	24	3	27
1962	Stan Musial	99	−23	76
1963	Billy Williams	81	13	94
1964	Rico Carty	97	−17	80
1965	Tommy Harper	82	−5	77
1966	Rico Carty	70	−8	62
1967	Tony Gonzalez	50	20	70
1968	Cleon Jones	111	−33	78

Year	Left Fielder	Bat	Field	Total
1969	Cleon Jones	111	18	119
1970	Billy Williams	160	10	170
1971	Willie Stargell	157	−9	148
1972	Billy Williams	157	−10	147
1973	Pete Rose	108	29	137
1974	Pete Rose	79	23	102
1975	George Foster	46	27	73
1976	George Foster	114	26	140
1977	George Foster	161	24	185
1978	George Foster	111	−10	101
1979	Dave Winfield	119	19	138
1980	Dusty Baker	71	5	76
1981	George Foster	95	4	99
1982	Lonnie Smith	93	−10	83
1983	Tim Raines	108	34	142
1984	Jose Cruz	77	−3	74
1985	Tim Raines	112	6	118
1986	Tim Raines	106	−4	102
1987	Tim Raines	128	12	140
1988	Kal Daniels	86	−1	85
1989	Kevin Mitchell	149	−3	146
1990	Barry Bonds	119	17	136
1991	Barry Bonds	120	24	144
1992	Barry Bonds	157	−1	156
1993	Barry Bonds	178	−9	169
1994	Barry Bonds	122	5	127
1995	Barry Bonds	109	7	116
1996	Barry Bonds	160	−10	150
1997	Barry Bonds	122	0	122
1998	Barry Bonds	138	−11	127
1999	Luis Gonzalez	98	−2	96
2000	Barry Bonds	129	4	133
2001	Barry Bonds	229	−17	212
2002	Barry Bonds	253	−29	224
2003	Barry Bonds	197	−1	196
2004	Barry Bonds	274	1	275
2005	Jason Bay	117	1	118
2006	Matt Holliday	108	−10	98

American Association. Charley Jones, who twice led American Association center fielders, repeated that feat as a left fielder. His record 135 Faber System points was exceeded only by Tip O'Neill, who logged 174 points in 1887. For many years O'Neill was credited with a major league record .492 batting average in 1887, but modern researchers have generally followed the decision of the Special Rules Committee announced in 1968 that the 1887 records be changed to no longer consider bases on balls as hits or times at bat. Consequently, O'Neill's 1887 average is now listed as .435. Jones, O'Neill, and Harry Stovey each led the Association's left fielders twice. Jones also had three other league-leading seasons — one in the Association as a center fielder and two in the National League as a left fielder. Stovey led the Association as a first baseman once.

AMERICAN ASSOCIATION LEADING LEFT FIELDERS

Year	Left Fielder	Bat	Field	Total
1882	Joe Sommer	77	46	123
1883	Mike Mansell	31	4	35
1884	Charley Jones	129	6	135
1885	Charley Jones	103	18	121
1886	Tip O'Neill	90	35	125
1887	Tip O'Neill	216	−42	174
1888	Harry Stovey	97	4	101
1889	Harry Stovey	110	21	131
1890	Spud Johnson	71	−32	39
1891	Charlie Duffee	27	42	69

Players' League. Hardy Richardson, who had a long National League career, mostly as a second baseman, was the Players' League's leading left fielder.

PLAYERS' LEAGUE LEADING LEFT FIELDER

Year	Left Fielder	Bat	Field	Total
1890	Hardy Richardson	90	15	105

American League. After he switched to the American League, Big Ed Delahanty was the junior circuit's best left fielder. In 1902 he set a league record for the position with 139 Faber System points. Unfortunately, that was his last full season in baseball as he died tragically during the next summer. In 1908 Matty McIntyre raised the record to 150 points, which stood until Babe Ruth amassed 204 points in 1919. The Bambino raised the mark to 254 points in 1921, before moving to right field. The Babe's record still stands. The only other junior circuit left fielder to compile 200 points in a season is Ted Williams, who reached that standard three times. Al Simmons led AL left fielders in six consecutive seasons from 1929 through 1934. Despite having his career interrupted twice by wartime service to his country Williams led 10 times in the 1940s and 1950s. Since then Carl Yastrzemski and Rickey Henderson have each led left fielders six times as well as being league leaders at other positions.

AMERICAN LEAGUE LEADING LEFT FIELDERS

Year	Left Fielder	Bat	Field	Total
1901	Tommy Dowd	−5	23	18
1902	Ed Delahanty	125	14	139
1903	Patsy Dougherty	95	1	96
1904	Jesse Burkett	47	9	56
1905	Topsy Hartsel	74	−28	46
1906	George Stone	129	−10	119
1907	Davy Jones	66	26	92
1908	Matty McIntyre	108	42	150
1909	Clyde Engle	39	8	47
1910	Duffy Lewis	16	24	40
1911	Birdie Cree	67	5	72
1912	Amos Strunk	0	60	60
1913	Duffy Lewis	36	28	64
1914	Tilly Walker	53	51	104

Year	Left Fielder	Bat	Field	Total
1915	Bobby Veach	98	21	119
1916	Joe Jackson	70	2	72
1917	Joe Jackson	78	30	108
1918	Bobby Veach	27	0	27
1919	Babe Ruth	143	67	210
1920	Joe Jackson	130	−10	120
1921	Babe Ruth	254	4	254
1922	Ken Williams	144	12	156
1923	Ken Williams	114	14	128
1924	Goose Goslin	100	−20	80
1925	Al Wingo	85	13	98
1926	Goose Goslin	115	28	143
1927	Goose Goslin	76	−14	62
1928	Heinie Manush	98	0	98
1929	Al Simmons	147	39	186
1930	Al Simmons	169	20	189
1931	Al Simmons	145	16	161
1932	Al Simmons	111	−5	106
1933	Al Simmons	62	41	103
1934	Al Simmons	62	24	86
1935	Moose Solters	42	39	81
1936	Joe DiMaggio	41	37	88
1937	Bob Johnson	67	10	77
1938	Bob Johnson	61	25	86
1939	Bob Johnson	104	8	112
1940	Hank Greenberg	161	−20	141
1941	Ted Williams	240	−30	210
1942	Ted Williams	208	15	223
1943	Charlie Keller	87	13	100
1944	Bob Johnson	113	6	119
1945	George Case	26	28	54
1946	Ted Williams	210	−17	193
1947	Ted Williams	186	−12	174
1948	Ted Williams	176	−6	170
1949	Ted Williams	213	−6	207
1950	Hoot Evers	68	28	96
1951	Ted Williams	142	5	147
1952	Gene Woodling	46	19	65
1953	Gus Zernial	78	−5	73
1954	Ted Williams	174	−28	146
1955	Roy Sievers	56	−13	43
1956	Charlie Maxwell	81	5	86
1957	Ted Williams	169	−14	155
1958	Ted Williams	168	−57	111
1959	Minnie Minoso	73	19	92
1960	Minnie Minoso	86	1	87
1961	Rocky Colavito	130	9	140
1962	Rocky Colavito	70	24	94
1963	Carl Yastrzemski	109	13	122
1964	Boog Powell	111	−9	102
1965	Carl Yastrzemski	83	15	98

Year	Left Fielder	Bat	Field	Total
1966	Carl Yastrzemski	65	24	89
1967	Carl Yastrzemski	141	4	145
1968	Carl Yastrzemski	130	17	147
1969	Carl Yastrzemski	87	15	102
1970	Frank Howard	143	−31	112
1971	Don Buford	97	−5	92
1972	Carlos May	100	−11	89
1973	Tommy Harper	53	7	60
1974	Cesar Tovar	42	12	54
1975	Roy White	59	11	70
1976	Roy White	78	3	81
1977	Larry Hisle	99	18	117
1978	Jim Rice	153	33	186
1979	Jim Rice	141	−11	130
1980	Ben Oglivie	109	22	131
1981	Rickey Henderson	99	13	112
1982	Brian Downing	76	11	87
1983	Rickey Henderson	86	16	102
1984	Rickey Henderson	104	−14	90
1985	Phil Bradley	71	2	73
1986	Jim Rice	109	10	119
1987	George Bell	117	−25	92
1988	Mike Greenwell	135	−7	128
1989	Rickey Henderson	46	6	52
1990	Rickey Henderson	158	6	164
1991	Rickey Henderson	75	−24	51
1992	Shane Mack	97	−8	89
1993	Juan Gonzalez	110	7	117
1994	Albert Belle	149	−36	113
1995	Albert Belle	130	−5	125
1996	Albert Belle	134	−12	122
1997	Rusty Greer	87	−19	68
1998	Albert Belle	162	−17	145
1999	Johnny Damon	38	2	40
2000	Darin Erstad	110	35	145
2001	Garret Anderson	53	9	62
2002	Garret Anderson	62	0	62
2003	Manny Ramirez	123	−9	114
2004	Carlos Lee	69	13	82
2005	Manny Ramirez	133	−4	129
2006	Manny Ramirez	102	−24	78

Federal League. Although Chet Chadbourne was the Federal League's top left fielder in 1914 and Claude Cooper was best in 1915, neither man had a long or distinguished major league career. Neither played as many as 100 games in a season in either the American or National League.

FEDERAL LEAGUE LEADING LEFT FIELDERS

Year	Left Fielder	Bat	Field	Total
1914	Chet Chadbourne	33	39	72
1915	Claude Cooper	51	34	85

Player of the Year

National League. In 1876 second baseman Ross Barnes of the Chicago White Stockings became the first major league Player of the Year with 201 Faber System points. His point total was first exceeded by his teammate Cap Anson with 207 points in 1881. Five years later the mark was raised to 218 points by another White Stocking, Michael Joseph "King" Kelly. Kelly's points all came from his batting prowess, as he did not perform at any position in enough games to be eligible for fielding points, splitting his time between the outfield, first base, second base, shortstop, and catching. In 1894 Billy Hamilton amassed 230 points, a record that was smashed the following season by Hughie Jennings, who accumulated 320 points in an outstanding year both at the plate and in the field.. The record of the Oriole shortstop has stood now for well over 100 years. No other National Leaguer has attained 300 points in a season, although several have had 200-point seasons— Ed Delahanty, John McGraw, Honus Wagner (twice), Rogers Hornsby, Frankie Frisch, Chuck Klein, Stan Musial, Ernie Banks, Willie Mays, Ryne Sandberg, Jeff Bagwell, Todd Helton (twice), Barry Bonds (three times), and Albert Pujols.

From 1898 through 1898 Hughie Jennings was Player of the Year four times in a row. Wagner earned that honor seven times, including five consecutively. Hornsby was the league's top layer six times, while Musial, Mays, Sandberg, and Bonds each earned the honor five times. Middle infielders and outfielders have won the majority of the Players of the Year designations. No catcher has captured the honors. (Bonus points for catchers were not included in these calculations.)

NATIONAL LEAGUE PLAYER OF THE YEAR, 1876–2006

Year	Player	Pos.	Bat	Field	Total
1876	Ross Barnes	2b	184	17	201
1877	Jim O'Rourke	cf	102	2	104
1878	Orator Shaffer	rf	88	23	111
1879	Charley Jones	lf	113	37	150
1880	George Gore	cf	147	−3	144
1881	Cap Anson	1b	176	31	207
1882	Dan Brouthers	1b	131	23	134
1883	Jack Glasscock	ss	15	121	136
1884	Fred Pfeffer	2b	90	106	196
1885	Roger Connor	1b	151	12	163
1886	King Kelly		218	*	218
1887	Sam Thompson	rf	164	15	179
1888	Cap Anson	1b	137	26	163
1889	Jimmy Ryan	cf	98	79	177
1890	George Pinckney	3b	88	40	128
1891	Billy Hamilton	lf	154	−12	142
1892	Bid McPhee	2b	50	108	160
1893	Ed Delahanty	lf	130	71	201
1894	Billy Hamilton	cf	190	40	230
1895	Hughie Jennings	ss	134	186	320
1896	Hughie Jennings	ss	126	107	233
1897	Hughie Jennings	ss	106	128	234
1898	Hughie Jennings	ss	128	39	167
1899	John McGraw	3b	191	40	231
1900	Nap Lajoie	2b	32	118	150

*not enough games at one position to be eligible for fielding points

Year	Player	Pos.	Bat	Field	Total
1901	Jesse Burkett	lf	170	−20	150
1902	Ginger Beaumont	cf	115	24	139
1903	Honus Wagner	ss	99	121	220
1904	Roy Thomas	cf	85	49	134
1905	Honus Wagner	ss	143	42	185
1906	Honus Wagner	ss	128	54	182
1907	Honus Wagner	ss	144	22	166
1908	Honus Wagner	ss	163	9	172
1909	Honus Wagner	ss	130	73	203
1910	Sherry Magee	lf	141	−12	129
1911	Honus Wagner	ss	87	34	121
1912	Bill Sweeney	2b	81	88	167
1913	Miller Huggins	2b	41	81	122
1914	Zach Wheat	lf	68	20	88
1915	George Cutshaw	2b	−19	135	116
1916	Max Carey	cf	40	75	115
1917	Heinie Groh	3b	86	58	144
1918	Heinie Groh	3b	96	25	121
1919	George Burns	lf	76	32	108
1920	Rogers Hornsby	2b	127	−3	124
1921	Rogers Hornsby	2b	174	−20	154
1922	Rogers Hornsby	2b	200	10	210
1923	Frankie Frisch	2b	76	30	106
1924	Rogers Hornsby	2b	207	−17	190
1925	Rogers Hornsby	2b	205	−37	168
1926	Paul Waner	rf	141	10	151
1927	Frankie Frisch	2b	79	154	233
1928	Paul Waner	rf	141	10	151
1929	Rogers Hornsby	2b	199	−33	166
1930	Chuck Klein	rf	173	57	220
1931	Woody English	ss	72	31	103 tie
	Mel Ott	rf	73	30	103 tie
1932	Chuck Klein	rf	164	35	199
1933	Chuck Klein	rf	161	26	187
1934	Paul Waner	rf	129	1	130
1935	Billy Herman	2b	83	63	146
1936	Mel Ott	rf	152	21	173
1937	Joe Medwick	lf	187	2	189
1938	Mel Ott	3b	143	10	153
1939	Frank McCormick	1b	100	20	120
1940	Johnny Mize	1b	152	−15	137
1941	Pete Reiser	cf	123	30	153
1942	Mel Ott	rf	137	3	140
1943	Stan Musial	rf	138	5	143
1944	Stan Musial	rf	132	18	150
1945	Tommy Holmes	rf	142	8	150
1946	Stan Musial	1b	166	−29	137
1947	Ralph Kiner	lf	138	12	150
1948	Stan Musial	lf	200	1	201
1949	Stan Musial	rf	154	1	155

Year	Player	Pos.	Bat	Field	Total
1950	Duke Snider	cf	71	26	97
1951	Jackie Robinson	2b	103	35	138
1952	Hank Sauer	lf	88	14	102
1953	Duke Snider	cf	147	15	162
1954	Willie Mays	cf	127	41	168
1955	Willie Mays	cf	134	46	189
1956	Duke Snider	cf	118	16	134
1957	Willie Mays	cf	127	31	158
1958	Willie Mays	cf	144	29	173
1959	Ernie Banks	ss	136	68	204
1960	Ernie Banks	ss	90	94	184
1961	Frank Robinson	rf	134	14	148
1962	Frank Robinson	rf	163	19	182
1963	Hank Aaron	rf	149	−15	134
1964	Ron Santo	3b	119	52	171
1965	Willie Mays	cf	167	41	208
1966	Ron Santo	3b	106	35	141
1967	Ron Santo	3b	119	52	171
1968	Pete Rose	rf	112	32	144
1969	Willie McCovey	1b	184	1	185
1970	Billie Williams	lf	160	10	170
1971	Joe Torre	3b	190	−3	187
1972	Joe Morgan	2b	125	51	176
1973	Joe Morgan	2b	108	54	162
1974	Mike Schmidt	3b	122	26	148
1975	Joe Morgan	2b	138	50	188
1976	Joe Morgan	2b	151	−3	148
1977	George Foster	lf	161	24	185
1978	Dave Parker	rf	141	−16	125
1979	Keith Hernandez	1b	123	37	160
1980	Mike Schmidt	3b	133	14	147
1981	Mike Schmidt	3b	146	22	168
1982	Ozzie Smith	ss	−26	166	140
1983	Dale Murphy	cf	133	17	150
1984	Ryne Sandberg	2b	96	82	178
1985	Ryne Sandberg	2b	97	52	149
1986	Mike Schmidt	3b	128	42	170
1987	Ozzie Smith	ss	59	114	173
1988	Ozzie Smith	ss	22	85	107
1989	Will Clark	1b	141	12	153
1990	Ryne Sandberg	2b	104	35	139
1991	Ryne Sandberg	2b	93	126	219
1992	Ryne Sandberg	2b	81	70	151
1993	Barry Bonds	lf	178	−9	169
1994	Jeff Bagwell	1b	191	24	215
1995	Barry Bonds	lf	109	7	116
1996	Eric Young	2b	84	92	176
1997	Larry Walker	rf	193	5	198
1998	Mark McGwire	1b	203	−9	194
1999	Larry Walker	rf	160	10	170

Year	Player	Pos.	Bat	Field	Total
2000	Todd Helton	1b	198	35	233
2001	Barry Bonds	lf	229	−17	212
2002	Barry Bonds	lf	253	−29	224
2003	Todd Helton	1b	182	30	212
2004	Barry Bonds	lf	274	1	275
2005	Derrek Lee	1b	164	19	183
2006	Albert Pujols	1b	165	35	200

American Association. Second baseman of the Cincinnati Red Stockings Bid McPhee was Player of the Year in the American Association three times and holds the league record with 234 Faber System points, set in 1886. Jack Crooks, also a second baseman, is the only other Association player to score 200 points in a season. Guardians of the keystone led the loop in six of its ten years of existence.

AMERICAN ASSOCIATION PLAYER OF THE YEAR, 1882–91

Year	Player	Pos.	Bat	Field	Total
1882	Hick Carpenter	3b	113	18	131
1883	Hugh Nichol	rf	76	60	136
1884	Bid McPhee	2b	75	96	171
1885	Pete Browning	cf	134	20	154
1886	Bid McPhee	2b	75	159	234
1887	Tip O'Neill	lf	216	−42	174
1888	Bid McPhee	2b	5	159	164
1889	Lou Bierbauer	2b	−13	161	148
1890	Cupid Childs	2b	89	82	171
1891	Jack Crooks	2b	22	185	207

American League. When Napoleon Lajoie jumped from the Philadelphia Phillies to their new crosstown rivals, the Athletics, he gave the fledgling American League instant credibility. Lajoie earned Player of the Year honors with 253 Faber System points, a mark that stood as the circuit's record until Tris Speaker amassed 278 points in 1920. The Grey Eagle's record still holds, with the closest challenge being posted by Babe Ruth with 269 points in 1923. No one else has collected as many as 250 points in a season, but 14 individuals have led the league with more than 200 points., with Ruth doing so five times. The latest to reach that level was Cal Ripken, Jr., with 228 points in 1991.

Lajoie was the American League Player of the Year six times. Babe Ruth and Ted Williams each won the honor seven times, and Williams almost certainly would have added to that total had he not spent several seasons in service to his country during World War II and the Korean conflict. Although middle infielders and outfielders dominated the early lists of junior circuit Players of the Years, hard-hitting first basemen made their presence felt, starting with George Sisler and Lou Gehrig in the 1920s. From 1932 through 1937 first sackers took Player of the Year honors seven consecutive years, with Gehrig, Jimmie Foxx, and Hank Greenberg providing the firepower. Third basemen were missing from the list for half a century until Al Rosen was Player of the Year in 1953. Since then Brooks Robinson, George Brett, Wade Boggs, and Alex Rodriguez have been Player of the Year while guarding the hot corner. No catcher has been the league's best player, but two designated hitters—Edgar Martinez and David Ortiz—have earned the accolades. In 1970 Carl Yastrzemski played 94 games at first base, not enough to make him eligible for consideration as Leading First Baseman of the Year. However, when the 69 games he played in the outfield are added to his total he has enough games to be eligible for the title Player of the Year.

AMERICAN LEAGUE PLAYER OF THE YEAR, 1901–2006

Year	Player	Pos.	Bat	Field	Total
1901	Nap Lajoie	2b	198	55	253
1902	Ed Delahanty	lf	125	14	139
1903	Nap Lajoie	2b	94	89	183
1904	Nap Lajoie	2b	157	32	189
1905	George Davis	ss	68	85	153
1906	Nap Lajoie	2b	109	124	233
1907	Ty Cobb	rf	139	19	158
1908	Nap Lajoie	2b	59	118	177
1909	Eddie Collins	2b	140	46	186
1910	Nap Lajoie	2b	146	95	241
1911	Ty Cobb	cf	190	16	206
1912	Tris Speaker	cf	175	60	235
1913	Tris Speaker	cf	117	74	191
1914	Eddie Collins	2b	159	68	227
1915	Ty Cobb	cf	206	5	211
1916	Tris Speaker	cf	155	33	188
1917	Ty Cobb	cf	172	39	211
1918	Ty Cobb	cf	135	38	173
1919	Babe Ruth	lf	143	67	210
1920	Tris Speaker	cf	165	113	278
1921	Babe Ruth	lf	254	4	258
1922	George Sisler	1b	163	−1	162
1923	Babe Ruth	rf	248	21	269
1924	Babe Ruth	rf	211	−10	201
1925	Joe Sewell	ss	29	103	132
1926	Babe Ruth	rf	244	−3	241
1927	Lou Gehrig	1b	226	6	232
1928	Babe Ruth	rf	191	−25	166
1929	Al Simmons	lf	147	39	186
1930	Lou Gehrig	1b	207	−9	198
1931	Babe Ruth	rf	221	−31	190
1932	Jimmie Foxx	1b	223	9	232
1933	Jimmie Foxx	1b	191	7	198
1934	Lou Gehrig	1b	195	−3	192
1935	Hank Greenberg	1b	150	9	159
1936	Lou Gehrig	1b	174	0	174
1937	Hank Greenberg	1b	178	14	192
1938	Jimmie Foxx	1b	173	−3	170
1939	Joe DiMaggio	cf	148	46	194
1940	Joe DiMaggio	cf	136	13	149
1941	Ted Williams	lf	240	−30	210
1942	Ted Williams	lf	208	15	223
1943	Lou Boudreau	ss	34	95	129
1944	Lou Boudreau	ss	73	148	221
1945	George Stirnweiss	2b	90	28	118
1946	Ted Williams	lf	210	−17	193

Year	Player	Pos.	Bat	Field	Total
1947	Ted Williams	lf	186	−12	174
1948	Ted Williams	lf	176	−6	170
1949	Ted Williams	lf	213	−6	207
1950	Phil Rizzuto	ss	82	80	162
1951	Ted Williams	lf	142	5	147
1952	Larry Doby	cf	83	30	113
1953	Al Rosen	3b	176	13	189
1954	Bobby Avila	2b	122	44	166
1955	Mickey Mantle	cf	135	29	164
1956	Mickey Mantle	cf	174	28	202
1957	Mickey Mantle	cf	210	−2	208
1958	Mickey Mantle	cf	168	−4	164
1959	Al Kaline	cf	110	19	129
1960	Luis Aparicio	ss	7	144	151
1961	Norm Cash	1b	190	11	201
1962	Norm Siebern	1b	112	16	128
1963	Carl Yastrzemski	lf	109	13	122
1964	Brooks Robinson	3b	117	26	143
1965	Rocky Colavito	rf	100	18	118
1966	Frank Robinson	rf	179	−11	168
1967	Horace Clarke	2b	27	122	149
1968	Carl Yastrzemski	lf	130	17	147
1969	Rico Petrocelli	ss	115	48	163
1970	Carl Yastrzemski	1b	179	−6	173
1971	Bobby Murcer	cf	126	10	136
1972	Dick Allen	1b	162	4	166
1973	Rod Carew	2b	112	42	154
1974	Bobby Grich	2b	68	88	156
1975	Fred Lynn	cf	122	27	149
1976	Bobby Grich	2b	60	89	149
1977	Rod Carew	1b	176	26	202
1978	Jim Rice	lf	153	33	186
1979	Fred Lynn	cf	158	18	176
1980	George Brett	3b	187	9	196
1981	Dwight Evans	rf	101	13	114
1982	Robin Yount	ss	128	32	160
1983	Cal Ripken, Jr.	ss	111	87	198
1984	Cal Ripken, Jr.	ss	98	119	217
1985	Rickey Henderson	cf	144	24	168
1986	Don Mattingly	1b	145	1	146
	Kirby Puckett	cf	122	24	146 tie
	Robin Yount	cf	124	22	146 tie
	Wade Boggs	3b	145	1	146 tie
1987	Wade Boggs	3b	150	15	165
1988	Wade Boggs	3b	177	25	202
1989	Wade Boggs	3b	124	29	153
1990	Rickey Henderson	lf	158	6	164
1991	Cal Ripken, Jr.	ss	120	108	228
1992	Frank Thomas	1b	146	−12	134
1993	John Olerud	1b	158	2	160

Year	Player	Pos.	Bat	Field	Total
1994	Frank Thomas	1b	179	−19	160
1995	Edgar Martinez	DH	162	*	162
1996	Roberto Alomar	2b	101	49	150
1997	Ken Griffey, Jr.	cf	132	12	144
1998	Damion Easley	2b	25	126	151
1999	Manny Ramirez	rf	181	−25	156
2000	Alex Rodriguez	ss	124	51	175
2001	Alex Rodriguez	ss	146	24	170
2002	Alex Rodriguez	ss	136	39	175
2003	Alex Rodriguez	ss	117	57	174
2004	Miguel Tejada	ss	114	34	148
2005	Alex Rodriguez	3b	153	4	157
2006	David Ortiz	DH	125	*	125

not enough games at any position to qualify for fielding points

Federal League. Although his name was not the best known among the stars who jumped to the new Federal League in 1914, Benny Kauff proved to be by far the loop's best player. By a wide margin he won Player of the Year honors in both years of the league's life. If he had been able to maintain that pace for a decade or so in the National League, he would have become a viable Hall of Fame candidate. However, he ran afoul of the law and, although never convicted of any crimes, was banned from baseball by Commissioner Kenesaw Mountain Landis in 1920.

FEDERAL LEAGUE PLAYER OF THE YEAR, 1914–15

Year	Player	Pos.	Bat	Field	Total
1914	Benny Kauff	rf	160	28	188
1915	Benny Kauff	rf	153	44	195

Career Rankings of Players

In this section all eligible players are ranked in comparison to other players at the same position. Three separate rankings are provided for each position. First, the top ten players are identified based on their extended career; that is, all of their eligible seasons. Next, the best ten performers based on points per season are named. Finally, all eligible players are ranked according to their Faber System points earned during their ten best seasons (or all of their eligible seasons in case they have fewer than ten such years.)

First Base

Extended Careers. Based on his extended career of 20 eligible seasons (including stints at third base and in the outfield), Cap Anson is the best first baseman of all time. The Marshalltown, Iowa, native ranks fifth on the best ten years list, but his longevity enabled him to move to the top on the extended career rankings. The difficulty of performing at the same level of excellence for as long as 20 years caused him to drop out of the top ten in points per season. The same fate befell Eddie Murray, Rafael Palmeiro, and Roger Connor, among others. The only first basemen to rank in the top ten on all three lists are Jimmie Foxx, Lou Gehrig, and Jeff Bagwell, each of whom had 14 eligible seasons.

FIRST BASEMEN EXTENDED CAREERS

First Baseman	Eligible Years		Bat	Field	Other	Points
1. Cap Anson	1876–97	20	2729	630	95 3b, of	3454
2. Jimmie Foxx	1928–42	15	2610	703		3313
3. Eddie Murray	1977–96	20	2257	1038		3295
4. Lou Gehrig	1925–38	14	2716	545		3261
5. Rafael Palmeiro	1988–2003	18	2137	913		3050
6. Roger Connor	1880–96	17	2118	736		2854
7. Jeff Bagwell	1991–2004	14	1988	865		2853
8. Rod Carew	1967–85	17	2061	432	221 2b	2714
9. Mark Grace	1988–2002	15	1513	951		2464
10. Dan Brouthers	1881–94	13	1927	457		2384

ADRIAN C. ANSON.
ALLEN & GINTER'S
RICHMOND. *Cigarettes.* VIRGINIA

Points Per Season. In computing the average points per season, the number of points earned at each position is divided by the total number of eligible seasons. For multi-position players, the points per season may seem quite low. For example, Albert Pujols has six eligible big league seasons—three at first base, two in the outfield, and one in which he did not play enough games at a single position to earn fielding points. Dividing his first base points (224) by six yields 37.3 points. Dividing his outfield points (77) by six provides 12.8 points. Adding these two together results in 50.1 points, which is his correct total. However, at first glance this appears to undervalue his performance at each position. If we were to calculate his points based on the number of years he played at each position, the results would be 74.7 at first base and 38.5 in the outfield. If we were judging his performance at either of those positions, these numbers could be used. But as a player, however, the 50.1 statistic is the right one to use. Todd Helton leads first basemen in points per season. Pujols is second. Both of these players are still active. Helton may have reached his peak. Barring injury or other misfortune, Pujols bids fair to improve his rating, especially if he remains at first base. He

Adrian Constantine Anson was nicknamed "Cap" in honor of his many years as playing manager of the Chicago White Stockings. Twice he was the National League's leading third baseman and eight times he was the best at first base. For an extended career of 20 years he was baseball's greatest first baseman (Library of Congress).

is an excellent fielder but as of this writing has only five seasons with enough games at the same position to earn fielding points. Among players no longer active Gehrig has the most points per season. He, Foxx, and Bagwell were mentioned above. Of the other first basemen in the top ten in points per season, each retired with from nine to twelve eligible seasons. Both Hank Greenberg at number five and ninth-place Johnny Mize lost time due to wartime military service. Greenberg lost five years and Mize three. Both almost certainly would have ranked higher on the other lists had not their country needed them elsewhere.

FIRST BASEMEN POINTS PER SEASON

First Baseman	Eligible Years		Bat	Field	Other	Points
1. Todd Helton	1998–2006	9	189.2	79.3		268.3
2. Albert Pujols	2001–06	6	207.2	37.3	12.8 of	258.3
3. Lou Gehrig	1925–38	14	192.9	38.9		231.8
4. Jimmie Foxx	1928–42	15	174.0	46.9		220.9
5. Hank Greenberg	1933–42	9	156.7	46.4	4.8	207.9
6. Jeff Bagwell	1991–2004	14	142.0	61.8		203.8
7. Bill Terry	1925–35	10	129.2	74.0		203.2
8. Keith Hernandez	1976–87	12	121.2	77.1		198.3
9. Johnny Mize	1936–51	12	143.8	44.1		187.9
10. Mark McGwire	1987–99	11	144.1	40.5		184.6

Career Rankings— Best Ten Years. According to Faber System's preferred methods of rating ball players— their best ten years— Lou Gehrig is the highest ranking first baseman of all time. His contemporary Jimmie Foxx is second, and, perhaps surprisingly, still-active Todd Helton is third. Every one of the top ten performers on the career list also made the top ten in one or the other of the extended career or points per season rankings. Gehrig, Foxx, and Jeff Bagwell made both of the others. Still active at number 15 on the career list, Jim Thome is the best performer not ranking in the top ten in any of the lists. The leading first basemen span the history of baseball; three of the top ten performed in the 19th century; four played exclusively in the 20th century; and three have careers that spanned the most recent turn of the century. The complete rankings show 213 names, including two (David Ortiz and Matt Franco) who have no eligible fielding seasons but have played more games at the initial sack than anywhere else on the field. Lou Gehrig, baseball's best hitting first baseman, comes out on top in the overall rankings, while Keith Hernandez the best fielder among first sackers, ranks eleventh as a Player. Although Keith was an excellent hitter, with a National League batting championship to his credit, he did not have the power that some of his competitors displayed.

RANKING OF FIRST BASEMEN (BEST YEARS)

First Baseman	Years		Bat	Field	Other	Points
1. Lou Gehrig	1925–38	10	2247	444		2691
2. Jimmie Foxx	1928–42	10	1942	574		2516
3. Todd Helton	1999–2006	9	1703	714		2417
4. Jeff Bagwell	1991–2004	10	1728	678		2406
5. Cap Anson	1876–97	10	1801	494		2295
6. Dan Brouthers	1881–94	10	1842	366		2208
7. Eddie Murray	1977–96	10	1456	734		2190
8. Roger Connor	1880–96	10	1578	598		2176
9. Johnny Mize	1936–49	10	1683	474		2157
10. Rafael Palmeiro	1988–2005	10	1474	664		2138

First Baseman	Years		Bat	Field	Other	Points
11. Keith Hernandez	1976–87	10	1301	796		2097
12. Rod Carew	1969–82	10	1489	405	155 2b	2049
13. Bill Terry	1925–35	10	1292	740		2032
14. Mark McGwire	1987–99	10	1555	445		2000
15. Jim Thome	1994–2006	10	1478	414	69 3b	1961
16. Fred McGriff	1988–2001	10	1400	541		1941
17. Mark Grace	1988–2002	10	1148	784		1932
18. Harmon Killebrew	1959–72	10	1576	196	159 3b, of	1931
19. Frank Thomas	1991–2006	10	1775	139		1914
20. Don Mattingly	1984–95	10	1291	603		1894
21. Will Clark	1986–2000	10	1290	592		1882
22. Hank Greenberg	1933–47	9	1410	418	43 of	1871
23. Willie McCovey	1960–79	10	1516	353		1869
24. George Sisler	1916–30	10	1293	567		1860
25. Orlando Cepeda	1958–70	10	1428	423		1851
26. Andres Galarraga	1987–2001	10	1334	513		1847
27. Norm Cash	1960–72	10	1245	577		1822
28. John Olerud	1990–2004	10	1176	623		1799
29. Gil Hodges	1948–62	10	1163	626		1789
30. Boog Powell	1962–75	10	1297	483		1780
31. Dick Allen	1964–75	10	1529	94	94 3b, of	1717
32. Tony Perez	1965–81	10	1254	381	75 3b	1710
33. Fred Tenney	1897–1908	10	1037	653		1690
34. Carlos Delgado	1996–2006	10	1223	461		1684
35. Steve Garvey	1974–85	10	1103	562		1665
36. Kent Hrbek	1982–94	10	1120	539		1659
37. Cecil Cooper	1975–85	10	1123	526		1649
38. Jake Beckley	1889–1905	10	1042	598		1640
39 Jake Daubert	1910–24	10	988	646		1634
40. Wally Joyner	1986–2000	10	971	660		1631
41. Ed Konetchy	1908–21	10	892	695		1587
42. George Scott	1966–79	10	1062	510		1572 tie
43. Jason Giambi	1996–2006	10	1374	198		1572 tie
44. Bill Buckner	1972–86	10	908	658		1566
45. Mickey Vernon	1941–58	10	962	593		1555
46. Rudy York	1937–47	10	1038	445	70 c	1553
47. Albert Pujols	2001–06	6	1243	224	77 of	1544
48. Dolf Camilli	1934–42	10	1125	413		1538
49. Bill White	1956–68	10	963	568		1531
50. Mark Hargrove	1974–85	10	1044	464		1508
51. Chris Chambliss	1971–85	10	813	678		1491
52. Frank McCormick	1938–46	9	881	599		1480
53. Lee May	1967–79	10	970	509		1479
54. John Mayberry	1972–81	10	969	506		1475
55. Jim Bottomley	1923–36	10	1140	323		1463
56. Joe Start	1889–1905	10	939	469		1408
57. Joe Judge	1917–30	10	800	597		1397 tie
57. Tino Martinez	1992–2005	10	866	531		1397 tie
59. Stuffy McInnis	1911–24	10	699	688		1387
60. Mo Vaughn	1992–2002	10	1175	205		1380

First Baseman	Years		Bat	Field	Other	Points
61. Eric Karros	1992–2003	10	733	644		1377
62. Lu Blue	1921–31	10	886	490		1376
63. Dan McGann	1898–1908	10	702	646		1348
64. Bob Watson	1971–80	9	970	280	95 of	1345
65. George Kelly	1920–29	9	667	527	136 2b	1330
66. Ted Kluszewski	1948–58	10	948	381		1329
67. Joe Adcock	1951–65	10	768	472	66 of	1306
69. Jason Thompson	1976–85	10	864	416		1280
70. Wally Pipp	1915–27	10	628	630		1258
71. George McQuinn	1938–47	10	612	574		1250
72. Elbie Fletcher	1937–49	10	694	544		1238
73. Harry Davis	1896–1910	10	844	385		1229
74. Ron Fairly	1961–77	10	884	178	161 of	1223
75. Jack Fournier	1914–27	10	990	229		1219
76. Cecil Fielder	1990–98	8	866	350		1216
77. Vic Power	1954–65	10	522	613	75 of	1210
78. Bill Skowron	1955–66	10	717	486		1203
79. J. T. Snow	1993–2005	10	640	555		1195
80. George Burns	1914–27	10	721	473		1194
81. Henry Larkin	1885–92	9	940	143	108 of	1191
82. Hal Trosky	1934–44	8	835	351		1186
83. Norm Siebern	1958–66	7	778	310	97 of	1185
84. Willie Montanez	1971–80	10	655	382	136 of	1173
85. Tommy Tucker	1887–99	10	716	445		1161
86. Richie Sexson	1999–2006	7	761	391		1152
87. Long John Reilly	1880–91	10	810	337		1147
88. Joe Kuhel	1932–45	10	654	491		1145
89. John Morrill	1876–1888	10	692	399	49 3b	1140
90. Pete O'Brien	1983–92	10	581	543		1124
91. Hal Chase	1905–19	10	785	330		1115
92. Charlie Grimm	1922–33	10	485	624		1109
93. John Kruk	1986–94	9	898	139	69 of	1106
94. Derrek Lee	1998–2005	7	691	413		1104
95. Phil Cavarretta	1935–49	10	819	192	75 of	1086
96. Ferris Fain	1947–55	8	690	392		1082 tie
96. Bruce Bochte	1975–86	10	708	282	92 of	1082 tie
98. Frank Chance	1903–08	6	716	362		1078
99. Wes Parker	1964–72	10	562	486		1048
100. Zeke Bonura	1934–40	7	597	447		1044
101. Fred Luderus	1911–19	9	598	444		1042
102. Mike Sweeney	1997–2005	7	769	201	70 c	1040
103. Fred Merkle	1910–19	10	609	428		1037
104. Dave Orr	1884–90	7	777	258		1035
105. Andre Thornton	1974–86	10	764	267		1031
106. Dan Driessen	1973–85	10	647	377		1024
107. Gus Suhr	1930–39	9	609	406		1015
108. Donn Clendennon	1963–70	8	635	373		1008
109. Paul Konerko	1999–2006	8	657	341		998
110. Alvin Davis	1984–91	8	710	263		973
111. Earl Sheely	1921–31	8	538	434		972

First Baseman	Years		Bat	Field	Other	Points
112. Whitey Lockman	1948–57	10	522	257	188 of	967
113. Earl Torgeson	1947–57	10	608	356		964
114. Sean Casey	1999–2006	8	671	290		961
115. Ripper Collins	1932–38	7	631	292		923
116. Joe Pepitone	1963–71	9	459	355	108 of	922
117. Darin Erstad	1997–2005	8	504	145	269 of	918
118. Don Mincher	1964–71	9	543	363		906
119. Chick Gandil	1912–19	8	409	496		905
120. Charlie Comiskey	1882–92	10	514	386		900
121. Deron Johnson	1954–75	10	687	140	70 3b, of	897
122. Hal Morris	1990–98	8	614	275		889
123. Dick Hoblitzell	1909–17	9	499	349		848
124. Leon Durham	1981–87	7	600	195	45 of	840
125. David Segui	1993–2000	9	444	384		828
126. Dick Stuart	1959–65	7	621	201		822
127. Don Hurst	1928–33	6	562	251		813
128. Jim Spencer	1969–81	10	346	466		812
129. Bill Phillips	1879–88	10	400	391		791
130. Jim Gentile	1960–64	5	582	205		787
131. Ed Kranepool	1964–77	10	370	415		785
132. George Stovall	1905–15	10	270	505		775
133. Willie Upshaw	1982–88	7	457	317		774
134. Eddie Robinson	1948–56	6	493	272		765
135. Dots Miller	1909–17	9	419	187	158 2b	764
136. Kitty Bransfield	1901–10	9	356	399		755
137. Glenn Davis	1985–92	6	537	216		753
138. Kevin Millar	1999–2006	8	532	149	63 of	744
139. Mike Epstein	1967–73	7	446	297		743
140. Tony Clark	1996–2005	8	524	213		737
141. Jack Doyle	1892–1903	9	551	180		731
142. David Ortiz	2000–06	6	716	*		716
143. Nick Etten	1941–46	6	533	156		689
144. Nate Colbert	1969–74	6	439	242		681
145. Joe Harris	1917–27	6	447	146	75 of	668
146. Greg Brock	1983–90	7	321	327		648
147. Walt Dropo	1950–56	6	387	251		638
148. Eddie Waitkus	1946–52	6	249	381		630
149. Danny Cater	1965–71	7	404	191	32 of	627
150. Tom Jones	1904–10	7	172	450		622
151. Walter Holke	1917–25	8	171	435		606
152. John Milner	1972–80	8	452	92	60 of	604
153. Dave Magadan	1988–97	8	433	126	43 3b	602
154. Sid Bream	1986–93	6	281	300		581
155. Charlie Hickman	1900–06	7	577	5	–15 2b, of	567
156. Jake Stahl	1904–10	6	333	229		562
157. Vic Saier	1912–16	5	369	191		560
158. Willie Aikens	1979–83	5	437	117		554
159. Candy La Chance	1895–1904	9	184	353		537
160. Scott Hatteberg	1997–2006	7	272	170	93 c	535

*not enough games at a position in any season to be eligible for fielding points.

First Baseman	Years		Bat	Field	Other	Points
161. Dick Siebert	1939–45	7	237	295		532
162. Patsy Tebeau	1889–98	7	203	246	81 3b	530
163. Babe Dahlgren	1935–45	7	271	257		528
164. Dave Foutz	1887–93	5	427	120	−21 of	526
165. Jack Burns	1931–36	6	183	342		525
166. Randy Milligan	1989–93	5	332	190		522
167. Dale Long	1955–62	7	271	246		517
168. Paul Sorrento	1992–98	7	286	223		509
169. Buddy Hassett	1936–42	7	270	235		505
170. Sid Farrar	1883–90	8	144	356		500
171. Shea Hillenbrand	2001–06	6	395	52	37 3b	484
172. John Ganzel	1901–08	5	159	312		471 tie
173. Dee Fondy	1952–57	6	219	252		471 tie
174. Travis Lee	1999–2006	7	197	270		467
175. Pat Tabler	1983–89	7	385	80	1 of	466
176. Mike Jorgenson	1972–76	5	256	207		463
177. Lee Thomas	1961–65	5	263	114	68 of	445
178. Perry Werden	1890–97	5	214	239		453
179. Dick Gernert	1952–59	5	250	173		423 tie
180. Kevin Young	1993–2002	5	204	219		423 tie
181. Buck Jordan	1933–37	5	214	204		418
182. Frank Isbell	1901–09	6	83	295	21 2b	399
183. Lee Stevens	1992–2002	5	204	184		388
184. Ron Jackson	1976–83	5	181	168	36 3b	385
185. Mike Ivie	1975–79	5	281	101		382
186. Tommy McCraw	1963–72	6	160	191	25 of	376
187. Babe Young	1940–47	5	277	94		371
188. Bob Oliver	1969–74	5	238	98	32 of	368
189. Phil Todt	1925–30	6	−57	420		363
190. Nick Esasky	1984–89	5	257	101	3 3b	361
191. Lamar Johnson	1977–82	5	295	65		360
192. Harvey Hendrick	1927–32	5	303	51		354
193. Doc Johnston	1913–21	7	132	211		343 tie
194. Steve Balboni	1984–89	5	216	127		343 tie
195. Joe Collins	1950–55	6	246	87		333
196. Dick Sisler	1948–52	5	173	69	88 of	330
197. Fred Whitfield	1963–67	5	204	120		324
198. Danny Meyer	1975–82	5	192	97	8 of	297
199. Gerald Perry	1984–91	5	199	82		281
200. Doug Mientkiewicz	1999–2004	5	96	144		240
201. Brad Fullmer	1998–2002	5	215	21		236
202. Rich Reese	1968–72	5	137	96		233
203. Larry Biittner	1972–79	5	187	41		228
204. Dave Bergman	1982–90	5	179	48		227
205. Russ Wrightstone	1921–27	5	155	45	19 of	219
206. Todd Benzinger	1988–92	5	90	102		192
207. Franklin Stubbs	1986–91	5	19	117	46 of	182
208. Frank Torre	1956–62	5	58	114		172
209. Mike Squires	1979–83	5	−23	130		107
210. Pete LaCock	1975–80	5	−6	57		51

First Baseman	Years		Bat	Field	Other	Points
211. Dalton Jones	1964–69	5	42	28	-72	−2
212. Tony Muser	1973–77	5	−37	−8		−45
213. Matt Franco	1997–2003	5	−189	*		−189

*not enough games at a position in any season to be eligible for fielding points.

Second Base

Extended Careers. Based on an extended career of all eligible seasons, Eddie Collins is the leading major league second baseman. Bid McPhee is second and Nap Lajoie third. Regardless of which method of ranking is used, these three second sackers come out as the top three, albeit not always in the same order. Joe Morgan and Craig Biggio, in fourth and seventh place respectively, make the top ten career list, but not the points per season rankings. All the other extended career leaders are among the leaders in all three systems. Biggio is the only active player in the top ten. All of the extended career leaders had at least 13 years of full-time major league service. McPhee, Lajoie, and tenth-ranking Bobby Doerr each earned more Faber System points in the field than at the plate; the others got the majority of their points with the bat.

SECOND BASEMEN EXTENDED CAREERS

Second Baseman	Eligible Years		Bat	Field	Other	Points
1. Eddie Collins	1908–26	19	2453	1497		3950
2. Bid McPhee	1881–96	17	1138	2241		3379
3. Nap Lajoie	1897–1916	15	1662	1712		3374
4. Joe Morgan	1965–84	19	1986	906		2892
5. Rogers Hornsby	1916–31	15	2503	210	141 ss, 3b	2854
6. Charlie Gehringer	1926–41	16	1659	1052		2711
7. Craig Biggio	1989–2006	17	1773	633	261 c, of	2667
8. Ryne Sandberg	1983–97	13	1354	1254		2608
9. Roberto Alomar	1988–2003	16	1603	937		2540
10. Bobby Doerr	1938–51	13	1102	1368		2470

Points Per Season. Lajoie moved ahead of Collins and McPhee to become the all-time leader in points per season. Bobby Grich and Hardy Richardson replaced Morgan and Biggio in the top ten when ratings are based on points per year. Otherwise, the same eight players were in both rankings. No active second sackers are in the top ten on points per season. Among the leaders only Roberto Alomar was active since 2000. The apparent discrepancy between fielding points per year shown in this table and the comparable figure depicted in the tables in Part 2 of the book is because some players had fewer eligible seasons as fielders than they did as players. For example, in 1908 Eddie Collins appeared in 102 games, so he is an eligible player that season. He did not appear in sufficient games at any position to be eligible for fielding points, but the season still counts as one of his 19 eligible seasons in this section of the book.

However, it is not included in the section on fielding. For fielding purposes, he had only 18 eligible seasons. This is only one of several examples that could be given.

SECOND BASEMEN POINTS PER SEASON

Second Baseman	Eligible Years		Bat	Field	Other	Points
1. Nap Lajoie	1897–1916	15	103.9	107.0		210.9
2. Eddie Collins	1908–26	19	129.1	78.8		207.9
3. Bid McPhee	1881–96	17	66.9	131.8		198.7

Second Baseman	Eligible Years		Bat	Field	Other	Points
4. Rogers Hornsby	1916–31	15	166.9	14.0	9.4 ss, 3b	190.3
5. Bobby Doerr	1938–51	13	84.8	105.2		190.0
6. Ryne Sandberg	1892–97	14	96.7	89.6		186.3
7. Bobby Grich	1972–85	13	88.8	84.6		173.4
8. Charlie Gehringer	1926–41	16	103.7	64.8		168.5
9. Roberto Alomar	1988–2003	16	100.2	58.6		160.8
10. Hardy Richardson	1879–90	11	110.4	23.4	24.2 3b, of	158.0

Career Rankings — Best Years. Nap Lajoie, Eddie Collins, and Bid McPhee rank one, two, three in the career rankings, just as they do in points per season listing. All of the other top ten career second basemen are among the ten leaders in points per year, with the sole exception of sixth-place Joe Morgan, who did not make the prior list. He replaces Hardy Richardson, who falls to 19th in the career rankings. Of the top ten McPhee and the two Bobbys—Doerr and Grich—attained more Faber System points in the field than at the plate; the reverse was true of the other leaders. Among the ten leaders McPhee played his entire career in the 19th century, fielding without a glove most of the time. Lajoie played in both the 19th and 20th, and Alomar participated in both the 20th and 21st centuries. Rogers Hornsby, the best hitting second baseman of all time, ranks fifth as a player, his below average glove work holding him out of the top spot. The best fielder McPhee comes in third as a player. The two men ahead of him, Lajoie and Collins, were superb both at the plate and in the field. Bill Mazeroski, the best fielder since McPhee, ranks 17th as a player. The best currently active player, Craig Biggio, ranks 12th among 216 eligible second basemen.

RANKING OF SECOND BASEMEN (BEST YEARS)

Second Baseman	Best Years		Bat	Field	Other	Points
1. Nap Lajoie	1897–1916	10	1567	1329		2896
2. Eddie Collins	1908–26	10	1624	1063		2687
3. Bid McPhee	1882–99	10	878	1587		2465
4. Ryne Sandberg	1982–93	10	1177	1165		2342
5. Rogers Hornsby	1916–31	10	1959	231	73 ss	2263
6. Joe Morgan	1965–84	10	1428	783		2211
7. Charlie Gehringer	1927–41	10	1322	850		2172
8. Bobby Doerr	1939–51	10	970	1160		2130
9. Bobby Grich	1972–85	10	989	1081		2070
10. Roberto Alomar	1998–2003	10	1270	792		2062
11. Nellie Fox	1951–61	10	967	995		1962
12. Craig Biggio	1991–2006	10	1308	638		1946
13. Frankie Frisch	1921–34	10	1044	829		1873
14. Billy Herman	1932–46	10	1037	789		1826 tie
14. Willie Randolph	1977–91	10	964	862		1826 tie
16. Jeff Kent	1992–2006	10	1193	631		1824
17. Bill Mazeroski	1952–70	10	365	1452		1817
18. Red Schoendienst	1945–58	10	754	1029		1783
19. Hardy Richardson	1879–90	10	1138	257	266 of	1661
20. Lou Whitaker	1978–94	10	986	664		1650 tie
20. Miller Huggins	1904–15	10	943	707		1650 tie
22. Jackie Robinson	1947–56	10	1166	294	98 1b-3b-of	1558
23. Chuck Knoblauch	1991–2000	10	977	409	40 of	1426
24. Cupid Childs	1890–1900	10	994	425		1419

Second Baseman	Best Years		Bat	Field	Other	Points
25. Del Pratt	1912–22	10	688	676		1364 tie
25. Fred Pfeffer	1882–96	10	531	833		1364 tie
27. Johnny Evers	1903–14	10	762	584		1346
28. Claude Ritchey	1897–1908	10	528	814		1342
29. Jimmy Williams	1899–1909	10	695	493	85 3b	1273
30. Ray Durham	1995–2006	10	818	439		1257
31. Buddy Myer	1926–38	10	729	415	90 3b	1234
32. Pete Runnels	1952–62	10	817	248	158 1b, ss	1223
33. Jim Gilliam	1953–65	10	852	240	121 3b	1213
34. Joe Gordon	1938–50	10	755	447		1202
35. Bret Boone	1994–2003	10	673	519		1192
36. Manny Trillo	1975–87	10	262	919		1181
37. Bobby Lowe	1891–1904	10	481	6138	59 3b	1178
38. Frank White	1975–89	10	345	832		1177
39. Glenn Hubbard	1980–88	9	222	949		1171
40. Tommy Herr	1981–90	10	504	634		1138
41. Steve Sax	1982–92	10	703	427		1130
42. Lonny Frey	1934–46	10	542	536	42 ss	1120 tie
42. Ron Hunt	1963–74	10	773	347		1120 tie
44. Robby Thompson	1986–93	8	492	617		1109
45. Johnny Ray	1982–90	9	557	549		1106
46. Davey Johnson	1966–74	9	570	528		1098
47. Luis Castillo	1999–2006	8	645	436		1081
48. Fred Dunlap	1880–89	7	555	524		1079
49. Dave Cash	1971–79	8	495	584		1079
50. Horace Clarke	1967–73	7	292	761		1053
51. Max Bishop	1925–33	9	705	338		1043 tie
51. Eric Young	1993–2005	10	677	366		1043 tie
53. Eddie Stanky	1943–51	8	659	377		1036
54. George Cutshaw	1912–22	10	215	815		1030
55. Billy Goodman	1948–58	10	727	97	185 1b, 3b	1009
56. Jody Reed	1988–96	9	372	636		1008
57. Jim Gantner	1980–91	10	332	647	16 3b	995
58. Phil Garner	1975–86	10	499	292	199 3b	990
59. Larry Doyle	1908–20	10	967	14		981
60. Placido Polanco	2000–06	7	382	418	180 3b	980
61. Lou Bierbauer	1886–95	10	128	851		979
62. Gil McDougald	1951–60	10	586	160	231 ss, 3b	977
63. Tony Cuccinello	1930–45	10	534	410	16 3b	960 tie
63. Felix Millan	1968–76	9	480	480		960 tie
65. Davey Lopes	1973–83	10	728	213		941
66. Tony Lazzeri	1926–36	10	819	106		925
67. George Grantham	1923–32	10	850	−52	123 1b	921
68. Carlos Baerga	1990–2003	10	572	344	3 3b	919
69. Cookie Rojas	1965–75	10	428	489		917
70. Bill Doran	1983–91	10	643	270		913

Opposite: Napoleon Lajoie was baseball's best second baseman when he jumped to the American League in 1901, giving the new loop instant creditability as a major league. In 1912 his adoring Cleveland fans presented him with this giant horseshoe festooned with more than 1000 silver dollars (Library of Congress).

Second Baseman	Best Years		Bat	Field	Other	Points
71. Mark McLemore	1987–2002	10	353	556		909
72. Glenn Beckert	1965–73	9	515	379		894
73. Fernando Vina	1994–2002	7	346	541		887
74. Bobby Avila	1951–58	8	561	321		882
75. Michael Young	2001–06	6	451	246	181 ss	878
76. Don Blasingame	1956–65	9	387	488		875
77. Jack Burdock	1876–88	10	479	394		873
78. Frank Bolling	1958–65	10	351	515		866
79. Danny Murphy	1903–11	9	681	−72	248 of	857
80. Bucky Harris	1920–27	8	309	542		851
81. Harold Reynolds	1986–93	8	348	492		840
82. Dick McAuliffe	1962–73	10	768	46	21 ss	835
83. Tommy Helms	1966–74	9	171	590	64 3b	825
84. Tony Taylor	1958–70	10	458	292	73 3b	823
85. Mark Grudzielanek	1996–2006	10	461	272	82 ss	815
86. Hughie Critz	1924–34	10	109	697		806
87. Gerry Priddy	1943–51	7	302	494		796
88. Jorge Orta	1973–86	10	650	19	118 of	787
89. Delino DeShields	1990–2001	10	596	187	22 of	785
90. Jose Vidro	1999–2006	7	585	198		783
91. Tom Daly	1887–1903	10	518	47	210 c	775
92. Johnny Temple	1954–63	9	544	229		773
93. Sparky Adams	1924–33	8	361	233	175 3b	769
94. Alfonso Soriano	2001–06	6	590	102	67 of	759 tie
96. Hobe Ferris	1901–09	9	68	534	157 3b	759 tie
96. George Stirnweiss	1944–50	6	433	289	35 3b	757
97. Jerry Lumpe	1959–66	8	340	412		752
98. Rennie Stennett	1972–79	8	245	496		741
99. Danny Richardson	1887–94	7	169	283	288 ss	740
100. Joe Gerhardt	1876–90	10	32	650	56 1b	738
101. Bump Wills	1977–82	6	351	386		737
102. Otto Knabe	1907–15	9	268	460		728
103. Jack Crooks	1890–95	5	218	452	57 3b	727
104. Mark Loretta	1997–2006	8	508	218		726
105. Bobby Knoop	1964–70	7	88	635		723
106. Bobby Richardson	1959–66	8	357	363		720
107. Damion Easley	1997–2005	6	231	486		717
108. Ted Sizemore	1969–78	8	270	429		699
109. Marty Barrett	1984–88	5	298	399		697
110. Jerry Remy	1975–83	7	396	299		695 tie
110. Juan Samuel	1984–91	8	473	153	69 of	695 tie
112. Bill Sweeney	1907–14	7	329	281	82 3b	692
113. Mickey Morandini	1992–99	8	259	422		681
114. Mike Andrews	1967–72	6	506	174		680
115. Julio Cruz	1978–84	7	180	499		679
116. Tito Fuentes	1966–77	10	214	438	21 ss	673
117. Hub Collins	1887–91	5	522	108	41 of	671
118. Dick Green	1964–74	8	201	465		666
119. Jose Lind	1988–94	7	−10	667		657
120. Oscar Melillo	1927–35	7	−100	752		652

Second Baseman	Best Years		Bat	Field	Other	Points
121. Jose Offerman	1992–2002	9	535	36	77 1b, ss	648
122. Jerry Adair	1961–69	8	126	425	82 ss	633
123. Frank LaPorte	1906–15	8	405	191	21 3b	617
124. Tony Bernazard	1981–87	7	357	242		599
125. Kid Gleason	1895–1906	10	209	389		598
126. Ron Belliard	1999–2006	7	271	306		577
127. Mike Lansing	1993–2000	7	233	319	23 3b	575
128. Todd Walker	1998–2006	8	478	71		549
129. Sam Barkley	1884–88	5	157	388		545
130. Craig Counsell	1998–2006	6	166	219	155 ss, 3b	540
131. Max Alvis	1963–68	6	309	229		538
132. Heinie Reitz	1893–98	5	182	350		532
133. Bill Wambsganss	1915–25	10	219	309		528
134. John Castino	1979–83	5	193	161	170 3b	524
135. Germany Schaefer	1905–11	6	269	202	48 1b	519 tie
135. Randy Velarde	1992–2000	6	308	178	33 ss	519 tie
137. Jose Oquendo	1983–90	6	199	315	0 ss	514
138. Tony Womack	1997–2004	7	318	108	83 ss, of	509
139. Danny O'Connell	1951–61	7	160	263	77 3b	500 tie
139. Adam Kennedy	2000–06	7	204	296		500 tie
141. Jimmy Brown	1937–42	6	288	69	137 ss, 3b	494
142. Ron Oester	1980–89	8	228	265		493
143. Jim Delahanty	1904–11	7	437	−8	62 3b, of	491
145. Charlie Neal	1957–63	6	275	171	28 3b	474
146. Gene DeMont	1896–1902	5	329	71	68 ss	468
147. Cass Michaels	1945–54	9	214	173	78 ss, 3b	465
148. Julian Javier	1960–70	10	248	206		454
149. Pop Smith	1880–90	8	156	134	159 ss	449
150. John Hummel	1907–12	6	189	209	48 of	446 tie
150. Bill Hallman	1889–1901	9	160	231	55 ss	446 tie
152. Aaron Ward	1920–27	7	16	321	77 3b	414
153. Joe Quinn	1885–1900	8	−97	503	7 of	413
154. Cub Stricker	1882–92	10	262	143		405
155. Duane Kuiper	1975–82	5	86	307		393
156. Dick Padden	1897–1904	6	81	288	20 ss	389
157. Dick Egan	1909–14	5	76	383	−74 ss	385
158. Jack Farrell	1879–88	6	294	79		373
159. Rich Dauer	1978–84	7	175	192		367 tie
159. Jerry Royster	1976–86	6	164	130	73 3b	367 tie
161. Pokey Reese	1997–2002	5	−31	361	36 ss	366
162. Eddy Mayo	1943–48	5	76	204	84 3b	364
163. Sandy Alomar	1968–75	8	141	222		363
164. Art Howe	1977–81	5	247	76	39 1b, 3b	362
165. Burgess Whitehead	1934–41	5	63	289		352
166. Ralph Young	1915–22	7	124	215		339
167. Frankie Gustine	1940–48	8	198	4	135 3b	337
168. Jerry Browne	1987–94	6	318	40	−25 3b	333
169. Jackie Hayes	1929–37	5	−98	425		327 tie
169. Ed Abbaticchio	1903–08	5	259	51	17 ss	327 tie
171. Jim Lefebvre	1965–71	5	205	90	28 3b	323

Second Baseman	Best Years		Bat	Field	Other	Points
172. Damaso Garcia	1980–86	6	149	173		322
173. Connie Ryan	1943–53	7	117	204		321
174. Luis Alicia	1993–2001	7	247	71		318
175. Billy Gilbert	1901–05	6	128	173		301
176. Jimmy Bloodworth	1940–49	5	−33	325		292
177. Charley Bassett	1886–92	6	−31	144	174 ss, 3b	287
178. Mark Lemke	1992–97	7	51	235		286
179. Scott Spezio	1999–2006	5	72	136	74 1b	282
180. Don Gutteridge	1937–45	7	187	−9	78 3b	265
181. Billy Ripken	1988–92	5	−96	335		239
182. Don Kolloway	1942–50	6	64	121	53 2b	238
183. Joe Quest	1878–84	5	8	219		227
184. Marty Perez	1971–76	5	25	176	22 ss	223
185. Pete Coscarart	1939–45	6	107	101	13 ss	221
186. Emil Verban	1944–48	5	21	196		217
187. George Creamer	1880–84	5	−58	262		204
188. Carlos Garcia	1993–97	5	28	172		200
189. Bill Greenwood	1884–90	5	−21	220		199
190. Steve Yerkes	1911–15	5	120	101	−39 ss	182
191. Joey Cora	1993–98	6	338	−157		181
192. Bernie Allen	1962–70	6	131	45		176
193. Johnny Rawlings	1915–27	6	−52	137	88 ss	173
194. Miguel Cairo	1998–2005	5	−42	213		171
195. Pete Suder	1941–53	8	136	240	60 3b	164
196. Doug Flynn	1975–84	6	−124	272		148
197. Billy Gardner	1956–60	5	−15	132		117
198. Billy Martin	1952–60	6	34	71		105
199. Bill Regan	1926–30	5	−88	187		99
200. Marlon Anderson	1999–2006	6	85	8		93
201. Bill McClellan	1878–88	5	189	−116	17 ss	90
202. Mike Gallego	1988–94	5	−2	49	32 ss	79
203. Nelson Liriano	1989–96	5	45	22		67
204. Gary Sutherland	1967–76	7	29	24		53
205. Tony Piet	1932–37	5	39	−16	11 3b	34
206. Wayne Tolleson	1983–87	5	59	−17	-9 ss	33
207. Tom Foley	1984–89	5	22	31	-23 ss	30
208. Barry McCormick	1897–1904	5	−156	105	15 3b	−36
209. Al Myers	1885–91	5	43	−129		−86
210. Yank Robinson	1885–91	7	308	−400		−92
211. Mike Tyson	1973–80	6	−88	29	-42 ss	−101
211. Keith Lockhart	1995–2002	6	−40	−61		−101 tie
213. Al Newman	1987–92	5	−59	−59		−118
214. Denny Hocking	1997–2002	5	−127	0		−127
215. Wilton Guerrero	1997–2002	5	−139	−28		−167
216. Tim Cullen	1967–71	5	−161	−89		−250

Shortstop

Extended Careers. Honus Wagner ranks as the best shortstop of all time, based on an extended career of all eligible seasons. The Flying Dutchman also leads the career rankings based on his best ten years, and is third in points per season. He achieved his high ranking by playing excellent defense while being the National League's best hitter of his era. In second place is Cal Ripken, Jr., who also excelled both at the plate and in the field, as well as being baseball's all-time leader in consecutive games played. In third place is Robin Yount, who also played quite well in the outfield. Fourth place goes to Ozzie Smith, who is the best fielder ever to wield a glove at any position. Mr. Cub, the exuberant Ernie Banks, and old-time star Jack Glasscock joined Ozzie, Wagner, and Ripken as the only shortstops to rank in the top ten in all three ranking systems. Glasscock, who played without a glove, gained his honors in 14 seasons; all of the other extended career leaders played 15 or more eligible seasons. Smith, Aparicio, and Glasscock earned more fielding than batting points; the reverse was true of all others. Of the top ten shortstops only Glasscock played exclusively in the pioneer era. Wagner and Davis both played at the turn of the 19th and 20th centuries. The careers of Ripken and Rodriguez spanned the end of the 20th and beginning of the 21st. Among the leaders only A-Rod is still active. He bodes fair to move up in the rankings, if all goes well with him.

RANKING OF SHORTSTOPS EXTENDED CAREERS

Shortstop	Eligible Years		Bat	Field	Other	Points
1. Honus Wagner	1898–1916	19	2549	1305	84 1b, 3b, of	3938
2. Cal Ripken, Jr.	1982–2001	18	2118	1462	139 3b	3719
3. Robin Yount	1974–93	20	1665	920	658 of	3243
4. Ozzie Smith	1978–94	17	752	2405		3157
5. George Davis	1890–1908	18	1378	1054	437 3b, of	2869
6. Ernie Banks	1954–69	16	1632	583	552 1b	2767
7. Luis Aparicio	1956–73	18	874	1556		2430
8. Jack Glasscock	1880–91	14	1102	1236		2338
9. Alan Trammell	1978–94	15	1176	1139		2315
10. Alex Rodriguez	1996–2006	11	1692	538	84 3b	2314

Points Per Season. Fiery Hughie Jennings had only seven eligible seasons during his long and distinguished major league career, but he earned enough points during those few years to be the all-time leaders in points per season just ahead of Rodriguez, Ripken, and Wagner. Lou Boudreau ranks fifth, ahead of greats Ozzie Smith and Ernie Banks and the underrated Jack Glasscock. Still-active Nomar Garciaparra ranks ninth. Like A-Rod, Nomar has recently moved from shortstop to another infield position. Hall of Famer Joe Cronin rounds out the top ten.

RANKING OF SHORTSTOPS POINTS PER SEASON

Shortstop	Eligible Seasons		Bat	Field	Other	Points
1. Hughie Jennings	1892–1900	7	114.0	93.9	6.4 1b	214.3
2. Alex Rodriguez	1996–2006	11	153.8	48.9	7.6 3b	210.4
3. Honus Wagner	1898–1916	19	134.2	68.7	4.4 1b, 3b, of	207.3
4. Cal Ripken, Jr.	1982–2001	18	117.7	81.2	7.7 3b	206.6
5. Lou Boudreau	1940–49	9	82.3	112.1		194.4
6. Ozzie Smith	1978–94	17	44.2	141.5		185.7
7. Ernie Banks	1954–69	16	102.0	36.4	34.5 1b	172.9
8. Jack Glasscock	1880–91	14	78.7	88.3		167.0
9. Nomar Garciaparra	1997–2006	7	130.4	25.1	7.9 1b	163.4
10. Joe Cronin	1929–41	12	93.0	69.3		162.3

Career Rankings— Best Years. Of the 208 eligible shortstops Honus Wagner is the best in major league history. He was the best hitter, both in a ten-year career and an extended career, and was an outstanding fielder. Ozzie Smith ranks second. Although he was a weak hitter when he first entered the big leagues, Ozzie eventually became a better than average batsman and his sensational exploits in the field catapulted him into the runner-up spot. Steady Cal Ripken holds down third place, based on equally strong performance at the plate and in the field. Alex Rodriguez, in fourth, is the only active player in the top ten. Wagner, Smith, Ripken, and A-Rod as well as Ernie Banks and Jack Glasscock are in the top ten in career listings, extended careers, and points per season. Robin Yount, George Davis, and Alan Trammell each made one of the other top ten rankings. Holding down the tenth position in the career rankings is Barry Larkin. The Cincinnati star did not make the top ten in either of the other lists, but is close in both.

RANKING OF SHORTSTOPS (BEST YEARS)

Name	Years		Bat	Field	Other	Total
1. Honus Wagner	1898–1916	10	1730	1120		2850
2. Ozzie Smith	1978–94	10	688	1680		2368
3. Cal Ripken	1982–98	10	1144	1135		2270
4. Alex Rodriguez	1996–2006	10	1608	538	109 3b	2255
5. Robin Yount	1974–89	10	1249	928		2177
6. Ernie Banks	1954–69	10	1277	583	177 1b	2037
7. Jack Glasscock	1879–93	10	859	1151		2010
8. George Davis	1890–1908	10	955	1054		2009
9. Alan Trammell	1978–93	10	1086	907		1993
10. Barry Larkin	1987–2004	10	1099	856		1955
11. Luis Aparicio	1958–70	10	719	1230		1949
12. Joe Cronin	1929–41	10	1043	829		1872
13. Bill Dahlen	1891–1908	10	921	946		1867
14. Jay Bell	1990–2000	10	783	979	21 2b	1783
15. Bobby Wallace	1897–1911	10	688	1094		1782
16. Lou Boudreau	1940–49	9	741	1009		1750
17. Arky Vaughan	1932–43	10	1306	364	37 3b	1706
18. Derek Jeter	1996–2006	10	1314	316		1630
19. Tony Fernandez	1985–99	10	645	983		1628
20. Joe Sewell	1921–32	10	713	764	149 3b	1626
21. Omar Vizquel	1989–2006	10	618	998		1616
22. Donie Bush	1909–21	10	832	759		1591
23. Luke Appling	1933–49	10	1020	536		1556
24. PeeWee Reese	1941–55	10	916	637		1553
25. Dick Bartell	1929–41	10	622	915		1537
26. Vern Stephens	1942–51	10	1054	412	61 3b	1527
27. Hughie Jennings	1892–1900	7	798	657	45 1b	1500
28. Dave Bancroft	1915–28	10	705	794		1499
29. Herman Long	1889–1902	10	808	662		1470
30. Dave Concepcion	1974–87	10	557	909		1466
31. Larry Bowa	1971–84	10	427	1029		1456
32. Rabbit Maranville	1913–30	10	346	1069		1415
33. Joe Tinker	1902–14	10	405	993		1398
34. Miguel Tejada	1999–2006	9	865	500		1365
35. Johnny Pesky	1942–53	8	861	282	204 3b	1347
36. Rico Petrocelli	1965–75	10	714	374	243 3b	1331

Honus Wagner was baseball's greatest shortstop. An eight-time batting champion, he was also the best fielder of his era at the position (Library of Congress).

Name	Years		Bat	Field	Other	Total
37. Dick Groat	1955–66	10	585	740		1325
38. Julio Franco	1983–2005	10	1123	190	11 2b, 1b	1324
39. Maury Wills	1960–71	10	821	492		1313
40. Bert Campaneris	1965–77	10	661	624		1285
41. Phil Rizzuto	1941–54	10	487	759		1246
42. Edgar Renteria	1996–2006	10	700	542		1242
43. Rick Burleson	1974–81	8	464	774		1238
44. Don Kessinger	1966–76	10	460	766		1226
45. Jim Fregosi	1963–70	9	696	512		1208
46. Travis Jackson	1924–35	10	519	679		1198
47. Leo Cardenas	1962–72	10	406	780		1186
48. Marty Marion	1940–50	10	241	931		1172
49. Garry Templeton	1977–90	10	471	670		1163
50. Roger Peckinpaugh	1914–25	10	395	753		1148
51. Nomar Garciaparra	1997–2006	7	913	176	55 1b	1144
52. Al Dark	1948–58	10	676	446		1122
53. Monte Ward	1881–94	10	754	216	150 of	1120
54. Roy Smalley	1976–86	9	535	576		1111
55. Tommy Corcoran	1890–1904	10	83	1030		1103
56. Eddie Miller	1940–48	8	48	1033		1081
57. Johnny Logan	1952–60	9	333	740		1073
58. Mark Belanger	1968–78	10	109	960		1069
59. Chris Speier	1971–87	10	344	722		1066
60. Royce Clayton	1993–2005	10	213	847		1060
61. Art Fletcher	1911–22	10	478	568		1046
62. Roy McMillan	1952–65	10	104	932		1036
63. Billy Jurges	1932–43	10	197	807		1004
64. Ray Chapman	1913–20	8	608	394		1002
65. Bucky Dent	1974–83	9	52	948		1000
66. John Valentin	1993–99	7	505	256	229 3b	990
67. Eddie Joost	1941–52	9	433	460	88 3b	981
68. Spike Owen	1984–94	10	212	726	26 3b	964
69. Kid Elberfield	1901–11	9	464	405	88 3b	957
70. Terry Turner	1904–16	10	260	334	362 3b	956
71. Tim Foli	1972–82	10	–4	945		941
72. Everett Scott	1913–24	10	–204	1126		922 tie
72. Orlando Cabrera	1999–2006	8	226	696		922 tie
74. Ron Hansen	1960–68	7	275	634		909
75. Jimmy Rollins	2001–06	6	464	414		878
76. Neifi Perez	1998–2006	10	151	723		874
77. Rafael Furcal	2000–06	6	536	342		868
78. Germany Smith	1884–97	10	5	845		850
79. Freddy Parent	1901–09	9	464	379		843
80. Roger Metzger	1971–78	7	63	749		812
81. Ozzie Guillen	1985–97	10	45	755		800
82. Rich Aurelia	1996–2006	10	459	339		798
83. Scott Fletcher	1983–93	9	378	211	204 2b	793
84. Greg Gagne	1985–97	10	207	585		792
85. Mike Bordick	1992–2003	10	131	649		780
86. Mickey Doolan	1905–15	10	–47	824		777

Name	Years		Bat	Field	Other	Total
87. George McBride	1905–16	10	−150	921		771
88. Ed McKean	1887–98	10	931	−165		766
89. Buck Herzog	1910–19	9	376	−99	119 2b, 3b	758
90. Ed Brinkman	1963–74	10	−40	797		757
91. Chico Carrasquel	1950–59	8	212	537		749
92. Gene Alley	1965–72	7	169	576		745
93. Shawon Dunston	1986–99	8	245	496		741
94. Denis Menke	1963–73	10	554	46	137 1b-2b-3b	737
95. Woody English	1928–37	8	445	150	141 3b	736
96. Alfredo Griffin	1979–91	10	155	578		733
97. Billy Rogell	1928–38	8	212	518		730
98. Al Bridwell	1906–14	8	345	374		719
99. David Eckstein	2001–06	6	325	387		712
100. Lyn Lary	1930–38	7	252	456		708
101. Bill Russell	1972–83	10	305	393		698
102. Dick Schofield	1984–94	8	−48	734		686
103. Jose Vizcaino	1993–2002	6	222	449		671
104. Rey Sanchez	1993–2002	7	50	530	84 2b	664 tie
105. Walt Weiss	1988–97	7	158	506		664 tie
106. Jeff Blauser	1989–97	9	466	187		653
107. Bud Harrelson	1967–77	10	130	521		651
108. Buddy Kerr	1944–50	6	12	635		647
109. Jack Wilson	2001–06	6	82	562		644
110. Woody Held	1958–65	8	361	222	59 of, 2b	642
111. Ivan DeJesus	1977–84	8	315	303		618
112. Red Kress	1928–38	7	351	218	26 3b, 1b	595 tie
113. Tony Kubek	1957–65	8	201	394		595 tie
114. Freddie Patek	1969–78	8	219	351		570
115. Glenn Wright	1924–32	7	398	163		561
116. Johnny Peters	1876–1882	6	393	147		550
117. Buck Weaver	1912–20	9	291	114	130 3b	535
118. Dickie Thon	1982–91	5	198	318		516
119. Frank Fennelly	1884–89	6	453	44		497
120. Sam Wise	1882–93	10	550	−96	37 2b	491
121. Alex S. Gonzalez	1996–2005	9	−25	501	3 3b	479
122. Solly Hemus	1951–58	5	345	135	−8 2b	472
123. Julio Lugo	2000–06	6	270	201		471 tie
123. Heinie Wagner	1907–13	6	164	307		471 tie
125. Arthur Irwin	1880–90	9	139	294	25 3b	458
126. Jose Valentin	1995–2006	10	247	125	74 25, 3b	446
127. Frankie Crosseti	1933–45	9	210	220		430
128. Zoilo Versalles	1961–68	8	276	153		429
129. Davy Force	1876–84	8	−120	375	165 2b	420
130. Rey Ordonez	1996–2002	6	−107	514		407
131. Bill Spiers	1989–2000	5	243	127	25 3b	395
132. Frank Duffy	1972–77	6	21	366		387
133. Eddie Kasko	1957–64	6	140	189	55 3b	384
134. Craig Reynolds	1977–86	7	99	283		382
135. Leo Durocher	1928–39	7	−136	513		377 tie
135. Eddie Bressoud	1959–66	7	206	171		377 tie

Name	Years		Bat	Field	Other	Total
137. Wayne Causey	1961–67	7	239	131	5 2b, 3b	375
138. Bones Ely	1890–1902	10	−192	538	24 of	370
139. Dal Maxvill	1966–72	7	−45	400		355
140. Don Buddin	1956–61	5	142	210		352
141. Sadie Houck	1879–86	7	186	159	3 of	348
142. Deivi Cruz	1998–2004	8	6	315		321
143. Gene Michael	1969–73	5	−58	375		318
144. Monte Cross	1895–1906	10	−81	381		300
145. Tom Veryser	1975–81	6	24	275		299
146. Ed Caskin	1879–84	5	103	194		297
147. Alex Gonzalez	1999–2006	6	1	288		289
148. Johnny Lipon	1948–52	5	98	191		279
149. Jose Hernandez	1998–2003	5	121	125	29 3b	275
150. Billy Klaus	1955–62	5	122	96	53 3b	271
151. Hod Ford	1921–30	8	−190	251	206 2b	267
152. Rafael Ramirez	1981–90	8	165	100		265
153. Wally Gerber	1919–28	9	−85	347		262
154. Gary DiSarcina	1992–98	6	−95	349		254
155. George Strickland	1951–59	6	−41	265	29 3b	253
156. Mark Koenig	1926–35	7	226	25		252
157. Chris Gomez	1994–2004	6	−11	262		251
158. Carlos Guillen	2001–06	5	294	−46		248
159. Wil Cordero	1993–2000	6	196	−125	175 of, 3b	246
160. Granny Hamner	1948–57	10	204	19	20 2b	243
161. Eric McNair	1932–39	6	128	78	32 2b, 3b	238
162. Manny Lee	1988–94	5	14	121	101 2b	236
163. Bill Almon	1977–84	5	102	115	−2 3b	225
164. Jack Barry	1909–17	8	221	−30	33 2b	224
165. Ivy Olson	1911–22	9	173	23	23 2b	219
166. Skeeter Newsome	1936–46	6	−154	369		216
167. Ricky Gutierrez	1993–2001	5	134	81		215
168. Hal Lanier	1965–71	6	−268	385	95 2b	212
169. Jose Uribe	1985–90	5	−68	279		211
170. Mariano Duncan	1985–96	7	239	2	−34 3b	207
171. Kevin Stocker	1994–2000	6	−101	302		201
172. Bill Gleason	1882–88	7	494	−296		198
173. Heinie Sand	1923–28	6	91	103		194
174. Bill Urbanski	1932–36	5	69	123		192
175. Doc Lavan	1915–21	6	−8	198		190
176. Pat Mears	1994–2000	6	−22	187		165 tie
176. U. L. Washington	1972–83	5	99	66		165 tie
178. Alan Bannister	1977–83	5	201	−55	11 of	157
179. Larry Brown	1964–69	5	65	85		150
180. Charley O'Leary	1904–13	5	−103	247		144 tie
180. Bobby Wine	1962–71	7	−170	314		144 tie
182. Jose Pagan	1961–69	5	28	75	40 3b	143
183. Joe DeMaestri	1953–59	7	−184	308		125
184. Daryl Spencer	1953–60	6	117	−17	15 2b	115 tie
184. Ruben Amaro	1961–67	5	-66	181		115 tie
186. Frank Taveras	1976–81	5	187	−84		105 tie

Name	Years		Bat	Field	Other	Total
187. Alex Cora	2000–2004	5	3	68	34 2b	105 tie
188. Shorty Fuller	1889–95	7	35	53		88 tie
188. Bill Keister	1899–1903	5	336	−218	−30 2b, of	88 tie
190. Alvaro Espinosa	1989–96	5	−101	205	−49 3b	55
191. Alex Grammas	1954–60	5	−104	59		45
192. Tommy Thevenow	1926–35	5	−181	210	15 2b, 3b	44
193. Cristian Guzman	1999–2005	7	−27	64		37
194. Enzo Hernandez	1971–76	5	−111	147		36
195. Chick Galloway	1921–26	6	−67	102		35
196. Sonny Jackson	1966–71	5	61	−118	58 of	1
197. Johnnie LeMaster	1978–84	6	−118	109		−9
198. Chico Fernandez	1957–62	5	−45	28		−17
199. Desi Relaford	1998–2004	5	3	−31	−13 2b	−41
200. Rabbit Warstler	1932–38	6	−151	123	23 2b	−45 tie
200. Kurt Stillwell	1986–92	5	106	−151		−45 tie
202. Damian Jackson	1999–2005	5	−37	−18		−55
203. Woody Woodward	1965–71	5	−170	38	28 2b	−104
204. Frank Shugart	1892–1901	5	−4	−143	44 of	−112
205. Larry Kopf	1915–22	5	50	−140	−23 2b	−113
206. Felix Fermin	1989–94	5	−97	−32		−129
207. Bob Lillis	1961–65	5	−233	97		−136
208. Curtis Wilkerson	1984–92	5	−60	−126	−14 2b	−200

Third Base

Extended Careers. Over an extended career Mike Schmidt is baseball's greatest third baseman, edging out his contemporaries, George Brett and Wade Boggs. Hard-hitting Eddie Mathews is fourth, followed by slick-fielding Brooks Robinson and Buddy Bell. Ron Santo is seventh, followed by Paul Molitor, Graig Nettles, and Darrell Evans. Every one of these worthies played his entire career during the last half of the twentieth century. This fact is not true of the top ten rankings at any other position. Although they were good hitters, Robinson, Bell, and Nettles earned more Faber System points in the field than at the plate; the opposite is true of all the others.

RANKING OF THIRD BASEMEN EXTENDED CAREERS

Third Baseman	Eligible Years		Bat	Field	Other	Points
1. Mike Schmidt	1973–88	16	2179	1098	50 1b	3327
2. George Brett	1974–93	20	2458	666	120 1b	3244
3. Wade Boggs	1982–98	17	2119	1038		3157
4. Eddie Mathews	1952–67	16	1903	847		2750
5. Brooks Robinson	1958–75	17	1199	1370		2569
6. Buddy Bell	1973–87	16	1109	1240	64 of	2413
7. Ron Santo	1961–74	14	1539	873		2412
8. Paul Molitor	1978–98	19	1903	309	59 2b	2400
9. Graig Nettles	1970–86	16	1034	1079		2113
10. Darrell Evans	1972–89	18	1287	554	244 1b, of	2085

Points Per Season. Mike Schmidt, the best third baseman on an extended career basis, also leads in points per season. Boggs, Santo, Brett, and Mathews also appear in both rankings. Beyond those five superstars, there are considerable differences as players with shorter careers appear in

Over an extended career Mike Schmidt is baseball's greatest third baseman. He also leads in points per season. Although he did not have as high a batting average as Wade Boggs or George Brett, Schmidt hit with more power and was a better fielder than either of his chief rivals (National Baseball Hall of Fame Library, Cooperstown, New York).

the spotlight. In second place is still active Scott Rolen. Scrappy John McGraw is in third place. Like his fellow Baltimore Oriole infielder, shortstop Hughie Jennings, McGraw had a long major league career, including success as a manager, but he played enough games in a season to meet our eligibility criteria only a few times. Almost unknown to modern baseball fans, but recognized by experts as a fine hitter and remarkable fielder who still holds the all-time record for putouts in a season by a thirdsacker, oldtimer Denny Lyons is in sixth place. Stan Hack, long-time star of the Chicago Cubs, is eighth. Still-active Chipper Jones of the Atlanta Braves is in ninth place. All occupants of the top ten spots in these rankings earned more points at the bat than they did in the field.

RANKING OF THIRD BASEMEN POINTS PER SEASON

Third Baseman	Eligible Years		Bat	Field	Other	Points
1. Mike Schmidt	1973–88	16	136.2	73.2	3.1 1b	207.9
2. Scott Rolen	1997–2006	9	111.1	79.9		191.0
3. John McGraw	1893–1900	7	163.4	26.9		190.3
4. Wade Boggs	1982–98	17	124.6	61.1		185.7
5. Ron Santo	1961–74	14	109.9	62.4		172.3
6. Denny Lyons	1887–96	8	127.4	44.1		171.5
7. Eddie Mathews	1952–67	16	118.9	52.9		171.8
8. Stan Hack	1934–45	11	107.7	60.7		168.4
9. Chipper Jones	1995–2006	12	138.1	25.3	4.2 of	167.6
10. George Brett	1974–93	20	122.9	33.3	6.0 1b	162.2

Career Rankings — Best Years. When third basemen are ranked according to their best ten years, Wade Boggs rises to the top of the list, ahead of Mike Schmidt and George Brett, who outranked him on the extended career list. Eight of the top ten on the present list are also in the top ten in the earlier ranking. The exceptions are Chipper Jones and Stan Hack, who replace Graig Nettles and Darrell Evans.

Jones is the highest ranking active player. Hack is the only one of the ten leaders who started his career before World War II. The highest rank achieved by a player who started before 1900 is Jimmy Collins in 17th place. The highest ranking third baseman who completed his career before 1900 is Denny Lyons in 36th place. There were good third sackers in the pioneer era, but few of them played as many as ten eligible seasons. In fourth place in these rankings is Ron Santo, who may very well be the best player eligible for the Hall of Fame who has not yet been inducted. Among the top ten Buddy Bell, another underrated players, is the only one with more fielding than batting points. The five year eligibility requirement for ranking was met by 208 third basemen, the fewest at any fielding position.

RANKING OF THIRD BASEMEN (BEST YEARS)

Third Baseman	Best Years		Bat	Field	Other	Points
1. Wade Boggs	1982–98	10	1682	767		2449
2. Mike Schmidt	1974–87	10	1627	806		2433
3. George Brett	1975–90	10	1555	625		2180
4. Ron Santo	1961–74	10	1411	759		2170
5. Eddie Mathews	1952–67	10	1472	677		2149
6. Brooks Robinson	1960–75	10	1009	914		1923
7. Buddy Bell	1973–87	10	921	969		1890
8. Chipper Jones	1995–2006	10	1514	304	45 of	1863
9. Stan Hack	1934–45	10	1185	644		1829
10. Paul Molitor	1978–96	10	1508	309	8 2b	1825
11. Ken Boyer	1955–67	10	1176	607		1783
12. Ron Cey	1973–84	10	997	778		1775
13. Heinie Groh	1913–24	10	888	779	86 2b	1753
14. Scott Rolen	1997–2006	9	1000	719		1719
15. Edgar Martinez	1990–2001	10	1592	117		1709
16. Darrell Evans	1972–87	10	1026	509	165 1b	1700
17. Jimmy Collins	1897–1908	10	844	848		1692
18. Lave Cross	1891–1905	10	746	938		1684
19. Frank "Home Run" Baker	1909–19	10	1082	601		1683
20. Graig Nettles	1970–87	10	839	816		1657
21. Sal Bando	1968–79	10	1053	565		1618
22. Pie Traynor	1923–34	10	952	647		1599
23. Vinny Castilla	1993–2005	10	880	689		1589
24. Robin Ventura	1990–2004	10	908	668		1576
25. Gary Gaetti	1982–98	10	687	857		1544
26. Carney Lansford	1978–90	10	873	663		1536
27. Bob Elliott	1940–53	10	1071	400	49 of	1520
28. Matt Williams	1990–2001	10	827	680		1507
29. Eddie Yost	1948–60	10	934	568		1502
30. Harlond Clift	1934–45	10	846	647		1493
31. George Kell	1944–56	10	827	633		1460
31. Toby Harrah	1973–83	10	1005	312	143 ss	1460
33. Tim Wallach	1982–94	10	708	750		1458

Third Baseman	Best Years		Bat	Field	Other	Points
34. Bill Madlock	1974–86	10	1077	328		1405
35. Terry Pendleton	1985–96	10	572	832		1404
36. Denny Lyons	1887–96	8	1019	353		1372
37. Todd Zeile	1990–2002	10	760	488	119 c, 1b	1367
38. Travis Fryman	1991–2002	10	702	569	84 ss	1355
39. John McGraw	1893–1900	7	1144	188		1332
40. Arlie Latham	1883–95	10	842	475		1317
41. Doug DeCinces	1976–87	10	620	675		1295
42. Edgardo Alfonzo	1995–2005	10	722	339	220 2b	1281
42. Pinky Whitney	1928–37	9	571	706		1277
44. Ken Caminiti	1989–98	10	743	532		1266
45. Willie Kamm	1923–34	10	376	875		1251
46. Billy Nash	1886–97	10	608	620		1228
47. Richie Hebner	1969–81	10	861	289	60 1b	1210
48. Ken Keltner	1938–48	10	511	696		1207
49. Willie Jones	1949–59	10	465	720		1185
50. Ken Oberkfell	1979–86	10	490	553	134 2b	1177
51. Ned Williamson	1878–88	10	809	360		1169
52. Jeff Cirillo	1995–2006	9	632	521		1153
53. Eric Chavez	1999–2006	8	538	601		1139
54. Larry Gardner	1910–21	10	701	426		1127
55. Don Money	1969–78	10	528	417	181 2b, ss	1126
56. Bill Bradley	1900–08	8	574	550		1124
57. Deacon White	1876–88	10	1084	-91	119 c	1112
58. Al Rosen	1950–56	7	815	278		1093
59. Ken McMullen	1965–72	10	450	624		1074
60. Ezra Sutton	1876–88	10	802	270	21 ss	1051
60. Art Devlin	1904–12	8	600	451		1051
62. Mike Lowell	2000–06	7	483	560		1043
63. Harry Steinfeldt	1899–1910	10	501	526		1027
64. Frank Malzone	1957–65	9	565	466		1031
65. Bob Bailey	1963–74	10	735	218	78 1b-of	1021
66. Kevin Seitzer	1987–96	9	746	267		1013
67. Freddie Lindstrom	1925–33	8	606	254	148 of	1008
68. Clete Boyer	1960–70	10	271	735		1006
69. Red Rolfe	1935–41	7	547	458		1005
70. Larry Parrish	1975–87	10	751	177	72 of	1000
71. Heinie Zimmerman	1911–19	9	736	210	54 2b	997
72. Pinky Higgins	1933–44	10	716	278		994
73. Marty McManus	1922–34	10	564	269	145 2b	978
74. Milt Stock	1914–25	10	570	355	31 2b	956
75. Bob Horner	1979–86	7	683	149	116 1b	946
76. Whitey Kurowski	1942–47	6	583	355		938
77. George Pinckney	1885–93	8	564	374		937
78. Tom Burns	1880–90	10	577	260	96 ss, 2b	933
79. Billy Werber	1933–41	9	445	458		903
80. Jimmie Dykes	1920–35	10	383	324	192 2b, 1b	899
81. Troy Glaus	1999–2006	6	566	331		897
82. Adrian Beltre	1999–2006	8	527	368		895
83. Doug Rader	1969–76	8	340	544		884

Third Baseman	Best Years		Bat	Field	Other	Points
84. Don Hoak	1956–63	8	401	480		881
85. Aramis Ramirez	2001–06	6	600	264		864
86. Jerry Denny	1881–90	10	296	555		851
87. Ray Boone	1950–58	9	630	184	26 ss, 1b	840
88. Bill Mueller	1997–2005	8	482	355		837
89. Buddy Lewis	1936–47	8	547	123	149 of	819
90. Charlie Hayes	1990–98	9	374	440		814
91. Red Smith	1912–18	7	508	296		804
92. Jeff King	1990–98	8	414	190	198 1b	802
93. Aurelio Rodriguez	1969–82	10	80	721		801
94. Jimmy Austin	1909–19	10	202	588		790
95. Ken Reitz	1973–81	9	157	629		786
96. Ray Knight	1979–87	8	443	298	51 1b	782
97. Bill Shindle	1888–98	10	301	477		778
98. Enos Cabell	1975–85	10	429	155	182 1b	766
99. Brook Jacoby	1984–92	9	453	311		764
100. Wid Conroy	1901–11	10	280	249	218 of, ss	747
101. Steve Buechele	1986–94	8	325	518		743
102. Corey Koskie	1999–2004	6	369	370		739
103. Hans Lobert	1907–15	7	425	287	24 ss	736
104. Bill Melton	1969–75	6	507	213		720
105. Ed Charles	1962–68	7	375	343		718
106. Grady Hatton	1946–55	8	305	317	77 2b	699
107. Hubie Brooks	1981–91	10	467	148	81 of	696
108. Jimmy Johnston	1916–25	9	536	18	139 2b, of	693
109. Ossie Bluege	1923–33	10	203	483		686
110. Don Wert	1964–70	7	253	426		679
111. Mike Mowrey	1907–16	7	275	403		678
112. Bobby Byrne	1907–14	9	316	354		670
113. Cecil Travis	1934–46	9	456	152	57 ss	665
114. Jimmy Davenport	1958–69	7	274	391		665
115. Jim Ray Hart	1964–73	6	613	43		656
116. Bob Aspromonte	1962–71	8	190	461		651
117. Tony Batista	1998–2004	7	308	250	79 ss	637
118. Joe Stripp	1930–38	8	308	295	32 1b	635
119. Sammy Strang	1901–07	6	506	123		629
120. Phil Nevin	1999–2006	6	544	52	32 1b	628
121. Bill Coughlin	1901–08	8	217	404		621
122. Hank Majeski	1939–51	6	266	354		620
123. Eric Soderholm	1974–79	5	305	310		615
124. Mike Pagliarulo	1985–93	8	159	449		608
125. Eddie "Kid" Foster	1912–21	10	376	230		606
126. Pepper Martin	1931–36	5	465	33	96 of	594
127. Bill Joyce	1890–98	7	514	54	24 1b	592
128. Max Alvis	1963–68	6	360	230		590
129. Pete Ward	1963–69	6	407	162	16 of	585
130. Hick Carpenter	1884–88	10	404	172		576
131. Howard Johnson	1984–94	9	584	−39	23 of	568
132. Scott Brosius	1994–2001	8	140	414		554
133. Vance Law	1982–89	8	274	184	95 2b	553

Third Baseman	Best Years		Bat	Field	Other	Points
134. Lennie Randle	1974–81	6	310	131	108 2b	549
135. Melvin Mora	2000–06	6	339	105	104 ss, of	548
136. Merrill May	1939–43	5	154	390		544
137. Randy Jackson	1941–56	6	198	341		539
138. Dean Palmer	1992–2000	8	507	31		538
139. Bill Everitt	1895–99	5	379	75	83 1b	537
140. Harry Lord	1908–13	6	353	181		534
141. Jim Tabor	1939–46	7	312	202		514
142. Hank Thompson	1950–55	5	345	168		513
143. Dave Hollins	1992–98	5	405	98		503
144. Charlie Irwin	1894–1902	6	54	436		490
145. Barney Friberg	1923–31	7	194	214	64 2b	472
146. Joe Dugan	1918–27	9	110	313	44 ss	467
147. Lee Tannehill	1903–11	7	−80	350	183 ss	454
148. Marv Owen	1932–38	7	111	337		448
149. Billy Johnson	1943–51	6	244	198		442
150. Harry Wolverton	1900–05	6	59	378		437
151. Doc Casey	1899–1907	7	212	222		434
152. Dude Esterbrook	1880–86	5	255	193	−16 1b	432
152. Andy High	1922–29	7	243	182	7 2b	432 tie
154. Wayne Garrett	1970–76	6	267	148		415
155. Odell "Bad News" Hale	1934–39	6	237	139	36 2b	412
156. George Moriarty	1907–14	8	108	302		410
157. Cookie Lavagetto	1937–41	5	336	84	−12 2b	408
158. Charlie Deal	1917–21	5	56	351		407
159. Aaron Boone	1999–2006	5	204	195		399
160. Rance Mulleniks	1982–88	6	335	61		396
161. Luis Salazar	1981–91	8	157	226		383
162. Bill McKechnie	1911–18	5	105	274		379
163. Paul Schaal	1965–73	6	312	67		379
164. David Bell	1998–2006	8	186	192		378
165. Tony Boeckel	1919–23	5	196	180		376
166. Jim Presley	1985–90	5	230	143		373
167. Mike Shannon	1965–69	5	192	55	125 of	372
168. Andy Carey	1954–60	5	128	240		368
169. Frank Hankinson	1878–87	7	−14	380		366
170. Roy Howell	1975–81	7	257	105		362
171. Art Whitney	1880–91	8	−84	372	70 ss	358
172. Billy Clingman	1895–1901	6	−120	316	161 ss	357
173. Wayne Gross	1977–85	6	209	139		348
174. Billy Cox	1947–53	7	96	237	11 ss	344
175. Lee Handley	1937–47	6	88	247	2 2b	337
176. Bobby Adams	1950–54	5	171	156		327
177. Ron Coomer	1997–2001	5	155	113	49 1b	317
178. Sean Berry	1993–98	5	275	38		313
179. Bubba Phillips	1954–63	6	92	265		307
180. Jim Morrison	1980–87	5	156	118	19 2b	293
181. Dennis Walling	1978–87	6	221	51	19 of	291
182. Doug Baird	1915–19	5	32	246		278
183. Dave Brain	1903–07	5	146	123		269

Third Baseman	Best Years		Bat	Field	Other	Points
184. Joe Mulvey	1884–91	8	84	172		256
186. Gene Freese	1955–61	5	205	11		216
186. Charley Smith	1961–67	5	37	179		216
187. Dave Chalk	1974–78	5	101	104	9 ss	214
188. Babe Pinelli	1920–25	5	−53	238		185
189. Lenny Harris	1990–2002	7	166	33	−16 2b, of	183
190. Chippy McGarr	1887–96	5	−56	197	41 ss	182
191. Johnny Vergez	1931–35	5	5	174		179
192. Les Bell	1925–29	5	213	−43		170
193. Tom Brookens	1980–88	5	35	119		154
194. Rollie Zeider	1910–17	5	53	48	32 2b	133
195. Sibby Sisti	1940–51	5	38	29	53 2b	120
196. Sammy Hale	1923–29	6	77	24		101
197. Frank O'Rourke	1921–30	5	−88	97	84 2b, ss	93
197. Dick Williams	1957–61	5	61	32		93 tie
199. Mike Muldoon	1882–86	5	17	68		83
200. Mike Lamb	2000–06	5	145	−74		71
201. Dave Hansen	1992–2003	5	8	48		54
202. Garth Iorg	1982–86	5	28	15		45
203. Geoff Blum	2000–05	5	−9	53		44
204. Willie Kuehne	1883–91	9	−138	159		26
205. Craig Paquette	1993–2001	5	−78	29		−49
206. Greg Norton	1998–2003	5	−71	6	11 1b	−54
207. Abraham Nunez	2001–06	5	−79	27		−57
208. Ed Sprague	1993–2000	7	102	−208		−106

Catcher

Extended Careers. Over an extended career Bill Dickey is baseball's best catcher by a slim margin over Johnny Bench. These two stars, along with Gabby Hartnett, Yogi Berra, Mike Piazza, and Mickey Cochrane are in the top ten in all of the backstop rankings. Piazza is the only active player in the top ten, and none started their careers before the 1920s. Although there is no maximum amount of bonus points a catcher may earn in a single season, career bonus points are limited to an average of not more than 60 points per eligible year at the position.

RANKING OF CATCHERS EXTENDED CAREERS

Catcher	Eligible Seasons		Bat	Field	Other	Bonus	Total
1. Bill Dickey	1929–42	14	1039	975		840	2854
2. Johnny Bench	1968–83	15	1407	758	−41 3b	672	2796
3. Gabby Hartnett	1924–37	15	1030	1171		518	2719
4. Yogi Berra	1948–61	14	1249	731	31 of	660	2671
5. Gary Carter	1975–92	16	1078	1012		483	2573
6. Mike Piazza	1992–2006	13	1588	601		273	2462
7. Carlton Fisk	1972–91	16	1171	797		456	2414
8. Ted Simmons	1970–85	16	1432	717		171	2320
9. Mickey Cochrane	1925–35	11	828	723		660	2211
10. Joe Torre	1961–76	15	1453	430	273 1b, 3b	83	2156

For an extended career and in points per season Bill Dickey reigns as baseball's top catcher. He helped lead the New York Yankees to pennant after pennant by his stellar work at the plate, at the backstop, and as a handler of pitchers (National Baseball Hall of Fame Library, Cooperstown, New York).

Points Per Season. Dickey also leads catchers in points per season. Cochrane moves up to second place, and Roy Campanella enters the rankings in third place. Piazza is again the only one of the top ten to be currently active. Buck Ewing is the sole 19th century backstop among the leaders. Accidents caused the careers of three of these backstops to end prematurely. Cochrane suffered a skull fracture when struck by a pitch. Campanella became a quadriplegic after being injured in an automobile accident. Tragically, Thurman Munson lost his life in a plane crash during the 1979 baseball season. In the table below catcher bonus points are averaged by eligible years as a catcher, whereas total points are computed by averaging all eligible seasons.

RANKING OF CATCHERS POINTS PER SEASON

Catcher	Eligible Seasons		Bat	Field	Other	Bonus	Total
1. Bill Dickey	1929–42	14	74.2	69.6		60.0	203.8
2. Mickey Cochrane	1925–35	11	75.3	65.7		60.0	201.0
3. Roy Campanella	1948–57	10	65.5	68.5		60.0	194.0
4. Yogi Berra	1948–61	14	89.2	52.2	2.2 of	60.0	190.8
5. Mike Piazza	1993–2006	13	122.2	46.2		21.0	189.4
6. Johnny Bench	1968–83	15	93.8	50.5	2.7 3b	51.7	186.4
7. Buck Ewing	1881–95	11	89.0	57.9	14.5 of, 1b, 3b	37.4	185.3

Catcher	Eligible Seasons		Bat	Field	Other	Bonus	Total
8. Gabby Hartnett	1924–37	15	68.7	78.1		34.5	181.3
9. Jorge Posada	1998–2006	9	63.9	53.3		60.0	171.2
10. Thurman Munson	1970–79	10	84.5	47.7		34.3	169.5

Career Rankings — Best Years. When catchers are rated according to their best ten years, Bench moves to the top of the rankings. Berra moves up to second place, and Dickey drops to third. In fourth place is still active Piazza, while Ewing in tenth spot is the only 19th century backstop among the top ten. Every catcher in the leading ten in career rankings is also in the top ten in one of the other lists. There are 222 catchers in our career rankings, more than at any infield position, but fewer than at any outfield slot.

RANKING OF CATCHERS (BEST YEARS)

Catcher	Best Years		Bat	Field	Other	Bonus	Total
1. Johnny Bench	1968–80	10	1204	627		600	2431
2. Yogi Berra	1948–59	10	1051	695		600	2346
3. Bill Dickey	1929–42	10	902	831		600	2333
4. Mike Piazza	1993–2006	10	1495	563		273	2331
5. Gabby Hartnett	1924–37	10	867	965		487	2319
6. Gary Carter	1977–92	10	984	786		479	2249
7. Mickey Cochrane	1925–36	10	798	703		600	2101
8. Roy Campanella	1948–57	10	750	685		600	2035
9. Carlton Fisk	1972–91	10	962	621		438	2021
10. Buck Ewing	1881–95	10	958	637	160 of, 1b, 3b	262	2017
11. Ted Simmons	1971–83	10	1200	609		171	1980
12. Joe Torre	1961–74	10	1251	430	136 1b	83	1900
13. Bill Freehan	1964–75	10	741	769		334	1844
14. Lance Parrish	1978–91	10	687	820		276	1783
15. Ivan Rodriguez	1991–2006	10	849	651		268	1768
16. Javier Lopez	1994–2005	10	626	555		555	1736
17. Jorge Posada	1998–2006	9	647	533		540	1720
18. Thurman Munson	1970–79	10	845	477		343	1695
19. Ernie Lombardi	1932–45	10	883	560		232	1675
20. Sherman Lollar	1950–61	10	509	711		387	1607
21. Roger Bresnahan	1902–14	10	842	422	59 of	250	1573
22. Charlie Bennett	1878–91	10	528	847		189	1564
23. Elston Howard	1957–67	10	569	501		404	1474
24. Johnny Kling	1902–11	9	307	621		540	1468
25. Bob Boone	1973–89	10	312	668		447	1464
26. Jim Sundberg	1974–85	10	336	903		168	1407
27. Wally Schang	1914–28	10	630	389		364	1383
28. Jason Kendall	1996–2006	10	806	484		85	1375
29. Tony Pena	1981–95	10	406	722		228	1356
30. Johnny Roseboro	1958–69	10	256	676		422	1354
31. Ray Schalk	1913–23	10	84	843		410	1337
32. Del Crandall	1953–63	10	235	666		429	1330
33. Manny Sanguillen	1969–77	9	570	420		315	1305
34. Darrell Porter	1973–85	10	619	374		289	1282
35. Walker Cooper	1942–52	9	582	336		338	1256
36. Spud Davis	1930–40	10	510	597		147	1254

Catcher	Best Years		Bat	Field	Other	Bonus	Total
37. Frank "Pancho" Snyder	1914–25	10	160	751		336	1247
38. Tom Haller	1962–70	9	440	499		299	1238
39. Terry Steinbach	1987–98	10	367	525		310	1202
40. Benito Santiago	1987–2003	10	391	538		269	1198
41. Rick Dempsey	1977–86	10	102	621		473	1196
42. Muddy Ruel	1919–28	10	192	707		292	1191
43. Tim McCarver	1963–73	10	417	538		229	1184
44. Steve O'Neill	1913–24	10	261	533		360	1155
45. Jim Hegan	1947–56	10	–99	650		600	1151
46. Chief Zimmer	1889–1900	10	78	826		237	1141
47. Johnny Edwards	1962–73	10	191	731		187	1109
48. Mike Sciosia	1981–92	10	277	595		233	1105
49. Brad Ausmus	1994–2006	10	109	716		265	1090
50. Earl Battey	1960–66	7	445	435		204	1084
51. George Gibson	1906–15	9	98	494		481	1073
52. Mickey Tettleton	1985–96	10	680	362		26	1068
53. Al Lopez	1930–45	10	246	628		166	1040
54. Butch Wynegar	1976–85	9	316	580		139	1035
55. Chris Hoiles	1991–98	8	394	486		143	1023
56. Ernie Whitt	1980–89	10	306	577		132	1015
57. Jimmie Wilson	1924–35	10	109	656		242	1007
58. Dan Wilson	1994–2004	10	50	635		315	1000
59. Gus Mancuso	1932–43	9	152	440		403	995
60. Gene Tenace	1973–79	8	657	168	91 1b	66	982
61. Chief Meyers	1910–15	6	385	211		382	978
62. Ed Bailey	1956–64	9	401	398		170	969
63. Jason Varitek	1998–2006	8	248	345		332	925
64. Jerry Grote	1967–76	10	138	680		102	920
65. Paul Lo Duca	2001–06	6	378	371		165	914
66. Smokey Burgess	1952–62	8	474	292		147	913
67. Ossee Schreck	1899–1907	8	114	554		235	903
68. Rick Cerone	1978–89	10	116	586		196	898
69. Darren Daulton	1989–97	8	472	342		73	887
70. Bill Killefer	1912–19	8	–32	634		280	882
71. Gus Triandos	1955–63	8	363	381	39 1b	90	873
72. Terry Kennedy	1981–90	10	372	386		113	871
73. Jack Clements	1888–98	8	393	316		155	864
74. Damian Miller	1999–2006	8	–34	665		225	857
75. Wilbert Robinson	1890–1902	10	101	404		345	850
76. Silver Flint	1878–85	8	125	305		418	848
76. Mike Lieberthal	1997–2005	8	362	421		65	848
78. Jack Rowe	1880–90	10	729	48	68 ss	53	845
78. Don Slaught	1983–94	10	307	430		108	845
80. Joe Girardi	1990–2002	10	64	580		188	832
81. Joe Azcue	1963–70	8	174	603		54	831
82. Pop Snyder	1876–84	8	105	485		237	827
83. Bob O'Farrell	1920–31	10	200	435		188	823
84. Alan Ashby	1975–87	10	112	557		150	819
85. Frank "Shanty" Hogan	1928–34	7	186	444		188	818
86. Lou Criger	1898–1908	9	–22	633		204	815

Catcher	Best Years		Bat	Field	Other	Bonus	Total
87. Charles Johnson	1995–2004	10	131	615		66	812
88. Ramon Hernandez	2000–06	7	171	334		304	809
89. Bubbles Hargrave	1922–27	6	267	395		133	795
89. Harry Danning	1937–42	6	296	374		125	795
91. Jack Warner	1897–1906	8	−100	645		248	793
91. Milt May	1973–82	9	248	472		73	793
93. Steve Yeager	1974–83	9	3	464		309	776
94. Del Rice	1945–53	8	−64	558		275	769
95. Hank Severeid	1916–24	8	162	531		75	768
96. A. J. Pierzynski	2001–06	6	193	334		237	764
97. Darrin Fletcher	1993–2001	8	200	379		162	741
98. Deacon McGuire	1890–1904	10	277	374		87	738
99. Mickey Owen	1938–50	8	59	356		318	733
100. Mike Stanley	1990–99	8	436	179	8 1b	109	732
101. John Clapp	1876–81	6	505	97	48 of	70	720
101. Joe Ferguson	1973–79	6	363	249		108	720
102. Jody Davis	1982–88	7	247	402		70	719
103. Birdie Tebbetts	1939–49	8	57	384		270	711
104. Billy Sullivan	1901–11	8	−157	547		318	708
104. Bo Diaz	1980–88	7	168	401		139	708
106. Sandy Alomar	1990–2003	9	97	396		190	683
107. Bengie Molina	2000–06	7	106	464		109	679
108. Mike LaValliere	1986–92	6	138	324		214	676
109. Mike Matheny	1996–2005	9	−48	511		206	670
110. Todd Hundley	1992–2002	9	322	306		39	667
111. Duke Farrell	1889–1900	10	254	249	32 3b	131	666
112. Rick Ferrell	1930–45	10	182	599		56	655
113. Heinie Peitz	1893–1905	10	−8	459		202	653
114. Andy Seminick	1946–55	10	236	335		69	640
115. Mike Macfarlane	1990–99	8	150	381		103	634
116. Ron Hassey	1980–89	6	184	339		108	631
117. Sammy White	1952–59	8	165	351		114	630
118. Ray Fosse	1970–77	6	147	377		103	627
119. Luke Sewell	1926–37	10	−176	515		271	610
120. Phil Masi	1945–51	8	130	363		116	609
121. Mike Tresh	1939–47	8	−57	450		210	603
122. Clay Dalrymple	1961–68	8	77	421		104	602
123. Johnny Bassler	1921–25	5	188	326		84	598
124. Randy Hundley	1966–73	6	123	347		124	594
125. Cliff Johnson	1975–86	8	578	0		0	578
125. Brent Mayne	1991–2004	9	10	505		63	578
127. Eddie Taubensee	1992–2000	8	182	296		93	571
128. Bruce Benedict	1979–88	7	65	442		59	566
129. Bill Carrigan	1909–14	5	69	313		179	561
130. Brian Harper	1989–93	5	360	108		88	556
131. Buddy Rosar	1943–48	6	15	493		44	552
132. Ed Herrmann	1969–76	7	101	408		37	546
133. Ray Mueller	1938–49	5	46	358		133	537
134. Zach Taylor	1923–29	7	−120	527		128	535
135. Earl Smith	1920–26	5	182	162		190	534

Catcher	Best Years		Bat	Field	Other	Bonus	Total
136. John Romano	1960–66	6	341	136		54	531
137. Bill Rariden	1913–17	5	92	257		175	524
138. Fred Carroll	1885–90	6	408	80		31	519
138. Wes Westrum	1950–54	5	−14	299		234	519 tie
140. Hank Gowdy	1914–24	5	118	208		184	510
141. Kirt Manwaring	1989–98	8	−16	398		125	507
142. Rich Gedman	1982–89	6	119	264		126	504
142. Dave Valle	1987–93	7	39	453		12	504 tie
144. Frankie Hayes	1936–46	10	208	291		2	500
145. Jim Pagliaroni	1961–66	5	171	250		77	498
146. Bob Brenly	1983–87	5	130	329		36	497
147. Michael Barrett	1999–2006	6	179	278		39	496
148. John Stearns	1977–82	6	249	245		0	494
149. Jimmy Archer	1909–15	6	−44	311		221	488
149. Earl Williams	1971–76	6	313	81	24 1b	70	488 tie
151. Rollie Hemsley	1929–44	8	−52	388		149	485
152. Mike Heath	1981–90	8	214	215		56	484
153. Mal Kittridge	1890–1905	10	−201	577		96	472
153. Matt Nokes	1987–92	5	196	195		81	472 tie
155. Joe Oliver	1990–97	8	47	353		76	468
156. Pat Borders	1990–94	5	−3	288		173	458
157. Ozzie Virgil	1984–88	5	161	292		0	453
158. Larry McLean	1907–12	6	105	333		2	440
159. Ivy Wingo	1912–20	9	51	258		129	438
159. Ellie Rodriguez	1971–75	5	164	274		0	438 tie
161. Al Todd	1934–40	5	144	208		85	437
162. Jack Boyle	1887–95	8	−109	147	122 1b	274	434
163. Buck Martinez	1975–86	8	−114	371		176	433
164. Bill Bergen	1901–11	9	−349	778		0	429
164. George Mitterwald	1970–77	5	168	199		62	429 tie
166. Clint Courtney	1952–58	6	146	274		8	428
166. Charlie Moore	1977–85	7	132	93	104 of	99	428 tie
168. Stan Lopata	1953–58	5	163	232		16	411
169. John Flaherty	1995–2002	8	−44	425		28	409
170. Connie Mack	1887–94	6	−48	445		11	408
171. Mike Gonzalez	1914–26	6	16	352		36	404
171. Dave Nilsson	1994–99	5	351	53		0	404 tie
173. Jack O'Connor	1889–98	7	135	159	59 of	48	401
174. Clyde McCullough	1941–51	7	47	334		16	397
175. Otto Miller	1912–21	6	−108	410		90	392
176. Doc Bushong	1881–88	7	−116	254		243	381
177. Dave Duncan	1968–76	7	8	197		176	381 tie
178. Admiral Schlei	1904–09	5	7	282		85	374
179. Tom Pagnozzi	1991–96	5	41	268		63	372
180. Bob Rodgers	1962–67	7	−3	326		43	366
181. Walter Schmidt	1918–23	5	−117	377		101	361
181. Damon Berryhill	1988–94	5	−44	253		152	361 tie
183. Scott Servais	1993–98	6	−42	324		74	356
184. Ed Ott	1977–81	5	18	188		132	338
185. Cy Perkins	1919–24	6	−28	345		0	318

Catcher	Best Years		Bat	Field	Other	Bonus	Total
185. Dave Rader	1972–78	6	142	139		32	313 tie
187. Chad Kreuter	1993–2000	7	1	265		28	294
188. John Gooch	1922–29	6	−59	206		143	291
189. Jason Larue	2001–05	5	63	211		0	274
190. Mike Fitzgerald	1984–92	5	−40	224		86	270
190. Jeff Reed	1988–99	7	51	203		16	270 tie
192. Bob Swift	1940–48	7	−141	308		97	265
193. Ron Karkovice	1993–2000	5	−114	255		122	263
194. Harry Bemis	1902–08	5	−4	150		113	259
195. Andy Etchebarren	1966–77	5	−66	194		128	257
196. John Bateman	1963–72	5	69	185		0	254
197. Hal Smith	1955–62	6	69	197	35 3b	16	248
198. Dorf Ainsmith	1913–22	6	−103	215		135	247
199. Greg Myers	1990–2003	5	18	166		59	243
200. Oscar Stanage	1909–20	8	−136	119		256	239
201. Frank House	1954–59	5	−73	262		23	213
202. Ed Sweeney	1910–14	5	−97	271		33	208
203. Fred Kendall	1972–77	6	−31	237		0	206
204. Bill Holbert	1878–84	7	−191	307	4 of	80	202
205. Red Dooin	1904–10	8	−48	147		85	184
206. Jake Early	1941–48	5	−68	206		30	168
207. Paul Casanova	1966–73	7	−104	249		19	164
208. Doggie Miller	1884–96	7	311	−162	−30 of, 3b	0	119
209. Bob Melvin	1986–93	6	−208	271		47	110
210. Al Evans	1946–50	5	−136	241		0	105
211. Barney Gilligan	1882–86	5	−118	52		167	101
212. Red Kleinow	1905–09	5	−69	120		46	98
213. Charlie Berry	1930–34	5	−168	263		0	96
214. J. C. Martin	1961–67	5	−155	62		174	81
215. Tim Laudner	1982–89	5	−96	127		47	79
216. Henry Blanco	1999–2004	5	−304	305		71	72
217. Val Picinich	1922–29	5	−158	187		34	63
218. Greg Zaun	1998–2005	5	−130	145		0	15
219. Ray Hayworth	1930–36	5	−244	245		18	14
220. Mickey O'Neil	1920–24	5	−302	307		8	13
221. Al Spohrer	1929–34	5	−210	95		9	−106
222. John Grim	1893–97	5	−282	138		19	−125

Right Field

Extended Career. Over an extended career of 22 seasons Hank Aaron accumulated more Faber System points than any other right fielder. As stated in the section on fielding, outfield positions are considered generic in calculating fielding points. Aaron, second-ranking Babe Ruth, and third-place Frank Robinson had seasons in which they played more games in left field than in right. Fourth-ranking ranking Mel Ott had a year at third base. In fifth place is Al Kaline, who had some years in which he was a center fielder. Not until we reach Roberto Clemente in sixth position do we find one whose primary position was right field throughout his career. No active players are in the top ten, and only one whose career stated before 1900 makes the list.

RANKING OF RIGHT FIELDERS EXTENDED CAREER

Right Fielder	Eligible Seasons		Bat	Field	Other	Points
1. Hank Aaron	1954–75	22	3298	986	37 1b	4321
2. Babe Ruth	1918–34	16	3298	586		3884
3. Frank Robinson	1956–69	19	2825	849	73 1b	3747
4. Mel Ott	1928–45	18	2616	820	60 3b	3496
5. Al Kaline	1954–74	20	2366	1015		3379
6. Roberto Clemente	1955–72	18	1864	1004		2868
7. Tony Gwynn	1984–99	16	1987	877		2864
8. Dave Winfield	1974–93	19	2072	762		2834
9. Sam Crawford	1900–16	17	2001	766		2767
10. Willie Keeler	1894–1907	14	1970	762		2732

Points Per Season. Although Aaron's lengthy career helped him gain the top spot in extended career rankings, it cost him in points per season, where he falls to sixth position. Ruth moves up to the top spot. Two active players, Bobby Abreu and Vladimir Guerrero, occupy the next two positions. Robinson at number four joins Aaron, Ruth, Keeler and Ott as the only repeaters from the extended career top ten. Old-timer Sam Thompson comes in fifth. Modern players Larry Walker and Lance Berkman move into the top ten

RANKING OF RIGHT FIELDERS POINTS PER SEASON

Right Fielder	Eligible Seasons		Bat	Field	Other	Points
1. Babe Ruth	1918–34	16	206.1	36.6		242.7
2. Bobby Abreu	1998–2006	9	142.7	57.2		199.9
3. Vladimir Guerrero	1998–2006	9	158.0	40.7		198.7
4. Frank Robinson	1956–69	19	148.7	44.7	3.8 1b	197.2
5. Sam Thompson	1886–96	10	138.4	58.6		197.0
6. Hank Aaron	1954–75	22	149.9	44.8	1.7	196.4
7. Willie Keeler	1894–1907	14	140.7	54.4		195.1
8. Larry Walker	1990–2003	13	141.3	50.3		191.6
9. Lance Berkman	2000–06	7	156.0	27.6	7.9 1b	191.1
10. Mel Ott	1928–45	18	145.3	45.6	3.3 3b	194.2

Career Rankings — Best Ten Years. Ruth leads Aaron in the rankings for the best ten year career, followed in order by Robinson, Ott, and Keeler. Walker is sixth, Kaline seventh, Clemente eighth, Paul Waner ninth, and Tony Gwynn tenth. Among these only Waner did not also make at least one of the other top ten lists. None of the ten leaders was active in 2006, although 11th ranking Sammy Sosa is attempting a comeback in 2007. A total of 231 right fielders meet the five year eligibility requirement.

RANKING OF RIGHT FIELDERS (BEST YEARS)

Right Fielder	Best Years		Bat	Field	Other	Total
1. Babe Ruth	1919–32	10	2697	518		3215
2. Hank Aaron	1957–71	10	1856	662		2518
3. Frank Robinson	1956–70	10	1797	599		2396
4. Mel Ott	1929–44	10	1730	593		2323
5. Willie Keeler	1894–1907	10	1609	643		2252
6. Larry Walker	1990–2003	10	1657	577		2234

Right Fielder	Best Years		Bat	Field	Other	Total
7. Al Kaline	1955–67	10	1495	723		2218
8. Roberto Clemente	1955–71	10	1471	685		2156
9. Paul Waner	1926–42	10	1493	632		2125
10. Tony Gwynn	1984–97	10	1459	639		2098
11. Sammy Sosa	1990–2005	10	1516	541		2057
12. Sam Crawford	1901–15	10	1454	583		2037
13. Sam Thompson	1886–96	10	1384	586		1970
14. Harry Heilmann	1917–30	10	1589	357		1946
15. Gary Sheffield	1990–2005	10	1524	419		1943
16. Dave Winfield	1974–94	10	1335	558		1893
17. Dwight Evans	1973–90	10	1234	581		1815
18. Reggie Smith	1967–82	10	1282	519		1801
19. Chuck Klein	1929–40	10	1384	416		1800
20. Bobby Abreu	1998–2006	9	1284	515		1799
21. Vladimir Guerrero	1998–2006	9	1422	366		1790
22. Reggie Jackson	1968–82	10	1407	378		1785
23. Rocky Colavito	1956–66	10	1232	542		1774
24. Harry Stovey	1886–96	10	1353	269	129 1b	1751
25. King Kelly	1878–91	10	1589	149		1738
26. Dave Parker	1975–90	10	1307	414		1721
27. Kiki Cuyler	1924–36	10	1147	569		1716
28. Enos Slaughter	1939–53	10	1211	500		1711
29. Rusty Staub	1965–78	10	1226	477		1703
30. Paul O'Neill	1988–2001	10	1091	584		1675
31. Jack Clark	1977–90	10	1211	348	114 1b	1673
32. Elmer Flick	1898–1907	10	1259	403		1662
33. Dante Bichette	1990–2000	10	1249	412		1661
34. Tony Oliva	1964–74	10	1285	371		1656
35. Bobby Murcer	1969–78	10	1111	496		1607
36. Juan Gonzalez	1991–2001	10	1225	363		1588
37. George Hendrick	1973–86	10	973	607		1580
38. Ken Singleton	1971–83	10	1286	260		1546
39. Sam Rice	1917–31	10	973	571		1544
40. Harry Hooper	1911–25	10	891	648		1539
41. Johnny Callison	1961–70	10	815	720		1535
42. Dixie Walker	1937–48	10	1064	387		1451
43. Joe Carter	1985–96	10	920	524		1444
44. Tim Salmon	1993–2003	10	1013	425		1438
44. Shawn Green	1995–2006	10	965	473		1438
46. Chili Davis	1982–94	10	1060	366		1426
47. Carl Furillo	1946–58	10	926	499		1425
48. Mike Tiernan	1887–98	10	1258	163		1421
49. Pedro Guerrero	1981–91	10	1160	118	98 3b, 1b	1413
50. Bobby Bonilla	1986–97	10	1109	169	131 3b	1409
51. Harold Baines	1980–99	10	1098	300		1398
52. Daryl Strawberry	1983–98	10	1003	376		1379
53. Ken Griffey	1975–87	10	978	356	40 1b	1374
54. David Justice	1990–2002	10	1053	295		1348
55. Jackie Jensen	1952–61	9	921	422		1343
56. Lance Berkman	2000–06	7	1090	193	55 1b	1338

Right Fielder	Best Years		Bat	Field	Other	Total
57. Patsy Donovan	1892–1904	10	741	582		1323
58. Tommy Holmes	1942–50	9	757	553		1310
59. Felipe Alou	1961–72	10	865	407	19 1b	1291
59. Jose Canseco	1986–99	10	1113	178		1291
61. Babe Herman	1926–36	10	1051	183	52 1b	1286
62. Chicken Wolf	1882–91	10	654	605		1259
63. Roger Maris	1957–68	10	798	474		1272
64. Vic Wertz	1947–60	10	974	153	137 1b	1264
65. Tom Brunansky	1982–92	10	698	550		1248
66. Bill Nicholson	1940–48	9	862	354		1216
67. Richie Zisk	1973–82	10	930	281		1211
68. Tommy Harper	1963–75	10	803	376	20 3b	1199
69. Bob Allison	1959–68	9	849	338	11 1b	1198
70. Jack Tobin	1914–27	10	811	370		1181
71. Jesse Barfield	1982–90	9	640	536		1176
72. Ross Youngs	1918–25	8	895	252		1147
73. Wally Moses	1936–49	10	635	499		1134
74. Ichiro Suzuki	2001–06	6	732	392		1124
75. Von Hayes	1982–90	9	710	294	119 1b	1123
76. John Titus	1904–12	8	769	351		1120
77. Magglio Ordonez	1998–2006	7	784	327		1111
78. Danny Tartabull	1986–96	9	923	179		1102
79. Jay Buhner	1991–2000	8	710	387		1097
80. Tommy McCarthy	1888–96	9	805	291		1096
81. Hal McRae	1974–83	10	1046	43		1089
82. Roy Cullenbine	1940–47	8	707	307	74 1b	1088
83. Raul Mondesi	1994–2003	9	629	442		1071
84. Gavvy Cravath	1912–18	7	818	245		1063
85. Ruben Sierra	1986–2004	10	789	272		1061
86. Max Flack	1914–23	9	589	472		1061
87. Jim Northrup	1966–74	9	667	391		1058
88. Terry Puhl	1978–89	9	574	479		1053
89. Jeromy Burnitz	1997–2006	10	702	343		1045
90. Reggie Sanders	1992–2004	10	597	436		1033
91. Brian Jordan	1995–2002	7	587	443		1030
92. Wildfire Schulte	1905–16	10	626	386		1012
93. Al Cowens	1974–85	10	546	466		1012
94. Tommy Henrich	1938–49	7	677	329		1006
95. Socks Seybold	1901–07	7	690	304		994
96. Elmer Valo	1942–56	10	730	263		993
97. Wally Moon	1954–63	9	746	231		977
98. Kirk Gibson	1981–94	10	868	100		968
99. Hank Bauer	1949–58	10	599	366		965
100. Orator Shaffer	1877–90	9	558	401		959
100. Mike Mitchell	1907–14	8	526	433		959
102. Claudell Washington	1975–89	10	652	298		950
103. Bake McBride	1974–80	6	530	403		933
104. Oyster Burns	1885–94	9	711	212		923
105. Sixto Lescano	1975–84	9	555	365		920
106. Tony Armas	1977–88	9	502	415		917

Right Fielder	Best Years		Bat	Field	Other	Total
107. Jermaine Dye	1999–2006	7	644	258		902
108. Owen "Chief" Wilson	1908–16	9	362	534		896
109. Willard Marshall	1942–53	9	468	391		859
110. Buck Freeman	1899–1906	8	703	123	23 1b	849
111. Curt Walker	1922–30	9	380	364		844
112. J. D. Drew	1999–2006	7	634	206		840
113. Ed Swartwood	1882–90	7	752	77		829
114. Joe Orsulak	1985–97	10	334	494		828
115. Derek Bell	1993–2002	8	491	320		811
116. Lee Lacy	1975–86	10	563	229		792
117. Pete Fox	1933–44	8	414	373		787
118. Bing Miller	1926–31	10	360	416		776
119. Keith Moreland	1982–89	8	544	170	54 3b	768
120. Danny Green	1899–1905	7	517	241		758
121. Jim Eisenreich	1989–97	9	438	319		757
122. Wally Post	1954–62	8	456	299		755
122. Oscar Gamble	1973–82	9	623	121		755 tie
124. Floyd Robinson	1961–66	6	510	242		752
125. George Harper	1922–29	6	462	277		739
126. Johnny Grubb	1973–82	8	443	292		735
127. Charlie Hemphill	1901–10	8	436	294		730
127. Jay Johnstone	1969–82	9	396	334		730 tie
129. Pat Kelly	1969–78	9	493	235		728
130. Greg Gross	1974–87	10	521	204		725
131. Clifton Heathcote	1919–26	7	168	556		724
132. Rob Deer	1986–93	8	336	386		722
133. Ival Goodman	1935–40	6	448	268		716
134. Richard Hidalgo	1999–2004	6	392	311		703
135. Orlando Merced	1991–96	6	436	191	69 1b	696
136. Dan Ford	1975–83	8	460	234		694
137. Steve Evans	1909–15	6	537	151		688
138. Casey Stengel	1913–24	7	375	311		686
139. Tony Conigliaro	1964–70	5	496	187		683
130. Trot Nixon	1999–2006	7	406	277		683
141. Juan Encarnacion	1999–2006	8	298	381		679
142. Carl Reynolds	1929–38	7	331	345		676
143. Red Murray	1907–13	7	430	232		662
144. Tommy Griffith	1915–24	8	377	283		660
145. Bill Robinson	1967–80	9	394	245	16 1b	655
146. Shano Collins	1911–22	9	181	414	53 1b	648
147. Johnny Wyrostek	1946–53	8	316	332		648 tie
148. Kevin Bass	1984–94	9	363	283		646
149. Billy Southworth	1919–26	6	351	290		641
150. Matt Lawton	1997–2004	7	342	297		639
151. Ken Harrelson	1965–69	5	384	135	104 1b	623
152. Willie Crawford	1969–76	7	408	208		616
153. Hugh Nichol	1883–89	6	286	327		613
154. Johnny Moore	1932–36	5	367	231		598
155. Paul Radford	1883–94	10	272	219	104 ss	595
156. Glenn Wilson	1983–90	6	263	297	30 1b	590

Right Fielder	Best Years		Bat	Field	Other	Total
157. Roy Johnson	1929–35	7	415	172		587
158. Joe Cunningham	1957–62	6	529	0	53 1b	582
159. Bruce Campbell	1932–42	8	391	186		577
160. Doc Gessler	1904–11	6	446	112	13 1b	571
151. Mike Marshall	1983–89	7	392	179		571
162. Michael Tucker	1996–2005	10	206	364		570
162. George Altman	1959–64	6	299	271		570 tie
164. Matt Stairs	1997–2005	8	391	148	20 1b	559
165. Bill Hinchman	1907–16	5	384	167		551
165. Candy Maldonado	1984–92	8	309	242		551 tie
167. Cory Snyder	1986–93	7	212	328		540
168. Jose Guillen	1997–2005	6	329	205		534
169. Tom Paciorek	1976–84	7	401	83	46 1b	530
170. Gene Moore	1936–45	7	229	297		526
171. George Browne	1902–09	8	498	25		523
172. Mike Hershberger	1962–67	6	150	366		516
172. Felix Jose	1990–94	5	317	199		516 tie
174. Sam Mele	1947–54	6	300	214		514
175. Al Zarilla	1944–52	8	292	219		511
176. Russ Snyder	1960–70	8	240	266		506
177. Frankie Baumholtz	1947–55	5	260	245		505
178. Don Mueller	1950–57	8	258	244		502
179. Bobby Roth	1916–20	5	364	13		497
180. Mike Dorgan	1877–86	6	401	76		477
180. Ben Grieve	1998–2004	6	282	195		477 tie
182. Aubrey Huff	2002–06	5	394	52	29 3b	475
183. Ollie Brown	1966–71	5	218	256		474
184. Mark Whiten	1991–96	5	265	205		470
185. Willie Kirkland	1958–65	7	196	273		469
186. Jack Manning	1876–86	7	371	90		461
187. George Watkins	1930–36	7	344	116		460
188. Harry Lumley	1904–08	5	331	120		451
189. Jim King	1955–66	5	171	265		436
190. Walt Moryn	1956–60	5	254	172		430
191. Lon Knight	1876–84	5	247	181		428
192. Chet Laabs	1939–43	5	256	170		426
193. Elmer Smith	1915–21	5	258	165		423
194. Ellis Valentine	1977–82	5	205	201		406
195. Mike Davis	1983–88	6	231	173		404
196. Ron Northey	1942–47	5	274	129		403
197. John Cassidy	1877–84	6	271	125		396
198. Mike Lum	1968–74	7	169	210	17 1b	396
199. Jim Rivera	1952–58	7	167	274		389
200. Gino Cimoli	1957–63	6	168	218		386
201. Lee Stanton	1972–77	5	254	125		379
202. Ed Kirkpatrick	1962–77	7	148	134	94 c	376
203. Cozy Dolan	1901–06	6	257	115		372
204. Joel Youngblood	1978–84	6	227	172	−35 3b	364
205. Jake Evans	1879–84	5	−20	377		357
206. Ron Swoboda	1965–70	6	155	182		337

Right Fielder	Best Years		Bat	Field	Other	Total
207. Jack Rothrock	1927–35	5	160	174		334
208. Mike Kingery	1987–96	5	145	188		333
209. John Vander Wal	1995–2003	6	277	54		331
210. Suitcase Simpson	1951–58	5	220	106		326
211. Danny Moeller	1912–16	5	171	117		288
212. Randy Bush	1983–92	5	184	102		286
213. Chief Roseman	1882–86	5	166	116		282
214. Roger Repoz	1966–71	6	74	200		274
215. Tommy Dowd	1891–1901	10	121	149		270
216. Alex Ochoa	1997–2002	5	108	156		264
217. Roger Cedeno	1998–2003	5	172	87		259
218. Walter Williams	1967–73	5	156	103		259 tie
219. Homer Summa	1923–28	5	145	112		257
220. Bob Bailor	1977–83	5	124	160	−40 ss	244
221. Hosken Powell	1978–82	5	72	145		217
222. Bob Kennedy	1940–55	10	−15	126	94 3b	206
223. Butch Huskey	1996–2000	5	105	80	−4 1b	181
224. Lou Finney	1935–42	7	95	38	20 1b	153
225. John Mabry	1995–2006	6	76	39	28 1b	143
226. Jack McGeachy	1887–91	5	−120	256		136
227. Jim Holt	1970–75	5	−23	131	21 1b	130
228. Dave Clark	1989–97	5	111	−1		110
229. Orlando Palmeiro	1999–2006	6	4	80		84
230. Gene Stephens	1955–60	5	−42	46		4
231. Darren Bragg	1996–2003	5	−35	5		−30

Center Field

Extended Careers. Tris Speaker is baseball's greatest center fielder for an extended career. Ty Cobb is second, Willie Mays is third, and Mickey Mantle is fourth. These four rank in the same order at the top of the points per season leader board and appear with only one switch in rankings on the career list. Ken Griffey, Jr., in fifth place, is the only active player among the top ten extended career leaders. No players from the 19th century are in the elite group.

RANKING OF CENTER FIELDERS EXTENDED CAREERS

Center Fielder	Eligible Seasons		Bat	Field	Other	Total
1. Tris Speaker	1909–27	19	3183	1649		4832
2. Ty Cobb	1907–27	19	3407	1170		4577
3. Willie Mays	1951–71	19	3273	1258		4531
4. Mickey Mantle	1952–68	16	2579	700	71 1b	3350
5. Ken Griffey, Jr.	1989–2006	14	1818	887		2705
6. Andre Dawson	1977–94	18	1546	1046		2592
7. Richie Ashburn	1948–62	15	1474	1106		2580
8. Max Carey	1911–28	17	1223	1215		2438
9. Joe DiMaggio	1936–51	12	1675	750		2425
10. Vada Pinson	1959–75	17	1279	928		2207

Points Per Season. There are no changes among the top four from the extended career rankings. New to the points per season list are Roy Thomas in fifth, Benny Kauff in sixth. Billy

Hamilton in ninth, and Carlos Beltran in the tenth spot. All of these except Kauff and Beltran played at least part of their major league career in the 1800s. Kauff had only five eligible seasons before he was banned from baseball by Commissioner Landis.

RANKING OF CENTER FIELDERS POINTS PER SEASON

Center Fielder	Eligible Seasons		Bat	Field	Other	Total
1. Tris Speaker	1909–27	19	167.5	86.8		254.3
2. Ty Cobb	1907–27	19	179.2	61.6		240.9
3. Willie Mays	1951–71	19	172.3	66.2		238.5
4. Mickey Mantle	1952–68	16	161.1	43.8	4.4 1b	209.4
5. Roy Thomas	1899–1908	10	122.7	85.1		207.8
6. Benny Kauff	1914–19	5	136.6	66.4		203.0
7. Joe DiMaggio	1936–51	12	139.6	62.5		202.1
8. Ken Griffey, Jr.	1989–2006	14	129.9	63.4		193.2
9. Billy Hamilton	1889–1901	11	168.1	24.5		192.6
10. Carlos Beltran	1999–2006	7	106.1	79.6		185.7

Career Rankings — Best Years. When career rankings are based on each player's best ten years Cobb moves to the top of the list, ahead of Speaker. Mays and Mantle retain their third and fourth positions, respectively. Griffey is again fifth, and Joe DiMaggio makes his best showing at number six. Richie Ashburn and Kirby Puckett, neither of whom made either of the other top tens, come in at seventh and eighth. Roy Thomas and Billy Hamilton, two stars who started their major league careers before 1900 are ninth and tenth. Next to Griffey the best showing by an active player is Jim Edmonds in twelfth place. Two hundred thirty-seven center fielders played the requisite number of eligible seasons to make these rankings, the most by players at any position (excluding pitchers, of course.)

RANKING OF CENTER FIELDERS (BEST YEARS)

Center Fielder	Best Years		Bat	Field	Other	Total
1. Ty Cobb	1907–24	10	2128	722		2850
2. Tris Speaker	1909–26	10	1787	1034		2821
3. Willie Mays	1951–91	10	1849	818		2667
4. Mickey Mantle	1952–64	10	1959	619		2578
5. Ken Griffey, Jr.	1990–2006	10	1553	710		2258
6. Joe DiMaggio	1936–51	10	1561	642		2203
7. Richie Ashburn	1948–60	10	1177	936		2113
8. Kirby Puckett	1984–95	10	1330	761		2091
9. Roy Thomas	1899–1908	10	1227	851		2078
10. Billy Hamilton	1889–1901	10	1769	293		2062
11. Brett Butler	1983–94	10	1231	794		2025
12. Jim Edmonds	1995–2006	10	1246	758		2004
13. Mike Griffin	1887–98	10	1047	943		1990
14. Duke Snider	1949–63	10	1405	580		1985
15. Hugh Duffy	1889–94	10	1350	630		1980
16. Max Carey	1911–25	10	1030	874		1904
17. Andre Dawson	1977–92	10	1171	712		1883
18. Jimmy Wynn	1965–76	10	1168	698		1866
20. Fred Lynn	1975–86	10	1151	712		1863
21. George Gore	1879–91	10	1608	254		1862

Center Fielder	Best Years		Bat	Field	Other	Total
22. Bobby Bonds	1969–79	10	1278	540		1818
23. Kenny Lofton	1992–2006	10	1114	691		1805
24. Amos Otis	1970–82	10	1050	746		1796
25. Vada Pinson	1959–70	10	1121	671		1792
26. Andruw Jones	1997–2006	10	961	826		1787
27. Jimmy Ryan	1886–1903	10	1148	617		1765
28. Bernie Williams	1993–2006	10	1225	540		1765
29. Dom DiMaggio	1940–52	10	996	727		1723
30. Dale Murphy	1978–91	10	1124	596		1720
31. Larry Doby	1948–57	10	1136	581		1717
32. Edd Roush	1915–29	10	1013	700		1713
33. Paul Hines	1876–90	10	1286	418		1704
34. Fielder Jones	1896–1908	10	969	732		1701
35. Jim O'Rourke	1876–93	10	1444	248		1692
35. George Van Haltren	1889–1901	10	1204	488		1692
37. Curt Flood	1958–69	10	860	821		1681
38. Steve Finley	1990–2004	10	945	725		1670
39. Cy Williams	1915–27	10	974	689		1663
40. Ellis Burks	1987–2002	10	1105	532		1637
41. Ginger Beaumont	1899–1909	10	1105	511		1616
42. Lloyd Waner	1927–38	10	860	750		1610
43. Cesar Cedeno	1971–85	10	959	641		1606
44. Pete Browning	1882–92	10	1472	49	57 2b	1578
45. Chet Lemon	1976–90	10	885	689		1574
46. Earl Averill	1929–39	10	1200	563		1563
47. Earl Combs	1925–33	9	1052	478		1530
48. Tommy Leach	1902–15	10	922	411	196 3b	1529
49. Al Oliver	1971–82	10	1047	469		1516
50. Willie Davis	1961–76	10	791	713		1504
51. Johnny Damon	1996–2006	10	891	575		1466
52. Willie Wilson	1979–92	10	795	669		1464
53. Clyde Milan	1908–21	10	809	651		1460
54. Rick Monday	1967–78	10	870	588		1458
54. Ray Lankford	1991–2001	10	857	601		1458
56. Hack Wilson	1924–33	9	1141	316		1457
57. Marquis Grissom	1991–2004	10	714	720		1443
58, Dummy Hoy	1888–1901	10	936	483		1419
59. Dode Paskert	1908–20	10	706	704		1410
60. Gus Bell	1950–62	10	673	628		1401
61. Paul Blair	1965–75	10	627	770		1397
62, Chick Stahl	1897–1906	9	810	585		1395
63. Sam West	1928–38	10	497	890		1387
64. Curt Welch	1884–91	8	622	750		1372
65. Andy Van Slyke	1983–94	10	752	614		1366
66. Willie McGee	1982–96	10	741	622		1363
67. Tom Brown	1883–97	10	855	501		1356
68. Steve Brodie	1890–1902	10	577	768		1345
69. Pop Corkhill	1883–91	8	534	808		1342
70. Andy Pafko	1944–54	10	759	535	47 3b	1341
71. Jose Cardenal	1965–77	10	757	579		1336

Center Fielder	Best Years		Bat	Field	Other	Total
72. Wally Berger	1930–38	8	885	447		1332
73. Devon White	1987–2001	10	609	718		1327
74. Baby Doll Jacobson	1917–26	9	726	597		1323
75. Eric Davis	1986–98	8	889	428		1317
76. Garry Maddox	1972–85	10	585	730		1315
77. Cy Seymour	1901–08	8	829	479		1308
78. Carlos Beltran	1999–2006	7	743	557		1300
79. Lloyd Moseby	1981–90	10	640	636		1276
80. Tony Gonzalez	1960–70	10	693	577		1270
81. Doc Cramer	1933–45	10	556	697		1253
82. Bobby Thomson	1947–59	10	671	553		1224
83. Matty Alou	1964–73	10	779	441		1220
84. Bill Lange	1893–99	7	714	484		1198
85. Bill Bruton	1953–64	10	555	614		1169
86. Mickey Rivers	1974–84	9	650	503		1153
87. Jerry Mumphrey	1976–87	10	644	509		1153
88. Len Dykstra	1986–94	7	687	460		1147
88. Jimmy Slagle	1899–1908	10	630	517		1147
90. Jimmie Piersall	1953–62	10	446	695		1141
91. Amos Strunk	1912–21	9	489	647		1136
92. Cesar Tovar	1966–75	9	788	324	12 1b	1124
93. Ned Hanlon	1880–91	10	690	433		1123
94. Dave Henderson	1982–93	10	404	618		1112
95. Terry Moore	1935–47	8	450	632		1082
96. Jimmy Barrett	1900–07	6	607	402		1009
97. Bill Virdon	1955–65	10	383	668		1051
98. Dwayne Murphy	1979–85	7	481	562		1041
99. Billy North	1973–80	7	554	475		1029
100. Benny Kauff	1914–19	5	683	332		1014
101. Barney McCoskey	1939–48	7	621	387		1008
102. Daryl Hamilton	1991–99	8	521	486		1007
103. Johnny Bates	1906–14	8	627	379		1006
104. Gorman Thomas	1975–85	8	604	389		993
104. Otis Nixon	1985–98	10	408	585		993
106. Vince DiMaggio	1937–45	8	373	619		992
107. Del Unser	1968–77	10	362	629		991
108. Mike Cameron	1997–2006	9	412	576		988
109. Lance Johnson	1990–97	8	476	507		983
110. Jim Landis	1958–65	8	394	578		972
111. Brady Anderson	1991–2001	10	453	516		969
112. Mookie Wilson	1981–90	9	474	471		945
113. Sam Chapman	1938–51	10	369	572		941
113. Stan Spence	1942–49	7	532	409		941
115. Dave Martinez	1987–2001	10	412	528		940
116. Mark Kotsay	1999–2006	8	372	561		933
117. Ruppert Jones	1977–86	8	477	441		918
118. Johnny Mostil	1921–28	7	396	519		915
119. Preston Wilson	1999–2006	7	483	425		908
120. Mike Kreevich	1936–45	9	221	684		905
121. Happy Felsch	1915–20	5	431	442		873

Center Fielder	Best Years		Bat	Field	Other	Total
122. Frank Demeree	1933–40	7	604	267		871
123. Rick Manning	1975–84	9	310	560		870
124. Al Bumbry	1973–84	10	451	414		865
125. Juan Pierre	2001–06	6	502	360		862
126. Jim Fogarty	1883–90	6	226	634		860
127. Jim McTamany	1886–91	6	550	304		854
128. Brian McRae	1991–99	9	366	487		853
129. Tommie Agee	1966–73	8	485	363		848
130. Bug Holliday	1889–94	6	597	246		843
130. Harry Rice	1925–33	7	447	396		843
132. Dave Philley	1947–56	9	294	533		827
133. Johnny Hopp	1941–50	8	619	136	58 1b	813
134. Hy Myers	1915–22	8	325	487		812
135. Ken Berry	1965–73	9	238	572		810
136. Taylor Douthit	1926–31	6	400	406		806
137. Omar Moreno	1977–86	9	277	527		804
138. Fred Snodgrass	1910–16	7	394	407		801
139. Fred Schulte	1928–34	7	283	513		796
140. Cesar Geronimo	1972–80	9	231	560		791
141. Rick Miller	1973–83	9	361	425		786
142. Ping Bodie	1911–20	8	345	431		776
143. Jim Busby	1951–58	8	210	561		771
144. Bill Tuttle	1954–61	8	318	445		763
145. Gary Pettis	1984–90	8	224	528		752
146. Johnny Frederick	1929–34	6	390	339		729
147. Ira Flagstead	1919–28	7	259	468		727
148. Vernon Wells	2001–06	5	420	307		727 tie
149. Jake Stenzel	1894–98	5	557	169		726
150. Torii Hunter	1999–2006	7	305	420		725
151. Rube Oldring	1907–15	7	309	414		723
152. Stan Javier	1988–2000	10	348	374		722
153. Mickey Stanley	1967–73	7	280	440		720
154. Roberto Kelly	1989–97	7	417	298		715
155. Jackie Brandt	1956–64	7	326	380		706
156. Jay Payton	2000–06	7	287	418		705
157. Doug Glanville	1997–2002	6	241	458		699
158. Chad Curtis	1992–2000	7	309	386		695
159. Randy Winn	1998–2006	7	320	372		692
160. Pete Hotaling	1879–88	9	519	172		691
161. Mule Haas	1929–36	7	274	412		686
162. Milt Thompson	1987–94	8	365	321		686
163. Walt Judnich	1940–47	5	366	287	29 1b	682
164. Carl Everett	1997–2006	8	450	231		681
165. Ethan Allen	1927–37	7	216	457		673
166. Albie Pearson	1958–65	5	439	233		672
167. Jim Hickman	1962–72	8	441	184	44 1b	669
168. Lee Mazelli	1977–81	7	415	266	−12 1b	669 tie
169. Ken Landreaux	1979–87	8	344	323		667
170. Mike Devereaux	1989–96	8	280	384		664
171. Johnny Groth	1949–54	6	297	366		663

Center Fielder	Best Years		Bat	Field	Other	Total
172. Vic Davalillo	1964–72	7	345	315		660
173. Jimmie Hall	1963–67	5	392	266		658
174. Rebel Oakes	1909–15	7	284	372		656
175. Solly Hofman	1907–15	7	428	211	3 2b	642
176. Whitey Witt	1916–24	7	395	189	51 ss	635
177. Bobby Tolan	1967–76	6	331	303		632
178. Ted Uhlaender	1966–71	6	259	367		626
179. Eddie Milner	1982–87	6	236	385		621
180. Emmett Heidrick	1899–1904	5	336	281		617
181. Wally Westlake	1947–52	6	321	292		613
182. Jose Cruz, Jr.	1997–2006	7	241	359		600
183. Nemo Leibold	1914–23	7	284	312		596
184. Oliver Pickering	1897–1908	6	305	290		595
184. Jack Smith	1916–24	7	350	245		595 tie
186. Juan Beniquez	1974–86	8	341	245		586
187. Don Demeter	1959–66	7	379	194		573
188. Homer Smoot	1902–06	5	296	273		569
189. Don Lock	1963–67	5	282	283		565
190. Dave May	1970–77	6	227	332		559
191. Oddibe McDowell	1985–89	5	228	331		559 tie
192. Jimmy McAleer	1889–98	7	–11	568		557
193. Tom Goodwin	1995–2001	7	183	369		552
194. Marvin Benard	1996–2001	5	261	290		551
195. Barry Bonnell	1977–84	7	295	250		545
196. Mack Jones	1965–70	6	380	155		535
197. Joe Birmingham	1907–12	6	46	466		512
198. Johnny Cooney	1936–41	6	151	351		502
199. Jimmy Welsh	1925–30	5	131	360		491
200. Lennie Green	1959–65	6	340	139		479
201. Dick Johnston	1886–91	5	146	324		470
202. Harry Walker	1943–49	5	277	179		456
203. Eddie Brown	1924–28	5	230	218		448
204. Danny Hoffman	1905–10	5	184	262		446
205. Mitch Webster	1986–94	6	268	149		417
206. Rudy Law	1980–85	5	196	214		410
207. John Dobbs	1901–05	5	158	245		403
208. Farmer Weaver	1889–94	5	111	281		392
209. Rich Becker	1995–2000	6	90	293		383
210. Fred Mann	1883–87	5	271	110		371
211. Darren Lewis	1992–89	8	111	257		368
212. Gary Matthews, Jr.	2001–06	5	151	210		361
213. Elliott Maddox	1970–80	6	134	157	56 3b	347
214. Chris Singleton	1999–2003	5	79	267		346
215. Terrence Long	2000–06	6	155	190		345
216. Brian L. Hunter	1996–2000	5	40	294		334
217. Cito Gaston	1969–73	5	122	210		332
218. Marvell Wynne	1983–89	6	81	250		331
219. Gabe Kapler	1999–2004	5	74	250		324
220. John Shelby	1983–90	7	–44	261		305
221. Bob Dernier	1982–86	5	53	250		303

Center Fielder	Best Years		Bat	Field	Other	Total
222. Henry Cotto	1984–93	6	59	231		290
223. Bobby Del Greco	1956–63	5	10	247		257
224. Darrell Thomas	1972–84	10	98	108	43 2b	249
225. Rowland Office	1974–80	6	5	213		218
226. George Metkovich	1944–52	5	112	77	21 1b	210
227. Gerald Williams	1995–2001	7	53	150		203
228. Darrin Jackson	1988–98	5	60	202		202
229. John Moses	1986–90	5	53	138		191
230. Butch Huskey	1996–2000	5	105	80	−4 1b	181
231. Charlie Dexter	1896–1903	5	97	65		162
232. John Cangelosi	1986–95	5	125	36		161
233. Quinton McCracken	1996–2005	5	155	−2		153
234. Hal Jeffcoat	1948–53	5	−104	227		124
235. George Wright	1982–86	5	−87	217		120
236. Ty Cline	1962–69	5	−67	75		8
237. Herm Winningham	1985–92	5	−126	87		−39

Left Field

Extended Career. Barry Bonds has the best extended career record of any left fielder in major league history. He is followed by Stan Musial, Pete Rose, Carl Yastrzemski, and Rickey Henderson, all of whom had more than twenty years in the big leagues. In sixth place is Ted Williams with 15 years. The years Williams spent in service prevented him from competing for a spot at the top. Bonds is the only active player in the top ten. Ed Delahanty and Fred Clarke are the two old-timers on the list. Big Ed compiled his point total in only 13 seasons before his tragic death

Barry Bonds is ranked as baseball's best left fielder. Whether assessed by an extended career, points per season, or ten best years, Bonds heads the list. His batting average does not match that of Ted Williams or Stan Musial, but as a home run hitter he reigns supreme (National Baseball Hall of Fame Library, Cooperstown, New York).

RANKING OF LEFT FIELDERS EXTENDED CAREERS

Left Fielder	Eligible Seasons		Bat	Field	Other	Total
1. Barry Bonds	1986–2006	20	3446	1040		4486
2. Stan Musial	1942–63	21	3126	534	257 1b	3917
3. Pete Rose	1963–85	23	2673	569	525 1b,2b,3b	3767
4. Carl Yastrzemski	1961–83	23	2593	700	224 1b	3517
5. Rickey Henderson	1980–2001	21	2497	925		3422
6. Ted Williams	1939–60	15	2893	455		3348
7. Al Simmons	1924–38	16	1812	993		2805
8. Ed Delahanty	1890–1902	13	1932	823		2755

Left Fielder	Eligible Seasons		Bat	Field	Other	Total
9. Fred Clarke	1895–1911	16	1725	935		2660
10. Tim Raines	1981–95	16	1752	835		2587

Points Per Season. In points per season Bonds retains his place at the top. Williams and Delahanty move up to second and third, respectively. Among the other leaders from the extended career list only Musial and Al Simmons retain a place in the ten leaders in points per season. The other spots are taken by players with shorter careers, such as Shoeless Joe Jackson in fourth position. Besides Bonds, Manny Ramirez is an active player in this list. Delahanty is the sole representative of players who started their careers before 1900.

RANKING OF LEFT FIELDERS POINTS PER SEASON

Left Fielder	Eligible Years		Bat	Field	Other	Total
1. Barry Bonds	1986–2006	20	172.3	52.0		224.3
2. Ted Williams	1939–60	15	206.6	30.3		223.2
3. Ed Delahanty	1890–1902	13	148.6	63.3		211.9
4. Joe Jackson	1911–20	9	154.6	47.7		202.2
5. Stan Musial	1942–63	21	148.9	25.4	12.2 2b	186.5
6. Manny Ramirez	1994–2006	13	154.5	26.2		180.7
7. Joe Medwick	1933–44	12	130.6	46.3		177.0
8. Al Simmons	1924–38	16	113.3	62.1		175.3
9. Charlie Keller	1939–46	6	130.2	43.2		173.3
10. Albert Belle	1991–2000	10	137.2	34.8		172.0

Career Leaders — Best Years. Bonds completes a sweep of leftfield honors by topping the compendium of career leaders based on their best years. Williams is second, Delahanty third, and Musial fourth. Jesse Burkett in ninth place is the only top ten left fielder who does not rank among the leaders in one of the other compilations. Bonds, of course, is the top active player on the list, while Ramirez also makes the top ten. Delahanty and Burkett represent the pioneer contingent among the leaders. A total of 234 left fielders meet eligibility requirements.

RANKING OF LEFT FIELDERS (BEST YEARS)

Left Fielder	Best Years		Bat	Field	Other	Total
1. Barry Bonds	1986–2006	10	2329	656		2985
2. Ted Williams	1940–60	10	2335	401		2736
3. Ed Delahanty	1890–1902	10	1713	793		2506
4. Stan Musial	1942–62	10	1965	503		2468
5. Al Simmons	1924–37	10	1601	717		2318
6. Pete Rose	1965–81	10	1568	569	131 1b	2268
7. Carl Yastrzemski	1962–77	10	1570	647		2217
8. Rickey Henderson	1980–94	10	1555	628		2183
9. Jesse Burkett	1890–1905	10	1705	363		2068
10. Manny Ramirez	1994–2006	10	1707	319		2026
11. Billy Williams	1962–73	10	1519	475		2014
12. Fred Clarke	1897–1910	10	1334	675		2009
13. Jim Rice	1975–86	10	1489	513		2002
14. Tim Raines	1981–95	10	1349	640		1989
15. Joe Medwick	1933–44	10	1445	510		1955
16. Joe Kelley	1893–1906	10	1339	552	38 1b	1929

Left Fielder	Best Years		Bat	Field	Other	Total
17. George Foster	1971–85	10	1234	601		1835
18. Joe Jackson	1911–20	9	1391	429		1820
19. Sherry Magee	1905–17	10	1205	612		1817
20. Willie Stargell	1965–79	10	1475	246	80 1b	1801
21. Jimmy Sheckard	1899–1912	10	1048	746		1794
22. Minnie Minoso	1951–61	10	1316	464		1780
23. Goose Goslin	1922–36	10	1250	485		1735
24. Zack Wheat	1910–25	10	1119	603		1722
25. Albert Belle	1991–2000	10	1372	348		1720
26. Bobby Veach	1914–24	10	1103	600		1703
27. Bob Johnson	1934–45	10	1109	590		1699
28. Brian Giles	1997–2006	10	1217	462		1679
29. Luis Gonzalez	1991–2006	10	1138	528		1666
30. Moises Alou	1992–2006	10	1215	405		1620
31. George Burns	1913–22	10	1036	459		1595
32. Ralph Kiner	1946–55	10	1277	304		1581
33. Frank Howard	1960–71	10	1254	313		1567
34. Roy White	1966–77	10	1036	530		1566
35. Brian Downing	1975–92	10	1030	239	280 c	1549
36. Heinie Manush	1923–37	10	1048	485		1533
37. Lou Brock	1962–76	10	1230	296		1526
38. Dusty Baker	1972–83	10	947	570		1515
39. Roy Sievers	1949–63	10	1038	219	209 1b	1466
40. Del Ennis	1946–57	10	969	417		1464
41. Kip Selbach	1894–1905	10	830	609		1439
42. Charley Jones	1876–87	10	1010	418		1428
43. Jose Cruz	1972–86	10	971	449		1423
44. Ken Williams	1920–28	9	972	419		1391
45. Ryan Klesko	1994–2005	10	920	265	192 1b	1377
46. Joe Vosmik	1931–40	10	847	516		1363
47. Gary Mathews	1973–84	10	1052	298		1350
48. Harvey Kuenn	1953–63	10	916	189	241 ss	1346
49. Ben Chapman	1930–40	10	789	545		1334
50. Greg Luzinski	1972–83	10	1179	121		1300
51. Augie Galan	1935–47	9	887	412		1299
52. Tony Phillips	1983–97	10	978	122	186 2b, ss, 3b	1296
53. Garret Anderson	1995–2006	10	764	529		1293
54. Gene Woodling	1949–61	10	820	438		1258
55. Kevin McReynolds	1984–93	10	687	568		1255
56. Charlie Jamieson	1917–28	10	726	526		1252
57. Jeff Heath	1938–46	10	850	357		1207
58. Rico Carty	1964–79	10	1076	130		1206
59. Tip O'Neill	1884–92	8	1005	199		1204
60. Ben Oglivie	1975–85	10	804	395		1199
61. Topsy Hartsel	1901–08	7	858	339		1197
62. Ron Gant	1988–2002	10	836	314	41 2b	1191
63. Sid Gordon	1943–54	10	854	271		1125
64. Chick Hafey	1927–34	7	742	367		1109
65. Don Baylor	1972–86	10	978	127		1105
66. Jeff Burroughs	1973–83	10	870	233		1103

Left Fielder	Best Years		Bat	Field	Other	Total
66. B. J. Surhoff	1987–2004	10	488	337	278 c, 3b	1103
68. Bob Meusel	1920–30	10	795	295		1090
69. George Bell	1984–93	10	896	194		1090
70. George Wood	1880–91	10	791	293		1084
71. Don Buford	1964–72	9	817	192	73 2b, 3b	1082
72. Lou Piniella	1969–82	10	683	391		1074
73. Willie Horton	1965–79	10	1014	56		1070
74. Lonnie Smith	1980–91	9	865	200		1065
75. Duffy Lewis	1910–20	10	565	496		1061
76. Greg Vaughn	1990–2001	10	687	372		1059
77. Tommy Davis	1960–75	10	877	179		1056
78. Charlie Keller	1939–46	6	781	259		1040
79. Steve Kemp	1977–83	7	666	366		1032
80. Larry Hisle	1969–78	7	667	363		1030
81. Abner Dalrymple	1878–87	10	1002	26		1028
82. Geoff Jenkins	1999–2006	7	624	403		1027
83. Carlos Lee	1999–2006	8	691	331		1022
84. Ralph Garr	1971–79	9	759	255		1014
85. Irish Meusel	1918–26	9	759	253		1012
86. Al Smith	1954–63	10	780	226		1006
87. Hank Sauer	1948–57	8	672	332		1004
88. Cliff Floyd	1994–2006	9	730	263	10 1b	1003
89. Phil Bradley	1984–90	7	647	355		1002
90. Bobby Higginson	1995–2004	9	528	468		996
91. Joe Moore	1933–41	9	627	365		992
92. Kevin Mitchell	1986–94	7	732	169	80 1b	977
93. Ron LeFlore	1975–81	7	637	34		972
94. Mike Greenwell	1987–95	8	655	316		971
95. Joe Hornung	1879–90	10	496	474		970
95. Jeff Conine	1993–2004	10	627	211	132 1b	970
97. John Anderson	1895–1908	10	582	174	196 1b	957
97. Burt Shotten	1911–18	8	632	325		957
99. Bob Bescher	1909–16	8	594	350		944
100. Elmer Smith	1892–1900	8	713	229		942
101. Matty McIntyre	1904–11	6	494	446		940
102. Frank Thomas	1953–62	10	652	254	24 3b	930
103. Joe Rudi	1970–80	9	623	302		925
104. Gary Ward	1982–90	9	469	452		921
105. Tilly Walker	1914–22	8	421	478		899
106. Cleon Jones	1966–74	8	557	335		892
107. Carlos May	1969–76	8	659	189	34 1b	882
108. Greg Jefferies	1989–98	10	687	87	107 1b, 3b	881
108. Pat Burrell	2000–06	7	590	291		881
110. Tom York	1876–84	8	608	271		879
111. Sam Mertes	1899–1903	8	494	324	53 2b	861
112. Duff Cooley	1895–1904	7	504	358		862
113. Tom Tresh	1962–69	8	542	191	127 ss	860
114. Ken Henderson	1969–76	7	510	339		849
115. Leon Wagner	1961–68	8	706	141		847
116. Mike Donlin	1901–08	5	757	89		846

Left Fielder	Best Years		Bat	Field	Other	Total
116. Bibb Falk	1921–28	7	505	341		846
118. Vince Coleman	1985–95	8	475	367		842
119. John Stone	1930–37	8	479	353		832
120. Lefty O'Doul	1928–33	6	753	76		829
121. Carson Bigbee	1917–23	7	400	427		827
122. Gee Walker	1932–45	10	461	365		826
123. Dave Kingman	1972–86	10	730	72	23 1b	825
124. Rusty Greer	1994–2000	7	603	219		822
125. George Case	1938–46	9	428	393		821
126. George Stone	1905–10	5	567	227		794
127. Bernard Gilkey	1992–98	6	438	345		783
128. Charlie Maxwell	1956–60	5	458	318		776
129. Mel Hall	1983–92	9	461	314		775
130. Jack Graney	1910–19	8	369	403		772
131. Gene Richards	1977–82	6	501	266		767
132. Shannon Stewart	1998–2005	6	491	272		763
133. Patsy Dougherty	1902–10	8	707	48		755
134. Dale Mitchell	1947–53	7	505	235		740
135. Tito Francona	1956–68	9	515	158	65 1b	738
135. Shane Mack	1987–94	6	470	268		738
137. Warren Cromartie	1977–83	7	390	305	35 1b	730
138. Peanuts Lowrey	1943–52	9	329	372	27 3b	728
139. Luis Polonia	1987–94	7	470	247		717
140. Manny Mota	1964–72	8	533	175		708
141. Chuck Hinton	1961–70	8	455	252		707
141. Mike Easler	1980–86	7	603	104		707
143. Les Mann	1913–20	8	291	404		695
144. Johnny Briggs	1967–75	9	494	200		694
145. Joe Sommer	1882–89	7	311	357		668
146. Dan Gladden	1985–92	8	307	384		691
147. Riggs Stephenson	1927–32	5	520	167		687
147. Hoot Evers	1947–52	6	339	348		687
149. Cliff Carroll	1884–93	8	413	266		679
150. Jim Russell	1943–49	6	377	301		678
151. Lee Magee	1912–19	7	323	283	64 2b	670
152. Larry Herndon	1976–86	10	364	304		668
153. Hector Lopez	1955–65	10	476	89	102 1b, 3b	667
153. Jacque Jones	2000–06	7	306	361		667
155. Bob Nieman	1952–59	6	500	166		666
156. Jerry Morales	1972–81	9	304	362		666
157. Bob Skinner	1954–63	8	459	170	33 1b	662
158. Gus Zernial	1950–57	6	474	184		658
159. Blondie Purcell	1879–90	10	553	99		652
160. Billy Hatcher	1986–94	9	275	374		649
161. Rick Reichardt	1967–72	6	346	287		633
162. Spike Shannon	1904–08	5	342	288		630
163. Danny Litwhiler	1941–49	6	346	271		617
164. Al Martin	1993–2000	8	434	182		616
165. Adam Dunn	2002–06	5	533	79		612
166. Freddy Leach	1926–31	6	296	306		602

Left Fielder	Best Years		Bat	Field	Other	Total
166. Dave Collins	1977–86	8	380	220		600
167. Marty Cordova	1994–2002	7	299	301		600 tie
168. Irv Noren	1950–55	6	278	319		597
169. Raul Ibanez	2001–06	6	431	157		588
170. Jeff Leonard	1979–89	6	369	217		586
171. Monte Irvin	1950–56	5	421	160		581
172. Taft Wright	1938–48	7	389	190		579
173. Bernie Carbo	1970–75	6	401	171		572
174. Emmett Seery	1886–91	6	368	192		560
175. Walter Wilmot	1888–95	7	367	190		557
176. Rondell White	1995–2004	6	312	244		556
177. Henry Rodriguez	1994–2000	6	325	230		555
178. Max West	1938–42	5	268	244	39 1b	551
179. Jim Lemon	1956–61	6	424	124		548
180. Mike Menosky	1917–22	5	279	252		547
181. Steve Braun	1971–77	7	469	70	8 3b	547
182. Troy O'Leary	1995–2001	7	325	220		535
183. Darby O'Brien	1887–92	5	320	214		534
184. Gary Roenicke	1979–85	7	298	233		531
185. Roy Hartzell	1906–15	9	303	166	57 2b, 3b	526
186. Moose Solters	1934–40	5	298	227		525
187. Steve Henderson	1978–84	5	393	132		525 tie
188. Dmitri Young	1997–2005	8	443	81		524
189. Curt Blefary	1965–69	5	355	131	36 1b	522
190. Lee Maye	1961–70	9	381	138		519
191. Jesus Alou	1964–71	8	250	267		517
192. Alex Johnson	1968–76	7	489	17		506
193. Dion James	1984–93	6	305	197		502
194. Pete Incaviglia	1986–96	9	389	113		502
195. Pete Gillespie	1880–86	7	300	195		495
196. Greasy Neale	1916–20	5	179	316		495
197. Jack McCarthy	1898–1904	5	202	287		489
198. John Lowenstein	1974–83	5	314	159		473
199. Rip Radcliff	1935–41	7	375	97		472
200. Possum Whitted	1913–21	6	166	234	54 3b	454
201. Eddie Burke	1890–97	7	286	163		449
202. Frank Catalanotto	1999–2006	5	291	158		449 tie
203. Beals Becker	1909–15	5	285	162		447
204. Fatty Fothergill	1923–32	7	376	63		439
205. Rube Bressler	1921–30	6	266	157		423
206. Shad Barry	1902–08	6	265	126	28 1b	419
207. Jimmy Delsing	1951–55	5	137	267		412
208. Howard Shanks	1912–23	10	54	240	106 ss, 2b	400
209. Clyde Barnhart	1921–27	5	237	105	54 3b	396
210. Clyde Engle	1909–15	5	246	104	40 1b, 3b	390
211. Mickey Hatcher	1981–87	6	186	185		371
212. Hal Lee	1932–36	5	147	207		354
213. Carmelo Martinez	1984–88	5	223	131		354 tir
214. Rip Repulski	1953–57	5	197	133		330
215. Mike Felder	1987–93	6	92	227		319

Left Fielder	Best Years		Bat	Field	Other	Total
216. Glenallen Hill	1992–2000	6	224	92		316
217. Chris James	1987–92	5	145	158		303
218. Todd Hollandsworth	1996–2006	5	87	204		291
219. Larry Sheets	1985–90	5	212	71		283
220. Jerry Lynch	1958–64	6	259	17		276
221. Dan Pasqua	1986–91	5	183	97		270
222. Gene Clines	1972–78	6	148	116		264
223. Dick Harley	1898–1903	5	79	181		260
224. Daryl Boston	1987–93	7	127	128		255
225. Eric Owens	1999–2003	5	11	221		232
226. George Tebeau	1888–95	5	147	82		229
227. Wes Covington	1959–65	6	240	−25		215
228. Derrick May	1992–96	5	134	74		208
229. Gil Coan	1948–52	5	8	190		198
230. Dwight Smith	1989–95	5	122	68		190
231. Gary Thomasson	1973–79	7	115	66		181
232. Pat Sheridan	1983–1989	5	101	64		165
233. Thomas Howard	1991–96	6	20	98		118
234. Mark Sweeney	1997–2006	5	22	0		22

4

STARTING PITCHERS

In rating pitchers (in this section whenever the word pitcher is used without a modifier, it refers to starting pitchers) it is necessary to remember that the primary purpose of the pitcher is to win games for his team. Keeping this fundamental objective in mind will prevent the rater from being sidetracked by secondary goals, such as strikeouts, no-hitters, or shutouts. Strikeouts may be dramatic and exciting, but they are only one means to an end. The end is to win. If the win is not attained, what good is the strikeout? It is better for a pitcher to get all 27 outs via grounders or fly balls and win than it is to strike out a record number but lose the game.

No-hitters are always exciting for spectators to watch, but pitching a no-hitter should never be the pitcher's primary objective. A no-hitter that results in a win is worth as much as any other win, no more, no less. And not all no-hitters result in wins; sometimes a hurler can toss a no-hitter and lose the game. A no-hitter that results in a loss is still a loss. Each win or loss counts as one game in the standings, and the pennant winner is the team that has the best won-lost record. A pitcher could conceivably strike out 27 batters in every game and pitch a no-hitter each time he takes the mound, yet lose all of his games because of bases on balls forcing runners across the plate.

Shutouts are another overrated aspect of pitching. A whitewash is worth no more than any other victory. Winning a game 8–6 is as good as winning it 8–0 and far better than losing it 2–1. The measure of a pitcher is not the number of shutouts he hurls, nor is it his earned run average. It is his won-lost record. The Faber System does not confuse the issue by giving points for strikeouts, shutouts, or earned run average. It concentrates solely on the primary objective. Nothing else counts.

The primary objective is winning. The most effective moundsman is the one who wins the most frequently and consistently. The more wins the better. Other things being equal, the pitcher who wins 20 games has made a greater contribution than the one who wins 10. The Faber System gives one point for each game won. Consistency is also important. If two hurlers on the same team each win 20 games in a season, but one of them loses 20 while the other tastes defeat only 10 times, clearly the latter has made a greater contribution to his team's pennant drive. Standings are based on a won-lost percentage. Therefore, the moundsman with the better won-lost ratio deserves credit for the consistency of his performance.

A pitcher's winning percentage demonstrates the *quality* of his work; the total number of decisions represents the *quantity* of work done. Another variable arises from the fact that it is far more difficult to win for a weak team than for a strong one. A pitcher who wins 20 and loses

10 games for a team that has a record of 80 wins and 80 losses has accomplished far more than the one who achieves the same record for a team with 100 wins and 60 losses.

In order to rate fairly pitchers who labor for weak teams or strong teams, the Faber System utilizes the weighted rating system devised by Ted C. Oliver. (Ted C. Oliver, *Kings of the Mound*, 2nd ed., Los Angeles, 1947.) A pitcher's weighted rating is determined by the difference in his personal winning percentage and the team's winning percentage in games wherein the particular moundsman is not the pitcher of record. This difference is multiplied by the number of decisions charged to the pitcher being rated. Quality of performance is represented by the difference between individual and team winning percentages; quantity by the number of decisions. The highest weighted ratings thus go to the pitchers who exceed their team's winning percentage by a wide margin and also have a large number of decisions. Both quality and quantity are taken into account. The only weakness in the weighted rating is that it assumes that exceeding the club's winning percentage by a certain amount is of identical worth regardless of what that percentage is. This, in actuality, is not quite true. In reality, exceeding the winning percentage of a great team is a much more remarkable achievement that exceeding the winning percentage of a team of modest accomplishments. For example, in order to exceed by 100 points the percentage of a team winning two-thirds of its games, a hurler would have to post a .767 mark, whereas to exceed by the same margin the record of a team winning two-fifths of its games, the moundsman would have to produce only a .500 figure. The Faber System is superior to that devised by Oliver in that it uses weighted ratings as only one component along with the number of wins and the winning percentage. The exact formula is: $R=W + 100p/2 + WR/200$, where R is Faber System rating, W is wins, p is percentage, and WR is weighted rating. In order to equalize ratings for hurlers pitching different distances the rating is multiplied by .74 in those seasons (1876–80) when the pitching distance was 45 feet and by .83 in those years (1881–92) when it was 50 feet.

The weighted rating system was developed to rate moundsmen who are a part of a pitching staff. It does not work well when applied to the early part of the pioneer era when one pitcher might account for all or virtually all of his team's decisions. In 1876, for example, Jim Devlin of the Louisville Grays won 30 games and lost 35 for a winning percentage of .462. The Grays lost the only game in which Devlin was not the pitcher of record, for a percentage of .000, giving Devlin a mark 462 points higher than the "rest of the staff" and a weighted rating of 30,030 points. Suppose the Grays had somehow won the one decision in which Devlin did not figure. Then the team without Devlin would have had a winning percentage of 1.000, and Devlin would have been 538 points below his staff's average for a weighted rating of -34,970 points, a swing of 65,000 points based entirely on the outcome of a single game. Obviously, this is not the way the weighted rating is supposed to work. The solution is to adjust the rating in cases wherein one pitcher is responsible for more than one-half of his club's outcomes. For each percentage point over 50 per cent of the decisions, .02 is deducted from a multiplier of 1.00. In 1876 Devlin was the pitcher of record in nearly 99 per cent of the Grays' decisions. Thus, the multiplier applied to his weighted rating is .02, and the rating is a more realistic 601, instead of 30,030. Use of the multiplier is confined almost exclusively to the first 10 years of the pioneer era. Only once after 1886 did a major league pitcher figure in more than one-half of his teams decisions. That was in 1889 when John Clarkson of Boston was the pitcher of record in 53 per cent of the Beaneaters' games. The resulting multiplier of .94 reduced his weighted rating from 10,472 to 9844, still high enough to be the best in the league. In that season Clarkson won 49 games and lost 19, while the rest of the staff won 34 and lost 26. Clarkson's league-leading status was well earned.

Because starting pitchers are occasionally used in relief, wins and losses in that role are included in their records. Everyone credits Lefty Grove with 300 lifetime wins; no one claims he fell short of that milestone because 33 of his victories came in relief. However, saves are not counted in rating starters. Relievers who made only occasional starts are not included among starting pitchers.

Leading Pitchers by Year

In order to be listed among the yearly leaders, a pitcher usually must be involved in 15 or more decisions in the year under consideration. There are two exceptions to this rule. During the early years of organized professional baseball, seasons were very short by modern standards, sometimes consisting of as few as 75 or 80 games per team. During the short seasons, however, pitching was from a distance of 45 or 50 feet, the type of deliveries utilized did not necessitate long rests between starts, and the schedules typically allowed many off days during the season. In those days pitchers had no difficulty meeting the criterion of 15 decisions per year. However, after 1893 when the pitching distance was lengthened to 60 feet 6 inches, hurlers needed more rest between starts. So from 1893 to date whenever the season consists of fewer than 150 games, the eligibility requirement for pitchers is approximately 10 percent of the games played by their teams. The other exception is that we omit pitchers who were primarily relievers and met the 15 decisions criterion by games won and lost in relief.

In 1883–84 Tim Keefe of the New York Giants became the first National League hurler to be the league's best pitcher two years in a row. Tommy Bond, Jim McCormick, Charlie "Old Hoss" Radbourn, and Jouett Meekin also won two crowns, but not back to back. In 1892–93 Cy Young of the Cleveland Spiders matched Keefe's feat of two consecutive league-leading seasons, then Young went Keefe one better by garnering his third crown in 1895. After the turn of the century Young took three consecutive Pitcher of the Year titles for Boston in the new American League in 1901–03, giving him a total of six league-leading seasons. Counting only seasons in the National League, the great Christy Mathewson of the New York Giants was the first to lead more than three times, with four seasons as the league's best, including three in a row. Grover Cleveland "Pete" Alexander topped Matty by leading six times, including four consecutively. Five of Alex's leading seasons came when he was with the Philadelphia Phillies; the other when he toiled for the Chicago Cubs. The only other pitchers to be National League Pitcher of the Year as many as three times are Dazzy Vance, Warren Spahn, Juan Marichal, and Tom Seaver.

The 60 wins recorded by Old Hoss Radbourn of the Providence Grays in 1884 are the most victories ever posted by a major league pitcher in a single season. The most wins posted in a season since the pitching distance was increased to the present 60 feet 6 inches are the 37 tallied by Mathewson in 1908. The last NL hurler to post 30 wins in a season was Dizzy Dean of St. Louis's Gashouse Gang in 1934. Radbourn's .833 in 1884 is the best percentage by a pioneer league-leader, but trails the .875 recorded by Fred Goldsmith of the Chicago White Stockings in 1880. This record was broken by Freddie Fitzsimmons of the Brooklyn Dodgers with .889 in 1940 and by Elroy Face of the Pittsburgh Pirates with an all-time best of .947 compiled from 18 wins and only one loss in 1959. (However, Face's record was compiled as a reliever. Greg Maddux's .905, based on 19 wins and two losses in 1995, is best for a starting pitcher.) The highest weighted rating was achieved by Sadie McMahon in 1890 with 18,851 points. Sadie divided his season between the Philadelphia Athletics and the Baltimore Orioles. That record has stood unmatched for well over 100 years. The nearest approach to it is Steve Carlton's 17,057 points for the Philadelphia Phillies in 1972. Amazingly, Carlton won 27 games and lost 10 that season. The last-place Phillies won 32 and lost 87 games in which Lefty was not the pitcher of record.

NATIONAL LEAGUE PITCHER OF THE YEAR, 1876–2006

Year	Pitcher	Club	W	L	Pct.	WR	Points
1876	Jack Manning	Bos	18	5	.783	7728	71
1877	Tommy Bond	Bos	40	17	.702	200	56
1878	Monte Ward	Pro	22	13	.629	6233	62

Year	Pitcher	Club	W	L	Pct.	WR	Points
1879	Tommy Bond	Bos	43	19	.694	12283	103
1880	Jim McCormick	Cle	45	28	.616	8237	87
1881	Old Hoss Radbourn	Pro	25	11	.694	8496	85
1882	Jim McCormick	Cle	36	29	.554	5487	76
1883	Pud Galvin	Buf	46	29	.613	11730	113
1884	Old Hoss Radbourn	Pro	60	12	.833	12079	134
1885	Mickey Welch	NY	44	11	.800	4455	88
1886	Charlie Ferguson	Phi	30	9	.769	8658	92
1887	Tim Keefe	NY	35	19	.648	9180	94
1888	Tim Keefe	NY	35	12	.745	7614	91
1889	John Clarkson	Bos	49	19	.721	9844	111
1890	Kid Gleason	Phi	38	17	.691	7740	93
1891	Bill Hutchinson	Chi	44	19	.698	9765	106
1892	Cy Young	Cle	36	12	.750	8928	99
1893	Cy Young	Cle	34	16	.680	9000	113
1894	Jouett Meekin	NY	33	9	.786	7350	109
1895	Cy Young	Cle	35	10	.778	9090	119
1896	Jouett Meekin	NY	26	14	.650	9280	105
1897	Amos Rusie	NY	28	10	.737	5548	93
1898	Bert Cunningham	Lou	28	15	.651	11266	117
1899	Jim Hughes	Brk	28	6	.824	6256	100
1900	Joe McGinnity	Brk	29	9	.763	8436	109
1901	Noodles Hahn	Cin	22	18	.550	9800	99
1902	Jack Taylor	Chi	23	11	.676	8126	98
1903	Sam Leever	Pit	25	6	.781	6014	94
1904	Joe McGinnity	NY	35	8	.814	7224	112
1905	Christy Mathewson	NY	31	8	.795	5694	99
1906	Sam Leever	Pit	22	7	.759	5423	87
1907	Tully Sparks	Phi	22	8	.733	6270	90
1908	Christy Mathewson	NY	37	11	.771	9408	123
1909	Christy Mathewson	NY	25	6	.806	7967	105
1910	Christy Mathewson	NY	27	9	.750	7488	102
1911	Grover Alexander	Phi	28	13	.683	9143	108
1912	Claude Hendrix	Pit	24	9	.727	5247	86
1913	Tom Seaton	Phi	27	12	.692	5733	91
1914	Grover Alexander	Phi	27	15	.643	9408	106
1915	Grover Alexander	Phi	31	10	.756	9225	115
1916	Grover Alexander	Phi	33	12	.733	8820	114
1917	Grover Alexander	Phi	30	13	.698	7525	103
1918	Burleigh Grimes	Brk	19	9	.679	8148	94
1919	Jesse Barnes	NY	25	9	.735	5100	88
1920	Grover Alexander	Chi	27	14	.659	9594	108
1921	Burleigh Grimes	Brk	22	13	.629	5565	81
1922	Eppa Rixey	Cin	25	13	.658	5016	83
1923	Dolf Luque	Cin	27	8	.771	8155	107
1924	Dazzy Vance	Brk	28	6	.824	9894	118
1925	Dazzy Vance	Brk	22	9	.710	10323	110
1926	Remy Kremer	Pit	20	6	.769	6890	92
1927	Larry Benton	Bos/NY	17	7	.708	5160	78
1928	Dazzy Vance	Brk	22	10	.688	7488	86

Year	Pitcher	Club	W	L	Pct.	WR	Points
1929	Red Lucas	Cin	19	12	.613	7161	86
1930	Phil Collins	Phi	16	11	.593	8370	88
1931	Ed Brandt	Bos	18	11	.621	7337	86
1932	Lon Warneke	Chi	22	6	.786	6916	96
1933	Ben Cantwell	Bos	20	10	.667	4770	77
1934	Dizzy Dean	StL	30	7	.811	9287	117
1935	Paul Derringer	Cin	22	13	.671	8400	98
1936	Carl Hubbell	NY	16	6	.813	8704	111
1937	Lou Fette	Bos	20	10	.667	5520	81
1938	Bill Lee	Chi	22	9	.710	4867	82
1939	Paul Derringer	Cin	25	7	.781	6112	95
1940	Freddie Fitzsimmons	Brk	16	2	.889	6408	92
1941	Elmer Riddle	Cin	19	4	.826	6877	94
1942	Claude Passeau	Chi	19	14	.576	5643	76
1943	Rip Sewell	Pit	21	9	.700	6750	90
1944	Bucky Walters	Cin	23	8	.742	6386	92
1945	Hank Borowy	NY (AL)/Chi	21	7	.750	6152	90
1946	Schoolboy Rowe	Phi	11	4	.733	4740	72
1947	Ewell Blackwell	Cin	22	8	.733	9660	107
1948	Harry Brecheen	StL	20	7	.741	6183	88
1949	Warren Spahn	Bos	21	14	.600	5110	77
1950	Sal Maglie	NY	18	4	.818	6666	92
1951	Preacher Roe	Brk	22	3	.880	7800	105
1952	Robin Roberts	Phi	28	7	.800	10640	121
1953	Warren Spahn	Mil	23	7	.767	6336	93
1954	Robin Roberts	Phi	23	15	.605	5966	83
1955	Don Newcombe	Brk	22	5	.800	4775	84
1956	Don Newcombe	Brk	27	7	.794	8296	108
1957	Jack Sanford	Phi	19	8	.704	6669	87
1958	Warren Spahn	Mil	22	11	.667	2904	70
1959	Vance Law	Pit	18	9	.667	5265	77
1960	Ernie Broglio	StL	21	9	.700	5280	82
1961	Johnny Podres	LA	18	5	.783	5543	85
1962	Bob Purkey	Cin	23	5	.821	7308	101
1963	Juan Marichal	SF	25	6	.806	9207	109
1964	Larry Jackson	Chi	24	11	.686	9695	106
1965	Sandy Koufax	LA	26	8	.765	7140	100
1966	Juan Marichal	SF	25	6	.806	8773	109
1967	Mike McCormick	SF	22	10	.688	5024	81
1968	Juan Marichal	SF	26	9	.743	8925	108
1969	Tom Seaver	NY	25	7	.781	6528	97
1970	Bob Gibson	StL	23	7	.767	11190	117
1971	Ferguson Jenkins	Chi	24	13	.649	6549	89
1972	Steve Carlton	Phi	27	10	.730	17057	149
1973	Ron Bryant	SF	24	12	.667	5724	86
1974	Mike Caldwell	SF	14	5	.737	6289	82
1975	Tom Seaver	NY	22	9	.710	7416	97
1976	Randy Jones	SD	22	14	.611	7416	90
1977	Tom Seaver	NY/Cin	21	6	.778	8397	103
1978	Gaylord Perry	SD	21	6	.778	8397	102

Year	Pitcher	Club	W	L	Pct.	WR	Points
1979	Joe Niekro	Hou	21	11	.656	4256	75
1980	Steve Carlton	Phi	24	9	.727	6864	94
1981	Tom Seaver	Cin	14	2	.875	4960	83
1982	Phil Niekro	Atl	17	4	.810	6279	89
1983	John Denny	Phi	19	6	.760	6050	87
1984	Mario Soto	Cin	18	7	.720	8500	97
1985	Dwight Gooden	NY	24	4	.857	8540	110
1986	Fernando Valenzuela	LA	21	11	.656	8192	95
1987	Rick Sutcliffe	Chi	18	10	.643	5768	79
1988	Danny Jackson	Cin	23	8	.742	7719	99
1989	Mike Scott	Hou	20	10	.667	5010	78
1990	Doug Drabek	Pit	22	6	.786	7712	100
1991	Jose Rijo	Cin	15	6	.714	6216	82
1992	Greg Maddux	Chi	20	11	.646	9393	99
1993	Mark Portugal	Hou	18	4	.818	7459	96
1994	Bret Saberhagen	NY	14	4	.778	6226	84
1995	Greg Maddux	Atl	19	2	.905	6888	98
1996	John Smoltz	Atl	24	8	.750	6304	94
1997	Shawn Estes	SF	19	5	.792	6672	92
1998	John Smoltz	Atl	17	3	.850	4460	82
1999	Mike Hampton	Hou	22	4	.847	7670	102
2000	Scott Elarton	Hou	17	7	.709	7416	89
2001	Curt Schilling	Ari	22	8	.786	7392	98
2002	Randy Johnson	Ari	24	5	.828	7772	104
2003	Mark Prior	Chi	18	6	.750	5832	85
2004	Roger Clemens	Hou	18	4	.818	6358	91
2005	Chris Carpenter	StL	21	5	.808	5902	91
2006	Carlos Zambrano	Chi	16	7	.696	7728	90

American Association

The American Association was led by a different pitcher in each of its ten seasons as a major league. Guy Hecker posted the most wins in a season with 52 in 1884. Matt Kilroy had the best weighted rating and the most Faber System points with 138 in 1887, the most attained by any 19th century major league hurler.

AMERICAN ASSOCIATION PITCHER OF THE YEAR, 1882–91

Year	Pitcher	Club	W	L	Pct	WR	Points
1882	Will White	Cin	40	12	.769	8481	100
1883	Frank Mountain	Col	26	33	.441	13023	94
1884	Guy Hecker	Lou	52	20	.722	13211	128
1885	Ed Morris	Pit	39	24	.619	13356	114
1886	Toad Ramsey	Lou	38	27	.585	12415	107
1887	Matt Kilroy	Bal	46	19	.708	16900	138
1888	Icebox Chamberlain	Lou-StL	25	11	.694	9381	89
1889	Bob Caruthers	Brk	40	11	.784	8568	101
1890	Sadie McMahon	Bal-Phi	36	21	.632	18851	134
1891	Gus Weyhing	Phi	31	20	.608	6943	80

Players' League

Gus Weyhing was the Players' League's best pitcher in 1890. The following year he returned to the American Association and was that circuit's best pitcher. Before hanging up his glove the Louisville native also pitched in the National League and in the American League in that loop's first season as a major.

PLAYERS' LEAGUE PITCHER OF THE YEAR, 1890

Year	Pitcher	Club	W	L	Pct	WR	Points
1890	Gus Weyhing	Brk	30	16	.652	5382	75

American League

In its first year as a major league, the American League was led in pitching by Denton "Cy" Young of the Boston Somersets, who won 33 games and garnered 129 Faber System points. If the Cy Young award to outstanding pitchers had been available from the league's inception, its first winner would have been Cy Young himself! And he would have repeated the next two seasons, winning 32 games in 1902 and 28 in 1903, while racking up 126 points and then 91 points. In 1904 Young's best effort was topped by Jack Chesbro of the New York Highlanders with a league record 41 wins and 147 Faber System points. Happy Jack's win total remains unmatched. His point total, however, fell to second place, when Walter Johnson of the Washington Nationals compiled 153 points, the most ever in major league history. In 1913 the Big Train won 36 games and lost only seven for a team that otherwise had a losing record of 54 wins and 57 losses. Not far behind the achievements of Johnson and Chesbro is Big Ed Walsh of the Chicago White Sox, who won 40 games and compiled 140 points in 1908. The only pitcher to win as many as 30 games in a season in the last 70 years is Denny McLain who led the Detroit Tigers to the 1968 pennant with 31 victories.

The best winning percentage of a pitcher during the league's first decade was the .862 by Wild Bill Donovan of the 1907 Detroit Tigers. Five years later Smoky Joe Wood of the Boston Red Sox turned in a mark of .872. In his fabulous 1931 season for the Philadelphia A's, Lefty Grove raised the record to .886. Finally, Johnny Allen of the Cleveland Indians had a 15 wins and one loss season in 1937 for a percentage of .939.

Young set the early AL standard with three consecutive league-leading seasons. (Earlier he had led the National League three times.) Johnson led five times, but these seasons were spread out over more than a decade. Robert Moses "Lefty" Grove put together four league-leading seasons back-to-back from 1930 through 1933. No other American League hurler has led four years in a row. The only other pitchers to lead the circuit more than twice are Bob Feller and Roger Clemens. Feller, the Van Meter Meteor, led in 1940 and 1941 and then after serving nearly four years in the Navy during World War II came back to be the loop's outstanding pitcher again in 1946, his first full year back from the service. Feller led three times, and technically only twice in a row, but he led in three consecutive seasons in which he was eligible. If his streak had not been interrupted by naval service, could he have led seven times in a row? Clemens led the American League three times and the National League once for a total of four seasons as the best pitcher in his circuit.

AMERICAN LEAGUE PITCHER OF THE YEAR, 1901–2006

Year	Pitcher	Club	W	L	Pct	WR	Points
1901	Cy Young	Bos	33	10	.767	11696	129
1902	Cy Young	Bos	21	11	.744	11428	126

Year	Pitcher	Club	W	L	Pct	WR	Points
1903	Cy Young	Bos	28	9	.757	4921	91
1904	Jack Chesbro	NY	41	12	.744	13462	147
1905	Jesse Tannehill	Bos	22	9	.710	7626	96
1906	Eddie Plank	Phi	19	6	.760	6700	91
1907	Wild Bill Donovan	Det	25	4	.862	8961	113
1908	Ed Walsh	Chi	40	15	.727	12760	140
1909	George Mullin	Det	29	8	.784	6808	102
1910	Russ Ford	NY	26	6	.813	9344	114
1911	Walter Johnson	Was	25	13	.658	12236	119
1912	Smoky Joe Wood	Bos	34	5	.872	9360	125
1913	Walter Johnson	Was	36	7	.837	15093	153
1914	Chief Bender	Phi	17	3	.850	4540	83
1915	Walter Johnson	Was	27	13	.675	6480	93
1916	Bob Shawkey	NY	24	14	.632	5662	84
1917	Walter Johnson	Was	23	16	.590	5577	81
1918	Scott Perry	Phi	21	19	.525	6920	83
1919	Eddie Cicotte	Chi	29	7	.806	8604	112
1920	Jim Bagby	Cle	31	12	.721	5031	92
1921	Red Faber	Chi	25	15	.625	12000	116
1922	Eddie Rommel	Phi	27	13	.675	13680	129
1923	Howard Ehmke	Bos	20	17	.541	6840	81
1924	Walter Johnson	Was	23	7	.767	6330	93
1925	Stan Coveleskie	Was	20	5	.800	4925	85
1926	George Uhle	Cle	27	11	.711	6992	98
1927	Ted Lyons	Chi	22	14	.579	6992	98
1928	Al Crowder	StL	21	5	.808	8608	104
1929	Wes Ferrell	Cle	21	10	.677	5611	83
1930	Lefty Grove	Phi	28	5	.848	7821	109
1931	Lefty Grove	Phi	31	4	.886	8295	116
1932	Lefty Grove	Phi	25	10	.714	4690	99
1933	Lefty Grove	Phi	24	8	.750	9126	108
1934	Lefty Gomez	NY	26	5	.839	8866	112
1935	Wes Ferrell	Bos	25	14	.641	6864	91
1936	Vern Kennedy	Chi	21	9	.700	6120	87
1937	Johnny Allen	Cle	15	1	.938	6960	97
1938	Buck Newsom	StL	20	16	.556	9180	94
1939	Dutch Leonard	Was	20	8	.718	9828	105
1940	Bob Feller	Cle	27	11	.711	6726	97
1941	Bob Feller	Cle	25	13	.658	8654	112
1942	Tex Hughson	Bos	22	6	.786	5992	91
1943	Spud Chandler	NY	20	4	.833	5992	90
1944	Hal Newhouser	Det	29	9	.763	9652	115
1945	Dave Ferriss	Bos	21	10	.677	8370	97
1946	Bob Feller	Cle	26	15	.634	10742	112
1947	Phil Marchildon	Phi	19	9	.679	5908	83
1948	Ray Scarborough	Was	15	8	.652	7751	87
1949	Mel Parnell	Bos	25	7	.781	6368	96
1950	Bob Hooper	Phi	15	10	.600	7825	84
1951	Ned Garver	StL	20	12	.625	11616	109
1952	Bobby Shantz	Phi	24	7	.774	10137	114

Year	Pitcher	Club	W	L	Pct	WR	Points
1953	Mel Parnell	Bos	21	8	.724	6264	88
1954	Sandy Consuegra	Chi	16	3	.842	5016	83
1955	Billy Hoeft	Det	16	7	.696	4945	76
1956	Billy Pierce	Chi	20	9	.690	4930	80
1957	Jim Bunning	Det	20	8	.714	7112	92
1958	Bob Turley	NY	21	7	.750	5236	85
1959	Camilio Pascual	Was	17	10	.630	7236	85
1960	Gaylord Perry	Cle	18	10	.643	5124	76
1961	Whitey Ford	NY	35	4	.862	6670	101
1962	Dick Donovan	Cle	20	10	.667	6360	85
1963	Bill Monbouquette	Bos	20	10	.667	7200	89
1964	Dean Chance	LA	20	9	.690	6496	87
1965	Mel Stottlemyre	NY	20	9	.690	7569	93
1966	Jim Kaat	Min	25	13	.658	5396	85
1967	Jim Lonborg	Bos	22	9	.710	5456	85
1968	Denny McLain	Det	31	6	.838	9674	121
1969	Denny McLain	Det	24	9	.727	7095	95
1970	Sam McDowell	Cle	20	12	.625	6208	82
1971	Dave McNally	Bal	21	5	.808	5252	87
1972	Gaylord Perry	Cle	24	16	.600	7440	91
1973	Jim "Catfish" Hunter	Oak	21	5	.808	7046	96
1974	Ferguson Jenkins	Tex	25	12	.676	7252	95
1975	Jim "Catfish" Hunter	NY	23	14	.622	4958	79
1976	Mark Fidrych	Det	19	9	.679	7420	90
1977	Dave Rozema	Det	15	7	.782	5742	78
1978	Ron Guidry	NY	25	3	.893	9436	117
1979	Tommy John	NY	21	9	.700	5310	83
1980	Steve Stone	Bal	25	7	.781	6528	97
1981	Pete Vuckovich	Mil	14	4	.778	4518	76
1982	Pete Vuckovich	Mil	18	6	.750	4608	79
1983	Rich Dotson	Chi	22	7	.759	5220	86
1984	Bert Blyleven	Cle	19	7	.731	8060	96
1985	Ron Guidry	NY	22	6	.786	6216	92
1986	Roger Clemens	Bos	24	4	.857	9094	112
1987	Roger Clemens	Bos	20	9	.690	7221	91
1988	Mark Gubicza	KC	20	8	.714	6524	89
1989	Brett Saberhagen	KC	23	6	.793	7946	103
1990	Bob Welch	Oak	27	6	.818	7524	106
1991	Mark Langston	Cal	19	8	.704	6615	87
1992	Kevin Brown	Tex	21	11	.657	7232	90
1993	Randy Johnson	Sea	19	8	.704	6399	86
1994	David Cone	KC	16	5	.762	5271	80
1995	Randy Johnson	Sea	18	2	.900	8240	104
1996	Pat Hentgen	Tor	20	10	.667	7740	92
1997	Roger Clemens	Tor	21	7	.750	9520	107
1998	Roger Clemens	Tor	20	6	.769	6994	93
1999	Pedro Martinez	Bos	23	4	.852	8802	110
2000	Tim Hudson	Oak	20	6	.769	6318	90
2001	Roger Clemens	NY	20	3	.870	7429	101
2002	Pedro Martinez	Bos	20	4	.833	7296	98

Year	Pitcher	Club	W	L	Pct	WR	Points
2003	Roy Halladay	Tor	22	7	.759	8062	100
2004	Johan Santana	Min	20	6	.769	6240	89
2005	Cliff Lee	Cle	18	5	.783	5589	93
2006	Johan Santana	Min	19	6	.760	4950	82

Federal League

Claude Hendrix of the Chi-Feds was the best pitcher in the Federal League during its initial season of 1914. He slipped a bit the next year, but his teammate George McConnell helped pitch the Whales to the 1915 pennant. That was McConnell's only winning season in the big leagues. In contrast, Hendrix had several very successful seasons, both before and after his Federal League tenure, until his career came to a premature end after he was accused of betting against his own team in 1920.

FEDERAL LEAGUE PITCHER OF THE YEAR, 1914–15

Year	Pitcher	Club	W	L	Pct	WR	Points
1914	Claude Hendrix	Chi	29	11	.725	8280	106
1915	George McConnell	Chi	25	10	.714	6755	95

Leading Pitchers by Career

Extended Career. In an extended career of 22 seasons Denton True "Cy" Young compiled the most Faber System points of any pitcher in major league history. Walter Johnson is second, Roger Clemens third, Grover Cleveland "Pete" Alexander is fourth, and Tom Seaver fifth. Young has 511 wins, more than 100 more than Johnson. Young also leads in weighted rating, with Johnson again second. The highest winning percentage turned in over an extended career belongs to Whitey Ford, who edged out Pedro Martinez and Lefty Grove for the honor. Mordecai Peter Centennial (Three-Finger) Brown had only 12 eligible seasons, the fewest of anyone in the top 50 extended career list. The careers of Young, Kid Nichols, and Clark Griffith included years both before and after 1900. Pud Galvin is the only one among the 50 leaders who pitched exclusively in the 19th century. Clemens heads list of 11 hurlers whose careers spanned the most recent turn of the century.

Cy Young was baseball's greatest pitcher. Pitching in both the 19th and the 20th centuries and in both the National and American leagues, he won 511 games, a record that will likely never be broken. Appropriately, the award presented annually to the best pitcher in each league is named in his honor (Library of Congress).

LEADING PITCHERS—EXTENDED CAREER

Pitcher	Eligible Seasons		W	L	Pct	WR	Points
1. Cy Young	1890–1911	22	511	316	.618	98541	1570
2. Walter Johnson	1908–26	19	406	264	.606	96078	1452
3. Roger Clemens	1986–2005	20	326	153	.681	72047	1349
4. Grover Alexander	1911–29	18	371	204	.645	84426	1333
5. Tom Seaver	1967–86	20	311	205	.603	61097	1210
6. Greg Maddux	1987–2006	20	331	199	.625	45452	1190
7. Christy Mathewson	1901–15	15	369	180	.672	60548	1178
8. Randy Johnson	1989–2006	16	266	139	.657	67949	1132
9. Warren Spahn	1947–65	19	355	240	.597	43270	1128
10. Phil Niekro	1967–87	21	312	268	.538	46617	1082
11. Lefty Grove	1925–39	15	286	128	.691	56259	1077
12. Steve Carlton	1967–87	18	325	232	.583	44394	1072
13. Nolan Ryan	1968–91	23	318	274	.537	21488	1040
14. Tom Glavine	1988–2006	19	288	187	.606	31601	1015
15. Don Sutton	1966–87	22	321	250	.562	15273	1011
16. Gaylord Perry	1964–83	20	310	258	.546	28215	989
17. Tommy John	1965–88	21	275	200	.579	26327	982
18. Bert Blyleven	1970–92	21	285	248	.535	21767	961
19. Ted Lyons	1924–42	18	253	219	.536	43513	959
20. Eddie Plank	1901–16	16	322	187	.633	30902	934
21. Robin Roberts	1948–65	17	280	227	.552	36397	927
22. Kid Nichols	1890–1905	14	361	207	.636	29328	911
23. Mike Mussina	1992–2006	15	236	129	.647	37722	909
24. Pedro Martinez	1993–2006	13	199	88	.693	48343	883
25. Ferguson Jenkins	1967–83	17	271	209	.565	27879	880
26. Carl Hubbell	1928–42	15	249	150	.624	30696	865
26. Bob Feller	1937–54	14	252	148	.630	35150	865
28. Jim Palmer	1966–82	15	255	140	.646	23797	858
29. Whitey Ford	1953–65	13	223	96	.699	34187	846
30. Red Faber	1914–31	16	241	188	.562	30660	838
31. Burleigh Grimes	1917–32	14	261	197	.570	25099	828
31. Bob Gibson	1961–74	14	242	153	.613	38149	828
33. Clark Griffith	1891–1905	12	230	134	.632	43491	816
34. Curt Schilling	1992–2006	14	196	122	.616	39432	814
35. Frank Tanana	1974–93	19	232	227	.504	18372	799
36. David Wells	1990–2005	15	208	124	.627	25778	794
37. Pud Galvin	1879–92	14	361	308	.540	53543	791
38. Jack Morris	1979–94	16	250	189	.581	18524	790
39. Early Wynn	1942–62	18	280	232	.547	1712	782
40. Juan Marichal	1961–73	13	232	138	.627	30299	779
41. Herb Pennock	1914–31	13	211	137	.605	24807	765
41. Sad Sam Jones	1918–35	18	225	206	.522	13098	765
43. Kenny Rogers	1990–2006	13	180	111	.619	36278	763
44. Jim Kaat	1961–81	18	256	217	.541	5658	761
45. Kevin Brown	1989–2004	14	192	128	.600	27119	755
46. Rick Reuschel	1972–89	15	205	177	.537	21181	754
47. Jamie Moyer	1987–2006	15	190	144	.569	23003	746
48. Mordecai Brown	1903–15	12	232	120	.659	39393	744
49. Jerry Koosman	1968–84	17	216	203	.516	6853	739
50. Jim "Catfish" Hunter	1965–78	14	196	130	.586	20679	730

Christy Mathewson won 373 games to tie Grover Cleveland Alexander for the National League lifetime record. Matty leads all pitchers in Faber System points per season. His performance in the 1905 World Series was sensational, as he pitched three shutouts, a feat that may never be equaled (Library of Congress).

Points Per Season. When pitchers are ranked according to Faber System points earned per season, Christy Mathewson moves to the top of the list. Cy Young, who led the extended career rankings, drops to eighth. Walter Johnson retains his spot in second place. In fourth place is Grover Cleveland Alexander, who makes the top five in both rankings. Near the top in points per season are several hurlers who did not have enough longevity to join the extended career

Russ Ford had the highest weighted average per season of all big league pitchers. The Canadian-born right hander was one of the American League's dominant pitchers for a time, surreptitiously scuffing the baseball with emery paper to cause it to break sharply. After only five years of stardom, he saw his career prematurely ended by chronic arm trouble (Library of Congress).

leaders. Among these stars Russ Ford, Ed Walsh, Dizzy Dean, and Roy Halladay all make the top ten. Halladay is one of six hurlers among the top 50 who are still active into the 21st century. Randy Johnson is the best of this august group. On the other hand, the major league careers of nine of the top 50 were confined to the 19th century, with Frank Killen being the best of these. Seven of the leaders, headed by Young, pitched both before and after 1900.

The pitcher with the highest average number of wins per season is Tommy Bond. As a teenager Bond pitched in the old National Association of Professional Base Ball Players, the precursor to the major leagues. When the National League was founded the Irish-born youngster quickly became its dominant pitcher. In 1876 he won 31 games. Then he improved and won at least 40 in each of the next three seasons. In a three-year span he led the league in Faber System points twice, in wins twice, in winning percentage twice, in earned run average twice, in strikeouts twice, and in shutouts all three years. He is said to have had one of baseball's first curve balls. In five years he won 180 games. He never won another. His last big league victory came at the age of 24. (He won 13 games in the Union Association in 1884, but the Faber System does not consider that circuit a major league.)

Bob Caruthers has the highest winning percentage. Known as Parisian Bob because he conducted salary negotiations from France after the 1885 season, he became the highest paid player in the American Association. He was not only an outstanding pitcher, but was also an excellent

Opposite: Rival pitchers Ernie Shore (left) of the Boston Red Sox and Grover Cleveland Alexander of the Philadelphia Phillies shake hands before the opening of the 1915 World Series. Alexander and his Phillies won the first game, but the Sox came back to sweep the next four. For a few years Shore was an excellent pitcher. Alexander was one of the best ever. His 273 lifetime wins ties him with Christy Mathewson for the National League record (Library of Congress).

hitter, and appeared in more major league games as an outfielder than he did as a pitcher. He twice won 40 games in a season, leading first the St. Louis Browns and then the Brooklyn Bridegrooms to their first-ever pennants. In 1893 he had a sore arm and was unable to handle the new 60 foot, 6 inch pitching distance. His major league pitching career ended at the age of 28.

Russ Ford has the highest weighted average per season of all big league pitchers. The Canadian-born righthander was one of the American League's dominant pitchers for a while, surreptitiously scuffing the baseball with emery paper to cause it to break sharply. His career lasted only five years before chronic arm trouble brought his big league tenure to an early end. The leaders in all three categories (wins, percentage, and weighted rating) all had relatively short careers. Two of the three pitched all their games when the distance from mound to the plate was less than it is now. All of this makes the achievements of men like Mathewson, both Johnsons, Alexander, Grove, and Young all the more impressive.

LEADING PITCHERS POINTS PER SEASON

Pitcher	Eligible Seasons		W	L	Pct.	WR	Points
1. Christy Mathewson	1901–15	15	25	12	.672	4037	78.53
2. Walter Johnson	1908–26	16	21	14	.606	5057	76.42
3. Russ Ford	1910–14	5	18	12	.597	5408	76.00
4. Grover Alexander	1911–29	18	21	11	.645	4690	74.05
5. Ed Walsh	1906–12	7	24	16	.600	3982	73.43
6. Lefty Grove	1925–39	15	19	9	.691	3761	71.80
7. Dizzy Dean	1932–37	6	22	13	.639	3568	71.50
8. Cy Young	1890–1911	22	23	14	.618	4479	71.36
9. Randy Johnson	1989–2004	15	17	9	.660	4601	72.67
10. Roy Halladay	1999–2005	6	14	7	.675	4667	70.67
11. Joe McGinnity	1899–1908	10	25	14	.641	4035	70.60
12. Frank Killen	1892–98	6	23	19	.556	4675	70.50
13. Sandy Koufax	1958–66	8	19	9	.676	3587	70.38
14. Noodles Hahn	1899–1904	6	20	15	.578	3899	70.30
15. Amos Rusie	1889–98	9	27	19	.587	3601	70.11
16. Roy Oswalt	2001–06	6	16	8	.676	3770	69.00
17. Denny McLain	1965–71	6	20	12	.618	3643	68.67
18. Bob Caruthers	1885–91	7	30	12	.706	3597	68.43
19. Sadie McMahon	1889–96	8	22	15	.589	4847	68.25
20. Wes Ferrell	1929–38	10	19	12	.607	2764	68.20
21. Jesse Tannehill	1897–1906	10	19	10	.644	3692	68.10
22. Clark Griffith	1891–1905	12	19	11	.632	3624	68.00
23. Pedro Martinez	1993–2006	13	15	7	.693	3719	67.92
24. Addie Joss	1902–09	8	19	11	.629	3451	67.50
25. Roger Clemens	1986–2005	20	16	8	.681	3451	67.25
26. John Clarkson	1885–94	10	32	17	.647	2946	65.80
27. J. R. Richard	1975–79	5	17	12	.585	3635	65.40
28. Eddie Rommel	1921–28	7	18	14	.564	3677	65.14
29. Urban Shocker	1919–27	9	19	12	.619	3083	65.11
30. Kid Nichols	1890–1905	14	26	15	.636	2095	65.07
31. Smoky Joe Wood	1909–15	6	18	9	.671	2793	65.00
31. Whitey Ford	1953–65	13	17	7	.699	2630	65.00
33. Jim Maloney	1962–69	8	16	8	.667	3335	64.88
34. Mel Parnell	1948–53	6	18	9	.661	2803	64.80
35. Vean Gregg	1911–18	5	17	11	.606	3762	64.20

Pitcher	Eligible Seasons		W	L	Pct.	WR	Points
36. Ron Guidry	1977–86	10	16	8	.664	2874	64.10
37. Sal Maglie	1950–56	7	15	6	.696	2950	63.57
38. Matt Kilroy	1886–90	5	26	23	.535	4907	63.20
39. Dazzy Vance	1922–32	11	17	12	.592	3202	62.91
40. Dwight Gooden	1984–96	10	16	8	.650	2971	62.50
41. Babe Ruth	1914–19	5	17	9	.659	2266	62.40
42. Schoolboy Rowe	1934–48	9	15	9	.637	3011	62.20
43. Mordecai Brown	1903–15	12	19	10	.659	3283	62.00
44. Bartolo Colon	1998–2005	8	16	9	.625	2535	61.88
45. Bob Feller	1937–54	14	18	11	.630	2511	61.79
46. Jack Chesbro	1899–1908	10	20	13	.612	2480	61.70
47. Charlie Buffinton	1883–91	9	25	16	.619	3671	61.67
48. Will White	1878–85	7	32	23	.584	3351	61.57
49. Bob Gibson	1961–74	14	17	11	.613	2725	61.29
50. Larry Corcoran	1880–84	5	34	17	.667	1474	61.00

Career Rankings of Top 200 Starting Pitchers

Career Leaders — Best Ten Years. Cy Young is the greatest pitcher of all time when rankings are based on a player's best ten years. He leads in victories, averaging nearly 32 wins a season for ten years, and in weighted rating. Lefty Grove, who ranks sixth overall, leads in winning percentage. The leaders in these rankings also fare well in the other lists, with Young, Grove, Walter Johnson, Grover Cleveland Alexander, Christy Mathewson, and Randy Johnson making the top ten in all three calculations. Roger Clemens and Tom Seaver both make the extended career best ten, as well. Young's record, of course, spanned the 19th and 20th centuries. Walter Johnson is the best who pitched entirely in the 1900s. Clemens is the top performer of those active into the present century. James Francis "Pud" Galvin is the leader among those who finished their careers before 1900.

One pitcher with only nine eligible seasons ranks among the top 50 in the career rankings. He is Amos Rusie, the Hoosier Thunderbolt, whose fastball has been credited with being the principal cause of lengthening the distance between the mound and the plate. (Jack Kavanagh in *The Ballplayers,* ed. Mike Shatzkin, New York: William Morrow and Company, 1990.) Rusie sat out the entire 1896 season in a dispute with management and retired in 1898 after tearing muscles in his shoulder in a successful pickoff attempt. Urban Shocker, the spitballer who died of heart trouble at the age of 37, was the only other pitcher with an abbreviated career to make the top 100. Sandy Koufax heads up the second 100 after only eight eligible seasons. He retired at the age of 30 because of arthritis. After suffering from control problems early in his career, he became one of baseball's dominant pitchers and compiled over 100 Faber System points each year from 1963 through 1966.

Although we computed Faber System points for all eligible pitchers, we have ranked only the top 200. As there are 887 starting pitchers rated, it will be easier for readers to find the rating of individual pitchers by consulting the alphabetical list that follows the rankings.

CAREER LEADERS — BEST TEN YEARS

Pitcher	Best Ten Years		W	L	Pct.	WR	Points
1. Cy Young	1891–1908	10	318	129	.711	81985	1010
2. Walter Johnson	1910–25	10	259	124	.676	80196	998
3. Grover C. Alexander	1911–27	10	253	112	.693	70436	954

Roger Clemens, the highest ranking active pitcher, is in the top five all time in ten-year career and extended career listings. At the age of 45 he essayed a comeback during the 2007 season (National Baseball Hall of Fame Library, Cooperstown, New York).

Pitcher	Best Ten Years		W	L	Pct.	WR	Points
4. Christy Mathewson	1901–14	10	276	113	.710	58917	936
5. Roger Clemens	1986–2004	10	197	66	.749	70756	900
6. Lefty Grove	1928–39	10	218	70	.757	56683	879
7. Randy Johnson	1989–2004	10	183	74	.712	63887	861
8. Tom Seaver	1967–81	10	190	87	.686	57690	823
9. Steve Carlton	1969–84	10	198	89	.690	54003	817
10. Warren Spahn	1947–63	10	213	118	.644	44728	773
11. Kid Nichols	1890–1904	10	297	145	.672	33600	766
12. Bob Feller	1937–54	10	199	99	.668	45430	761
12. Greg Maddux	1988–2002	10	181	76	.704	43503	761 tie
14. Pedro Martinez	1993–2005	10	163	66	.712	47907	753
15. Juan Marichal	1961–71	10	203	97	.677	38902	732
16. Clark Griffith	1891–1902	10	207	117	.639	42371	729
17. Eddie Plank	1903–14	10	215	102	.678	33515	725
18. Curt Schilling	1992–2006	10	167	95	.663	44177	717
19. Robin Roberts	1950–64	10	202	134	.601	42235	716
20. Whitey Ford	1953–65	10	184	74	.713	34735	713
21. Bob Gibson	1962–72	10	190	105	.655	39243	708
22. Joe McGinnity	1899–1908	10	247	144	.632	16786	706
23. Jim Palmer	1969–82	10	200	94	.680	30172	701
24. Gaylord Perry	1966–79	10	193	131	.596	41393	699
24. Tom Glavine	1988–2006	10	178	76	.701	39438	699 tie
24. Mike Mussina	1992–2006	10	165	76	.695	38696	699 tie
27. Burleigh Grimes	1918–31	10	201	118	.630	35529	694
28. Ted Lyons	1924–42	10	159	100	.614	43254	686
29. Wes Farrell	1929–38	10	190	123	.607	27643	682
30. Jesse Tannehill	1897–1906	10	185	106	.636	33742	681
31. Phil Niekro	1969–84	10	194	148	.567	41364	680
32. Dazzy Vance	1922–32	10	176	116	.603	36878	666
32. Carl Hubbell	1929–41	10	190	102	.651	30572	666 tie
34. Pud Galvin	1879–91	10	300	231	.565	53236	665
34. Mordecai Brown	1903–15	10	213	98	.685	20550	665 tie
36. Ferguson Jenkins	1967–82	10	200	133	.601	32402	664
36. Tommy John	1965–87	10	157	68	.698	31589	664 tie
38. Jamie Moyer	1987–2005	10	146	65	.682	34327	660
39. John Clarkson	1885–94	10	315	172	.647	29459	658
40. Red Faber	1914–29	10	175	117	.600	34395	646
41. Herb Pennock	1914–30	10	170	89	.658	28565	645
42. David Wells	1990–2005	10	162	75	.680	28298	644
43. Bert Blyleven	1971–89	10	158	103	.606	34253	640
43. Ron Guidry	1977–86	10	163	79	.674	28737	640 tie
45. Mark Langston	1984–95	10	166	141	.541	35631	638
45. David Cone	1988–2001	10	154	78	.664	29948	638 tie
47. Kenny Rogers	1990–2006	10	145	80	.644	34174	637
48. Tony Mullane	1882–92	10	259	183	.586	39070	635
49. Jim "Catfish" Hunter	1965–78	10	175	107	.621	29716	633
49. Nolan Ryan	1972–91	10	164	118	.597	35146	633 tie
51. Amos Rusie	1889–98	9	246	173	.587	32408	631
52. Kevin Brown	1989–2003	10	156	92	.629	29011	630
53. Jack Morris	1979–94	10	175	89	.663	26369	627

Pitcher	Best Ten Years		W	L	Pct.	WR	Points
54. Jim Bunning	1957–69	10	174	110	.613	29716	626
55. Wilbur Cooper	1914–25	10	184	135	.577	31231	625
55. Dwight Gooden	1984–96	10	156	84	.650	29710	625 tie
57. Chief Bender	1903–14	10	173	82	.678	20526	620
58. Mickey Welch	1880–90	10	276	181	.604	35596	618
59. Jack Chesbro	1899–1908	10	199	126	.612	24800	617
60. Charlie Radbourn	1881–91	10	304	178	.631	44191	616
61. Rick Reuschel	1973–89	10	149	103	.591	34107	616 tie
62. Tim Keefe	1883–93	10	278	155	.642	27618	614
62. Babe Adams	1909–23	10	159	91	.636	26530	614 tie
64. Don Sutton	1972–85	10	163	93	.637	25952	612
65. Hal Newhouser	1940–52	10	177	108	.621	25912	606
65. Bob Welch	1980–92	10	153	81	.654	23383	606 tie
67. Lon Warneke	1932–41	10	175	100	.636	21062	605
68. Early Wynn	1943–59	10	189	108	.636	18770	604
69. Vic Willis	1898–1909	10	213	147	.592	14466	601
69. Emil "Dutch" Leonard	1934–51	10	146	117	.557	35065	601 tie
71. Jerry Koosman	1968–82	10	156	102	.605	24287	600
72. Luis Tiant	1966–79	10	161	97	.624	15063	599
73. Freddie Fitzsimmons	1926–40	10	157	90	.636	23699	594
74. Sam Leever	1899–1908	10	179	94	.656	16714	591
74. Wild Bill Donovan	1901–11	10	172	111	.608	21835	591 tie
74. Red Ruffing	1930–42	10	179	83	.687	13497	591 tie
74. Mickey Lolich	1964–75	10	172	126	.577	15404	591 tie
78. Allie Reynolds	1944–54	10	160	80	.667	18651	590
78. Dave Stieb	1979–90	10	145	98	.597	29452	590 tie
80. Orel Hershiser	1984–98	10	153	100	.605	24620	589
81. Stan Coveleskie	1916–26	10	193	125	.607	18574	587
81. Jesse Haines	1921–33	10	153	83	.648	21505	587 tie
83. Urban Shocker	1919–27	9	169	104	.619	27750	586
84. Eddie Cicotte	1908–20	10	173	98	.638	20155	585
84. Vida Blue	1971–85	10	160	108	.597	24819	585 tie
86. Rube Marquard	1911–23	10	165	107	.607	24088	584
86. Chuck Finley	1989–2000	10	149	107	.582	28729	584 tie
88. Jim Kaat	1962–75	10	178	124	.589	21904	581
89. Bob Lemon	1947–57	10	197	111	.640	12812	580
90. Jimmy Key	1985–97	10	150	83	.644	19594	579
91. George Mullin	1902–13	10	190	147	.564	21230	578
91. Art Nehf	1917–28	10	160	99	.618	21243	578 tie
91. Tommy Bridges	1932–43	10	160	98	.651	22034	578 tie
91. Frank Tanana	1974–92	10	148	110	.573	27241	578 tie
95. Hippo Vaughn	1910–20	10	170	125	.576	25222	575
95. Bucky Walters	1935–46	10	164	113	.592	24303	575 tie
97. Virgil Trucks	1942–57	10	151	96	.611	23603	574

Opposite: Leslie "Bullet Joe" Bush (right) and Walter Johnson pose with President Warren G. Harding before a game at Yankee Stadium on April 24, 1923. Bush pitched the first shutout ever thrown in the new stadium, and the Yankees won, 4–0. At the time Bush was one of the American League's best pitchers. Johnson was the circuit's best ever. His 416 lifetime wins are still the league record (Library of Congress).

Pitcher	Best Ten Years		W	L	Pct.	WR	Points
98. John Smoltz	1989–2006	10	150	87	.633	21401	573
99. Hools Dauss	1913–26	10	174	118	.596	20039	571
100. Rick Sutcliffe	1979–93	10	149	103	.591	23552	570
101. George Uhle	1919–31	10	155	120	.564	26562	567
102. Eppa Rixey	1912–28	10	177	127	.582	20387	566
103. Gus Weyhing	1887–99	10	248	203	.550	21858	565
104. Sandy Koufax	1958–66	8	148	71	.676	28699	563
105. John Candelaria	1976–88	10	133	78	.630	22632	561
106. Schoolboy Rowe	1934–48	9	137	78	.637	27097	560
107. Ed Reulbach	1905–15	10	163	80	.671	12483	558
107. Sad Sam Jones	1918–35	10	135	92	.595	24704	558 tie
109. Lew Burdette	1953–64	10	162	99	.621	17307	558 tie
110. Lefty Gomez	1931–41	10	178	89	.667	13974	557
110. Paul Derringer	1931–45	10	176	130	.575	20944	557 tie
110. Mike Cuellar	1966–76	10	169	105	.617	17328	557 tie
110. Frank Viola	1984–93	10	163	120	.576	21481	557 tie
114. Slim Sallee	1909–19	10	151	117	.564	25796	556
115. Charlie Buffinton	1883–91	9	227	140	.619	33037	555
115. Earl Whitehill	1924–36	10	159	120	.576	21909	555 tie
117. Al Orth	1896–1908	10	165	134	.552	22155	554
118. Kevin Appier	1990–2001	10	136	97	.584	24793	553
119. Deacon Phillippe	1899–1910	10	181	104	.635	10140	552
120. Claude Passeau	1935–45	10	151	135	.528	26879	551
121. Bill Doak	1914–27	10	139	106	.567	26059	549
122. Waite Hoyt	1921–37	10	168	98	.635	13568	548
122. Billy Pierce	1950–62	10	162	109	.598	17288	548 tie
124. Milt Pappas	1959–72	10	150	98	.605	18334	547
124. Joe Niekro	1967–85	10	156	112	.582	19749	547 tie
124. Sadie McMahon	1889–96	8	175	122	.589	38776	546
127. Camilo Pascual	1957–68	10	141	117	.547	26641	544
128. Buck Newsom	1934–47	10	161	133	.548	22041	543
129. Addie Joss	1902–09	8	155	92	.628	27658	541
129. Carl Mays	1916–26	10	180	104	.634	16021	541 tie
131. Guy Bush	1926–35	10	155	94	.622	15132	540
132. Ted Breitenstein	1892–1900	9	162	166	.494	31147	539
133. Jeff Pfeffer	1914–24	10	157	111	.586	18659	538
133. Red Lucas	1927–37	10	134	117	.534	27019	538 tie
135. Lee Meadows	1915–27	10	154	130	.542	21977	536
135. Claude Osteen	1962–73	10	152	133	.533	13193	536 tie
137. Eddie Lopat	1944–54	10	149	87	.631	13185	535
137. Jim Perry	1959–74	10	157	106	.597	16098	535 tie
139. Rick Wise	1967–79	10	147	118	.555	21194	534
140. Dave McNally	1963–74	10	164	95	.633	11179	533
141. Don Newcombe	1949–60	10	149	90	.623	15789	528
142. Jerry Reuss	1973–89	10	145	95	.604	16139	527
143. Doc White	1901–10	10	170	129	.569	13693	526
143. Charlie Hough	1976–91	10	144	125	.535	22867	526 tie
143. Al Leiter	1993–2004	10	129	92	.581	21272	526 tie
146. Jack Quinn	1910–28	10	161	123	.567	16026	524
146. Johnny Allen	1932–42	8	122	57	.682	19062	524 tie
148. Brickyard Kennedy	1892–1903	10	183	150	.550	13141	523

Pitcher	Best Ten Years		W	L	Pct.	WR	Points
148. Charlie Root	1926–41	10	162	106	.604	4635	523 tie
148. Don Drysdale	1957–68	10	167	124	.574	14360	523 tie
148. Jim Maloney	1962–69	8	126	67	.653	26676	519
152. Curt Davis	1934–45	10	140	107	.567	16315	518
153. Bob Forsch	1975–88	10	126	83	.603	18191	517
154. Doyle Alexander	1973–88	10	140	93	.601	14206	516
155. Ed Walsh	1906–12	7	168	112	.600	27871	514
156. Vern Law	1950–66	10	127	94	.575	20519	512
156. Danny Darwin	1980–96	10	106	76	.582	20851	512 tie
156. Andy Pettitte	1995–2006	9	146	81	.643	15226	512 tie
159. Bob Buhl	1953–65	10	142	101	.584	15312	511
160. Rip Sewell	1939–48	9	131	91	.590	20370	508
161. Larry French	1930–42	10	163	105	.608	8703	505
163. Mel Harder	1930–44	10	155	116	.572	12719	503
163. Sam McDowell	1964–73	10	132	115	.581	21065	503 tie
163. Wilbur Wood	1968–78	10	155	143	.520	18678	503 tie
166. Larry Jackson	1957–68	10	155	128	.548	15071	502
167. Bob Shawkey	1914–26	10	173	120	.590	7378	500
168. Bruce Hurst	1983–92	10	136	101	.574	15216	500 tie
168. Andy Benes	1990–2000	10	131	111	.541	19528	500 tie
168. Jason Schmidt	1998–2006	9	118	77	.605	16494	500 tie
171. Larry Dierker	1965–76	10	130	110	.542	19699	499
172. Joe Bush	1913–25	10	162	136	.544	12105	498
172. Mike Torrez	1970–82	10	143	102	.584	12193	498 tie
174. Bret Saberhagen	1984–99	9	130	83	.610	17268	497
175. Curt Simmons	1950–64	10	139	101	.579	13487	494
176. Bill Gullickson	1980–93	10	137	109	.557	14147	491
177. Steve Rogers	1973–83	10	135	111	.549	15330	488
178. Rick Rhoden	1976–88	10	122	100	.550	15108	482
179. Bob Caruthers	1885–91	7	209	87	.706	25182	479
179. Sonny Siebert	1964–74	10	126	96	.568	15379	479 tie
181. Bill Sherdel	1920–30	10	138	100	.580	10171	478
182. Bill Lee	1934–46	10	142	111	.561	12142	476
182. Jim Lonborg	1965–78	10	132	108	.550	13860	476 tie
184. Remy Kremer	1924–31	8	158	82	.658	17442	475
185. Howard Ehmke	1917–28	10	146	145	.502	15013	472
185. Bob Friend	1952–63	10	142	140	.504	13948	472 tie
187. Dennis Eckersley	1975–85	10	136	104	.567	9947	471
188. Pat Hentgen	1993–2003	9	122	94	.565	19554	470
189. Al Crowder	1927–35	9	156	100	.591	10915	469
190. Jack Stivetts	1889–97	9	204	126	.618	2616	467
191. Mel Stottlemyre	1965–73	9	149	129	.536	14301	464
192. Chick Fraser	1896–1908	10	149	168	.470	14258	462
192. Harvey Haddix	1953–62	10	123	100	.552	12332	462 tie
194. Willis Hudlin	1927–39	10	135	113	.544	10609	460
195. Jouett Meekin	1891–99	9	153	131	.539	15741	459
195. Charlie Liebrandt	1980–93	10	129	100	.563	10049	459 tie
197. Joe Nuxhall	1953–65	10	117	89	.568	12865	458
198. Frank Dwyer	1889–95	9	169	140	.547	12887	457
198. Red Donahue	1896–1906	10	159	148	.518	6829	457 tie

Pitcher	Best Ten Years		W	L	Pct.	WR	Points
198. Jim Slaton	1971–83	10	127	118	.518	11276	457 tie
198. Dave Stewart	1982–94	10	142	104	.577	7562	457 tie

Career Ratings of All Eligible Starting Pitchers (Listed Alphabetically)

ALL PITCHERS WITH FIVE OR MORE ELIGIBLE SEASONS

Pitcher	Years		W	L	Pct.	WR	Points
Abbott, Jim	1989–96	8	80	100	.444	−12847	198
Adams, Babe	1909–23	10	159	91	.636	26530	614
Aldridge, Vic	1922–27	6	87	66	.569	2212	270
Alexander, Doyle	1973–88	10	140	93	.601	14206	516
Alexander, Grover C.	1911–27	10	253	112	.693	70436	954
Allen, Johnny	1932–42	9	122	57	.682	19062	524
Alvarez, Wilson	1993–99	7	78	71	.523	3190	275
Ames, Leon "Red"	1905–17	10	137	114	.546	4255	437
Anderson, Brian	1995–2004	6	55	62	.470	309	196
Andrews, Ivy	1932–36	5	41	50	.451	4837	177
Andujar, Joaquin	1976–86	9	114	93	.551	3655	380
Antonelli, Johnny	1953–59	7	114	89	.562	10107	362
Appier, Kevin	1990–2001	10	136	97	.584	24793	553
Appleton, Pete	1930–39	5	42	50	.457	−3029	136
Ashby, Andy	1994–2002	7	88	77	.533	465	257
Astacio, Peter	1993–2005	10	108	98	.524	6995	399
Auker, Eldon	1932–42	9	127	98	.564	5301	409
Avery, Steve	1991–98	7	79	58	.577	−3904	257
Ayers, Doc	1914–20	6	59	69	.461	−7280	156
Bagby, Jim	1916–21	6	120	81	.597	3920	317
Bagby, Jim, Jr.	1938–45	6	76	76	.500	−4224	202
Bahnsen, Stan	1968–77	10	132	134	.496	−6124	349
Baldwin, James	1996–2002	6	69	57	.548	2314	252
Baldwin, Mark	1887–93	7	154	165	.483	−10459	227
Bannister, Floyd	1977–88	10	116	118	.496	7839	403
Barber, Steve	1960–67	8	101	84	.546	−598	319
Barker, Len	1980–84	5	57	51	.528	6774	220
Barnes, Jesse	1916–26	10	141	138	.505	1856	402
Barnes, Virgil "Zeke"	1924–28	5	58	55	.513	−4846	158
Barr, Jim	1972–78	8	90	101	.471	−4811	254
Barrett, Red	1943–48	5	62	66	.484	−4935	155
Batista, Miguel	1999–2006	6	58	54	.518	2687	229
Beattie, Jim	1978–84	5	41	67	.380	−8062	94
Beebe, Fred	1906–10	5	55	78	.414	3142	172
Belcher, Tim	1988–98	10	112	98	.534	4806	437
Bell, Gary	1958–68	8	97	95	.505	−2209	286
Bender, Chief	1903–14	10	173	82	.677	20576	620
Benes, Andy	1990–2000	10	131	111	.541	19528	500
Benge, Ray	1928–36	9	108	129	.456	2984	308
Benson, Kris	1999–2006	6	63	64	.496	5492	242
Benton, Al	1934–49	7	68	59	.535	409	258
Benton, Larry	1925–33	9	115	108	.516	10554	396

Pitcher	Years		W	L	Pct.	WR	Points
Benton, Rube	1912–25	10	137	121	.531	4258	427
Benz, Joe	1912–18	5	58	66	.468	−6105	146
Bere, Jason	1993–2001	5	49	50	.495	2309	175
Bernhard, Bill	1900–06	7	110	72	.604	12780	386
Bibby, Jim	1973–83	8	85	89	.489	−532	282
Bickford, Vern	1948–52	5	64	51	.557	6868	238
Billingham, Jack	1970–79	10	135	103	.567	822	421
Black, Bud	1983–92	8	89	94	.489	−532	276
Blackwell, Ewell	1946–52	6	75	72	.510	12528	282
Blaeholder, George	1928–35	8	96	120	.444	2625	286
Blake, Sheriff	1925–30	6	75	82	.478	−15055	144
Blankenship, Ted	1922–28	6	68	70	.493	−299	215
Blanton, Cy	1935–41	5	62	60	.508	68	189
Blass, Steve	1966–72	6	89	51	.636	12288	341
Blue, Vida	1971–85	10	160	108	.597	24819	585
Blyleven, Bert	1971–89	10	158	103	.606	34253	640
Boddicker, Mike	1983–91	9	129	106	.549	14254	448
Bolin, Bobby	1963–70	6	58	47	.552	1583	229
Bond, Tommy	1876–80	5	180	97	.650	13582	303
Bones, Ricky	1992–96	5	47	56	.456	−2037	148
Bonham, Ernie	1974–79	6	63	75	.457	−4101	186
Borowy, Hank	1942–49	8	104	76	.578	6753	361
Bosio, Chris	1987–95	8	86	76	.531	2121	303
Bosman, Dick	1969–75	6	64	62	.508	9481	262
Bowman, Joe	1935–45	7	66	85	.437	−628	221
Boyd, Oil Can	1984–90	5	62	48	.564	3760	220
Boyle, Henry	1885–89	5	74	108	.407	3525	160
Bradley, George	1876–83	6	110	108	.505	−2254	201
Branca, Ralph	1947–51	5	68	47	.591	−710	210
Brandt, Ed	1928–37	10	116	142	.450	3413	346
Brazle, Al	1946–52	6	72	46	.610	4105	277
Brecheen, Harry	1943–53	9	118	83	.587	964	385
Breitenstein, Ted	1892–1900	9	162	166	.494	31147	539
Brett, Ken	1970–77	6	54	65	.454	3844	232
Brewer, Tom	1954–60	7	88	80	.524	4607	292
Bridges, Tommy	1932–43	10	160	98	.651	22034	578
Briles, Nelson	1966–76	7	91	77	.542	−2016	271
Broglio, Ernie	1959–64	6	74	62	.544	2939	243
Brown, Buster	1905–12	6	47	95	.331	−4620	126
Brown, Clint	1930–39	5	59	62	.488	−6355	149
Brown, Kevin	1989–2003	10	156	92	.629	29011	629
Brown, Lloyd	1929–36	8	79	89	.470	−11668	229
Brown, Mordecai	1904–15	10	212	95	.691	22021	665
Brown, Skinny	1953–64	8	68	67	.504	1541	276
Browning, Tom	1985–91	7	106	75	.586	14949	382
Brunet, George	1965–70	6	63	79	.444	−4206	177
Buehrle, Mark	2001–06	6	93	65	.589	9525	321
Buffinton, Charlie	1883–91	9	227	140	.619	33037	555
Buhl, Bob	1953–65	10	142	101	.584	15312	511
Bunning, Jim	1957–69	10	174	110	.613	28898	626
Burba, Dave	1996–2001	7	87	61	.588	6962	330

Pitcher	Years		W	L	Pct.	WR	Points
Burdette, Lew	1952–64	10	162	99	.621	17307	558
Burkett, John	1990–2003	10	133	96	.581	12888	497
Burns, Britt	1980–85	6	70	58	.547	12202	292
Burris, Ray	1975–85	9	93	109	.460	−4321	274
Bush, Guy	1926–35	10	155	94	.622	15132	540
Bush, Joe	1913–25	10	162	136	.544	12105	498
Butcher, Max	1937–45	8	84	92	.477	939	281
Buzhardt, John	1960–66	6	48	73	.397	−11227	113
Byrd, Paul	1999–2006	5	62	49	.559	9889	238
Byrne, Tommy	1949–55	5	59	46	.652	1669	205
Cadore, Leon	1917–22	5	63	68	.481	−5254	156
Caldwell, Mike	1972–84	10	125	101	.554	8305	436
Caldwell, Ray	1911–20	10	126	114	.525	13054	454
Callahan, Nixey	1897–1902	6	97	69	.584	11420	331
Camnitz, Howie	1907–14	8	131	101	.565	−3112	341
Candelaria, John	1976–88	10	133	78	.630	22632	561
Candiotti, Tom	1986–98	10	118	109	.520	10455	430
Cantwell, Ben	1929–36	8	71	103	.408	−4441	213
Cardwell, Don	1959–69	8	81	104	.438	−2910	239
Carleton, Tex	1932–38	7	94	70	.573	154	294
Carlson, Hal	1917–29	9	103	107	.490	7537	359
Carlton, Steve	1969–84	10	198	89	.690	54003	817
Carpenter, Chris	1997–2006	7	93	56	.624	12683	375
Carroll, Ownie	1927–33	5	58	69	.457	2367	187
Carsey, Kid	1891–97	7	111	116	.489	343	277
Caruthers, Bob	1885–91	7	209	87	.706	25182	479
Casey, Dan	1886–90	5	91	81	.529	−3290	168
Castillo, Frank	1992–2002	7	66	78	.458	−7110	193
Chamberlain, Icebox	1887–94	8	157	116	.575	8848	376
Chance, Dean	1962–70	8	119	103	.536	10196	385
Chandler, Spud	1938–46	5	78	29	.729	14188	328
Chase, Ken	1938–43	5	44	80	.355	−15281	77
Cheney, Larry	1912–18	7	112	90	.554	4882	323
Chesbro, Jack	1899–1908	10	199	126	.612	24800	617
Christensen, Larry	1975–82	7	74	61	.548	−1867	249
Cicotte, Eddie	1908–20	10	173	98	.638	20155	585
Clancy, Jim	1978–88	10	122	124	.496	−1176	364
Clark, Mark	1994–99	5	57	43	.570	7821	214
Clark, Watty	1928–36	7	95	82	.537	8304	323
Clarkson, John	1885–94	10	315	172	.647	29459	658
Clemens, Roger	1986–2004	10	197	66	.749	70359	900
Clement, Matt	1999–2005	7	80	81	.497	−2736	256
Cleveland, Reggie	1971–80	8	97	86	.530	2543	323
Cloninger, Tony	1963–70	6	86	71	.548	1297	255
Coffman, Dick	1930–35	5	37	61	.378	−6241	101
Colburn, Jim	1973–78	6	72	79	.477	837	218
Coleman, Joe	1967–76	10	130	131	.498	6886	403
Collins, Phil	1929–35	7	79	85	.482	10388	301
Collins, Ray	1910–14	5	77	52	.597	2219	236
Collins, Rip	1920–30	9	100	70	.588	12889	427

Pitcher	Years		W	L	Pct.	WR	Points
Colon, Bartolo	1998–2005	8	125	75	.625	20282	495
Cone, David	1988–2001	10	154	78	.664	29948	638
Conley, Gene	1954–62	8	88	83	.515	2082	306
Coombs, Jack	1906–18	10	151	104	.592	2503	437
Cooper, Mort	1939–46	7	114	60	.658	5915	370
Cooper, Wilbur	1914–25	10	184	135	.577	31231	625
Corcoran, Larry	1880–84	5	170	84	.669	7370	305
Corridon, Frank	1904–10	6	71	68	.511	277	224
Coveleskie, Stan	1916–26	10	193	125	.607	18524	587
Craig, Roger	1956–64	8	41	56	.423	−8970	106
Crandall, Doc	1908–15	6	91	52	.636	10454	322
Crowder, Al	1927–35	9	156	108	.591	10915	469
Cuellar, Mike	1966–76	10	169	105	.617	17328	557
Culp, Ray	1963–71	8	108	83	.565	6623	365
Cunningham, Bert	1888–99	9	138	161	.462	15281	400
Cuppy, Nig	1892–99	8	150	88	.630	12304	442
Curtis, John	1972–80	7	68	72	.486	−2591	233
Daal, Omar	1998–2003	6	56	67	.455	−7427	155
Danforth, Dave	1917–25	5	55	56	.495	−2175	167
Daniels, Benny	1959–65	6	44	69	.389	−1282	153
Darling, Ron	1984–94	10	126	97	.565	450	412
Darwin, Danny	1980–96	10	106	76	.582	20851	512
Dauss, Hooks	1913–26	10	174	118	.596	20039	571
Davenport, Dave	1914–18	5	71	72	.497	4844	217
Davis, Curt	1934–45	10	140	107	.567	16315	518
Davis, Dixie	1920–25	5	68	54	.557	4953	234
Davis, Doug	2001–06	5	52	52	.500	3626	200
Davis, Storm	1983–93	8	92	74	.554	3425	327
Dean, Dizzy	1932–37	6	133	35	.639	21408	429
DeLeon, Jose	1984–90	6	56	85	.347	−9779	134
Delock, Ike	1955–61	7	71	55	.563	8827	310
Demeree, Al	1913–18	6	73	66	.525	−8276	195
Denny, John	1975–86	10	108	93	.537	9749	423
Derringer, Paul	1931–45	10	176	130	.575	20944	557
Deshaies, Jim	1986–94	8	80	86	.482	−1437	266
Dickson, Murry	1946–58	10	128	136	.485	15710	453
Dierker, Larry	1965–76	10	130	110	.542	19699	499
Dietrich, Bill	1934–45	10	92	108	.460	−4227	299
Dinneen, Big Bill	1898–1908	10	157	154	.505	2643	415
Ditmar, Art	1955–60	5	61	60	.504	3821	209
Doak, Bill	1914–27	10	139	106	.567	26059	549
Dobson, Chuck	1967–71	5	68	57	.544	2419	220
Dobson, Joe	1941–52	9	120	82	.594	3180	402
Dobson, Pat	1969–77	9	116	119	.494	−4874	304
Doheny, Ed	1896–1903	7	71	76	.483	−9002	198
Donahue, Pete	1922–30	9	127	110	.536	1711	369
Donahue, Red	1896–1906	10	160	148	.519	6891	457
Donovan, Bill	1901–11	10	172	111	.608	21835	591
Donovan, Dick	1955–64	9	115	91	.558	8442	394
Dotson, Rich	1980–89	9	106	105	.502	3425	335

Pitcher	Years		W	L	Pct.	WR	Points
Douglas, Phil	1914–22	8	94	92	.505	−6528	268
Downing, Al	1963–73	9	109	86	.559	8334	389
Drabek, Doug	1986–97	10	133	94	.581	11541	479
Drabowsky, Moe	1957–69	6	50	71	.413	−2699	160
Drago, Dick	1969–79	8	85	94	.475	−3782	257
Dravecky, Dave	1983–87	5	55	52	.514	1836	192
Drysdale, Don	1957–68	10	167	124	.574	14360	523
Dubiel, Monk	1944–50	5	43	51	.457	−1758	146
Duboc, Jean	1912–16	5	73	60	.549	4580	233
Duggleby, Bill	1901–06	6	87	97	.473	2031	240
Dwyer, Frank	1889–98	9	169	140	.547	12887	457
Earnshaw, George	1929–36	8	120	86	.583	2629	348
Eckersley, Dennis	1975–85	10	136	104	.567	9947	471
Ehmke, Howard	1917–28	10	146	145	.502	15013	472
Ehret, Red	1889–97	9	133	158	.457	−12609	248
Elliott, Jumbo	1927–33	6	61	68	.473	1763	207
Ellis, Dock	1969–78	10	128	102	.557	2051	417
Ellsworth, Dick	1960–69	9	106	125	.459	6813	343
Erickson, Scott	1991–2002	10	127	116	.523	8085	424
Erskine, Carl	1951–56	6	92	58	.613	−2499	264
Escobar, Kelvim	1999–2006	5	59	61	.492	−4631	160
Esper, Duke	1890–96	7	97	89	.522	5837	286
Estes, Shawn	1997–2005	9	96	81	.542	4137	341
Ewing, Long Bob	1903–10	8	119	111	.517	7401	354
Faber, Red	1914–28	10	175	117	.600	34395	646
Falcone, Pete	1975–82	5	45	61	.425	−1055	144
Falkenburg, Cy	1906–15	7	110	99	.526	9247	326
Farrell, Dick	1958–67	9	88	92	.489	13250	382
Fassero, Jeff	1992–2000	9	98	86	.533	1298	345
Feller, Bob	1937–54	10	199	99	.668	45430	761
Ferguson, Alex	1922–28	5	45	72	.385	662	143
Fernandez, Alex	1991–99	8	98	78	.557	4770	340
Fernandez, Sid	185–94	8	92	69	.571	1268	326
Ferrell, Wes	1929–38	10	190	123	.607	37643	682
Finley, Chuck	1989–2000	10	149	107	.582	28729	584
Fischer, Bill	1957–63	5	37	45	.451	−1454	145
Fisher, Jack	1960–68	8	71	116	.380	−12831	167
Fisher, Ray	1911–20	8	92	84	.523	7122	340
Fitzsimmons, Freddie	1926–40	10	157	90	.636	23699	594
Flaherty, Patsy	1903–08	5	64	79	.448	−5758	148
Flanagan, Mike	1977–88	10	142	105	.575	636	432
Flores, Jesse	1943–47	5	41	55	.427	1421	134
Fogg, Josh	2002–06	5	50	51	.495	5037	198
Foreman, Frank	1889–1901	6	93	79	.541	10113	281
Forsch, Bob	1975–88	10	126	83	.603	18191	517
Forsch, Ken	1971–83	9	93	82	.526	4569	358
Ford, Russ	1910–14	5	92	62	.600	27039	380
Ford, Whitey	1953–65	10	184	74	.713	34735	713
Foutz, Dave	1884–92	6	139	63	.688	5963	309
Fowler, Dick	1942–51	6	62	68	.477	3328	234
Fox, Howie	1945–51	5	40	63	.388	−3653	119

Pitcher	Years		W	L	Pct.	WR	Points
Foytack, Paul	1956–62	6	79	68	.537	2137	252
Frankhouse, Fred	1930–37	7	84	79	.515	13353	326
Fraser, Chick	1896–1908	10	149	168	.470	14258	462
French, Larry	1930–42	10	163	105	.608	8703	505
Frey, Benny	1930–36	6	50	76	.397	195	170
Friend, Bob	1942–63	10	142	140	.504	13948	472
Fromme, Art	1907–12	5	67	78	.462	1383	167
Fryman, Woody	1966–78	10	101	116	.465	3568	349
Gale, Rich	1978–82	5	49	47	.510	−3417	165
Galehouse, Denny	1936–48	10	93	98	.487	−7378	291
Gallia, Bert	1915–19	5	63	57	.515	2096	208
Galvin, Pud	1879–91	10	300	231	.565	53236	665
Garcia, Freddy	1999–2006	7	107	66	.618	9333	376
Garcia, Mike	1949–57	9	138	90	.605	1200	412
Gardner, Mark	1990–2000	7	71	67	.514	1086	259
Garland, Jon	2002–06	5	72	53	.576	4520	239
Garrelts, Scott	1985–90	5	59	38	.608	10240	265
Garver, Ned	1948–59	10	119	130	.478	21022	456
Garvin, Ned	1899–1904	6	57	96	.373 -	13176	103
Gaston, Milt	1925–34	10	92	161	.364	−13158	226
Genewich, Joe	1923–28	6	68	78	.466	9730	259
German, Les	1890–96	5	31	58	.348	−19122	20
Getzein, Charlie	1884–90	7	136	125	.521	9177	298
Gibson, Bob	1962–72	10	190	105	.644	39243	708
Glavine, Tom	1989–2006	10	178	78	.701	39438	699
Gleason, Kid	1888–94	7	132	130	.504	2595	275
Goldsmith, Fred	1880–84	5	110	63	.636	−4839	198
Goltz, Dave	1974–80	7	94	83	.531	5803	305
Gomez, Lefty	1931–41	10	178	89	.667	13974	557
Gomez, Ruben	1953–58	6	71	72	.497	−444	218
Gooden, Dwight	1984–96	10	156	84	.650	29710	625
Gordon, Tom	1989–97	9	97	88	.525	3668	351
Grant, Jim "Mudcat"	1958–69	10	120	103	.538	5402	411
Gray, Sam	1924–32	9	104	111	.448	−3101	306
Gray, Ted	1949–53	5	49	63	.438	−1977	151
Gregg, Vean	1911–18	5	83	54	.606	19515	321
Griffin, Tom	1969–81	6	51	56	.477	−383	189
Griffith, Clark	1891–1902	10	207	117	.639	42371	729
Grimes, Burleigh	1918–31	10	201	118	.630	35529	694
Grimsley, Ross	1971–79	9	117	88	.571	2956	385
Gromek, Steve	1944–55	7	83	76	.522	8396	301
Groom, Bob	1944–55	9	117	148	.442	−6539	280
Gross, Kevin	1985–96	10	110	119	.480	−3776	336
Grove, Lefty	1928–39	10	218	70	.757	56682	879
Gubicza, Mark	1984–96	10	116	114	.504	−1733	362
Guidry, Ron	1977–86	10	163	79	.674	28736	640
Gullett, Don	1971–77	6	89	43	.674	11475	348
Gullickson, Bill	1980–93	10	137	109	.557	14147	491
Gumbert, Ad	1889–95	7	115	92	.556	1846	288
Gumbert, Harry	1937–48	9	111	88	.558	3131	379

Pitcher	Years		W	L	Pct.	WR	Points
Gura, Larry	1975–84	8	106	81	.567	6481	366
Guzman, Jose	1986–93	6	75	70	.517	5561	259
Guzman, Juan	1992–99	7	78	69	.531	3748	284
Haas, Moose	1977–84	7	81	67	.547	4212	299
Hacker, Warren	1952–56	5	47	69	.405	−5076	118
Haddix, Harvey	1953–62	10	123	100	.552	12332	462
Haddock, George	1889–93	5	91	78	.538	6651	215
Hadley, Bump	1927–39	10	128	114	.529	1680	412
Haefner, Mickey	1943–49	7	77	83	.481	3878	275
Hahn, Noodles	1899–1904	6	122	89	.578	23394	422
Haines, Jesse	1921–33	10	153	83	.648	21505	587
Halladay, Roy	1999–2006	6	85	41	.675	27999	424
Hallahan, Wild Bill	1930–36	7	92	69	.571	−663	287
Hamilton, Earl	1911–23	10	122	128	.443	−4484	291
Hamilton, Joey	1994–98	5	55	44	.556	4877	217
Hammaker, Atlee	1982–88	5	46	48	.489	−995	162
Hamlin, Luke	1937–44	6	66	69	.489	−2717	197
Hampton, Mike	1995–2004	20	130	94	.580	7349	454
Hands, Bill	1966–73	8	99	86	.535	−929	292
Hanson, Erik	1990–96	6	73	68	.518	5672	260
Harder, Mel	1930–44	10	155	116	.572	12719	503
Hargan, Steve	1966–76	7	69	79	.466	−703	248
Harmon, Bob	1909–16	8	105	126	.455	8210	324
Harnish, Pete	1990–99	8	94	73	.563	13059	385
Harper, Harry	1916–20	5	48	68	.414	−8618	107
Harper, Jack	1901–05	5	78	55	.586	6710	252
Harriss, Slim	1920–28	9	95	135	.413	1689	289
Harshman, Jack	1954–59	6	67	59	.532	−2706	213
Hart, Bill	1886–1901	6	60	109	.355	−9228	121
Hawkins, Andy	1984–90	6	70	63	.527	6317	258
Hawley, Pink	1892–1901	10	167	178	.484	2976	407
Haynes, Jimmy	1998–2002	5	53	61	.464	−409	168
Healy, Egyptian	1886–91	6	75	129	.368	−3468	138
Hearn, Jim	1947–56	8	90	74	.549	−242	307
Heaton, Neal	1983–90	6	63	73	.463	−3715	189
Hecker, Guy	1883–89	7	167	133	.557	27317	399
Heimach, Lefty	1922–31	5	47	48	.495	1253	177
Heintzleman, Ken	1940–51	8	71	85	.455	−2316	239
Helling, Rick	1998–2003	6	79	62	.560	7067	282
Hemming, George	1891–96	5	78	70	.527	13852	279
Hendrix, Claude	1912–20	9	139	111	.556	−2316	405
Hentgen, Pat	1993–2003	9	122	94	.565	19554	470
Herbert, Ray	1958–63	6	78	65	.545	12435	301
Hermanson, Dustin	1997–2004	6	63	69	.477	1493	213
Hernandez, Levan	1998–2006	9	114	108	.514	1608	335
Hernandez, Orlando	1998–2006	5	61	46	.570	−3354	190
Hershiser, Orel	1984–98	10	153	100	.605	24620	589
Hess, Otto	1904–13	5	57	73	.438	−8855	122
Higbe, Kirby	1939–48	8	115	96	.545	11449	392
Higuera, Teddy	1985–90	6	89	42	.623	21274	380

Pitcher	Years		W	L	Pct.	WR	Points
Hildebrand, Oral	1933–38	6	62	66	.440	4524	231
Hill, Ken	1989–98	9	103	82	.557	2546	365
Hitchcock, Sterling	1995–99	5	55	51	.519	1367	193
Hobbie, Glenn	1958–63	6	61	66	.480	2442	206
Hoeft, Billy	1953–58	6	71	70	.540	3507	237
Hogsett, Chief	1930–37	5	45	62	.421	263	154
Hollingsworth, Al	1935–45	7	56	84	.400	−5480	179
Holtzman, Ken	1966–79	10	153	129	.580	2999	416
Honeycutt, Rick	1978–86	9	85	103	.452	2007	304
Hooten, Burt	1972–83	10	126	100	.558	5617	433
Horlen, Joel	1963–71	9	105	104	.502	1469	341
Hough, Charlie	1976–91	10	144	125	.535	22867	526
Houtteman, Art	1948–55	7	78	84	.481	−11387	193
Howell, Harry	1899–1908	9	122	140	.466	−1941	335
Hoyt, LaMarr	1981–86	6	89	65	.578	10392	317
Hoyt, Waite	1921–37	10	168	98	.635	13568	548
Hubbell, Carl	1929–41	10	190	102	.651	30572	666
Hudlin, Willia	1927–39	10	135	113	.544	10609	460
Hudson, Charles	1983–87	5	44	49	.473	−4221	136
Hudson, Sid	1940–53	10	97	132	.424	−2146	294
Hudson, Tim	2000–06	7	108	58	.651	14457	407
Hughes, Tom	1901–12	10	122	154	.443	−1435	339
Hughson, Tex	1942–47	5	84	48	.636	11905	301
Humphries, Johnny	1938–45	5	46	55	.456	−4491	141
Hunter, Jim "Catfish"	1965–78	10	175	107	.621	29716	633
Hurst, Bruce	1983–90	10	136	101	.574	15216	500
Hutchinson, Fred	1946–51	6	87	57	.604	8480	309
Hutchison, Bill	1889–95	7	182	158	.535	5762	332
Jackson, Al	1962–66	5	53	88	.376	5962	176
Jackson, Danny	1985–95	9	99	103	.490	−4837	286
Jackson, Larry	1957–68	10	155	128	.548	15071	502
Jacobs, Elmer	1916–24	5	41	63	.394	−2568	131
James, Big Bill	1914–19	6	62	68	.477	−2215	192
Jansen, Larry	1947–53	7	118	84	.584	12320	382
Jarvis, Pat	1967–72	6	77	70	.524	4873	257
Jay, Joey	1954–65	7	84	80	.512	−11570	199
Jenkins, Ferguson	1967–82	10	200	133	.601	32402	664
Jennings, Jason	2002–06	5	54	55	.495	6705	210
John, Tommy	1965–87	10	157	68	.698	31589	664
Johnson, Jason	1999–2006	7	52	83	.385	−8056	146
Johnson, Ken	1960–67	7	77	86	.472	7460	280
Johnson, Randy	1989–2004	10	183	74	.712	63887	861
Johnson, Si	1931–42	10	73	142	.340	−9257	181
Johnson, Syl	1923–39	7	71	63	.530	3369	271
Johnson, Walter	1910–25	10	259	124	.676	80196	998
Jones, Bobby J.	1994–2002	8	84	76	.525	6485	347
Jones, Percy	1922–29	5	44	45	.494	−759	166
Jones, Randy	1974–83	8	92	109	.458	6220	298
Jones, Sad Sam	1918–35	10	135	92	.595	24704	558
Jones, Toothpick Sam	1955–61	7	96	93	.508	2979	288

Pitcher	Years		W	L	Pct.	WR	Points
Joss, Addie	1902–09	8	155	92	.628	27658	541
Kaat, Jim	1962–75	10	178	124	.589	21904	581
Kaufman, Tony	1922–26	5	59	54	.522	1872	198
Keefe, Tim	1883–93	10	278	155	.642	27618	614
Kellner, Alex	1949–55	7	79	97	.449	4555	257
Kennedy, Brickyard	1892–1903	10	183	150	.550	13141	523
Kennedy, Joe	2001–05	5	35	51	.407	807	140
Kennedy, Vern	1935–45	8	94	101	.482	3746	307
Keough, Matt	1978–82	5	47	69	.405	−6368	116
Key, Jimmy	1985–1997	10	150	83	.644	19594	579
Kile, Daryl	1991–2001	10	124	103	.546	8557	434
Killen, Frank	1892–98	6	140	112	.556	28049	423
Killian, Ed	1904–08	6	95	73	.565	7629	306
Kilroy, Matt	1886–90	5	131	114	.535	24536	316
Kinder, Ellis	1947–54	6	73	54	.575	4785	266
King, Eric	1985–91	5	44	38	.537	3844	200
King, Silver	1887–97	9	206	149	.580	5992	421
Kirby, Clay	1969–75	7	74	96	.489	−60	230
Kison, Bruce	1972–83	8	87	62	.504	2920	315
Kitson, Frank	1899–1906	8	116	109	.516	−1325	308
Kline, Ron	1955–68	8	83	97	.461	−288	271
Klinger, Bob	1938–43	5	53	54	.495	453	183
Klippstein, Johnny	1952–57	6	52	68	.433	−8416	139
Knell, Phil	1890–95	5	78	88	.470	8525	197
Knepper, Bob	1977–89	10	122	105	.538	14725	454
Knetzer, Elmer	1911–16	5	60	60	.500	6906	213
Knott, Jack	1935–41	7	69	81	.460	6633	267
Kolp, Ray	1921–33	8	67	74	.475	1579	264
Koosman, Jerry	1968–82	10	156	102	.605	24287	600
Koslo, George	1946–53	8	87	100	.465	−6781	244
Koufax, Sandy	1958–66	8	148	71	.676	28699	563
Kralick, Jack	1961–65	5	56	53	.514	182	184
Kramer, Jack	1939–48	6	78	76	.506	6119	261
Krausse, Lew	1966–71	5	52	67	.437	−1774	154
Kremer, Remy	1924–31	8	158	82	.658	17442	475
Krukow, Mike	1977–86	9	98	101	.492	8187	360
Kucks, Johnny	1955–59	5	50	46	.521	−6640	147
LaCoss, Mike	1979–89	5	57	53	.528	−3839	168
Lake, Joe	1908–13	6	62	90	.408	6396	223
Lamp, Dennis	1978–84	6	54	61	.470	−2536	186
Langford, Rick	1977–82	6	69	86	.445	803	205
Langston, Mark	1984–95	10	166	141	.541	35621	638
Lanier, Max	1940–52	8	93	71	.567	−9140	274
LaPoint, Dave	1983–90	6	54	66	.450	187	192
Lary, Frank	1955–61	7	117	93	.557	9945	360
Lavender, Jim	1912–16	5	57	68	.456	−10290	119
Law, Vern	1950–66	10	127	94	.575	20519	512
Lawrence, Brooks	1954–59	5	65	54	.546	4274	220
Leary, Tim	1986–93	6	65	75	.464	−3444	187
Lee, Big Bill	1934–46	10	142	111	.561	12142	476

Pitcher	Years		W	L	Pct.	WR	Points
Lee, Bill "Spaceman"	1973–81	6	82	61	.573	1443	258
Lee, Thornton	1935–45	7	96	79	.543	8628	326
Leever, Sam	1899–1908	10	179	95	.653	16155	591
Leibrandt, Charlie	1980–93	10	129	100	.563	10049	459
Leifield, Lefty	1906–11	6	103	79	.566	−9902	225
Leiter, Al	1993–2004	10	129	92	.581	21272	526
Leiter, Mark	1991–97	5	41	55	.438	−2197	138
Lemaster, Denny	1963–70	8	85	99	.462	−8967	224
Lemon, Bob	1947–57	10	197	111	.640	12812	580
Leonard, Dennis	1975–86	9	139	99	.582	7734	437
Leonard, E. "Dutch"	1934–51	10	146	118	.557	35065	601
Leonard, H. "Dutch"	1913–25	10	136	111	.551	−943	416
Lerch, Randy	1977–82	6	60	57	.513	−10927	142
Lewis, Ted	1897–1901	5	93	60	.608	5383	270
Lidle, Cory	2001–06	6	70	64	.522	−3893	210
Lieber, Jon	1997–2006	8	101	88	.534	9305	358
Lima, Jose	1998–2005	6	68	67	.504	−1293	208
Loaiza, Esteben	1995–2006	10	112	100	.528	5405	404
Lockwood, Skip	1970–78	6	45	74	.378	−8072	119
Lohrman, Bill	1938–42	5	54	49	.524	1203	196
Lolich, Mickey	1964–75	10	172	126	.577	15404	591
Lonborg, Jim	1965–78	10	132	108	.550	13860	476
Lopat, Eddie	1944–54	10	149	87	.631	13185	535
Lopez, Rodrigo	2002–06	5	60	57	.513	8967	229
Lovett, Tom	1885–94	5	85	54	.612	7256	222
Lowe, Derek	2001–06	5	71	48	.597	9282	261
Lucas, Red	1927–37	10	134	117	.534	27029	538
Lundgren, Carl	1902–08	7	90	54	.625	−1776	295
Luque, Dolf	1920–30	10	147	138	.516	−5044	393
Lush, John	1906–10	5	64	79	.448	9690	224
Lynch, Jack	1881–87	6	110	104	.514	3548	229
Lyons, Ted	1924–42	10	159	100	.614	43254	686
McCaskill, Kirk	1985–92	6	78	75	.510	−4684	209
McCatty, Steve	1979–84	5	53	56	.486	1763	184
McCormick, Jim	1879–87	9	239	202	.542	34254	459
McCormick, Mike	1958–69	9	115	107	.518	−1416	338
McDermott, Mickey	1951–55	5	53	52	.505	3510	195
McDonald, Ben	1992–97	5	60	51	.541	1874	205
McDowell, Jack	1988–96	8	116	77	.601	10710	401
McDowell, Sam	1964–73	10	132	115	.581	21065	503
MacFayden, Danny	1928–39	10	113	139	.448	9180	379
McGill, Willie	1890–95	5	65	69	.485	−2049	161
McGinnity, Joe	1899–1908	10	247	144	.632	26786	706
McGlothen, Lynn	1972–80	6	77	75	.507	4360	251
McGlothin, Jim	1967–72	6	61	69	.469	−6605	170
McGregor, Scott	1978–86	9	133	92	.591	8587	445
McIntire, Harry	1905–11	7	70	114	.380	−11726	155
McLain, Denny	1965–71	6	118	73	.618	21858	412
McLish, Cal	1957–63	7	82	66	.554	6481	304
McMahon, Sadie	1889–96	8	175	122	.589	38776	546

Pitcher	Years		W	L	Pct.	WR	Points
McNally, Dave	1963–74	10	164	95	.633	11179	533
McQuillan, George	1908–15	5	70	69	.504	1857	207
McQuillan, Hugh	1920–27	7	83	88	.485	−5962	224
McWilliams, Larry	1980–88	6	57	59	.491	2159	213
Maddux, Greg	1988–2002	10	181	76	.704	43503	761
Maglie, Sal	1950–56	7	103	45	.696	22003	476
Mahler, Rick	1981–88	8	87	101	.463	3565	297
Malone, Pat	1928–36	8	127	83	.605	3036	387
Maloney, Jim	1962–69	8	126	67	.653	26676	519
Marchildon, Phil	1941–48	5	68	69	.496	12659	264
Marichal, Juan	1961–71	10	203	97	.677	38902	732
Marquard, Rube	1911–23	10	165	107	.607	24088	584
Martinez, Dennis	1977–94	10	142	86	.623	22989	574
Martinez, Pedro	1993–2005	10	163	66	.712	47907	753
Martinez, Ramon	1990–2000	9	119	75	.613	20362	494
Masterson, Walt	1940–53	5	43	65	.398	−3860	119
Mathews, Bobby	1876–86	8	158	126	.556	19594	383
Mathewson, Christy	1901–14	10	276	113	710	58917	936
Matlack, Jon	1972–81	9	111	108	.507	3069	348
Maul, Al	1890–98	5	69	60	.535	17507	283
May, Jakie	1919–29	9	33	56	.371	611	175
May, Rudy	1970–81	10	113	115	.496	−9166	306
Mayer, Erskine	1913–18	5	78	56	.582	7065	261
Mays, Al	1885–89	5	53	89	.373	−7983	97
Mays, Carl	1916–26	9	180	104	.634	16021	541
Mays, Joe	1999–2005	5	44	57	.436	−5396	126
Meadows, Lee	1915–27	10	154	130	.542	21977	536
Medich, Doc	1973–82	10	124	105	.541	5397	424
Meeker, Jouett	1891–99	9	153	131	.539	15741	459
Melton, Cliff	1937–43	7	84	78	.519	712	274
Menefee, Jocko	1893–1903	5	49	63	.438	2090	173
Mercer, Win	1894–1902	9	131	164	.444	20650	429
Merritt, Jim	1966–73	6	74	71	.510	−3118	209
Messersmith, Andy	1969–76	8	119	86	.580	19378	429
Meyer, Russ	1948–54	7	83	63	.568	3047	299
Miller, Frank	1916–22	5	52	62	.456	5136	194
Millwood, Kevin	1998–2006	8	111	87	.561	−915	342
Milton, Eric	1998–2006	8	86	80	.518	8874	337
Minner, Paul	1950–55	6	60	74	.448	2227	207
Mitchell, Clarence	1916–31	10	94	119	.441	−5239	292
Mitchell, Willie	1910–17	7	78	76	.506	8269	309
Mizell, Vinegar Bend	1952–61	8	89	85	.511	−1765	283
Mlicki, Dave	1995–2001	6	56	61	.479	−5194	162
Moehler, Brian	1997–2006	6	60	73	.451	−576	195
Mogridge, George	1916–26	9	112	106	.514	3229	355
Monbouquette, Bill	1960–66	7	93	88	.514	13609	337
Montefusco, John	1975–82	5	59	55	.518	3824	206
Moore, Earl	1901–14	10	153	140	.522	6813	452
Moore, Mike	1982–94	10	134	117	.534	121	421
Moose, Bob	1968–73	6	69	55	.556	891	244

Pitcher	Years		W	L	Pct.	WR	Points
Morgan, Cy	1907–11	5	73	60	.549	−5219	175
Morgan, Mike	1982–99	10	111	126	.468	−11111	280
Morris, Ed	1884–90	7	171	123	.582	29902	423
Morris, Jack	1979–94	10	175	89	.663	16369	627
Morris, Matt	1997–2006	7	101	69	.594	7069	342
Morrison, Johnny	1921–29	6	92	68	.575	1819	272
Morton, Carl	1971–75	5	65	69	.485	3698	205
Morton, Guy	1915–22	6	75	57	.568	9855	295
Mossi, Don	1957–62	6	70	55	.560	5910	263
Moyer, Jamie	1993–2005	10	146	95	.606	34327	660
Mulder, Mark	2000–05	6	97	60	.618	10096	343
Mulholland, Terry	1990–2000	10	99	104	.488	−1791	330
Mullane, Tony	1882–92	10	259	183	.586	39070	635
Mullin, George	1902–14	10	190	147	.564	21230	578
Muncrief, Bob	1941–49	7	69	70	.496	4706	263
Mungo, Van Lingle	1932–45	8	108	99	.522	15681	391
Murphy, Tom	1969–78	5	48	65	.425	−1916	144
Mussina, Mike	1992–2006	10	165	76	.695	38696	699
Myers, Elmer	1916–21	6	54	72	.429	5273	214
Nagy, Charles	1991–99	8	117	76	.606	14137	432
Nash, Jim	1967–71	5	55	54	.505	4175	205
Navarro, Jaime	1989–99	10	104	85	.550	7244	374
Naylor, Rollie	1919–23	5	40	76	.344	−736	119
Neagle, Denny	1994–2002	8	106	71	.599	15322	419
Nehf, Art	1917–28	10	160	99	.618	21243	578
Newcombe, Don	1949–60	10	149	90	.623	15789	528
Newhouser, Hal	1940–52	10	177	108	.621	25912	606
Newsom, Buck	1934–47	10	161	133	.548	22041	543
Nichols, Kid	1890–1904	10	297	145	.672	33600	766
Niekro, Joe	1967–85	10	156	112	.582	19749	547
Niekro, Phil	1969–84	10	194	148	.567	41364	680
Niggeling, Johnny	1940–45	6	56	61	.479	−1509	189
Nolan, Gary	1967–76	7	97	61	.614	4687	335
Nomo, Hideo	1995–2004	10	118	101	.539	2924	386
Norman, Fred	1971–79	9	98	94	.510	−9783	280
Nuxhall, Joe	1953–65	10	117	89	.568	12865	458
O'Day, Hank	1884–90	5	64	101	.388	−8741	97
O'Dell, Billy	1958–65	7	83	73	.532	−1029	264
Odom, Blue Moon	1968–73	6	70	54	.565	823	242
Oeschger, Joe	1917–23	6	67	95	.414	−6705	153
Ojeda, Bob	1983–92	8	92	78	.542	−88	309
Oliveras, Omar	1991–2001	7	63	71	.470	3654	247
Oliver, Darren	1996–2003	5	68	60	.531	8703	267
Ortega, Phil	1964–68	5	46	58	.442	−553	153
Orth, Al	1896–1906	10	165	134	.552	22155	554
Ortiz, Ramon	2001–06	5	64	60	.516	4294	219
Ortiz, Russ	1999–2005	7	104	67	.608	11439	369
Osteen, Claude	1962–73	10	152	133	.533	13193	536
Ostermueller, Fritz	1934–48	9	97	88	.524	5296	355
Oswalt, Roy	2001–06	6	98	47	.676	22618	414

Pitcher	Years		W	L	Pct.	WR	Points
O'Toole, Jim	1960–64	5	81	55	.596	7150	266
Overall, Orval	1905–10	6	103	67	.606	−6285	153
Packard, Gene	1913–19	7	85	67	.556	19902	376
Palmer, Jim	1969–82	10	200	94	.680	30172	701
Pappas, Milt	1959–72	10	150	98	.605	18334	547
Park, Chan Ho	1997–2002	6	84	57	.596	14847	335
Parmalee, Roy	1933–37	5	55	43	.561	−3179	179
Parnell, Mel	1948–63	6	109	56	.661	16819	389
Pascual, Camilo	1957–68	10	141	117	.547	26641	544
Passeau, Claude	1936–45	10	151	135	.528	26879	551
Patten, Case	1901–07	7	103	124	.454	26981	403
Patterson, Roy	1901–06	5	73	61	.545	−1384	202
Pattin, Marty	1969–76	7	85	90	.486	−1267	245
Pearson, Monte	1933–39	6	83	50	.624	3481	286
Pelty, Barney	1904–11	7	80	101	.442	8231	275
Pennock, Herb	1914–30	10	170	89	.656	28565	645
Penny, Brad	2000–06	7	72	62	.537	4643	282
Perdue, Hub	1911–15	5	51	64	.443	3052	173
Perez, Melido	1988–94	7	72	79	.477	−4632	220
Perritt, Pol	1913–18	6	87	76	.534	2495	257
Perry, Gaylord	1966–79	10	193	131	.596	41393	699
Perry, Jim	1959–74	10	157	106	.597	16098	535
Peters, Gary	1963–71	9	121	99	.550	4532	381
Peterson, Fritz	1966–75	10	132	128	.508	1184	389
Petry, Dan	1980–90	9	111	85	.566	3895	378
Pettitte, Andy	1995–2006	9	146	81	.643	15226	512
Petty, Jesse	1925–29	5	65	69	.485	948	192
Pfeffer, Jeff	1914–24	10	157	111	.586	18659	538
Phillippe, Deacon	1899–1910	10	181	104	.635	10140	538
Phillips, Bill	1895–1902	5	62	61	.504	5265	211
Piatt, Wiley	1898–1903	6	85	78	.521	−3685	211
Pierce, Billy	1950–62	10	162	109	.598	17288	548
Pineiro, Joel	2002–06	5	51	53	.490	26	169
Pipgras, George	1928–33	5	84	59	.587	−1685	221
Pittinger, Togie	1901–06	6	105	100	.512	11907	316
Pizarro, Juan	1961–68	6	76	57	.571	3576	259
Plank, Eddie	1903–15	10	215	102	.678	33515	725
Podres, Johnny	1954–63	9	120	92	.566	−563	375
Pollet, Howie	1946–54	7	98	90	.521	2268	310
Ponson, Sidney	1998–2005	8	76	91	.455	−2061	244
Porterfield, Bob	1951–56	6	70	76	.479	4177	227
Portugal, Mark	1986–99	9	91	80	.532	8930	372
Potter, Nelson	1939–49	7	75	69	.521	9441	303
Powell, Jack	1897–1910	10	163	155	.513	8040	455
Purkey, Bob	1957–65	9	124	99	.556	12157	430
Quinn, Jack	1910–28	10	161	123	.567	16026	524
Radbourn, Charlie	1881–91	10	304	178	.631	44191	616
Radke, Brad	1995–2006	10	130	122	.516	13800	456
Raffensberger, Ken	1940–53	10	119	147	.447	5758	369
Ragan, Pat	1912–18	7	72	98	.424	−9399	171

Pitcher	Years		W	L	Pct.	WR	Points
Ramos, Pedro	1955–64	10	105	142	.425	−747	315
Ramsey, Toad	1886–90	5	111	118	.485	5436	204
Rapp, Pat	1994–2001	6	55	68	.447	−2148	177
Raschi, Vic	1948–54	7	118	57	.676	13291	419
Rasmussen, Dennis	1984–91	7	83	68	.550	4290	295
Rasmussen, Eric	1976–84	6	50	70	.417	−8947	138
Rau, Doug	1974–78	5	73	49	.598	1818	233
Rawley, Shane	1982–89	8	90	87	.508	3527	312
Redman, Mark	2000–05	5	50	59	.458	−1383	136
Reed, Rick	1997–2003	7	84	61	.579	6130	317
Reed, Ron	1968–79	10	104	104	.500	−2318	345
Renko, Steve	1970–82	10	108	104	.509	6099	398
Reulbach, Ed	1905–15	10	163	80	.671	12483	558
Reuschel, Rick	1973–89	10	149	103	.591	34107	616
Reuss, Jerry	1973–89	10	145	95	.604	16139	527
Reynolds, Allie	1944–54	10	160	80	.667	18651	590
Reynolds, Shane	1995–2003	8	102	81	.557	4102	340
Reynoso, Armando	1993–2000	5	48	45	.516	567	187
Rhem, Flint	1925–34	9	101	89	.532	−5792	306
Rhines, Billy	1890–98	5	97	82	.542	6906	248
Rhoades, Bob	1903–08	6	88	65	.575	6787	289
Rhoden, Rick	1976–88	10	122	100	.550	15108	482
Richard, J. R.	1975–79	5	86	61	.585	18174	327
Richie, Lew	1906–12	6	66	55	.545	1605	237
Rijo, Jose	1986–93	7	89	58	.605	15602	380
Ring, Jimmy	1918–28	10	115	138	.455	7746	377
Rixey, Eppa	1912–28	10	177	127	.582	20387	566
Roberts, Dave	1970–77	8	90	103	.466	3809	310
Roberts, Robin	1950–64	10	202	134	.601	42235	736
Robinson, Don	1978–90	9	92	77	.544	3902	355
Roe, Preacher	1944–51	7	99	67	.596	8143	345
Rogers, Kenny	1990–2006	10	145	80	.644	34174	637
Rogers, Steve	1973–83	10	135	111	.549	15330	488
Rommel, Eddie	1921–28	7	124	96	.564	25738	456
Rooker, Jim	1969–78	8	90	87	.508	−2051	283
Root, Charlie	1926–41	10	162	106	.604	4635	523
Ross, Buck	1936–43	6	45	71	.388	1031	166
Rowe, Schoolboy	1934–48	9	137	78	.637	27097	560
Rowley, Shane	1981–88	8	88	78	.530	8083	335
Rucker, Nap	1907–13	7	116	123	.485	27215	422
Rudolph, Dick	1913–19	7	117	95	.552	10308	360
Rueter, Kirk	1997–2004	8	102	71	.590	5071	364
Ruether, Dutch	1919–27	9	135	92	.595	7135	438
Ruffing, Red	1930–42	10	179	83	.687	13497	591
Rusch, Glendon	1998–2005	6	52	71	.403	−8440	125
Rush, Bob	1948–58	10	112	126	.471	9896	399
Rusie, Amos	1889–98	9	246	173	.587	32408	631
Russell, Allan	1916–23	6	55	56	.495	468	194
Russell, Jack	1928–34	7	59	100	.371	−9177	147
Russell, Reb	1913–18	6	81	61	.570	4061	270

Before he was a Yankee, Babe Ruth starred for the Boston Red Sox on the mound, at the plate, and in the field. In the 1918 World Series he pitched a record 29 2/3 scoreless innings against the Chicago Cubs. The following season he set a major league record with 29 home runs and was the American League's best left fielder (Library of Congress).

Pitcher	Years		W	L	Pct.	WR	Points
Ruth, Babe	1915–19	5	87	45	.659	11330	312
Ruthven, Dick	1973–84	10	110	113	.493	580	356
Ryan, Nolan	1972–91	10	164	118	.582	35146	633
Sabathia, C.C.	2001–06	6	81	56	.591	14715	330
Saberhagen, Bret	1984–99	9	130	83	.610	17268	497
Sadecki, Ray	1960–74	8	91	87	.511	−6135	356
Sain, Johnny	1946–53	8	127	98	.564	2342	362
Sallee, Slim	1909–19	10	150	117	.562	24853	556
Sanders, Ben	1888–92	5	81	69	.540	8400	218
Sanderson, Scott	1980–94	10	121	99	.550	8134	434
Sanford, Jack	1957–66	8	122	83	.595	15831	440
Scanlan, Doc	1904–10	5	57	52	.523	16918	272
Scarborough, Ray	1946–51	6	66	70	.485	10491	258
Schilling, Curt	1992–2006	10	167	95	.663	44177	717
Schmidt, Jason	1998–2006	9	118	77	.605	16494	500
Schmitz, Johnny	1946–55	7	81	89	.476	10325	298

Pitcher	Years		W	L	Pct.	WR	Points
Schneider, Pete	1914–18	5	59	85	.410	−9254	117
Schromm, Ken	1983–87	5	49	51	.490	3775	216
Schumacher, Hal	1933–42	10	148	110	.574	3279	448
Scott, Jack	1920–26	6	77	92	.456	−5620	196
Scott, Jim	1909–16	7	99	103	.490	−6451	245
Scott, Mike	1981–90	10	121	105	.536	11326	436
Seaver, Tom	1967–81	10	190	87	.686	57690	823
Segui, Diego	1963–71	6	54	62	.466	2873	212
Sele, Aaron	1994–2003	9	112	85	.569	2747	366
Sewell, Rip	1939–48	9	131	91	.590	20370	508
Shantz, Bobby	1950–57	5	64	56	.582	16255	287
Shaute, Joe	1923–31	8	89	96	.481	1838	290
Shaw, Bob	1959–66	7	93	76	.550	5655	313
Shaw, Dupee	1883–87	5	62	103	.375	816	129
Shaw, Jim	1914–20	6	78	90	.464	−4651	191
Shawkey, Bob	1914–26	10	173	120	.590	7378	500
Sheets, Ben	2001–05	5	55	62	.470	8381	198
Sherdel, Bill	1918–31	10	138	100	.581	10172	478
Shirley, Bob	1977–82	5	47	70	.402	−4637	125
Shocker, Urban	1919–27	9	169	104	.619	27750	586
Short, Chris	1960–71	10	122	110	.526	11953	434
Show, Eric	1982–87	6	76	65	.539	6445	273
Siebert, Sonny	1964–74	10	126	96	.568	15379	479
Siever, Ed	1901–07	6	81	77	.513	2962	246
Simmons, Curt	1950–64	10	139	101	.579	13487	494
Singer, Bill	1967–76	8	101	109	.481	−1988	300
Slaton, Jim	1971–83	10	127	118	.518	11276	457
Smiley, John	1988–96	8	106	75	.586	7570	376
Smith, Al	1935–45	8	90	88	.506	−4171	322
Smith, Bob	1926–35	9	91	125	.421	4341	305
Smith, Bryn	1982–91	9	99	84	.541	8297	380
Smith, Charlie	1906–13	6	52	76	.406	−1045	173
Smith, Edgar	1937–46	7	67	96	.411	−14456	140
Smith, Frank	1904–15	9	133	105	.559	6883	414
Smith, George	1918–22	5	35	72	.327	−8059	78
Smith, Sherry	1915–26	10	108	116	.482	−3025	344
Smith, Zane	1985–95	8	91	89	.506	2666	321
Smithson, Mike	1983–89	5	60	69	.465	−1922	165
Smoltz, John	1989–96	10	150	87	.633	21401	573
Sorensen, Larry	1977–84	8	87	92	.486	−5933	249
Sorrell, Vic	1928–34	7	82	89	.480	1357	253
Sothoron, Allen	1917–25	7	88	94	.484	4367	278
Soto, Mario	1980–86	7	88	75	.540	11536	331
Spahn, Warren	1947–63	10	213	118	.644	44728	772
Sparks, Tully	1901–09	9	113	129	.467	3774	337
Splitorff, Paul	1971–83	10	138	105	.568	4116	441
Staley, Gerry	1949–60	7	97	80	.548	1909	293
Staley, Harry	1888–95	8	137	119	.535	−387	306
Stange, Lee	1963–69	5	41	47	.466	−5550	130
Stein, Ed	1890–95	5	100	64	.610	11338	290

Pitcher	Years		W	L	Pct.	WR	Points
Stewart, Dave	1982–94	10	142	104	.577	7562	457
Stewart, Lefty	1927–34	8	95	91	.511	11511	357
Stieb, Dave	1979–90	10	145	98	.597	29452	590
Stivetts, Jack	1889–97	9	204	126	.618	2616	467
Stobbs, Chuck	1949–59	10	101	109	.481	2925	361
Stone, Steve	1973–81	7	85	64	.570	5962	304
Stottlemyre, Mel	1965–73	9	149	129	.536	14301	464
Stottlemyre, Todd	1990–2000	10	121	101	.545	5310	414
Stratton, Scott	1888–94	7	95	112	.459	5673	231
Sudhoff, Willie	1898–1905	8	101	126	.445	6626	374
Suggs, George	1910–15	6	100	88	.541	18285	349
Sullivan, Frank	1954–61	8	92	95	.482	2226	297
Sullivan, Mike	1892–97	5	46	50	.479	–4575	137
Suppan, Jeff	1999–2006	8	96	88	.522	4910	336
Surkont, Max	1951–55	5	51	66	.436	–394	162
Sutcliffe, Rick	1979–93	10	149	103	.591	23552	570
Sutton, Don	1972–85	10	163	93	.637	25952	612
Swan, Craig	1976–82	5	49	45	.521	11171	235
Swift, W. C. "Bill"	1985–98	5	54	46	.540	3852	204
Swift, W. V. "Bill"	1932–37	6	79	67	.541	–674	238
Swindell, Greg	1988–95	8	94	84	.528	8383	350
Tanana, Frank	1974–92	10	148	110	.574	27241	578
Tannehill, Jesse	1897–1906	10	188	104	.644	36915	681
Tapani, Kevin	1990–2000	10	123	106	.537	12962	452
Taylor, Dummy	1901–07	7	103	98	.512	–6121	247
Taylor, J. B. "Jack"	1899–1906	8	140	135	.509	9494	390
Taylor, J. W. "Jack"	1893–99	7	119	116	.506	11815	355
Terrell, Walt	1983–92	9	100	104	.493	–6442	302
Terry, Adonis	1886–96	10	180	115	.582	–16591	373
Terry, Ralph	1957–65	9	105	91	.536	–8310	297
Tesreau, Jeff	1912–17	6	115	68	.628	11054	358
Tewksbury, Bob	1990–96	7	84	73	.535	11149	377
Thomas, Tommy	1926–36	9	110	117	.485	12493	385
Thomson, John	1997–2004	5	51	56	.477	–128	169
Thurston, Sloppy	1923–32	6	71	66	.518	4143	245
Tiant, Luis	1966–79	10	161	97	.624	25063	599
Tobin, Jim	1938–45	7	92	106	.465	3712	277
Tomko, Brett	1997–2006	7	74	67	.525	5762	290
Toney, Fred	1915–23	8	130	91	.588	17683	455
Torrez, Mike	1970–82	10	143	102	.584	12193	498
Trachsel, Steve	1994–2006	10	115	106	.520	11384	430
Travers, Bill	1975–80	6	63	64	.496	1050	214
Trout, Dizzy	1939–52	10	143	116	.552	4095	434
Trout, Steve	1979–85	6	66	68	.493	620	245
Trucks, Virgil	1942–57	10	151	96	.611	23603	574
Tudor, John	1982–90	7	94	60	.610	16680	393
Turley, Bob	1954–59	5	73	52	.584	6094	252
Twitchell, Wayne	1973–78	5	34	50	.405	–7176	97
Tyler, Lefty	1911–20	9	122	114	.517	5723	386
Uhle, George	1919–31	10	155	120	.564	26562	567

Pitcher	Years		W	L	Pct.	WR	Points
Underwood, Tom	1975–83	9	84	87	.491	236	309
Valdes, Ismael	1995–2004	8	88	83	.518	629	297
Valenzuela, Fernando	1981–96	10	143	109	.567	13642	495
Vance, Dazzy	1922–32	10	176	116	.603	36878	666
Vander Meer, Johnny	1938–49	8	105	101	.510	3907	325
Van Gilder, Elam	1921–28	8	95	93	.505	4141	311
Vaughn, Hippo	1910–20	10	170	125	.576	25222	575
Vazquez, Javier	1998–2006	9	100	103	.493	2787	330
Veale, Bob	1964–70	7	103	87	.542	2874	308
Viau, Lee	1888–92	5	83	77	.519	−124	168
Viola, Frank	1984–93	10	163	120	.576	21481	557
Voiselle, Bill	1944–49	6	73	77	.487	28	215
Vuckovich, Pete	1978–85	6	77	51	.602	14847	331
Waddell, Rube	1900–09	10	181	141	.562	9002	491
Waits, Rick	1976–81	6	66	68	.493	855	218
Wakefield, Tim	1993–2005	10	124	101	.551	573	401
Walberg, Rube	1925–35	10	140	115	.549	−20341	292
Walk, Bob	1980–93	7	77	64	.546	6624	303
Walker, Bill	1929–35	7	89	65	.578	2566	306
Walsh, Ed	1906–12	7	168	112	.600	27871	514
Walters, Bucky	1935–46	10	164	113	.592	24303	575
Ward, Monte	1878–83	6	162	97	.625	9749	300
Warhop, Jack	1909–15	6	64	85	.430	−6835	159
Warneke, Lon	1932–41	10	175	100	.636	21062	605
Washburn, Jerrod	2001–06	6	66	61	.520	1807	231
Washburn, Ray	1962–68	5	56	44	.560	2734	211
Weaver, Jeff	1999–2006	8	86	101	.460	−6197	274
Wegman, Bill	1986–94	7	70	75	.483	−6811	204
Wehmeier, Herman	1948–57	9	90	100	.474	2400	320
Weidman, Stump	1882–87	6	92	141	.395	3480	188
Weiland, Bob	1932–39	5	55	67	.417	−1703	156
Weilman, Carl	1913–20	6	84	86	.488	7682	271
Weimer, Jake	1903–08	6	98	70	.583	11550	328
Welch, Bob	1980–92	10	153	81	.654	23383	606
Welch, Mickey	1880–90	10	276	181	.604	35596	618
Wells, David	1990–2005	10	162	75	.684	28298	644
Wells, Ed	1925–32	5	49	45	.521	797	192
Wells, Kip	2000–05	5	46	61	.430	−9050	108
Weyhing, Gus	1887–99	10	248	203	.550	21858	565
White, Doc	1901–10	10	170	129	.569	13693	526
White, Will	1878–85	7	226	161	.584	23455	431
Whitehill, Earl	1924–36	10	159	120	.572	21909	555
Whitney, Jim	1881–88	8	187	195	.490	14564	378
Whitson, Ed	1979–90	9	101	93	.521	1965	342
Wicker, Bob	1902–06	5	63	57	.525	−7175	157
Wight, Bill	1948–56	5	50	71	.413	3858	174
Wilcox, Milt	1972–84	9	105	94	.528	176	347
Wilhelm, Kaiser	1904–14	5	49	97	.336	−9504	79
Willett, Ed	1908–14	7	99	88	.529	1363	286
Williams, Stan	1958–69	7	80	74	.519	−3886	240

Pitcher	Years		W	L	Pct.	WR	Points
Williams, Woody	1997–2006	9	106	96	.525	4863	401
Willis, Vic	1898–1910	10	206	140	.595	17292	601
Wilson, Don	1967–74	8	103	92	.528	8492	340
Wilson, Earl	1962–69	8	112	94	.534	9077	372
Wilson, Jack	1937–41	5	58	55	.513	−6115	153
Wilson, Jim	1952–58	5	61	63	.492	3357	203
Wilson, Paul	1996–2004	5	38	49	.437	2509	160
Wiltse, Hooks	1904–12	9	135	84	.616	−3078	402
Winter, George	1901–08	7	75	97	.436	−12100	167
Wise, Rick	1967–79	10	147	118	.555	21194	534
Witt, Bobby	1986–97	10	117	113	.507	3565	386
Witt, Mike	1981–89	8	101	98	.508	2370	314
Wolf, Randy	1999–2003	5	54	48	.529	4652	208
Wood, Kerry	1998–2004	6	67	50	.573	9492	287
Wood, Smoky Joe	1909–15	6	106	52	.671	16759	390
Wood, Wilbur	1968–78	10	155	143	.520	18678	503
Worthington, Al	1956–67	5	44	48	.478	−3286	149
Wright, Clyde	1968–74	6	86	85	.503	3031	254
Wright, Jamey	1997–2006	7	61	85	.418	−2580	189
Wyatt, Whit	1932–43	6	83	60	.580	1792	261
Wynn, Early	1943–59	10	189	108	.636	18770	604
Wyse, Hank	1943–50	6	76	67	.531	5336	257
Young, Cy	1891–1908	10	318	129	.711	81985	1010
Zachary, Tom	1920–33	10	128	119	.518	10289	436
Zachry, Pat	1976–82	6	53	59	.473	1759	204
Zahn, Geoff	1977–84	8	103	93	.526	7643	354
Zito, Barry	2001–06	6	95	59	.617	6469	311

Fourteen pitchers are omitted from the above list because they were primarily relievers who met the 15 decisions criterion only when wins and losses in relief were included. They are: Clay Carroll, Elroy Face, Rollie Fingers, Gene Garber, John Hiller, Lindy McDaniel, Fred Marberry, Mike Marshall, Stu Miller, Phil Regan, Bob Stanley, Kent Tekulve, Dick Tidrow, and Hoyt Wilhelm.

5

CLOSERS

For many years pitchers were just pitchers. No differentiation was made between starters and relievers. The pitcher who started the game was expected to finish it. The goal was to hurl a complete game every time out. If the starter ran into trouble and could not finish the game, a fellow starter came in to bail him out. In the 1920s we began to see the emergence of the relief specialist — the pitcher who seldom, if ever, started and was used almost exclusively in relief. After World War II relief pitchers became standard members of almost every team. Official recognition that pitchers were no longer expected to finish what they started came in 1951, when the major leagues dropped the requirement that a hurler had to have 10 or more complete games to qualify for league leadership in earned run average or fielding percentage. Henceforth, eligibility for these honors was based on innings pitched, not complete games. For the next 20 or 30 years most teams had two types of pitchers, starters and relievers. The relievers were expected to finish the game, to close it out. We now call them closers. Specialization among relievers was not the dominant mode until a little later.

The primary objective of a relief pitcher is to help secure a win for his team. The two principal ways of doing this are by winning the game himself or by saving it for another hurler. The save became an official statistic in 1973. However, baseball historians have calculated retroactively the number of unofficial saves earned by each pitcher back to the beginning of the major leagues. A pitcher who enters the game in a save situation, but loses the lead is charged with a blown save. (The blown save is not recognized as an official statistic but has been calculated by researchers for seasons from 1969 to date. We refigured the ratings for the leading closers, subtracting one point for each blown save and found it had little impact on the rankings. Therefore, we are not using this unofficial statistic in this publication.)

In the Faber System closers acquire an eligible season if the number of total decisions in relief plus the number of saves add up to 15 or more. Relievers meeting this criterion are rated as closers whether or not they actually finish the game. They are rated by a multi-step method. First, the formula used with starters is applied.* The point total derived from this procedure is divided by two, for this represents one-half of the reliever's record. Then one point is added for each relief win and for each save and one point is subtracted for each relief loss. In this section whenever the term reliever is used without a qualifying adjective it is synonymous to closer.

*One modification in this procedure is used. If a pitcher is involved in fewer than 15 decisions, his point total for winning percentage is adjusted by applying a multiplier (the percentage his total decisions are of 15.) This is to avoid the obvious unfairness of awarding 50 points for a percentage of 1.000 based on one win and no losses, for example.

Leading Closers by Year

National League. In the early years of major league baseball there were no relief specialists. It was not until 1911 that a National League pitcher met the eligibility criteria for rating as a reliever. The trailblazer was Mordecai (Three Finger) Brown, whose nickname came from his having lost parts of two fingers in a farm accident. The righthander started 27 games for the Cubs that year and finished 21 of them. He also appeared in 26 games in relief, winning five, losing three, and saving 13. Most early relievers were, like Brown, starters pressed into occasional relief. One of the first exceptions was Tom Hughes of the Boston Braves. In 1915 he appeared in 50 games, starting 25 and relieving in an equal number. However, in 1916 he relieved in more games than he started. In 1921 Lou North of the St. Louis Cardinals became perhaps the first true relief specialist, when he relieved 40 times and made no starts. Our list of leading relievers by year starts with 1911 and includes only those seasons in which at least one pitcher met the eligibility requirements.

Trevor Hoffman and Eric Gagne have both led the league in Faber System points three times in a row. Hoffman and Hugh Casey have led it a total of four times each. Tom Hughes's record of 10 wins in relief was bested by Ben Cantwell with 12 in 1932. Mace Brown of the Pittsburgh Pirates raised the bar to 15 in 1938. Jim Konstanty exceeded that with 16 relief wins as he led the Philadelphia Whiz Kids to a pennant in 1950. Nine years later Elroy Face raised the mark to 18 wins in a sensational year in which he also set records for weighted rating and Faber System points. These records may never be broken. Before Face's outstanding year Hughes had held the weighted rating mark with 4860, set in 1915, only to see it broken by Johnny Morrison with 4884 in 1929 and Anton Karl with 5085 in 1945. Face's 9557 weighted rating was nearly twice as high as the previous record. Hughes and Morrison had set points marks with 49 and 50, respectively, in their record years. Clyde Shoun of Cincinnati raised the mark to 55 in 1943, and Konstanty pushed it to 64 in 1950. Hoyt Wilhelm posted 66 points for the New York Giants in 1952, which lasted until Face's 84 points in 1959. The record for the number of saves in a season continues to rise. It has been broken at least 14 times since 1913. The current record of 55 was set by John Smoltz in 2002 and tied by Eric Gagne the following year.

NATIONAL LEAGUE LEADING CLOSER, 1911–2006

Year	Reliever	Club	W	L	Pct.	WR	Sv	Pts
1911	Mordecai Brown	Chi	5	3	.625	232	13	27
1912	Larry Cheney	Chi	4	0	1.000	1744	11	29
1915	Tom Hughes	Bos	10	0	1.000	4860	5	49
1916	Tom Hughes	Bos	9	2	.818	2761	5	39
1920	Bill Sherdel	StL	8	8	.500	112	6	23
1921	Lou North	StL	4	4	.500	−576	7	15
1928	Jim Faulkner	NY	7	6	.538	−936	7	16
1929	Johnny Morrison	Brk	10	2	.833	4864	8	50
1930	Joe Heving	NY	7	5	.583	240	6	24
1931	Jack Quinn	Brk	5	3	.625	888	15	30
1932	Ben Cantwell	Bos	12	8	.600	2300	5	36
1933	Phil Collins	Ph	3	6	.333	−594	6	8
1934	Bob Smith	Bos	4	6	.400	−1240	5	9
1936	Dick Coffman	NY	7	3	.700	1110	7	30
1938	Mace Brown	Pit	15	8	.696	3151	5	45
1939	Bob Bowman	StL	7	0	1.000	2926	5	39
1940	Joe Beggs	Cin	12	3	.800	2430	7	48
1941	Hugh Casey	Brk	8	4	.667	228	7	29

Year	Reliever	Club	W	L	Pct.	WR	Sv	Pts
1942	Hugh Casey	Brk	6	1	.857	1330	13	35
1943	Clyde Shoun	Cin	13	3	.813	4432	7	55
1944	Xavier Rescigno	Pit	8	5	.615	377	5	27
1945	Anton Karl	Ph	9	6	.600	5085	15	50
1946	Hugh Casey	Brk	11	4	.733	1950	5	41
1947	Hugh Casey	Brk	10	4	.714	1596	18	50
1948	Harry Gumbert	Cin	10	8	.556	2808	17	45
1949	Ted Wilks	StL	10	3	.770	2080	9	43
1950	Jim Konstanty	Ph	16	7	.696	2829	22	64
1951	Emil "Dutch" Leonard	Ch	10	5	.667	4395	3	41
1952	Hoyt Wilhelm	NY	15	3	.833	4808	11	66
1953	Lew Burdette	Mil	8	0	1.000	3400	8	42
1954	Jim Hughes	Brk	8	4	.667	900	24	48
1955	Clem Labine	Brk	10	3	.833	2508	11	48
1956	Hershell Freeman	Cin	14	5	.737	3173	18	61
1957	Turk Farrell	Ph	10	2	.833	4212	10	51
1958	Roy Face	Pit	5	2	.714	1239	20	37
1959	Roy Face	Pit	18	1	.947	9557	10	84
1960	Lindy McDaniel	StL	12	2	.857	4592	26	74
1961	Stu Miller	SF	14	5	.737	4009	17	62
1962	Jack Baldshun	Ph	12	7	.632	2735	13	47
1963	Ron Perranoski	LA	16	3	.844	5016	21	76
1964	Al McBean	Pit	8	3	.727	2750	22	52
1965	Frank Linzy	SF	9	3	.750	2124	21	52
1966	Phil Regan	LA	14	1	.933	6060	21	80
1967	Ted Abernathy	Chi	6	3	.667	1242	28	47
1968	Phil Regan	Chi	12	5	.706	3553	25	65
1969	Wayne Granger	Cin	9	6	.600	1853	27	52
1970	Dave Giusti	Pit	9	3	.750	2604	26	58
1971	Clay Carroll	Cin	10	4	.714	3472	15	52
1972	Mike Marshall	Mon	14	8	.636	4796	18	59
1973	Mike Marshall	Mon	14	11	.560	1975	31	60
1974	Al Hrbosky	StL	8	1	.889	2484	9	40
1975	Al Hrbosky	StL	13	3	.813	5440	22	73
1976	Butch Metzger	SD	11	4	.800	4665	16	59
1977	Bruce Sutter	Chi	7	3	.700	2130	31	56
1978	Kent Tekulve	Pit	8	7	.533	−165	31	49
1979	Bruce Sutter	Chi	6	6	.500	84	37	50
1980	Rollie Fingers	SD	11	9	.550	2340	23	51
1981	Rick Camp	Atl	9	3	.750	3768	17	52
1982	Greg Minton	SF	10	4	.714	2716	30	65
1983	Jesse Orosco	NY	13	7	.650	5260	17	59
1984	Jesse Orosco	NY	10	6	.625	1230	31	59
1985	John Franco	Cin	12	3	.800	4095	12	57
1986	Ron Robinson	Cin	10	3	.769	3367	14	52
1987	Todd Worrell	StL	9	6	.600	225	33	56
1988	John Franco	Cin	6	6	.500	−528	39	51
1989	Tim Burke	Mon	9	3	.750	3240	28	62
1990	John Franco	NY	5	3	.625	536	33	48
1991	Mitch Williams	Ph	12	5	.706	4267	30	71

Year	Reliever	Club	W	L	Pct.	WR	Sv	Pts
1992	Doug Jones	Hou	11	8	.579	1691	36	63
1993	John Wetteland	Mon	9	3	.750	2112	43	74
1994	Trevor Hoffman	SD	4	4	.500	848	20	31
1995	Trevor Hoffman	SD	7	4	.636	1782	31	54
1996	Trevor Hoffman	SD	9	5	.643	1246	42	69
1997	Robb Nen	FL	9	3	.750	2352	35	67
1998	Trevor Hoffman	SD	4	2	.667	384	53	65
1999	Ugueth Urbina	Mon	6	6	.500	1044	41	57
2000	Antonio Alfonseca	FL	5	6	.455	−418	45	54
2001	Armando Benitez	NY	6	4	.600	1000	43	61
2002	Eric Gagne	LA	4	1	.800	1195	52	67
2003	Eric Gagne	LA	2	3	.400	−645	55	57
2004	Eric Gagne	LA	7	3	.700	1340	45	68
2005	Derrek Turnbull	Mil	7	1	.825	2152	39	66
2006	Chad Cordero	Was	7	4	.636	2332	29	53

American League. As in the senior circuit, the earliest American League relievers were starting pitchers who were called upon to rescue a fellow starter who ran into trouble. For example, Ed Walsh, who was the first ALer to meet eligibility requirements as a reliever, hurled more than 30 complete games in each of the two seasons in which he led the league in relief pitching. In 1917 Dave Danforth became the first leading reliever to relieve in more games than he started.

The record for Faber System points by a closer was set by Walsh with 23 in 1911 and broken by Bob Shawkey with 40 in 1916. New records were set in three consecutive years by Elam Vangilder with 45 in 1925, by Fred Marberry with 50 in 1926, and Wilcy Moore with 55 in 1927. Moore's record stood for nearly two decades until Earl Caldwell posted 56 points in 1946. That mark was broken successively by Dick Hyde, Luis Arroyo, Dick Radatz, and Bill Campbell. In 1982 Dennis Eckersley established the current record of 79 points, which has since been tied by Billy Koch and Keith Foulke. The three co-holders of the record all pitched for the Oakland Athletics. Although he never held the record, Johnny Murphy of the New York Yankees was the best fireman in the league in five different years. John Hiller of Detroit holds the record for relief wins with 14, Campbell has the highest weighted rating with 6314 points for the Minnesota Twins, and Bobby Thigpen of the Chicago White Sox the most saves with 57.

LEADING CLOSERS BY YEAR—AMERICAN LEAGUE

Year	Reliever	Club	W	L	Pct.	WR	Sv	Pts.
1911	Ed Walsh	Chi	7	5	.583	864	4	23
1912	Ed Walsh	Chi	3	2	.600	485	10	19
1916	Bob Shawkey	NY	8	2	.800	3000	9	40
1917	Dave Danforth	Chi	9	3	.750	1308	7	36
1918	George Mogridge	NY	6	7	.462	−377	5	16
1921	Jim Middleton	Det	4	8	.333	−1704	7	8
1922	Hub Pruett	StL	4	4	.500	−800	7	14
1923	Allan Russell	Was	9	7	.563	1296	9	33
1924	Hooks Dauss	Det	8	5	.615	806	6	29
1925	Elam Vangilder	StL	11	4	.733	3285	6	45
1926	Fred Marberry	Was	9	5	.643	1596	22	50
1927	Wilcy Moore	NY	13	3	.813	1760	13	55
1928	Fred Marberry	Was	7	9	.438	−880	3	14
1929	Bill Shores	Phi	6	2	.750	480	7	25

Year	Reliever	Club	W	L	Pct.	WR	Sv	Pts.
1930	Jack Quinn	Phi	8	3	.727	770	6	31
1931	Wilcy Moore	Bos	7	2	.778	3537	10	40
1932	Elon Hogsett	Det	6	3	.667	1566	7	27
1933	Jack Russell	Was	11	4	.733	1365	13	48
1934	Jack Russell	Was	2	7	.222	−2034	7	1
1935	Jack Knott	StL	5	4	.556	1224	7	37
1936	Pat Malone	NY	8	2.	.800	1430	9	36
1937	Johnny Murphy	NY	8	4	.667	1568	10	47
1938	Johnny Murphy	NY	8	1	.889	2277	11	41
1939	Joe Heving	Bos	11	2	.846	3653	7	49
1940	Johnny Murphy	NY	8	4	.667	1104	9	34
1941	Johnny Murphy	NY	8	3	.727	847	15	40
1942	Mace Brown	Bos	9	3	.750	1800	6	36
1943	Johnny Murphy	NY	12	4	.750	2032	8	46
1944	Gordon Maltzberger	Chi	10	5	.667	3420	12	47
1945	Joe Berry	Phi	8	7	.533	3105	5	32
1946	Earl Caldwell	Chi	13	4	.765	5440	8	56
1947	Joe Page	NY	14	7	.667	903	17	50
1948	Earl Johnson	Bos	9	2	.818	2354	5	38
1949	Joe Page	NY	13	8	.619	−273	27	54
1950	Tom Ferrick	NY	9	7	.563	−1312	11	28
1951	Ellis Kinder	Bos	10	1	.900	4081	14	55
1952	Harry Dorish	Chi	7	4	.636	1309	11	33
1953	Ellis Kinder	Bos	10	6	.625	1360	27	55
1954	Hal Newhouser	Cle	7	1	.875	1304	7	32
1955	Ray Narleski	Cle	8	1	.869	2727	19	51
1956	Ike Delock	Bos	11	2	.846	4264	9	53
1957	Bob Grim	NY	12	8	.600	−840	19	42
1958	Dick Hyde	Was	10	3	.769	6240	18	65
1959	Turk Lown	Chi	9	2	.818	2453	15	48
1960	Mike Fornieles	Bos	10	5	.667	4065	14	51
1961	Luis Arroyo	NY	15	5	.750	1760	29	70
1962	Dick Radatz	Bos	9	6	.600	2070	24	52
1963	Dick Radatz	Bos	15	6	.714	5838	25	75
1964	Dick Radatz	Bos	16	9	.640	5775	29	73
1965	Eddie Fisher	Chi	15	7	.682	2442	24	63
1966	Jack Aker	KC	8	4	.667	2652	32	60
1967	Minnie Rojas	Cal	12	9	.571	1197	27	54
1968	Wilbur Wood	Chi	12	11	.522	2898	16	43
1969	Ken Tatum	Cal	7	2	.778	3240	22	51
1970	Lindy McDaniel	NY	9	5	.643	1050	29	56
1971	Fred Scherman	Det	10	6	.625	1120	20	48
1972	Sparky Lyle	NY	9	5	.643	2058	35	64
1973	John Hiller	Det	10	5	.667	2355	38	71
1974	John Hiller	Det	17	14	.548	3968	13	48
1975	Rollie Fingers	Oak	10	6	.625	352	24	50
1976	Bill Campbell	Min	17	5	.773	6314	20	76
1977	Sparky Lyle	NY	13	5	.722	2124	26	64
1978	Bob Stanley	Bos	12	2	.857	3836	10	56
1979	Jim Kern	Tx	13	5	.722	4248	29	72

Year	Reliever	Club	W	L	Pct.	WR	Sv	Pts.
1980	Aurelio Lopez	Det	13	5	.722	4122	21	64
1981	Rollie Fingers	Mil	6	3	.667	1422	28	48
1982	Dan Quisenberry	KC	9	7	.563	144	35	56
1983	Rich "Goose" Gossage	NY	13	5	.722	3240	22	63
1984	Dan Quisenberry	KC	6	3	.667	1413	44	64
1985	Dave Righetti	NY	12	7	.632	627	29	58
1986	Dave Righetti	NY	8	8	.500	−992	46	60
1987	Dave Righetti	NY	8	6	.571	336	31	52
1988	Dennis Eckersley	Oak	4	2	.667	146	45	57
1989	Jeff Russell	Tx	6	4	.600	930	38	56
1990	Dennis Eckersley	Oak	4	2	.667	192	48	60
1991	Mike Henneman	Det	10	2	.833	4404	21	62
1992	Dennis Eckersley	Oak	7	1	.875	2376	51	79
1993	Jeff Montgomery	KC	7	5	.583	840	45	65
1994	Joe Boever	Det	9	2	.818	4345	3	41
1995	Jose Mesa	Cle	3	0	1.000	936	40	58
1996	Roberto Hernandez	Chi	6	5	.545	242	38	53
1997	Roberto Hernandez	Ch-SF	10	3	.770	3262	31	69
1998	Tom Gordon	Bos	7	4	.637	704	46	66
1999	Mariano Rivera	NY	4	3	.571	−245	45	58
2000	Billy Koch	Tor	9	3	.750	3084	33	66
2001	Troy Percival	Ana	4	2	.667	1272	39	53
2002	Billy Koch	Oak	11	4	.733	1605	44	79
2003	Keith Foulke	Oak	9	1	.900	3280	43	79
2004	Mariano Rivera	NY	4	2	.667	276	53	65
2005	Joe Nathan	Min.	7	4	.636	2152	43	65
2006	Joe Nathan	Min	7	0	1.000	2982	36	66

Other Leagues. There were no relief pitchers with eligible seasons in the American Association, the Players' League, or the Federal league.

Career Rankings of Closers

Extended Careers. Based on an extended career of 13 eligible seasons, Trevor Hoffman is baseball's all-time best closer. The lead has changed several times in the last few decades, passing from Hoyt Wilhelm to Rollie Fingers to Lee Smith before Hoffman took over the top spot during the 2006 season. Among the leaders Wilhelm has the most relief wins, Goose Gossage the highest weighted rating, and Hoffman the most saves.

LEADING EXTENDED CAREER CLOSERS

Reliever	Eligible Seasons		W	L	Pct.	WR	Sv	Pts.
1. Trevor Hoffman	1993–2006	13	49	55	.471	−564	473	589
2. Lee Smith	1982–95	14	63	77	.450	−7616	470	554
3. Rollie Fingers	1968–85	15	104	100	.510	−2628	339	543
4. Mariano Rivera	1996–2006	11	54	37	.593	−364	423	533
5. John Franco	1986–99	14	59	65	.476	−3152	400	518
6. Goose Gossage	1975–88	13	90	69	.566	5392	298	517
7. Jeff Reardon	1980–93	14	71	75	.486	−2087	363	507
8. Dennis Eckersley	1987–97	11	42	40	.525	−1777	386	476

Reliever	Eligible Seasons		W	L	Pct.	WR	Sv	Pts.
9. Hoyt Wilhelm	1952–70	15	113	92	.551	106	212	473
10. Sparky Lyle	1968–81	14	95	71	.572	4448	230	470

Points Per Season. The leading closer in points per year is Danny Graves. The first major leaguer to be born in Vietnam, Graves was a top closer for the Cincinnati Reds for four years, until the Reds tried to convert him to a starter. After one undistinguished season in that role, Graves returned to the bullpen, but never regained his former effectiveness. In second place is Dick Radatz, who like Graves had a short major league career. During each of his first three seasons with the Boston Red Sox, "The Monster," as he was called, was the best reliever in the American League. Among the leading closers, Radatz has the most relief wins per year and the highest weighted rating. Mariano Rivera of the New York Yankees has the most saves per season. Of the ten leaders in points per year, only Radatz and Al Hrabosky, "The Mad Hungarian," had eligible seasons before 1980.

LEADING CLOSERS—POINTS PER YEAR

Reliever	Eligible Seasons		W	L	Pct.	WR	Sv	Pts.
1. Danny Graves	1999–2004	5	6	5	.552	767	32	49.2
2. Dick Radatz	1962–66	5	10	7	.570	2559	23	48.8
3. Mariano Rivera	1996–2006	11	5	3	.593	−33	38	48.5
4. John Wetteland	1992–99	8	4	4	.548	178	37	47.3
5. Trevor Hoffman	1993–2006	13	4	4	.471	−43	36	45.3
6. Robb Nen	1994–2002	9	5	5	.512	−263	35	45.1
7. Dan Quisenberry	1980–86	7	6	6	.550	−215	32	44.9
8. Billy Koch	1999–2003	5	5	4	.551	−99	31	43.6
9. Dennis Eckersley	1987–97	11	4	4	.525	−162	35	43.3
10. Al Hrabosky	1974–79	6	9	4	.667	2134	14	43.0

Career (Best 10 Years). Trevor Hoffman and Mariano Rivera are tied for the best ten year career among closers. Although ranked in a slightly different order, the top ten in career rankings are almost the same as the ten leaders in the extended careers list. The only exception is Bruce Sutter replacing Hoyt Wilhelm. Wilhelm has the most relief wins, Lindy McDaniel the best weighted rating, and Hoffman the most saves. The highest ranking reliever to have pitched before World War II is Johnny Murphy in 61st place. Of the 137 eligible closers, not one pitched in the major leagues before 1920.

LEADING CLOSERS—BEST TEN YEARS

Reliever	Best Ten Years		W	L	Pct.	WR	Sv	Pts.
1. Trevor Hoffman	1993–2006	10	40	39	.506	−520	414	512
1. Mariano Rivera	1996–2006	10	53	33	.616	2081	387	512 tie
3. Lee Smith	1982–93	10	56	57	.496	−1149	354	475
4. Dennis Eckersley	1987–97	10	42	39	.513	1607	356	461
5. Goose Gossage	1975–86	10	78	79	.569	3453	254	439
6. John Franco	1986–97	10	54	48	.529	2896	303	437
7. Rollie Fingers	1972–82	10	89	73	.549	4581	233	434
8. Bruce Sutter	1976–88	10	65	67	.492	644	283	420
9. Jeff Reardon	1982–92	10	54	54	.500	−1593	300	417
10. Sparky Lyle	1968–81	10	81	47	.633	10366	181	414
11. Lindy McDaniel	1959–73	10	89	46	.659	16064	147	408

Trevor Hoffman is baseball's number one closer. He leads in extended career rankings and is tied with Mariano Rivera for the best ten-year career. In 2007 he became the first reliever to attain 500 saves (National Baseball Hall of Fame Library, Cooperstown, New York).

Reliever	Best Ten Years		W	L	Pct.	WR	Sv	Pts.
12. Robb Nen	1994–2002	9	43	41	.512	−2364	314	406
13. Roberto Hernandez	1992–2002	10	45	48	.484	−29	306	398
14. Rick Aguilera	1990–2000	10	38	43	.469	−2756	311	395
15. Hoyt Wilhelm	1952–70	10	91	57	.620	7526	212	388
16. Billy Wagner	1997–2006	9	33	28	.541	−1026	309	383

Reliever	Best Ten Years		W	L	Pct.	WR	Sv	Pts.
17. Randy Myers	1987–98	10	35	44	.444	−8390	341	382
18. John Wetteland	1992–99	8	34	28	.548	1425	295	378
19. Jose Mesa	1994–2004	10	44	47	.484	−4367	291	375
20. Armando Benitez	1997–2006	10	36	33	.522	−297	274	371
21. Tom Henke	1985–95	10	38	35	.521	871	274	362
22. Tug McGraw	1969–80	10	72	46	.610	6785	151	364
23. Troy Percival	1996–2002	9	26	36	.419	−5153	328	361
24. Mike Henneman	1987–96	10	57	42	.576	7882	201	357
25. Jeff Montgomery	1989–98	10	36	44	.450	−3000	291	352
26. Elroy Face	1956–68	10	77	63	.550	5304	163	341
27. Clay Carroll	1966–77	10	79	53	.598	3234	135	334
28. Ron Perranoski	1961–71	10	76	66	.535	−5135	172	329
28. Dave Righetti	1984–91	8	43	45	.486	−4616	247	329 tie
30. Doug Jones	1987–99	10	53	63	.457	−2560	268	321
31. Gene Garber	1973–87	10	72	77	.483	−3932	184	317
32. Gary Lavelle	1975–85	10	76	65	.539	3574	131	315
33. Dan Quisenberry	1980–86	7	44	40	.550	−1502	224	314
34. Mike Marshall	1971–79	8	83	83	.500	−87	173	310
35. Todd Jones	1995–2006	10	37	42	.468	−3884	258	306
36. Todd Worrell	1986–97	8	41	48	.461	−6045	243	305
37. Bob Wickman	1994–2006	9	24	41	.369	−9172	241	303
38. Dave Smith	1980–91	10	45	48	.484	−3496	205	301
39. Bob Stanley	1978–88	9	74	53	.583	7325	124	299
40. Don McMahon	1958–71	10	66	47	.584	8113	112	294
40. Steve Bedrosian	1982–90	8	53	50	.515	−23	178	294 tie
42. Stu Miller	1959–67	8	64	53	.566	−1931	144	283
43. Willie Hernandez	1977–89	9	57	47	.548	1685	142	280
43. Rod Beck	1992–99	8	25	36	.410	−5711	255	280 tie
45. Dave Giusti	1970–77	8	49	33	.598	4346	140	275
46. Roger McDowell	1985–95	9	64	62	.508	−4433	151	274
47. Ted Abernathy	1963–71	8	48	40	.545	7383	140	272
48. Jason Isringhausen	2000–06	6	22	22	.500	−4412	240	272
49. Mitch Williams	1986–94	9	44	53	.454	−4424	192	271
50. Ugueth Urbina	1997–2004	7	27	35	.435	−560	227	267
51. Gregg Olson	1989–99	7	27	28	.491	118	204	261
52. Al Hrbosky	1974–70	6	52	26	.667	12801	85	258
52. Keith Foulke	1999–2005	7	31	26	.544	−696	186	258 tie
54. Mark Clear	1979–87	7	65	40	.619	11848	76	255
55. John Hiller	1973–79	7	58	50	.537	9528	109	254
55. Jay Howell	1984–91	8	44	38	.537	1679	149	254 tie
57. Roger McDowell	1985–92	8	57	58	.496	−5885	147	248
57. Jeff Montgomery	1989–94	6	27	26	.509	448	186	248 tie
59. Danny Graves	1999–2004	5	32	26	.552	3833	162	246
60. Dick Radatz	1962–66	5	49	37	.570	12796	114	244
61. Johnny Murphy	1935–43	8	61	36	.629	−1564	88	240
62. Tim Burke	1985–91	7	45	29	.608	8439	102	236
63. Phil Regan	1966–71	6	52	33	.612	7798	87	234
63. Bobby Thigpen	1987–92	6	26	33	.441	3698	193	234 tie
65. Bill Campbell	1974–83	7	57	44	.564	3879	99	232
66. Bob Locker	1966–73	7	49	32	.605	8599	86	231

Reliever	Best Ten Years		W	L	Pct.	WR	Sv	Pts.
67. Kent Tekulve	1878–84	7	52	59	.468	−6447	148	228
68. Ron Reed	1976–84	9	54	43	.557	−267	102	226
69. Turk Farrell	1957–68	6	50	35	.588	11251	66	224
69. Darold Knowles	1966–76	9	50	56	.472	−2530	123	224 tie
71. Tippy Martinez	1976–84	8	48	32	.600	891	98	223
72. Pedro Borbon	1972–79	6	54	29	.651	5775	67	222
72. Ron Davis	1979–85	7	44	44	.500	−282	128	222 tie
74. Greg Minton	1980–89	8	42	47	.483	−1453	137	221
75. Jim Brewer	1968–73	6	42	35	.545	300	117	220
76. Billy Koch	1999–2003	5	27	22	.551	−495	155	218
77. Elias Sosa	1973–80	6	50	33	.602	8093	69	216
78. Jesse Orosco	1982–93	7	49	47	.510	−960	114	215
79. Aurelia Lopez	1979–85	5	45	27	.625	6472	99	212
80. Jeff Russell	1989–95	7	20	26	.435	−3652	178	209
81. Ellis Kinder	1950–56	6	40	25	.615	5774	72	208
82. Al Worthington	1957–68	7	45	39	.536	−114	99	205
83. Clem Labine	1953–59	7	50	39	.562	−2912	82	204
84. Jack Aker	1966–73	7	37	35	.514	2320	114	204
85. Fred Marberry	1924–32	7	42	32	.568	3214	88	203
86. Jeff Shaw	1996–2001	5	21	25	.457	−2160	164	203
87. Ron Kline	1963–68	5	38	30	.559	189	90	202
88. Dick Hall	1963–70	6	50	26	.658	6088	59	195
89. Frank Linzy	1965–73	7	50	46	.521	−3920	102	195
90. Bryan Harvey	1988–93	6	17	25	.405	−3024	171	193
91. John Wyatt	1962–67	6	37	36	.507	4964	100	190
92. Dave LaRoche	1971–79	7	40	32	.556	−1887	109	187
93. Jeff Brantley	1990–96	6	24	18	.571	568	128	184
94. Jim Kern	1976–82	6	47	48	.495	3740	72	183
95. Joe Heving	1930–44	5	42	17	.712	10873	31	176
95. Joe Hoerner	1966–71	6	30	20	.600	5596	78	176 tie
97. Tom Burgmeier	1971–83	7	41	37	.526	1730	78	176 tie
98. Steve Farr	1986–1993	7	30	28	.517	226	125	173
99. Larry Sherry	1960–66	5	39	24	.619	4684	64	172
100. Randy Moffitt	1973–83	7	43	37	.538	239	87	171
101. Grant Jackson	1973–80	5	37	18	.673	6610	49	167
102. Ed Roebuck	1955–64	5	36	15	.706	6648	49	166
103. Fred Gladding	1964–72	6	33	31	.516	−663	92	163
104. Tom Niedenfuer	1982–88	7	33	36	.478	−1471	93	161
105. Ron Taylor	1963–70	6	34	23	.586	3687	65	160
106. Terry Forster	1972–83	5	24	22	.522	−560	104	159
107. Antonio Alfonseca	1998–2002	5	19	26	.422	85	121	159
108. Craig Lefferts	1984–91	8	37	46	.446	−4717	99	158
109. Doug Bair	1977–83	6	37	32	.536	519	71	157
110. Mike Williams	1999–2003	5	15	27	.357	−4146	143	155
111. Mel Rojas	1992–96	5	23	19	.548	−607	102	154
112. Rob Dibble	1989–93	5	25	22	.532	1819	88	152
112. Stan Belinda	1990–95	5	28	16	.636	2525	71	152 tie
114. Tom Morgan	1954–62	5	32	16	.667	6720	47	150
115. Wilcy Moore	1927–33	5	36	23	.610	3718	47	149
116. Neil Allen	1979–84	5	32	34	.485	6665	70	148

Reliever	Best Ten Years		W	L	Pct.	WR	Sv	Pts.
117. Paul Lindblad	1969–76	5	36	24	.600	7166	38	147
117. Enrique Romo	1977–81	5	35	29	.547	6760	51	147 tie
119. Dale Murray	1975–82	5	41	40	.506	3651	45	146
120. Chuck Crim	1987–94	6	37	31	.544	3044	44	144
121. Turk Lown	1956–61	5	33	27	.550	2820	59	142
122. Dick Tidrow	1976–82	6	39	33	.542	4253	42	140
123. Sammy Stewart	1980–85	6	38	28	.576	453	41	135
124. Joe Sambito	1977–81	5	30	29	.508	−1711	67	132
124. Tom Hume	1979–83	5	28	30	.483	−2836	81	132 tie
126. Pete Mikkelsen	1964–72	5	36	27	.571	768	40	129
127. Don Elston	1958–62	5	37	40	.481	4544	50	126
128. Tim Stoddard	1980–87	5	26	19	.578	−614	62	125
129. Steve Howe	1980–94	5	26	24	.520	−2435	71	123
130. Bill Henry	1958–63	6	22	23	.489	−225	76	121
131. Ken Sanders	1966–73	5	27	38	.415	−1679	77	117
132. Jose Jimenez	2000–04	5	16	30	.348	−6038	110	116
133. Norm Charlton	1992–97	5	14	31	.312	−5248	92	112
134. Alejandro Pena	1987–94	5	20	18	.526	−286	60	107
135. Eddie Watt	1967–71	5	23	20	.535	−3347	58	106
136. Greg Harris	1989–94	5	28	32	.467	−877	45	88
137. Ryne Duren	1958–62	5	18	31	.367	−8723	53	57

6

MIDDLE RELIEVERS

The middle reliever is a fairly new phenomenon in the history of baseball. As noted above the specialization of relief pitcher began to emerge in the 1920s. For two or three decades there were two kinds of pitchers—starters and relievers. Eventually, the category of reliever subdivided into various subspecializations. The glamour reliever is now called the closer. The top closer is no longer a fireman who comes in to quench the rally when the previous pitcher is faltering. Now the closer comes into the game almost solely in a "save situation," that is when the team has a slight lead in the ninth inning. (Sometimes, but not frequently, he may enter the game in the eighth inning or when the score is tied, but almost never when his team is behind.) Naturally, the closers get the lion's share of the saves. The winner of the relief man of the year award is invariably a closer.

In addition to the closer the other subspecialties include long relief, middle relief, set-up man, and short relief in a non-save situation. Now we even have seventh and eighth inning specialists and pitchers whose only job is to retire a lefthanded batter in the eighth inning. As the nomenclature implies, the long reliever enters the game in the early innings, and the middle reliever comes in during the middle of the game. The set-up man comes in late in the game to hold the opposition until the closer is ready to do his thing. Long and middle relievers occasionally pick up a win or a loss, but a save is almost out of the question for them. Set-up men and other short relievers seldom get a decision unless there is a lead change. They can get a loss if they blow a lead or a win if their team comes from behind, but they seldom get a save, because if a save opportunity arises in the ninth inning out they go and in comes the closer.

Some relievers, like Lee Smith, have spent almost their entire careers as closers. Others, such as Kent Tekulve, have divided their time between closing and middle relief. (From this point on the term middle relief will be used to include all types of relief except closing.) Several middle relievers have been starters at some point in their careers. Some relievers have enjoyed a long and distinguished career coming out of the bullpen in non-save situations. One of the best of these was the unheralded Steve Reed, who never started a game in the big leagues, appeared in relief 833 times, and claimed a total of only 18 saves in 14 years.

Obviously, different eligibility criteria are needed for middle relievers. Number of appearances rather than number of decisions and saves per season seems more appropriate for this category of relief pitchers. Therefore, a minimum of 50 appearances in relief has been selected as the main criterion. Additionally, it is stipulated that in order to be classified as a middle reliever the pitcher must have fewer than 15 saves in a season and cannot lead his team in saves if he finishes more than half of the games in which he appeared.

Some baseball statisticians have started awarding a "hold" to relievers who enter the game in a save situation and do not relinquish the lead. However, a hold may be awarded to a pitcher who faces only one batter, which seems overly generous, especially since "blown holds" are not recorded. The number of wins, losses, and saves is not appropriate for rating middle relievers, nor is the winning percentage or weighted rating. Since the task of the middle relievers is to prevent the opposition from scoring, the earned run average is as useful a yardstick as is available for judging how well middle relievers do their jobs. As the difficulty of achieving a low ERA varies significantly over time, we calculate the ratings by subtracting the league ERA from each hurler's individual ERA.

Leading Middle Relievers by Year

National League. The first year that a National League middle reliever met our eligibility criteria was 1951. Since then someone has been eligible in every season except 1956 through 1958. Lindy McDaniel, Ramon Hernandez, and Al Holland have each led the league twice. In 1951 Hoyt Wilhelm recorded an ERA of 2.10 compared to the league mean of 4.07. The difference of 1.91 was the best mark attained in the National League for nearly 40 years. Eliminating the decimal point, we award him 191 points for the season. In 1989 Larry Andersen posted a record of 196 points. The very next year Rob Dibble came in with 205. Two years later Mel Rojas recorded 207, and two years after that Mike Jackson set a new mark at 272. Jackson's record stood until 2002, when Chris Hammond set the present standard at 316, with an amazing 0.95 ERA in a year when the league mean was 4.11.

LEADING MIDDLE RELIEVER BY YEAR—NATIONAL LEAGUE

Year	Pitcher	G	W	L	Sv	ERA	Mean	Points
1951	Bill Werle	50	4	2	6	5.65	3.96	−169
1952	Eddie Yuhas	52	11	1	6	2.72	3.73	101
1953	Hal White	59	6	5	7	2.94	4.29	135
1954	Hoyt Wilhelm	57	12	4	7	2.10	4.07	193
1955	Clem Labine	52	10	2	11	3.24	4.04	80
1956	none							
1957	none							
1958	none							
1959	Bill Henry	65	9	8	12	2.68	3.95	127
1960	Jim Brosnan	55	7	2	12	2.36	3.76	140
1961	Ron Perranoski	52	7	5	6	2.65	4.03	138
1962	Diomedes Olivo	61	5	1	7	2.77	3.94	117
1963	Tommie Sisk	53	1	1	1	2.92	3.29	37
1964	Ed Roebuck	62	5	3	12	2.30	3.54	124
1965	Lindy McDaniel	71	5	6	2	2.59	3.54	95
1966	Lindy McDaniel	64	10	5	6	2.66	3.61	95
1967	Ron Willis	65	4	6	8	2.34	3.38	104
1968	Ron Kline	56	12	5	7	1.68	2.99	131
1969	Ted Abernathy	56	4	3	3	3.18	3.60	42
1970	Howie Reed	56	6	4	5	3.13	4.05	92
1971	Bob Miller	56	8	5	10	1.64	3.47	183
1972	Ramon Hernandez	53	5	0	14	1.67	3.46	179
1973	Ramon Hernandez	59	4	5	11	2.41	3.67	126
1974	Clay Carroll	54	10	4	6	2.14	3.62	148
1975	Mike Garman	66	3	8	10	2.39	3.63	124

Year	Pitcher	G	W	L	Sv	ERA	Mean	Points
1976	Kent Tekulve	64	5	3	9	2.41	3.67	126
1977	Dave Heaverlo	56	5	1	1	2.55	3.91	136
1978	Darold Knowles	60	3	3	6	2.38	3.58	120
1979	Grant Jackson	72	8	5	14	2.96	3.73	77
1980	Al Holland	54	5	3	7	1.76	3.60	184
1981	Al Holland	44	6	5	7	2.41	3.49	108
1982	Rod Scurry	76	4	5	14	1.74	3.60	186
1983	Tom Niedenfuer	66	8	3	11	1.90	3.63	173
1984	Bill Dawley	60	11	4	5	1.93	3.59	166
1985	Don Carman	71	9	4	7	2.08	3.59	151
1986	Paul Assenmacher	61	7	3	7	2.50	3.72	122
1987	Frank Williams	85	4	0	2	2.30	4.08	178
1988	Alejandro Pena	53	6	7	12	1.91	3.45	154
1989	Larry Andersen	60	4	4	3	1.54	3.50	196
1990	Rob Dibble	68	8	3	11	1.74	3.79	205
1991	Chuck McElroy	71	6	2	3	1.95	3.68	173
1992	Mel Rojas	68	7	1	10	1.43	3.50	207
1993	Roger McDowell	54	5	3	2	2.25	4.04	179
1994	Mike Jackson	36	3	2	4	1.49	4.21	272
1995	Tony Fossas	58	3	0	0	1.47	4.18	271
1996	Scott Radinsky	58	5	1	1	2.41	4.52	211
1997	Tom Martin	55	5	3	2	2.09	4.20	211
1998	Dennis Cook	58	8	4	1	2.38	4.23	185
1999	Scott Sauerbeck	65	4	1	2	2.00	4.57	257
2000	Mike Myers	78	0	1	1	1.99	4.63	264
2001	Felix Rodriguez	80	9	1	0	1.68	4.36	268
2002	Chris Hammond	63	7	2	0	0.95	4.11	316
2003	Rheal Cormier	65	8	0	1	1.70	4.27	257
2004	Akinori Otsuka	73	7	2	2	1.75	4.30	255
2005	Hector Carrasco	61	5	4	2	2.04	4.22	218
2006	Pedro Feliciano	64	7	2	0	2.09	4.48	239

American League. The first eligible season in the junior circuit was claimed by Marlin Stuart in 1953. Only twice since then — in 1954 and 1960 — has the league failed to provide at least one eligible middle reliever. Darold Knowles, Ron Davis, and Paul Quantrill have each led the league twice, but Mark Eichhorn went them one better by having three league-leading seasons. The best early mark was attained by Tom Morgan in 1961 with 166 points. In 1972 Knowles exceeded that with a 210 mark. That record stood for over a decade until Eichhorn achieved 246 points in 1986. In 1995 Troy Percival set a new record with a 276, and Mariano Rivera surpassed him the very next year with 294 points. In 2006 Dennys Reyes of the Minnesota Twins established a new record with an astonishing ERA of 0.89 against a league mean of 4.48 for 359 points.

LEADING MIDDLE RELIEVER BY YEAR — AMERICAN LEAGUE

Year	Middle Reliever	W	L	Sv		ERA	Mean	Points
1953	Marlin Stuart	58	8	1	7	3.94	4.00	6
1954	none							
1955	Don Mossi	56	4	3	9	2.42	3.96	154
1956	Ellis Kinder	51	5	1	9	3.09	4.16	107

Year	Middle Reliever	W	L	Sv		ERA	Mean	Points
1957	Dick Hyde	50	4	3	1	4.12	3.79	−33
1958	Murray Wall	51	8	8	10	3.62	3.77	15
1959	Gerry Staley	67	8	5	14	2.24	3.86	162
1960	none							
1961	Tom Morgan	59	8	2	10	2.36	4.02	166
1962	Jack Spring	57	4	2	6	4.02	3.97	−5
1963	Art Fowler	57	5	3	10	2.42	3.63	121
1964	Wes Stock	64	8	3	5	2.30	3.63	133
1965	Johnny Klippstein	56	9	3	5	2.24	3.46	122
1966	Bob Humphreys	57	6	8	3	2.82	3.44	62
1967	Dave Baldwin	58	2	4	12	1.70	3.23	153
1968	Bob Locker	70	5	4	10	2.29	2.98	69
1969	Hoyt Wilhelm	52	7	7	14	2.20	3.63	143
1970	Paul Lindblad	62	8	2	3	2.71	3.72	101
1971	Dave LaRoche	56	5	1	9	2.50	3.47	97
1972	Darold Knowles	54	1	11	.833	1.36	3.46	210
1973	none							
1974	Bob Reynolds	54	7	5	7	2.74	3.62	88
1975	Jim Todd	58	8	3	12	2.29	3.79	150
1976	Steve Mingori	55	5	5	10	2.33	3.52	119
1977	Bob McClure	68	2	1	6	2.54	4.07	153
1978	Bob Lacey	74	8	9	5	3.01	3.77	76
1979	Sparky Lyle	67	5	8	13	3.13	4.22	109
1980	Ron Davis	53	9	3	7	2.95	4.03	108
1981	Ron Davis	43	4	5	6	2.71	3.66	95
1982	Ed VandeBerg	78	9	4	5	2.37	4.07	170
1983	Salome Barojas	52	3	3	12	2.47	4.06	159
1984	Jay Howell	60	8	4	7	2.69	3.99	130
1985	Gary Lavelle	69	5	7	8	3.10	4.15	105
1986	Mark Eichhorn	69	14	6	10	1.72	4.18	246
1987	Mike Henneman	55	11	3	7	2.98	4.46	148
1988	Mike Jackson	62	6	5	4	2.63	3.97	134
1989	Jesse Orosco	69	3	4	3	2.08	3.88	180
1990	Gene Nelson	51	3	3	5	1.57	3.91	234
1991	Mark Eichhorn	70	3	3	1	1.98	4.09	211
1992	Derek Lilliquist	71	5	3	6	1.75	3.94	219
1993	Jim Poole	55	2	1	2	2.15	4.32	217
1994	Mark Eichhorn	43	6	5	1	2.15	4.58	243
1995	Troy Percival	62	3	2	3	1.95	4.71	276
1996	Mariano Rivera	61	8	3	5	2.09	5.03	294
1997	Paul Quantrill	77	6	7	5	1.94	4.58	264
1998	Graeme Lloyd	50	0	0	0	1.67	4.65	298
1999	Keith Foulke	67	3	3	9	2.22	4.86	264
2000	Jeff Nelson	73	8	4	0	2.45	4.91	246
2001	Arthur Rhodes	71	8	0	3	1.72	4.45	273
2002	Buddy Groom	70	3	2	2	1.60	4.46	286
2003	Brendan Donnelly	63	2	2	3	1.58	4.52	294
2004	Francisco Rodriguez	69	4	1	12	1.82	4.63	281
2005	Cliff Politte	68	7	1	1	2.00	4.36	236
2006	Dennys Reyes	66	5	0	0	0.89	4.48	359

Leading Middle Relievers by Career

Middle Relievers — Extended Career. In computing career rankings 50 points are added to each a middle reliever's total for each eligible season completed. Only five pitchers have more than ten eligible seasons as middle relievers. Mike Stanton heads the list with 15 years, followed by Jesse Orosco with 14. Steve Reed, Mike Myers, and Dan Plesac have 11 seasons each. Stanton and Orosco also rank one-two in Faber System points. Mark Eichhorn ranks third with only seven eligible seasons. He is followed by Reed, Mike Timlin, Steve Kline, Paul Quantrill, Jeff Nelson, Mike Jackson, and Graeme Lloyd. All hurlers in the top ten started their career as middle relievers after 1985, and all but Eichhorn were still active after the year 2000.

Mark Eichhorn has the most points per season of any middle reliever. Pitching mainly for the Toronto Blue Jays and the California Angels, Eichhorn helped win recognition for his specialty (National Baseball Hall of Fame Library, Cooperstown, New York).

LEADING MIDDLE RELIEVERS — ALL ELIGIBLE SEASONS

Middle Reliever	Eligible Seasons		G	W	L	Sv	ERA	Points
1. Mike Stanton	1991–2006	15	1019	61	49	47	3.76	1666
2. Jesse Orosco	1988–2003	14	846	38	37	35	3.28	1540
3. Mark Eichhorn	1986–94	7	450	42	30	31	2.56	1496
4. Jeff Nelson	1993–2001	8	561	36	33	25	3.29	1433
5. Steve Reed	1993–2004	10	715	35	34	13	3.48	1423
6. Steve Kline	1998–2006	8	599	28	28	20	3.15	1343
7. Paul Quantrill	1997–2005	8	618	38	32	18	3.11	1330
8. Mike Jackson	1988–2002	10	644	51	47	47	3.26	1301
9. Graeme Lloyd	1993–2003	7	446	28	27	9	3.43	1235
10. Mike Timlin	1991–2006	9	613	52	39	39	3.60	1227

Middle Relievers — Points Per Season. In points per season Mark Eichhorn is the best of all middle relievers. Arthur Rhodes is second He is followed by the sensational young K-Rod, Francisco Rodriguez, who had his first eligible season at the age of 21. In fourth place is Kent Mercker, who is followed in turn by Mike Remlinger, Jeff Nelson, Graeme Lloyd, Steve Kline, Paul Quantrill, and Jim Mecir. All of the leaders in points per season have from five to eight years as middle relievers. All of the top ten started their middle relief careers since 1985. All except Eichhorn have continued into the 21st century.

LEADING MIDDLE RELIEVERS — POINTS PER SEASON

Middle Reliever	Eligible Seasons		G	W	L	Sv	ERA	Points
1. Mark Eichhorn	1986–94	7	64	4	4	4	2.56	213.7
2. Arthur Rhodes	1997–2003	5	62	7	4	2	3.10	198.0

Middle Reliever	Eligible Seasons		G	W	L	Sv	ERA	Points
3. Felix Rodriguez	2000–04	5	74	4	1	1	2.98	185.8
4. Kent Mercker	1991–2005	6	65	2	1	1	2.78	181.8
5. Mike Remlinger	1997–2003	6	70	4	3	3	3.06	179.3
6. Jeff Nelson	1992–2003	7	70	5	4	3	3.27	179.1
7. Graeme Lloyd	1993–2003	7	64	4	4	1	3.43	176.4
8. Steve Kline	1998–2006	8	74	4	3	3	3.15	167.9
9. Paul Quantrill	1997–2005	8	77	4	2	2	3.11	166.3
10. Jim Mecir	1998–2005	6	61	4	2	2	3.41	164.3

Middle Relievers Best Years. When ranked by performance over his best ten years, Jesse Orosco is baseball's best middle reliever. All of the ten leaders in extended career rankings are also among the top ten in rankings based on their best years, albeit in a slightly different order. This phenomenon does not occur in the rankings of any other position in baseball. Mike Stanton is second, Mark Eichhorn is third, Jeff Nelson fourth, and Steve Reed is fifth. Sixth place goes to Steve Kline, followed by Paul Quantrill, Mike Jackson, Graeme Lloyd, and Mike Timlin, familiar names all. All of the top ten started their careers in the 1980 or 1990s, and all but Eichhorn continued into the 21st century. The highest ranking middle reliever who started before 1980 is Hoyt Wilhelm in 29th place. His first eligible year at the position was 1952. Somewhat surprisingly, eight of the top ten played the majority of their major league careers in the American League. Only Steve Kline and Steve Reed played mostly in the senior circuit. A total of 91 middle relievers have had five or more eligible years at the position. Eighty-one of them have earned runs averages better than the league average, which speaks to the quality of the middle relievers and perhaps to the way in which they are now used.

LEADING MIDDLE RELIEVERS—BEST YEARS

Middle Reliever	Best Years		G	W	L	Sv	ERA	Points
1. Jesse Orosco	1988–2003	10	619	34	31	31	3.30	1863
2. Mike Stanton	1991–2006	10	730	47	34	28	3.38	1614
3. Mark Eichhorn	1986–94	7	450	42	30	31	2.56	1496
4. Jeff Nelson	1992–2001	8	561	36	33	25	3.29	1433
5. Steve Reed	1993–2004	10	651	35	34	13	3.48	1417
6. Steve Kline	1998–2006	8	599	28	28	20	3.15	1343
7. Paul Quantrill	1997–2005	8	618	38	32	18	3.11	1330
8. Mike Jackson	1988–2002	10	644	43	43	45	3.35	1301
9. Graeme Lloyd	1993–2003	7	446	28	27	9	3.43	1235
10. Mike Timlin	1991–2006	9	613	52	39	39	3.60	1227
11. Dan Plesac	1986–2003	10	633	42	37	36	4.04	1176
12. Larry Andersen	1984–93	8	475	31	31	32	2.75	1171
13. Mike Remlinger	1997–2003	6	421	34	23	16	3.06	1076
14. Paul Assenmacher	1986–98	10	632	37	30	36	3.45	1054
15. David Weathers	1999–2006	7	493	32	34	26	3.40	1042
16. Tony Fossas	1989–97	8	584	14	18	7	3.42	1036
17. Ricardo Rincon	1997–2004	7	535	18	23	21	3.53	1012
18. Eric Plunk	1992–99	7	397	37	24	12	3.61	1006
19. Arthur Rhodes	1997–2003	5	329	36	18	9	3.10	990
20. Jim Mecir	1998–2005	6	363	26	26	9	3.41	986
21. Rick Honeycutt	1988–96	8	443	21	17	37	3.51	977
22. Mike Myers	1996–2006	10	734	20	23	24	2.96	967
23. Damaso Marte	2002–06	5	354	15	19	31	3.06	965

Middle Reliever	Best Years		G	W	L	Sv	ERA	Points
24. Mark Guthrie	1992–2002	8	460	20	22	11	4.11	943
25. Felix Rodriguez	2000–04	5	371	34	19	6	2.98	929
26. Scott Radinsky	1990–98	6	397	33	16	33	3.18	914
27. Bob Patterson	1990–97	8	487	29	27	26	3.55	909
28. Kent Mercker	1992–2005	5	327	12	7	11	2.75	909 tie
29. Julian Tavarez	1995–2006	7	479	38	23	21	3.86	909 tie
30. Rheal Cormier	1999–2006	8	508	33	25	2	3.92	816
31. Ray King	2001–06	6	468	16	20	2	3.43	816 tie
32. Tony Castillo	1993–97	5	266	18	17	20	3.52	810
33. Bobby Howry	2000–06	5	364	20	23	20	3.54	795
34. Kent Tekulve	1976–88	6	414	40	25	30	2.87	792
35. Gene Nelson	1986–93	5	261	21	23	22	3.13	790
36. Greg Swindell	1997–2001	5	336	20	22	7	3.48	788
37. Dennis Cook	1994–2001	7	431	34	18	6	3.95	779
38. Buddy Groom	1994–2003	9	611	22	10	13	4.13	770
39. Chuck McElroy	1991–99	6	390	21	19	17	3.35	769
40. Terry Adams	1996–2004	5	325	23	30	10	3.64	758
41. Turk Wendell	1997–2003	6	414	28	24	14	3.62	754
42. Dave Veres	1995–2002	5	327	21	16	18	3.24	752
43. Gary Lavelle	1975–85	6	406	42	37	53	2.93	747
44. Mike Fetters	1992–2002	6	331	20	21	29	3.74	747 tie
45. Clay Carroll	1966–77	5	303	41	26	36	2.68	745
46. Darold Knowles	1969–78	5	280	29	17	47	2.49	734
47. Shigetoshi Hasegawa	1997–2004	6	312	37	30	17	3.97	727
48. Rich Rodriguez	1991–2001	8	505	24	12	6	3.69	718
49. Tim Worrell	1997–2002	5	320	19	21	6	3.50	718 tie
50. Tug McGraw	1970–78	5	271	39	28	52	2.73	710
51. Craig Lefferts	1983–88	6	402	29	34	34	3.08	661
52. Hector Carrasco	1995–2005	7	426	19	19	8	4.32	657
53. Scott Sauerbeck	1999–2005	6	425	20	16	5	3.79	656
54. Scott Eyre	2002–06	5	387	9	12	2	3.58	635
55. Ken Dayley	1985–90	5	293	23	23	34	2.92	629
56. Jason Grimsley	1999–2004	6	410	22	30	3	3.97	624
57. Eddie Guardado	1996–2001	6	431	25	20	28	4.27	615
58. Jeff Parrett	1988–96	6	371	44	28	14	3.39	606
59. Rick White	1994–2006	8	482	32	35	12	4.22	602
60. Danny Patterson	1997–2001	5	281	24	16	4	4.11	599
61. Alan Embree	1997–2006	10	657	29	27	7	4.05	596
62. Jamie Walker	1997–2006	5	377	15	15	5	3.69	594
63. Scott Sullivan	1997–2003	7	499	37	24	9	3.99	592
64. Justin Speier	2002–06	5	320	16	12	1	3.74	571
65. John Franco	1984–2004	5	293	31	18	22	3.50	545
66. Gene Garber	1974–87	6	394	32	28	37	3.17	542
67. Willie Hernandez	1977–88	5	333	35	23	35	3.22	507
68. Bob Locker	1965–72	5	311	24	17	30	2.86	506
69. Paul Lindblad	1969–76	5	321	37	22	33	3.05	500
70. Ed VandeBerg	1982–87	5	337	15	14	13	3.59	500 tie
71. Jay Powell	1996–2003	7	446	28	19	22	3.74	492
72. Eddie Fisher	1969–71	5	281	25	17	26	3.05	466
73. Dan Miceli	1997–2004	6	386	27	27	11	4.05	449

Middle Reliever	Best Years		G	W	L	Sv	ERA	Points
74. Gabe White	1998–2002	5	315	24	17	14	4.01	434
75. Jason Christiansen	1995–2005	6	359	19	19	13	4.13	415
76. Luis Viscaino	2002–06	5	359	23	21	5	4.09	408
77. Joe Boever	1990–95	6	383	29	29	25	3.95	389
78. Pedro Borbon	1972–79	6	397	46	21	47	3.47	378
79. Curt Leskanic	1995–2004	8	507	46	22	38	4.39	371
80. Braden Looper	1999–2006	5	363	22	15	18	3.69	365
81. Chuck Crim	1988–94	6	384	39	33	33	3.92	351
82. Juan Agosto	1985–91	5	354	32	21	12	3.57	320
83. Aaron Fultz	2000–06	7	370	21	12	3	4.54	315
84. Kerry Ligtenberg	2000–04	5	289	13	18	17	3.86	293
85. Ted Abernathy	1964–70	5	303	31	26	49	3.42	277
86. Jeff Fassero	1991–03	5	332	23	29	24	3.95	269
87. J.C. Romero	2002–06	5	361	23	11	2	4.11	259
88. Greg Harris	1988–94	5	310	21	29	24	3.99	235
89. Rob Murphy	1987–94	8	547	25	36	29	3.92	230
90. Frank DiPino	1985–90	6	367	25	22	22	3.92	211
91. Mark Davis	1985–93	5	320	18	30	23	3.98	195
92. Mike De Jean	1997–2001	5	298	18	11	6	4.41	140
93. George Frazier	1982–87	6	338	32	31	23	4.54	66

Appendixes

A. Most Underrated Players

Perhaps the greatest honor that a baseball player can receive is election to the National Baseball Hall of Famer in Cooperstown. Players are normally eligible for selection after having been retired at least five years. Among those players eligible for the Hall but who have not been admitted to membership, the ones with the highest Faber System ratings might be acclaimed as the game's most underrated players. Two highly ranked players—Pete Rose and Joe Jackson—are not on the list because Organized Baseball has declared them ineligible. Mark McGwire is probably not underrated by fans, but aspersions about his use of performance enhancing substances may have prevented his election to the Hall during his first season of eligibility. Ron Santo is the highest rated player not in the Hall of Fame. Wes Ferrell tops the starting pitchers, Lee Smith the closers, and Mark Eichhorn the middle relievers.

HIGHEST RATED ELIGIBLE PLAYERS NOT IN HALL OF FAME

Player	Points	Player	Points
1. Ron Santo	2170	11. Don Mattingly	1894
2. Keith Hernandez	2097	12. Buddy Bell	1890
3. Roy Thomas	2078	13. Andre Dawson	1883
4. Bobby Grich	2070	14. Will Clark	1882
5. Brett Butler	2025	15. Bill Dahlen	1867
6. Jack Glasscock	2010	16. Jimmy Wynn	1866
7. Jim Rice	2002	17. Fred Lynn	1863
8. Mark McGwire	2000	18. George Gore	1862
9. Alan Trammell	1993	19. George Foster	1835
10. Mike Griffin	1990	20. Stan Hack	1829

HIGHEST RANKING PITCHERS NOT IN HALL OF FAME

Starter	Points	Closer	Points
1. Wes Ferrell	682	1. Lee Smith	475
2. Jesse Tannehill	681	2. Goose Gossage	439
3. Tommy John	664		
4. Bert Blyleven	640	*Middle Reliever*	
4. Ron Guidry	640 tie	1. Mark Eichhorn	1496

273

B. Most Overrated Players

No player named in this publication is overrated *as a ballplayer*. During the past 130 years, millions of aspiring athletes have played baseball on the sandlots, in Little Leagues, in high schools and in colleges. A few of the very best of these have tried their hands at professional baseball. Some 16,000 have made it, however briefly, to the major leagues. Fewer than 2400 of these have played enough games over enough years to be included in this book. The least talented of these was an incredibly better player than the typical prep school star. We reiterate: "No one mentioned in this book is overrated as a ballplayer."

However, from another perspective all stars of the entertainment world are overrated. Like movie actors, television performers, and popular musicians, ballplayers receive much more recognition than others who may make a far greater contribution to the good of mankind. What baseball player is worth more to his country than a good teacher, an honest policeman, or a hard-working farmer?

There are some true heroes named in this book: Jackie Robinson, who showed so much remarkable courage and self-control; Roberto Clemente, who gave his life for others; and Curt Flood who sacrificed part of his own career to fight the unjust reserve clause. Hundreds of ballplayers have been devoted husbands, superb parents, and ideal role models. So have millions of non-players. Dave Stewart, Dave Winfield, Jim Thome and many others have received well-deserved praise for their community service and charitable activities. As players, however, they are ranked amidst others in no way deserving of such praise. Yet the vast majority of the adulation that entertainment stars receive is for their performance as entertainers, not for the good works they may or may not do. The point being made here is that being an entertainer, however worthy that may be, is not the greatest contribution one can make to the world in which we live. In that sense, they are all overrated.

In comparison with their fellow major leaguers, some baseballers may be said to be overrated. Listed below are the 12 members of the National Baseball Hall of Fame who have the fewest Faber System points . Listed are only those members who were selected primarily for their performance as major league position players. We are not saying they do not deserve to be in the Hall; we are saying that some others deserve it more.

Player	Points		Player	Points
1. Rick Ferrell	655		7. Ross Youngs	1147
2. Tony Lazzeri	925		8. Travis Jackson	1198
3. Freddie Lindstrom	1008		9. Phil Rizzuto	1246
4. Frank Chance	1078		10. George Kelly	1330
5. Tommy McCarthy	1096		11. Ray Schalk	1337
6. Chick Hafey	1109		12. Johnny Evers	1346

Clearly, playing in New York is an advantage to a ballplayer in getting the media coverage and national exposure that helps in election to the Hall of Fame. Five of the 12 listed above played the majority of their careers for New York teams: Tony Lazzeri and Phil Rizzuto for the Yankees and Freddie Lindstrom, Ross Youngs, and Travis Jackson for the Giants. In contrast, only one of the top 20 underrated position players performed mainly in the nation's media capital.

Media attention comes from playing in New York, but not exclusively from playing for clubs based in the city; sometimes it comes from playing against them. In the early years of the 20th century baseball's fiercest rivalry was between the New York Giants and the Chicago Cubs. In 1908 Franklin P. Adams of the New York *Globe* wrote a brief poem about a trio of Cubs "Ruthlessly pricking our gonfalon bubble, Making a Giant hit into a double." Tinker, Evers, and Chance were immortalized; the equally fine fourth infielder on that Cub team, third baseman

Tony Mullane is sometimes considered the major league's only ambidextrous pitcher. Although Mullane usually threw right handed, he pitched without a glove and could shift the ball between his hands and occasionally deliver a pitch from the port side (Library of Congress).

Harry Steinfeldt, is now known primarily as the answer to a trivia question. Tinker, Evers, and Chance are all in the Hall of Fame. Steinfeldt is not. He was not mentioned in the poem.

C. Righthanders and Lefthanders

As is well known, the majority of Americans are right-handed. (The exact percentages are unknown, but we estimate that 85 percent are right-handed, 13 percent are left-handed, and two percent are to some extent ambidextrous.) Most aspects of American society are therefore arranged for the convenience of righties, much to the annoyance of port-siders, who, like other minorities, do not enjoy being the victims of discrimination. The right-handers advantages, however, do not extend to the batter's box. The left-handed batter can get out of the box and down to first base in a fraction of a second less than his right-handed colleague. Furthermore, the majority of pitchers are right-handed and a curve ball that curves out away from a righty would curve in toward a lefty, and thus be easier for the left-handed batter to hit. Therefore, many natural righties have learned to hit from the port side. In order to equalize opportunities against right-handed and left-handed pitchers, some ballplayers have become adept at hitting from either side of the plate. These are the switch hitters.

The left-handed advantage is demonstrated by a look at the list of career leaders in hitting. Of the top 50, 24 batted left, 24 batted right, and two were switch hitters. Exactly half of the leading left-handed hitters (12 of 24) threw right-handed. Only one of the leading right-handed hitters, threw from the port side (Rickey Henderson.) At the top of the list the first six all hit from the left side.

LEADING HITTERS BY HANDEDNESS

LEFT-HANDED		RIGHT-HANDED		SWITCH HITTERS	
Hitter	*Points*	*Hitter*	*Points*	*Hitter*	*Points*
1. Babe Ruth	2697	1. Rogers Hornsby	1959	1. Mickey Mantle	1951
2. Ted Williams	2335	2. Jimmie Foxx	1942	2. Pete Rose	1568
3. Barry Bonds	2329	3. Hank Aaron	1856	3. Chipper Jones	1514
4. Lou Gehrig	2232	4. Willie Mays	1849	4. Eddie Murray	1456
5. Ty Cobb	2128	5. Cap Anson	1801	5. Tim Raines	1349
6. Stan Musial	1965	6. Frank Robinson	1797	6. Reggie Smith	1282
7. Dan Brouthers	1842	7. Frank Thomas	1775	7. Roberto Alomar	1270
8. Tris Speaker	1787	8. Honus Wagner	1730	8. Bernie Williams	1225
9. Billy Hamilton	1769	9. Jeff Bagwell	1728	9. Ted Simmons	1200
10. Mel Ott	1730	10. Ed Delahanty	1713	10. Bobby Bonilla	1109

The advantage that left-handers have at the plate does not carry over onto the mound. Of the 50 leading pitchers, 34 were primarily right-handers and 16 were left-handers. All of the top five were right-handers. A few hurlers have been ambidextrous, most notably Tony Mullane. The Count, as he was known, usually pitched right-handed, but could pitch with either hand. Playing without a glove, he could hold the ball in both hands before throwing it with either one. A few other old-timers, including Larry Corcoran and Elton "Icebox" Chamberlain, occasionally threw with either hand. The most recent pitcher to switch hands during a game was Greg Harris. Wearing a reversible glove with two thumbs in the final game of his major league career on September 28, 1995, Harris of the Montreal Expos started the ninth inning pitching right-handed against the Cincinnati Reds. He retired Reggie Sanders, then he switched to his left hand, walked Hal Morris and got Eddie Taubensee to ground out, and then reverted to his right hand to retire Brett Boone and end the game.

LEADING PITCHERS BY HANDEDNESS

LEFT-HANDED		RIGHT-HANDED	
Pitcher	Points	Pitcher	Points
1. Lefty Grove	879	1. Cy Young	1010
2. Randy Johnson	861	2. Walter Johnson	998
3. Steve Carlton	817	3. Grover Alexander	954
4. Warren Spahn	773	4. Christy Mathewson	936
5. Eddie Plank	725	5. Roger Clemens	900
6. Whitey Ford	713	6. Tom Seaver	823
7. Tom Glavine	699	7. Kid Nichols	766
8. Jesse Tannehill	681	8. Bob Feller	761
9. Carl Hubbell	666	9. Greg Maddux	761 tie
10. Tommy John	664	10. Pedro Martinez	753

D. Multi-Position Players

Most major leaguers have played at more than one position during their careers, if only for a few games. Stan Musial, Rod Carew, and Ernie Banks, for example, could be ranked among the leaders at first base or at another position. Pete Rose was among those who played very well at a number of different positions during a long career. As the Faber System permits points to be cumulated from one position to another, infielders, outfielders, and catchers need to be ranked at only their primary position.

Pitchers, however, are a different matter. Points as a starter, closer, and mid-reliever are not computed on a comparative base and are not additive to batting and fielding points. Therefore, a player who divides his time between pitching and another position must be ranked both as a player and as a pitcher if he has five or more eligible seasons as each. The same thing is true of pitchers with different specializations during their careers. Three baseball stars are ranked both as players and as pitchers: Dave Foutz, Babe Ruth, and Monte Ward. Several pitchers are ranked in two of the pitching specializations. Dennis Eckersley, Ron Kline, and Ron Reed are numbered among both starters and closers. John Franco, Jesse Orosco, Kent Tekulve, and Hoyt Wilhelm are listed both as closers and as middle relievers.

Index

277

4916 029